Praise for the third edition of *Work and Labour in Canada*

"For all the breathless talk of dramatic changes currently reshaping the world of work, there is precious little understanding of what exactly is changing, let alone the broader social, political, and economic forces that are doing the reshaping. Mark P. Thomas's timely revision of Andrew Jackson's essential text is a welcome antidote to that. Written in an accessible style, *Work and Labour in Canada* offers a masterful analysis of the challenges and changes that workers face today, using meticulous, clearly presented data, combined with vivid case studies that dig beneath the numbers. The result is an engaging introductory text for undergraduates, as well as an indispensable reference for work and labour scholars."

—Barry Eidlin, Department of Sociology, McGill University

"This book provides a useful, critical introduction to the forces shaping work and the challenges confronting workers in Canada today. Most helpfully, the authors proceed from their detailed, contextualized examination of various problems associated with work (e.g., precariousness, continuing areas of inequality, and health and safety concerns) to assess the potential of various avenues for change (e.g., union renewal, labour market policy initiatives, and forms of workplace democracy) to counter the economic and political forces that continue to adversely impact work."

—Lee Chalmers, Department of Social Science, University of New Brunswick

Work and Labour in Canada

Work and Labour in Canada

Critical Issues
Third Edition

Andrew Jackson and Mark P. Thomas

CANADIAN
SCHOLARS

Toronto | Vancouver

Work and Labour in Canada: Critical Issues, Third Edition
Andrew Jackson and Mark P. Thomas

First published in 2017 by
Canadian Scholars
425 Adelaide Street West, Suite 200
Toronto, Ontario
M5V 3C1

www.canadianscholars.ca

Library and Archives Canada Cataloguing in Publication

Jackson, Andrew, 1952-, author
    Work and labour in Canada : critical issues / Andrew Jackson and Mark Thomas. — Third edition.

Includes bibliographical references and index.
Issued in print and electronic formats.
ISBN 978-1-55130-957-6 (softcover). — ISBN 978-1-55130-958-3 (PDF). — ISBN 978-1-55130-959-0 (EPUB)

    1. Labor--Canada--Textbooks. 2. Labor movement--Canada--Textbooks. 3. Textbooks. I. Thomas, Mark P. (Mark Preston), 1969-, author II. Title.

HD8106.5.J32 2017   331.0971   C2017-900677-0
                                                                 C2017-900678-9

Text design by Brad Horning
Cover design by Susan MacGregor, Digital Zone
Cover image adapted from Gary Waters / Alamy Stock Photo

The editors and publisher would like to thank the Faculty of Liberal Arts & Professional Studies, York University, Toronto, for the contribution it made toward this publication.

17   18   19   20   21   5   4   3   2   1

Printed and bound in Canada by Webcom

Canadä

MIX
Paper from
responsible sources
FSC
www.fsc.org   FSC® C004071

Table of Contents

List of Tables and Figures

Chapter 9

Chapter 10

Chapter 12

List of Boxes

Preface to the Third Edition

I began using *Work and Labour in Canada: Critical Issues* by Andrew Jackson in my undergraduate teaching in Sociology at York University when the first edition came out in 2005. Over the years, my students consistently found the text to be a highly valuable resource, particularly for its extensive statistical documentation of both changing patterns of work and the connections between poor working conditions and growing inequality in Canadian society. When I was approached by Canadian Scholars' Press in the fall of 2014 with the opportunity to update the text for a third edition, I didn't hesitate to take up the offer. I was not only grateful for the opportunity to work on a text that had proven to be such a great resource over the years, but also thankful to Andrew Jackson for expressing confidence in passing along his project to me.

For two years (2012–2014), I was fortunate to have an office beside Andrew while he was a Packer Visiting Professor of Social Justice at York University. During this time, I benefited greatly from his insight into many matters related to subjects covered by the text, including the changing workplace and labour market in Canada, the challenges faced by contemporary workers' movements, and the important role played by critical social science research in informing strategies to improve work. As I began planning the new edition, maintaining the critical orientation that Andrew had so carefully crafted in earlier editions was of paramount concern.

Work and Labour in Canada provides a detailed overview of many contemporary issues facing workers in Canada, and is designed for undergraduate students, those teaching about work and labour, and those researching labour market issues. The third edition builds on the original text and takes that material in some new directions. The edition is thoroughly updated, and includes new tables and data, new examples and text boxes, and new lists of recommended readings for all chapters. This edition also includes two new chapters. A new Chapter 7, "The Inaccessible Canadian Workplace," presents a significantly expanded exploration of disability and work, introducing the "social model" of disability that draws attention to the multiple barriers that inhibit access to work for people with disabilities. A new Chapter 8, "Troubled Transitions: Into and Out of the Labour Force," is based on a merger of Chapters 7 and 8 from the second edition and covers issues faced by both young workers seeking to enter the labour market and older workers approaching retirement.

The third edition also includes new material in a number of chapters. Chapter 1 begins by discussing the concept of "alienated labour" and the idea of "work as a social problem" in order to understand the social basis for the problems people experience in the workplace and the labour market. Chapter

4 adds a discussion of occupational health and safety laws to the material on the unhealthy workplace to illustrate the ways in which laws that are meant to promote healthier work environments often fail to do so. In Chapter 5, a discussion of the relations of social reproduction is presented to further illustrate the interconnections between gendered divisions of labour in the household and the labour market. Chapter 6 has been extensively redeveloped to broaden the conceptual discussion of "racialization" in order to prompt consideration of the deep and longstanding processes of racism that continue to shape the contemporary labour market. As well, the section on immigration in this chapter has been expanded to include a discussion of the growth of temporary foreign labour programs, as an illustration of the ways in which Canada has grown its low-wage labour force through temporary migrant workers, while at the same time severely limiting the political and economic rights of those who participate in the programs. Chapter 6 also includes a discussion of how settler colonialism was formative to Canada's development in order to contextualize the inequality and racism experienced by Aboriginal peoples in the workplace and labour market. Chapter 9 has been expanded with a discussion of the ways in which labour laws have shaped (and constrained) the role and impact of trade unions, while the scope of Chapter 10 has been broadened to examine examples of contemporary workers' movements in addition to unions. Chapter 11 includes an expanded conceptual discussion of globalization, as well as a discussion of the connections between transnational labour activism and the emergence of the anti-globalization movement. Finally, in addition to outlining the social democratic approach to re-regulating the labour market, Chapter 12 now considers a range of additional strategies to improve work, including reduced working time, worker cooperatives, and the idea of moving beyond wage labour.

Though the book aims to be broad in scope, there are many more issues that could have been covered but were left for future study. For example, given Canada's diverse economic geography, the study of work requires more attention to differences in regional labour markets. Also, while the text has sought to map out patterns in the labour market and identify the social forces that shape work, it does not explore the micro-level social relations of the workplace, as is done with much greater detail through studies of the labour process, for example. As well, though some attention is given to developments in labour and employment laws, much more could be said about the role of the state in regulating the workplace and the labour market, particularly in this era of neoliberalism and austerity. Finally, when I started teaching with the first edition of this text, there was much less happening in terms of precarious worker organizing. Now, just over a decade later, workers in precarious jobs are leading a growing movement to improve wages and working conditions across Canada (and the U.S.) through campaigns such as the Fight for $15 and Fairness and the struggles for migrant worker justice. As these developments are fairly recent, the impact of precarious worker organizing on working conditions, and on broader working-class struggle, is a key question that requires more attention.

A resource for students, teachers, researchers, and labour activists, the first two editions of *Work and Labour in Canada* were written with a critical voice so as to prompt discussion and debate about how to improve work in the 21st century. It is my hope that the third edition of the text continues in this tradition.

Mark P. Thomas
Toronto, Canada
July 2016

Introduction

Over the last several decades, the workplace in Canada has experienced profound changes. Work has become increasingly insecure for a growing number of workers, income inequality has deepened, and so many find themselves "working on the edge." The organization of working time has become more "flexible," as people increasingly find themselves working too much, too little, or with erratic and unstable schedules. Entry into the labour market is itself a difficult process, as young workers struggle to match qualifications and credentials with jobs, while for many older workers, retirement with a secure income is a diminishing prospect. The composition of the labour market itself is changing—yet this change is conditioned by longstanding patterns of inequality. This is evidenced, for example, by both the growing numbers of immigrant and migrant workers, who continue to experience discrimination and unequal access to opportunities, and by the persistence of a gender wage gap, despite the high rates of labour market participation by women. Moreover, the organizations that emerged through the 20th century to provide regulatory protection for workers—trade unions—face many new challenges as they seek to counter the harsh effects of work reorganization in the context of a globalized economy.

Work and Labour in Canada presents an analysis of the contemporary Canadian workplace and situates the Canadian workplace in the context of these broad patterns and processes. The book aims to develop a critical understanding of the social processes contributing to the changing workplace and to identify progressive forces emerging to construct a more equitable, democratic, and meaningful experience of work.

In evaluating working conditions and the quality of jobs in Canada from a critical perspective, the book also seeks to initiate a discussion about how conditions might be improved. Making use of a wide array of resources and data, the book provides a substantial amount of detail on recent trends in employment, unemployment, the quality of jobs, conditions of inequality in the labour market, the role of Canadian unions, and how conditions in Canada are connected to global processes. In taking this focus, the book presents the workplace in Canada as a "contested terrain" (Edwards 1979): a space that is constantly undergoing change due to the conflict, competing interests, and power dynamics of capitalism as an economic system.

The book is organized into four parts. Part I, "Working in Precarious Times," presents an overview of conditions in the job market and in workplaces today, and a summary of trends over the past several decades. It focuses on wages, unemployment, forms of employment, opportunities for education and training, and workplace conditions. Differences in the experiences of different groups of workers are noted, setting the stage for further analysis later in the book. Part I is divided into four chapters. These cover the importance of jobs, recent trends in the job market and Canadian workplaces, and two important aspects of job quality: access to training and healthy working conditions. Chapter 1, "The World of Work in the 21st Century," sets out some key characteristics related to job quality, including wages, stability of employment, working conditions, and opportunities for promotion and training. The chapter also identifies social forces that are shaping employment conditions, such as work reorganization, government policies, and unions. The chapter introduces a discussion of why work (in the form of wage labour) remains a central social experience in everyday life and in shaping individual and collective identity, highlighting the importance of wages and of the quality of work to our livelihood and overall well-being. Through this discussion, the chapter explores the ways in which the organization of work can be seen as a "social problem" (Mills 1959; Rinehart 2006), thereby providing a framework that guides the discussion throughout the remaining chapters.

Chapter 2, "Work, Wages, and Living Standards in Canada," provides a detailed, statistically based analysis of trends in wages, employment, unemployment, and the quality of new jobs created over the past several decades. The chapter highlights inequality in the job market and the growing problem of precarious work—low-paying and insecure jobs—particularly in the aftermath of the 2008 financial crisis. Links are drawn from patterns in the labour market to a disturbing trend toward greater inequality in the wider society. Chapter 3, "Education, Training, and Lifelong Learning," focuses on a key aspect of job quality: opportunities for access to training and on-the-job learning. This is increasingly seen as crucial in a knowledge-based economy. A key dimension of precarious jobs is that they provide limited, if any, access to training and ladders to better jobs. It is disturbing that most opportunities for on-the-job training and career development go to higher-paid managers and professionals, compounding their relatively advantaged position in the job market. Finally, Chapter 4, "The Unhealthy Canadian Workplace," surveys workplace conditions that have implications for both the physical and mental health of workers. The focus here is on physical hazards at work, and on work and stress. Work can be, and often is, very stressful because of the pace and demands of the jobs and the low degree of control exerted by employees, and also because of conflict between work and family and community life. The chapter draws connections between the organization of work in contemporary capitalism and the prevalence of workplace danger, presenting health and safety as a part of the "contested terrain" of work, with the interests of workers and employers often at odds.

The job market is characterized by deep inequalities and differences along lines of gender, race, citizenship and immigration status, ability, and age, among other things, all of which intersect with differences in wages and the quality of employment. Part II, "Work, Inequality, and Difference," examines the labour market and workplace experiences of women, racialized groups, recent immigrants, Aboriginal peoples, people with disabilities, and younger and older workers.

Chapter 5, "Gender, Work, and Social Reproduction," compares and contrasts the occupational distribution, forms of employment, and earnings of women and men, and shows that there are deep and systematic differences based on gender. Women are more likely than men to be in lower-paid and precarious jobs, and the pay gap between women and men remains well entrenched. Despite a great deal of progress in terms of labour force participation through the 20th century, there are still deep and systematic differences of pay and job quality based on gender, as well as gendered dimensions to precarious employment.

Chapter 6, "Race, Racialization, and Racism at Work," examines the experiences of people of colour, immigrants and migrants, and Aboriginal people. Despite significant differences, these groups all encounter discrimination and racism in the job market, though the particular forms each group faces vary. This chapter highlights evidence of pay, employment, and opportunity gaps between racialized workers and other Canadians. These differences are disturbing in that they cannot be explained away with reference to education and ability. It is not just recent immigrants but also workers of colour born and educated in Canada who work at a disadvantage. Moreover, the very low level of economic well-being of many Aboriginal peoples and communities reflects the fact that their access to employment is highly limited, their pay levels are very low compared to the Canadian average, and their jobs are often very unstable.

As discussed in Chapter 7, "The Inaccessible Canadian Workplace," people with disabilities face many barriers when seeking employment. Building from a social model of understanding disability, the chapter outlines the many barriers to accessibility that are present in the workplace, developing an analysis of the social factors that create these barriers, including both those that exist within the workplace and those in society more generally that inhibit access to employment. The chapter argues that the lower employment rates for persons with disabilities, as well as their experiences of precariousness, reflect a collective failure to create accessible workplaces. The chapter also discusses the role of disability rights organizations and unions in pushing to make workplaces more accessible.

Chapter 8, "Troubled Transitions," highlights the different experiences of younger and older workers in the labour market. The chapter first looks at the barriers to entry into good jobs faced by many younger workers and notes the growing expectation of taking on forms of unpaid work through internships and volunteerism as a strategy to gain entry into the paid labour market. The chapter then looks at pathways from work to retirement, as well as the changing fortunes of older workers who are still active in the job market. The chapter also highlights the growing pressures on pension systems, and the challenge of income security in older age.

Part III, "Contemporary Workers' Movements in Canada," focuses on the role of unions and other workers' movements as a force for change in the contemporary Canadian workplace. This part of the book builds on key issues developed in Parts I and II, such as precarious work, growing inequality, and barriers to inclusion. Unions have historically been a major force for improving the quality of jobs, countering low pay, and promoting greater equality in the job market. However, union capacities to effect change have been undermined by declining union strength due to both neoliberal government policies and the global restructuring of work, as well as through labour market growth in sectors with traditionally low levels of union representation. In Canada, overall union coverage is stable, but very low among private service workers, particularly lower-paid women and racialized workers, who would gain the most from union representation. A key challenge for unions today is to win support among, and to make gains for, unorganized precarious workers.

Chapter 9, "The Impact of Unions," discusses the role and importance of collective bargaining, and closely examines union impacts on wages, benefits, and other dimensions of job quality. It also discusses how unions affect the way in which the economy and the labour market operate and critiques the often-heard argument that strong unions may be good for their members, but negatively affect economic performance. While outlining many of the positive effects on working conditions created by unions, the chapter also discusses the limits of unions in terms of their capacities to enact fundamental social change due to the ways in which they are constrained by, and integrated into, capitalist economies. Chapter 10, "Workers' Movements in the New Millennium," provides a detailed look at challenges facing unions as they attempt to organize and represent workers in today's changing labour market. There is a major ongoing process of union renewal, but whether it will be enough to ensure a continuing major role for unions in the workplaces of the future remains to be determined. The chapter also assesses new forms of workplace organizing that are taking place outside unions, as many non-unionized workers seek to collectively confront the social problems of work and improve their circumstances.

The book concludes by examining how Canada's increasing integration into the global economy has changed the world of work, and the extent to which the forces of free trade and global economic integration limit the possibilities for labour market alternatives. Part IV, "The Canadian Workplace in the Global Economy," looks at how globalization has fundamentally tilted the power dynamic of the "contested terrain" of work to an even greater extent in favour of employers and the corporate sector. Chapter 11, "Globalization and Work in Canada," focuses on the impacts of globalization, with specific attention to the ways in which, while operating according to a longstanding logic of the global extension of capitalist social relations, the contemporary global economy involves many processes that have reshaped work in historically distinct ways, with extreme implications for the organization and experience of work. The chapter looks specifically at the impacts of free trade agreements on work in Canada, arguing that there has been downward pressure on labour and social standards in the era of free trade. Nevertheless, as the concluding chapter, "Improving Work: Reforming or Transforming Wage Labour?," argues, the high-inequality and high-insecurity neoliberal labour market model is not universal: there are existing, viable alternatives that may offer solutions for improving work in Canada. This final chapter thus encourages the reader to think about the ways in which Canada's labour market model might be changed in order to improve the quality of jobs, and to address some of the many problems of work outlined in the book as a whole.

Overall, this book is intended for all those interested in better understanding the changing workplace in Canada in the initial decades of the 21st century. Taking a critical perspective, the book aims not only to encourage discussion of the many social problems associated with the experience of work, but also to raise the prospects of an alternative future of work, and in so doing to contribute to the social struggles needed to bring about such a future.

PART I

WORKING IN PRECARIOUS TIMES

CHAPTER 1

The World of Work in the 21st Century

The world of work is these days an ongoing source of concern. Whether one is currently employed, trying to enter the labour market for the first time, or approaching the end of one's career, there seems to be no end to the dilemmas stemming from the organization and experience of work in today's economy. The rise of precarious work, the pressures on retirement-age income security programs, the persistence of gendered and racialized divisions of labour and workplace-based inequalities, and the difficulties experienced by young people trying to develop a pathway into a career all point toward the tumultuous nature of the workplace in the early 21st century. These problems are heightened by the challenges facing trade unions (the collective organizations that workers have formed to advance their interests), by governments that seem intent on reducing or removing basic labour protections developed in the 20th century, and by the growing power of corporations acting in an increasingly global economic landscape.

For these and many other reasons to be explored in this book, work remains a central "social problem" in today's society (Rinehart 2006). Yet, despite these wide-ranging causes for concern, work nevertheless remains central to our daily lives. Work in the form of wage labour is the primary source of survival for the majority of people living in capitalist economies and, for many, constructs an ordering of our "everyday world." Moreover, the work we engage in may contribute more deeply to our sense of self and to our identity in both an individual and collective sense. Fraught with social problems including inequality, discrimination, stress, and physical risk, work is also constantly undergoing pressures for change as people seek to improve their working lives in order to make work a more rewarding and meaningful experience. In this way, the workplace can be seen as a "contested terrain" (Edwards 1979), shaped by tension, conflict, and struggle resulting from the competing interests of employers, labour organizations, individual workers, and governments. While the world of work in the early 21st century is indeed a very precarious place for many, there are also signs that the conflicts that arise through these competing interests could make possible an alternative future to this precarious present.

Work and Labour in Canada explores this changing world of work, mapping out major trends and patterns defining working life, and also identifying and exploring a number of the economic, social, and political factors that contribute to the "making" of the contemporary workplace. This chapter begins that journey by describing the fundamental importance of good jobs to well-being. It identifies some of the major recent changes in the Canadian workforce and the nature of work over the past several decades and summarizes key forces shaping the quality of jobs. In doing so, the chapter sets the stage for the more focused discussion of particular issues taken up in the rest of the book.

The Social Problem of Work

This book is premised on the idea that to understand work we must do so by locating work within a social context. This understanding of work builds from the writing of sociologist C. Wright Mills and his discussion of the "sociological imagination." For Mills (1959: 6), "the sociological imagination enables us to grasp history and biography and the relations between the two within society." This involves going beyond the personal element of our experiences by situating experience within a broader social context. Doing so provides the means to distinguish between "personal troubles" (matters that are unique to a specific individual) and "public issues" (matters that affect a larger public). This is particularly significant during times of social change, which can be disorienting and disruptive, and may generate high levels of anxiety and uncertainty. Building from Mills, the sociological imagination provides a way of understanding these moments of change (such as the changing world of work in the early 21st century) as it offers a way to think about the relationships between broad social patterns and how any given individual experiences those patterns.

For the purpose of this book, the sociological imagination introduces a way of recognizing the manner in which work, though in some ways experienced as an individual, is at the same time a deeply social matter. For example, when many individuals express concerns about working away the years of their lives, for Mills, we must inquire into the social basis of those concerns. Returning to a theme raised in the Introduction, this leads us to begin to recognize work as a *social* problem, specifically when we see that the organization of work is connected to adverse effects that transcend individual experiences. For example, we can begin to understand work as a social problem by looking at the ways in which work is shaped by *power differentials*, and is a source of *conflict* between competing groups, a source of *inequality* in terms of income distribution, and a source of *dissatisfaction* and *alienation* (Rinehart 2006). To use an example from Mills, we can understand the phenomenon of unemployment as a result of social conditions rather than individual failure. Similarly, thinking about the phenomena of low-wage work, the adverse health effects of work, and gendered and racialized inequalities in the labour market, these cannot be explained in individual terms: we must look to social factors to understand why, for example, low-wage work is on the rise these days, or why longstanding patterns of discrimination continue to persist.

What might be at the root of the social problems of work? Karl Marx addressed this question by looking at the class relations of capitalism, which involve control over the means of production by a small elite group (the capitalist class), a system of economic production that prioritizes capital accumulation and profit over human needs, and ways of organizing work that provide little or no capacity for people to control their labour. Marx (1964) argued that the social relations of capitalism produce conditions of alienated labour, whereby people are alienated from (separated from; lose control over) the products of their labour, from the labour process (the tasks of work), and from one another. Moreover, Marx also argued that since people derive meaning from their labour, within capitalism one also becomes alienated from oneself and one's human essence. Alongside the experience of alienation, Marx (1976) saw the workplace within capitalism as a site of exploitation, whereby wage labourers produce value for their employers that exceeds what they are paid through wages. While workers experience alienation and exploitation differently and to varying degrees depending on many factors (gender, race, age, ability, citizenship status, occupational status, etc.), these conditions affect all who sell their labour power for a wage in some way, from fast-food workers, to auto workers, to even well-paid scientists. Thus, as Thompson (1989: 4) describes, within capitalism, work becomes "not just something which a society organizes to meet social needs, or which people carry out in order to survive," but also "a framework within which those who own and control the economic resources seek to ensure the appropriation of surplus." Overall, Marx's analysis of work within capitalism points to the ways in which the organization of work itself is fundamentally connected to the production of inequality, conflict, and alienation—conditions he saw as endemic to capitalist society.

Of course, within capitalism, not everyone experiences these conditions in the same ways. As later chapters in the book will discuss, work is fundamentally shaped by many interconnected social relationships, such as those of gender, race, and ability, as well as political conditions, such as citizenship status. Thus, one's social location influences greatly the ways in which, and the extent to which, one may experience conditions of alienation and exploitation through wage labour. Moreover, while we often think of work in terms of employment, we must recognize that there are many forms of unpaid work as well, and that these forms of work must also be considered when discussing work in its social context. As will be discussed in Chapter 5, the organization of unpaid work—reproductive labour—remains centrally connected to the organization of the workplace and the labour market. While the book begins with the analysis below that is cast in some fairly general terms, as the chapters unfold we will begin to explore the ways in which the social problems of work are experienced in different ways by particular groups of workers, all set within the wider social context of contemporary capitalism in Canada.

Jobs and a Changing Workforce

The vast majority of Canadian families and households depend upon jobs and the labour market for their well-being. In 2014, almost 8 out of 10 of all people aged 15 to 64—including 86 percent of those aged 25 to 54, and 64 percent of those aged 15 to 24—participated in the paid workforce. This means that they were either working, or unemployed but actively seeking work. This is one of the highest participation rates among the advanced industrial countries, a bit higher than in the U.S., and only a little below the very high rates in the Scandinavian countries. Participation is understandably lower for teens and older workers, and participation and employment rates vary by gender, as shown in Chapter 5, but very few working-age Canadians other than the very marginalized have no attachment at all to the job market.

Earnings from employment make up the lion's share of all Canadian household income. In 2012, Canadian households had a total income of just over $1 trillion, about two-thirds of which came from employment.[1] Income transfers from governments—mainly public pensions, employment insurance, and welfare payments—contributed 13 percent of total income, with most of that amount going to retirees as Old Age Security and Canada Pension Plan payments. Some very affluent Canadians do collect very large amounts of dividends, capital gains, and interest income from their investments, but even these Canadians rely very heavily on employment and self-employment income for their livelihood.

In the 1950s and into the 1960s, the Canadian norm was for families to depend on the wages of an adult male breadwinner who worked from leaving school until retirement at age 65 to support his wife and children. A lot has changed, and several chapters in this book focus on the changing workforce. The importance of paid work over the life-course has shifted forwards and backwards. Well over one-half of all young people now complete some kind of post-secondary education. This has delayed entry into the permanent workforce for many young adults. However, the great majority of students work part-time or for part of the year, and increasingly rely on earnings to finance their studies. Meanwhile, the dream of "Freedom 55" is receding with the crisis of pensions and the increased interest of some older workers in continuing to work for non-monetary reasons. Many more older women work today than was the case a few years ago, simply because more women have been in the paid workforce for most of their lives.

By the mid-1970s, half of all women with employed spouses were working, and today that figure has risen to over 80 percent. The vast majority of women now want to participate in the paid workforce—perhaps with some time out for maternity and parental leaves—and their incomes make up a high and rising proportion of family incomes. Women have made substantial progress, but there are still huge gaps between women and men in terms of earnings and the quality of jobs. Because male wages have stagnated for so long, families have become increasingly dependent on the earnings of women (and on household debt) in order to maintain their living standards.

Today, Canada has one of the most diverse populations in the world, and one of the highest rates of immigration. New immigrants make up a high proportion of the workforce, and will—with Aboriginal Canadians—account for virtually all net job growth in the years ahead. New immigrants and racialized workers born in Canada are more highly educated than the Canadian-born, yet their earnings and job chances fall far short of equality.

To summarize, the great majority of Canadians work for a living, and paid work is absolutely central to the economic well-being of individuals and families. Some of our income comes from government transfers, and some of our basic needs—such as education for school-age children and health care—are met through government programs. But the fundamental reality is that we live in a capitalist society, and thus our income from employment centrally determines our standard of living. This is true in both absolute terms and as compared to our fellow citizens. The kinds of jobs we hold and the wages we earn largely determine our living standards, the extent to which we can buy the goods and services we want, the extent to which we can provide our children with opportunities, and our ability to balance work with family and community life and opportunities for leisure. As documented in Chapter 2, recent trends within the job market have driven the ever-increasing polarization of Canadian incomes and Canadian society, and have lowered the level of economic security enjoyed by many working Canadians and their families.

Without devaluing in any way the contribution and importance of unpaid work in the home and in the community, paid work is also a critical source of meaning and purpose in the lives of most Canadians, and a major source of personal identity. Jobs connect us to the wider society and provide us with a sense of participation in a collective purpose. Many people define themselves largely by what they do at work. Good jobs in good workplaces are needed if individuals are to be able to develop their individual talents and capacities, actively participate in society, and enjoy a broad equality of life chances. On the other hand, unemployment and bad jobs give rise to poverty and low income, stress, ill health, and alienation from the wider society in which we live.

Despite the central importance of paid work to our lives, Canada's progress as a country tends to be measured mainly on the basis of two key indicators: growth of Gross Domestic Product, or GDP, and the unemployment rate. GDP is the sum total of all income in the country, and the sum total of all output. The unemployment rate is the proportion of people in the labour force who want to work, but cannot find any work at all. The level of GDP is certainly important, and economic growth will usually lower unemployment and raise incomes, and thus directly benefit working people. But, it is important to go beyond the economic growth and unemployment numbers to ask the critical question: How is work working for people? This can be measured along many dimensions, including income, job security, and the quality of jobs at the workplace level.

GDP growth and low unemployment tell us nothing about the adequacy of wages or how earnings are distributed among households and families. One disturbing trend over the past several decades has been rapidly increasing inequality in the distribution of earnings. Wages and incomes from employment have risen for those at the very top, stagnated for those in the middle, and fallen for those at the bottom. Many Canadians work in very low-wage jobs. These trends have increased income gaps between families and kept poverty at high levels even in an economic recovery. Trends in employment and earnings also raise important issues of equality along lines of race, ethnicity, citizenship status, gender, age, and disability, among other factors.

Economic growth and unemployment numbers also tell us little about the security of employment and earnings. Many jobs are short-term and unstable, and government supports for frequently unemployed and lower-paid workers have been cut back. The cuts to Employment Insurance in the mid-1990s cut off access to the system for many, and lowered the level of benefits for those who did qualify. Low unemployment is obviously a good thing, but a low unemployment rate can and does hide the fact that many people—especially women and racial-ized workers—are working in low-wage jobs, in temporary jobs, or in part-time jobs even if they want to work full-time. Just having a job is a good thing, but there is a big difference between having a survival job and a job that offers a real ladder to better jobs. Economic growth and unemployment numbers also tell us nothing about the quality of jobs in terms of the pace and intensity of work, access to training and career ladders, and the consequences of jobs for our health.

For all of its central importance to economic, social, and individual well-being, the critical study of the labour market and work is relatively underdeveloped as an academic enterprise (Shalla 2007; Green 2006). Economists view work as a disutility or deprivation of leisure time that is endured to gain income in order to consume, rather than as a sphere for the development of human capacities and well-being. Sociologists tend to have a more critical perspective, stressing that human beings develop their individual potential and enter into social rela-tionships through their labour. However, many academics and management gurus have romanticized the post-industrial workplace as a sphere of liberation of individual talents and capacities. It is primarily critical sociologists, political economists, and labour studies scholars working in the traditions of Marxism and political economy that have charted growing inequalities in the job market, the intersections of such class-based inequalities with gender, race, ability, and citizenship status, and the power relations in the workplace that subordinate workers to managerial- and market-driven imperatives.

Drawing on a growing wealth of survey evidence, Green (2006) stresses that job quality should be assessed primarily from a worker perspective, and suggests that the quality of work has been in decline for several decades along several dimensions. Not only have many workers experienced decreasing job security and stagnant wages due to economic restructuring, but work effort and over-qualification for jobs have also grown in most countries. There has been a steady increase in the skills of the workforce, and even in the use of skills in the workplace, but the contemporary workplace is also marked by tight control of worker discretion on the job and by much greater stress due to the intensification of work. There is little persuasive evidence that new technologies and the so-called knowledge-based economy have significantly improved the quality of working life even for those at the top of the

Box 1.1: Decent Work for All
By the International Labour Organization

The primary goal of the International Labour Organization—a tripartite (government, employers, labour governed) United Nations agency based in Geneva—is to promote opportunities for women and men to obtain decent and productive work, in conditions of freedom, equity, security, and human dignity:

> Decent work sums up the aspirations of people in their working lives. It involves opportunities for work that is productive and delivers a fair income, security in the workplace and social protection for families, better prospects for personal development and social integration, freedom for people to express their concerns, organize and participate in the decisions that affect their lives and equality of opportunity and treatment for all women and men.

The ILO's Decent Work Agenda

Productive employment and decent work are key elements to achieving a fair globalization and poverty reduction. The ILO has developed an agenda for the community of work looking at job creation, rights at work, social protection and social dialogue, with gender equality as a crosscutting objective.

There has been an increased urgency among international policy-makers, particularly in the wake of the global financial and economic crisis of 2008, to deliver quality jobs along with social protection and respect for rights at work to achieve sustainable, inclusive economic growth, and eliminate poverty.

Decent Work and the Sustainable Development Goals

During the UN General Assembly in September 2015, decent work and the four pillars of the Decent Work Agenda—employment creation, social protection, rights at work, and social dialogue—became integral elements of the new 2030 Agenda for Sustainable Development. Goal 8 of the 2030 Agenda calls for the promotion of sustained, inclusive and sustainable economic growth, full and productive employment and decent work, and will be a key area of engagement for the ILO and its constituents. Furthermore, key aspects of decent work are widely embedded in the targets of many of the other 16 goals of the UN's new development vision.

Source: International Labour Organization (ILO). 2016. "Decent work." Geneva: ILO. http://www.ilo.org/global/topics/decent-work/lang--en/index.htm.

education and skills ladder. Moreover, there is a lot of evidence of deteriorating conditions and increased insecurity for those at the bottom of the job ladder.

Key Forces Driving the Quantity and Quality of Jobs

There are many factors that shape the quantity and quality of jobs in the labour market. These include the competing interests of employers, governments, labour organizations, and workers, with their conflicts and interactions making the workplace a "contested terrain." To understand how work is changing, and the social implications of these changes, it is necessary to examine a wide array of economic, social, and political forces, including those that follow.

Macroeconomic Conditions

In a capitalist economy, the great majority of jobs are created by private-sector employers. Workers are hired in order to produce goods and services, and workers are hired or laid off depending upon demand at home and outside Canada for those goods and services. In a downturn, many workers lose their jobs through layoffs, but the biggest impact comes from the fact that employers stop hiring. In Canada, deep recessions resulted in very high unemployment in both the early 1980s and the early 1990s. To some degree, these downturns are part of the workings of the capitalist business cycle, which often results in periods of economic restructuring in order to increase profitability. Government economic policies, too, have contributed to periodic high unemployment and ongoing slack in the job market.

Most orthodox economists believe that there is a "natural" or non-accelerating inflation rate of unemployment. The basic idea is that if unemployment falls too low, below about 7 percent in the case of Canada, wages will increase too fast, driving up the rate of inflation. In both the early 1980s and early 1990s, the Bank of Canada raised interest rates very sharply to deliberately slow down the economy, fearing that inflation was rising or about to rise too fast because of low unemployment. Critics argue that central banks tend to move too fast, too soon, and that the deliberate use of unemployment to fight even low rates of inflation is very costly (Maclean and Osberg 1996).

A wider issue at stake is how to make sure that very low unemployment does not result in wage-driven inflation. Virtually all economists would agree that, over time, the growth of wages must reflect improved worker productivity or higher output per hour. Mainstream economists think that this will result if labour markets are highly flexible. They take a critical view of the role of unions, minimum wages, and government income supports for the unemployed, all of which are seen to be possible sources of wages that are too high and too rigid. Other economists argue that some countries with strong unions have been able to achieve low inflation and low unemployment, basically because businesses and unions are able to agree on the right level of wages.

The important point in the case of Canada is that our job market usually runs with a bit of deliberate slack, which is with an unemployment rate of at least 6 percent, and often with a lot more slack. At any given time, there are more workers looking for jobs than there are available jobs. This means that jobs are hard to find, particularly for workers whose skills and education are not in very high demand, and for young people and new immigrants who lack Canadian job experience. The degree of slack in the job market is a huge influence upon employer investment in training for the unskilled, attention to the unrecognized skills and credentials of new immigrants, relative pay levels by skill, and employer willingness to balance demands of work and family. The very low unemployment rates reached in the U.S. after 1995 significantly reduced low pay and earnings inequality, as well as pay and opportunity gaps based upon race (Mishel et al. 2003), and there is no doubt that falling unemployment since the mid-1990s also had positive impacts in Canada. Still, as is argued in Chapter 2, even when unemployment fell to 6 percent, there remained some significant degree of slack in most of the job market.

Economic and Industrial Restructuring

Capitalism thrives on what Schumpeter (1975) called "creative destruction." In *The Communist Manifesto*, Marx and Engels (2002: 223) described this tendency as the "constant revolutionizing of production," whereby the capitalist class continually develops new methods, technologies, and spaces for production in order to sustain and enhance profitability. To relate this to the focus of this book, businesses in the Canadian economy are always adapting to changing economic circumstances. Some sectors and regions expand, while others shrink. This means that many workers are compelled to change jobs, often having to move in search of new work, and it means that workers must often gain new qualifications and learn new skills. Constant change and flux is disruptive for people and communities, and is another factor in the precarious nature of work.

Canada was highly dependent upon international markets long before anyone coined the term *globalization*. Resource industries, the auto industry, and most of the manufacturing sector were driven by export markets long before the Canada–U.S. Free Trade Agreement (FTA), the North American Free Trade Agreement (NAFTA), and the huge recent increase in trade in global markets. Canada has long imported a huge share of what is consumed. Nonetheless, trade deals in North America and the global shift of manufacturing to parts of the Global South have posed significant adjustment challenges, including the loss of many relatively good jobs in manufacturing.

A period of capitalist restructuring that began in the early 1970s initiated significant shifts in working conditions and in the organization of the labour market. Unionized private-sector employers, particularly those in large-scale manufacturing, undertook dramatic restructuring processes, attempting to downsize and reorganize workplaces along the principles of lean production (Moody 1997). So-called "flexible" production strategies, such as outsourcing and subcontracting, contributed to the rise of forms of precarious employment, leading toward an increasingly Just-in-Time workforce. Canada's economy has also been restructured by the ongoing shift from goods production to services, and by technological and organizational changes in how both goods and services are produced. Patterns of labour market change were part of this broader process of economic restructuring that was undertaken in an attempt to increase the productivity and profitability of labour.

Over time, there have been major shifts in the structure of occupations, with some movement toward jobs requiring higher levels of formal education and skills. However, the new economy hype has glossed over the fact that change is not new, or even more rapid, and that many jobs still do not look terribly different from those of a generation ago (Pupo and Thomas 2010). New occupations and new industries have certainly been produced by the information technology revolution and by growth in professional occupations. The share of all jobs in professional occupations has risen modestly, from a bit under one in five in the 1980s to almost one in four today. This includes: professional occupations in business and finance; jobs in the natural and applied sciences; professional occupations in health; teachers and professors; jobs in social sciences and government; and jobs in arts, culture, and recreation. But over one-third of men still work in good-producing industries (manufacturing, utilities, primary industry, trades, transport), and almost one in three women works in sales and service occupations, including in lower-paid and often part-time jobs in stores, hotels, and restaurants, and jobs as security guards, building cleaners, and so on. A low-wage, low-skill, private-service sector is very much a feature of Canada's new economy.

Neoliberalism and Labour Market Policies

Government policies also play an important role in shaping conditions of work, and in the changing patterns of work. The economic transformations referred to briefly above were accompanied by a major shift in public policy in many industrialized capitalist states, including Canada, with the emergence of the neoliberal policy paradigm. Neoliberalism is grounded in an ideological belief in the ability of market forces to generate productivity, efficiency, and prosperity. This approach to public policy represents a fundamental shift toward an emphasis on individualist and market-based mechanisms to address economic and social problems (Harvey 2003).

With respect to the regulation of work, supporters of neoliberalism advocate for a deregulation of labour markets, reductions in state spending on income security policies such as unemployment insurance, and the reduction of cross-border trade (McBride and Shields 1997). Labour market policy in this political context shifted away from social protection toward fostering conditions of labour "flexibility" by exposing workers to market forces (Peck 2001; Thomas 2009). This can include strategies such as privatization or contracting out, reductions in legal protections, and the lack of enforcement of existing legislation (Gellatly et al. 2011). While the principles of neoliberalism call for a reduction of state intervention in the economy, neoliberal state policies are in fact oriented toward changing the way in which the state intervenes, rather than simply "deregulation," as is often stated. What this has meant in practice is that neoliberalism has acted to increase the commodification of labour power—in other words, to heighten the exposure of workers to market forces. For example, with respect to labour policies and labour relations in Canada, successive federal and provincial governments have implemented legislative measures to restrict and eliminate workers' collective rights established in the postwar era through federal and provincial wage controls, the increasing use of back-to-work legislation, and the amendment or rewriting of progressive labour laws within provincial jurisdictions (Panitch and Swartz 2008).

Along with altering the conditions of work through new policy approaches, neoliberalism has also influenced peoples' expectations about work by creating greater pressure on individuals to adapt to the pressures of the "lean" society—which includes longer work hours, reduced pay, and increased user fees for public services (Sears 1999). With respect to labour and employment policies, neoliberalism has provided justification for more flexible and insecure forms of employment and has contributed to a lowering of expectations regarding employment rights.

Unions and Labour Market Institutions

As discussed in Chapters 9 and 10, workers form unions in order to protect and advance their interests and as a means to counter employer power in the workplace. In Canada, about one in three employees is covered by union agreements, double the number in the U.S. Union coverage in the private sector has been slowly falling, but collective agreements still play a major role in shaping wages and other dimensions of employment for many workers.

All advanced industrial countries are, with small differences of degree, exposed to the major structural forces of technological change and globalization. But, they differ profoundly in terms of the ways in which the job market is regulated or shaped by governments, employers, and unions. In most of continental Europe, the wages and employment conditions of the great majority of workers are still set by collective bargaining between unions and employers, with some intervention by governments in the form of minimum wages and employment standards legislation. These labour market rules make a big difference to the distribution of earnings and to the quality of jobs. For example, about 1 in 4 full-time workers in Canada is low paid—defined as earning less than two-thirds of the average national wage—compared to just 1 in 20 in Denmark, and only 1 in 8 in Germany (OECD 2016a).

Supporters of neoliberalism argue that more highly regulated job markets with stronger unions and better job and income protections come at the price of economic growth and job creation, resulting in major differences in the economic performance of North America and Europe. It is true that unemployment has been very high in some of the major European economies for much of the past 20 years, and this is a very serious problem. But some smaller European countries, such as the Netherlands and Denmark, have recently been able to achieve low unemployment along with higher job quality and more income equality than in North America. The main factors at play have included a strong tilt toward job creation in social services rather than private services, high levels of training for unemployed and low-wage workers, and close partnerships between governments, employers, and unions. Moreover, as discussed below, in the years following the financial crisis, the costs of creating a more open market and more "flexible" employment relations as called for by the neoliberal model have been high.

Canada and the Great Recession

The financial crisis across the global economy in late 2008, in what came to be referred to as the Great Recession, produced rising unemployment and inequality in Canada and around the world. Given that it takes economic growth of about 2 percent per year to offset annual increases of about 1 percent in the working-age population and in productivity (output per hour worked), unemployment tends to rise rapidly in downturns, and to take a long period of time to fall even after an economic recovery begins.

This crisis of insecurity and inequality that resulted from the Great Recession of 2008 is rooted in significant part in the so-called flexible labour markets created by governments enthralled with neoliberal economic doctrines and employer interests. The negative impact of the downturn upon Canadian workers was worsened by neoliberal austerity measures introduced in the years following the financial crisis. In response to the crisis, governments sought to further reduce expenditures, privatize public services, and redesign labour laws and labour market policies in order to enhance competitiveness and "labour flexibility" (Albo et al. 2010; Thomas and Tufts 2016). These initiatives contributed to the deterioration of working conditions experienced by many Canadians in the years since, pointing to the need for a fundamental and critical re-examination of Canada's labour market.

The immediate causes of the global economic crisis lay in the deregulation of finance, especially in the U.S. and the U.K., and a massive failure on the part of regulators to rein in rampant speculation and excessive risk-taking. As of early 2009, the International Monetary Fund estimated that total bad loans on the books of the global financial system flowing from the U.S. financial crisis stood at over $2 trillion. Part of these toxic assets originated in the explosion of bank-lending to finance so-called sub-prime mortgages in the U.S. — that is, loans to high-risk borrowers, conditions of the process of financialization (Bellamy Foster and Magdoff 2009). U.S. and U.K. banks also allowed many homeowners to use their houses as ATMs as a "housing bubble" developed out of cheap credit, further swelling the total volume of household debt to record levels.

The originators of high-risk debt, mainly the big investment banks, sliced and diced their loans into complex mortgage- and credit card–backed securities, which were in turn sold to other investors, such as banks, hedge funds, and pension funds, often with (supposed) guarantees against default. When the housing bubble burst in the U.S., the U.K., and other countries such as Ireland and Spain, the whole house of cards collapsed, leaving most large U.S., U.K., and European banks saddled with huge amounts of bad debt, which pushed them to the brink

Box 1.2: The Labour Market in Canada and the United States since the Last Recession

By Andre Bernard and Jeannine Usalcas

The [global financial crisis of 2008] resulted in more severe employment losses in the United States than in Canada. Proportionally, employment losses in the United States were more than double those in Canada, and lasted longer.

Since then, employment in both countries has increased at approximately the same rate, and has not exceeded the rate of growth of the working-age population. Accordingly, the employment rate remains below the pre-recession level in both countries. Since the beginning of 2014, however, employment growth has been higher in the United States than in Canada.

Since the end of the recession, the unemployment rate in both countries has declined, but the decreases have been largely driven by decreases in labour force participation. The decline in the participation rate in the United States has been more pronounced than in Canada, notably among prime-age workers. Therefore, the decrease in the unemployment rate has been more pronounced in the United States. Although Canada's unemployment rate has been lower than that of the United States since May 2008, the gap between the rates has now closed.

Source: Andre Bernard and Jeannine Usalcas. 2014, July. "The Labour Market in Canada and the United States since the Last Recession." *Economic Insights*, no. 036. Ottawa: Statistics Canada.

of insolvency. Even worse, the use of complex financial derivatives, such as credit default swaps, meant that no one was exactly sure who in the closely connected global financial system was ultimately on the hook for the bad debt. As a result, in 2008, banks were reluctant to do business with each other and tightened up greatly on new lending, choking off the economy from its needed oxygen of credit.

The financial crisis was a regulatory failure in the sense that governments generally stood by while financial institutions dealt themselves into insolvency by making highly risky loans, often financed by borrowing other people's money, and by spreading the risks through new financial products that virtually no one understood. In Canada, the federal government resisted calls from financial players to allow banks to merge and to reduce barriers to the entry of foreign banks, which kept our financial system relatively safe, if unexciting to those who wanted to take similarly huge risks. Many of the key players who fuelled the crisis, such as hedge funds, were not regulated at all, and more than a few were not so much reckless as out-and-out fraudulent. In the wake of the crisis, there have been many calls for and indeed even some action to tighten up regulatory controls and make sure that it never happens again. However, financial crises caused by the unwinding of speculative bubbles seem to be an enduring feature of capitalist economies.

All that said, and as compelling as the story of the financial crisis is, the roots of the global economic crisis lie much deeper, in the model of neoliberal global capitalism. The financial system not only drove speculative booms in real estate and shares (as in the dot-com boom, which crashed in 2000), but also generally failed to finance real, productive investments in the advanced capitalist countries. In Canada, as in the U.S. and much of Europe, investment in productive capacity—new plants, machinery and equipment, and so on—lagged despite record-high corporate profits. Instead, real investment mainly took place in developing countries, especially China and developing Asia.

One result of the globalization of manufacturing was the manufacturing job loss crisis and downward pressures on wages in the advanced industrial countries, including the U.S. and Canada. The profits of transnational corporations rose to record levels, as did the incomes of the top 1 percent of the workforce, but the wages of the great majority of the workforce rose only because families worked longer hours. In fact, since the mid-1980s the annual incomes of the top 1 percent of income earners grew by 80 percent, as compared to income growth of 19 percent for the bottom 90 percent of income earners over the same period (Grant and McFarland 2013).

Perversely, capital has flowed not from the rich countries to the poor countries, but from the poor countries to the rich countries, notably the U.S. The huge trade surplus of China with the U.S. was recycled into Chinese and other developing-country central bank purchases of U.S. financial assets, keeping the lopsided relationship between the two countries going. Japan and, to a lesser extent, Germany benefited by selling enough sophisticated machinery and equipment and production inputs to the developing low-wage countries to keep their manufacturing trade roughly in balance, and the resource boom helped offset the crisis in Canadian manufacturing to some degree. Meanwhile, the U.S. ran a huge and continuing trade deficit of about 5 percent of its national income over the past decade, keeping the global economy going, but at the price of ever-rising national debt, much of it held by U.S. households.

So-called free trade and liberalization of investment flows, as noted, put downward pressures on the bargaining power of workers and of trade unions. Adding to this, following the prescriptions of the Organisation of Economic Co-operation and Development Jobs Study of the early 1990s and most mainstream economists, many governments in the Global North consciously tried to make their labour markets more flexible and less inflation-prone by weakening the bargaining power of labour. Trade union rights came under attack. Parts of the job market that were once relatively insulated, such as public services and regulated industries like airlines and trucking, were opened up to lower-wage competition through privatization and deregulation. Minimum wages were not increased in line with inflation. Income support programs, such as unemployment insurance, were scaled back, increasing the pressure on unemployed workers to take pay cuts to get a new job.

Here in Canada, the employment rate rose to very high levels in the economic expansion of the past decade, and unemployment fell to very low levels. However, the proportion of the workforce in the most insecure forms of employment remained steady at about one in five workers. (In 2009, 12.1 percent of men and 12.9 percent of women were in temporary jobs, and 19.9 percent of men and 11.9 percent of women were in the most insecure form of self-employment, so-called own-account jobs, which are often disguised jobs that offer no security and low pay) (Ferrao 2010). The proportion of workers in low-wage jobs (1 in 10 adult women and 1 in 10 adult men)[2] has remained virtually constant, at a level second only to the U.S. in the advanced industrial world. High levels of precarious employment and low pay—especially for women and racialized workers—explain why poverty has not fallen significantly in the supposed good times. Indeed, the proportion of adults who are in working poor families has risen. Despite low unemployment, many working Canadians are far from secure.

In late 2008, Canada entered a recession not only with a higher proportion of precariously employed workers than in the 1980s, but also with much weaker private-sector unions. Minimum wages were raised in some provinces at the end of the expansion period, but remained well below the level of the 1980s when adjusted for inflation. Social assistance benefits were slashed deeply in the 1990s in Ontario and Alberta, and have not been raised in line with inflation elsewhere. Social assistance benefits fall well below the poverty line for almost all family types in all provinces, and can usually only be accessed by exhausting almost all financial assets. And, unlike in previous recessions, any increase in provincial social assistance caseloads will have to be paid for by provincial taxpayers, since federal cost-sharing was eliminated in 1994.

The Employment Insurance system, the first line of defence for workers losing their jobs, was "reformed" in the mid-1990s. When the recession took hold, maximum benefits in 2009 were $447 per week, down from more than $600 per week in today's dollars before the cuts. The average benefit is much less, just over $300 per week. Access to the system and the length of benefits vary on the basis of a complex grid reflecting the local area unemployment rate. In 2015, just one-third of unemployed women qualified for benefits (Canadian Labour Congress 2015a). To get in, a worker has to have essentially worked six months at full-time hours in the recent past (the 910-hour hurdle that has to be jumped by new entrants to the workforce, such as youth, recent immigrants, and women returning to work after an extended leave), and as many as 710 hours in the period immediately before a claim. The entrance requirement disqualifies many precariously employed workers, including half of all part-timers. Once qualified, benefits last for as few as 19 weeks and as many as 50 weeks, with the maximum being generally applicable only to those who lost full-time permanent jobs in a higher-unemployment region.

The key point is that Canada entered a period of high unemployment with many more insecurely employed workers than in previous recessions, with a weakened labour movement, and with a significantly reduced social safety net. The prospect is for the economic crisis to lead to a rapid increase in poverty and

Box 1.3: International Labour Organization Warns of Widespread Insecurity in the Global Labour Market
From the World Employment and Social Outlook 2015

GENEVA (ILO News) – Only one quarter of workers worldwide is estimated to have a stable employment relationship, according to a new report by the International Labour Organization (ILO).

The *World Employment and Social Outlook 2015* (WESO) finds that, among countries with available data (covering 84 per cent of the global workforce), three quarters of workers are employed on temporary or short-term contracts, in informal jobs often without any contract, under own-account arrangements or in unpaid family jobs.

Over 60 per cent of all workers lack any kind of employment contract, with most of them engaged in own-account [a worker who is self-employed, potentially with one or more partners, and has no employees on a continuous basis] or contributing family work in the developing world. However, even among wage and salaried workers, less than half (42 per cent) are working on a permanent contract.

The first edition of the new, annual flagship report, entitled *The Changing Nature of Jobs*, shows that while wage and salaried work is growing worldwide, it still accounts for only half of global employment, with wide variations across regions. For example, in the developed economies and Central and South-Eastern Europe, around eight in ten workers are employees, whereas in South Asia and Sub-Saharan Africa the figure is closer to two in ten.

Another current trend is the rise in part-time employment, especially among women. In the majority of countries with available information, part-time jobs outpaced gains in full-time jobs between 2009 and 2013.

"These new figures point to an increasingly diversified world of work. In some cases, non-standard forms of work can help people get a foothold into the job market. But these emerging trends are also a reflection of the widespread insecurity that's affecting many workers worldwide today," said ILO Director-General Guy Ryder.

"The shift we're seeing from the traditional employment relationship to more non-standard forms of employment is in many cases associated with the rise in inequality and poverty rates in many countries," added Ryder. "What's more, these trends risk perpetuating the vicious circle of weak global demand and slow job creation that has characterized the global economy and many labour markets throughout the post-crisis period."

Source: International Labour Organization (ILO). 2015. "ILO warns of widespread insecurity in the global labour market." *World Employment and Social Outlook*. Geneva: ILO. http://www.ilo.org/global/about-the-ilo/newsroom/news/WCMS_368252/lang--en/index.htm.

widespread economic insecurity, and also for workers to be forced into intense competition for the jobs that continue to exist, putting much more downward pressure on wages and working conditions.

There are economic and social dangers ahead. Economists rightly fear the prospect of deflation, an extended period of falling prices. Since interest rates cannot fall below zero, deflation can mean high real interest rates, reducing the willingness of households and businesses to borrow. And consumers will hold off spending on big-ticket items like cars if they know they can buy them for less in the future, particularly if they fear they may lose their jobs.

If and when wages start to fall, a country can enter a deflationary spiral. That is what happened in the Great Depression of the 1930s. Bank-lending and business investment came to a halt. Facing falling sales and falling prices, businesses tried to slash costs, including labour costs. The spiral came to an end only when governments began to invest, and only when the labour market found a floor. The fair wage legislation of the New Deal, plus the rise of industrial unions like the Autoworkers and Steelworkers, set the stage for the recovery. Ultimately, unions helped resolve the crisis by ensuring that wages would rise in line with productivity growth, driving consumer spending and then new business investment to meet higher demand.

In the immediate post-crisis period, Canadian governments did not seem very concerned about the prospect of wage deflation. To the contrary, the 2009 federal budget imposed a limit of just 1.5 percent on federal wage settlements, and government ministers were calling on the Canadian Auto Workers to cut auto sector wages. The "common sense" promoted in the mainstream media was that workers should tighten their belts in a recession, and accept wage cuts if demanded by employers.

The federal government also failed to make significant improvements to the Employment Insurance system (beyond extending benefits by up to five weeks) and instead doubled the Working Income Tax Benefit, which tops up very low earnings. This cushions the working poor against the impact of a downturn to some degree, but also allows employers to pay very low wages. Labour organizations have generally called for supplements to very low wages to be twinned with higher minimum wages.

In the context of a deep economic downturn, the focus should be on stabilizing the job market by reversing a slide into mass unemployment, and also by setting a stable floor. This would be best done by raising minimum wages, dramatically improving access to EI benefits as well as the level and duration of benefits, and encouraging unionization, particularly among lower-paid workers.

Conclusion

The quality of employment along a number of dimensions is critical to our individual and collective well-being. Yet work remains a profound social problem, heightened by the fallout from the Great Recession. The quality of jobs is shaped by many forces, including the overall state of the economy and industrial restructuring. It is also strongly influenced by the role of governments and unions. Labour market issues lay at the heart of the global economic crisis of 2008, and it is hoped that this book will help spur critical thinking about the current crisis of employment and the need for solutions to address the variety of economic, social, and political factors that contribute to the social problems of work.

Recommended Reading

International Labour Organization (ILO). 2015. *World Employment and Social Outlook: The Changing Nature of Jobs.* Geneva: ILO.
Marx, Karl. 1964. "Alienated Labour," in T. Bottomore (ed.), *Karl Marx: Early Writings.* New York: McGraw Hill, 120–34.
Organization for Economic Cooperation and Development. 2015. *OECD Employment Outlook 2015.* Paris: OECD.
Pupo, Norene, and Mark Thomas (eds.). 2010. *Interrogating the New Economy: Restructuring Work in the 21st Century.* Toronto: University of Toronto Press.

Notes

1. Statistics Canada CANSIM Table 111-0041. Accessed at: http://www5.statcan. gc.ca/cansim/a26?lang=eng&retrLang=eng&id=1110041&tabMode=dataTable &srchLan=-1&p1=-1&p2=9
2. Statistics Canada CANSIM Table 202-0802. Accessed at: http://www.statcan. gc.ca/pub/89-503-x/2010001/article/11388/tbl/tbl012-eng.htm

CHAPTER 2

Work, Wages, and Living Standards in Canada

From the mid-1990s to the present, precarious work has increasingly become the norm for many workers in Canada. Alongside growing precariousness in the labour market, Canadian society has experienced a dramatic increase in the inequality between the relatively small number of wealthy Canadians — the 1 percent — and the rest. In the years following the financial crisis of 2008, the persistence of this inequality, and its connections to capitalism as an economic system, was raised with the Occupy movement of 2011, and continues to fuel ongoing campaigns to improve work, such as the Fight for $15 and Fairness. In this chapter, we explore both the rise of precarious work and growing income inequality in Canada. The chapter surveys recent developments in the labour market, focusing on the period from the mid-1990s through to 2015. It looks at trends in wages and in the kinds of jobs that have been created, highlighting the significance and persistence of precarious forms of employment, the stagnation of real (inflation-adjusted) earnings, and the sharp rise in earnings and income inequality among workers and families. The chapter draws links between the organization of the labour market, rising income inequality, and continued high levels of poverty, particularly in the years following the 2008 financial crisis.

Jobs, Jobs, Jobs: Trends in Employment and Unemployment

By some measures, Canada did much better on the jobs front from the mid-1990s to the mid-2000s than was the case over the 1980s and early 1990s. There were two major economic downturns, one in the early 1980s and one in the early 1990s. The national unemployment rate peaked at 12 percent in 1983 and at 11.4 percent in 1993, and the periods 1982 through 1985 and 1991 through 1994 were all years of double-digit unemployment. Unemployment in the 1980s never fell below 7.5 percent. By contrast, the national unemployment rate fell steadily in the economic recovery, which began around 1993, and the employment rate (the proportion of the population aged 15 to 64 holding jobs) steadily increased. In fact, the national unemployment rate of 6 percent reached in 2007 was the lowest since the 1960s, and the national employment rate was at an all-time high of 63.5 percent. Post-

2008, the unemployment rate rose to as high as 8.6 percent in 2009 following the global economic downturn; however, since then it decreased to 6.9 percent in 2015.

Table 2.1 provides some detailed data on changes in employment and unemployment rates from 1976 to 2015. The decade from 1996 to 2006, just before the point of the financial crisis of 2008, shows some positive trends in overall employment. The national unemployment rate fell from 9.6 percent to 6.3 percent, about one-third, for both women and men, and by slightly less for younger workers. During this period, sustained economic growth drove the national employment rate, as the percentage of the working-age population (aged 15 to 64) holding jobs rose notably, from 58.5 percent in 1996 to 62.8 percent in 2006. During that period, the proportion of the Canadian population with jobs rose to one of the highest in the industrialized world. An unemployment rate of just over 6 percent represented a major step forward compared to the high unemployment levels of the mid-1970s through the mid-1990s. Post-2008, there was a notable increase in the unemployment rates for men, women, and workers of all age groups, though not to the higher levels of the mid-1980s or mid-1990s.

Table 2.1: Employment and Unemployment Trends, 1976–2015

	1976	1986	1996	2006	2015
Unemployment rate					
All	7.1	9.6	9.6	6.3	6.9
Men	6.4	9.5	9.9	6.5	7.5
Women	8.2	9.8	9.3	6.1	6.3
Age 15–24	12.4	14.7	15.4	11.7	13.2
Age 25–54	5.3	8.3	8.6	5.3	5.8
Age 55+	3.9	6.8	7.2	5.1	5.8
Newfoundland and Labrador	13.4	18.8	18.9	14.8	12.8
Prince Edward Island	9.3	13	14.6	11.1	10.4
Nova Scotia	9.2	13.3	12.4	7.9	8.6
New Brunswick	11	14.4	11.6	8.7	9.8
Quebec	8.7	11	11.8	8.1	7.6
Ontario	6.1	7	9	6.3	6.8
Manitoba	4.7	7.6	7.2	4.3	5.6
Saskatchewan	3.8	7.7	6.6	4.7	5
Alberta	3.9	9.9	6.9	3.5	6
British Columbia	8.4	12.7	8.7	4.8	6.2

Table 2.1 (continued)

	1976	1986	1996	2006	2015
Employment rate					
All	57.1	59.8	58.5	62.8	61.3
Men	72.7	69.6	65	67.6	65.3
Women	41.9	50.3	52.1	58.1	57.4
Age 15–24	55.7	59.5	52.7	58.5	55.8
Age 25–54	69.6	75.2	76.2	81.6	81.4
Age 55+	30.2	25.4	22	30.5	35.1
Newfoundland and Labrador	42.8	44.1	42.6	50.4	53.3
Prince Edward Island	51.9	54.5	56.3	60.7	60.5
Nova Scotia	50.5	51.9	52	57.7	57
New Brunswick	48	49.5	51.8	57.8	56.6
Quebec	53.7	56	54.6	60.1	59.9
Ontario	60.3	64	59.6	63.3	60.8
Manitoba	58.9	61.6	61.6	65.4	64.4
Saskatchewan	58.2	61.7	61	65.5	66.6
Alberta	64.7	65.4	67.4	70.9	68.6
British Columbia	56.6	57	59.9	62.2	59.5

Source: Statistics Canada CANSIM Table 282-0002.

During this period of employment growth between 1996 and 2006, the improve-ment in the availability of jobs was shared by virtually all parts of the country. In 2007, the employment rate hit record highs in all provinces with the single exception of Ontario, where the employment rate slipped slightly from 2003 as a result of major job losses in manufacturing and the forest industry. The unem-ployment rate fell notably from 1996 to 2006 across provinces, and particularly large declines were recorded in British Columbia and Alberta. While the picture was generally one of an improving job market across the country through the decade, significant regional differences remained very much in evidence in the years prior to the financial crisis of 2008. By 2006, the employment rate stood at a national high of 70.9 percent in Alberta, well above the low of 50.4 percent in Newfoundland and Labrador. Much of Atlantic Canada experienced significant job gains and declines in unemployment, but the gap between the east and the very low-unemployment provinces of the west remained evident. It is also notable that Quebec's job market performed much better than that of Ontario from 1996 to 2006, though Quebec still had a higher than average unemployment rate. Post-2008, the unemployment rates across the provinces have shown some variability, with continued declines in unemployment in some of the eastern provinces, but rising unemployment rates from Ontario moving west.

As defined by the *Labour Force Survey*, undertaken by Statistics Canada, being unemployed means that a person is not working at all *and* is actively seeking work. The headline unemployment rate is lower than alternative measures that count people who have recently worked but have given up looking for a job (known as discouraged workers), and that count the lost hours of people working part-time who want to work full-time, but cannot get the hours that they want.

Unemployment is generally a bit higher for men than for women. This reflects the fact that proportionately more men work in very seasonal industries, such as construction, and industries subject to frequent layoffs, like manufacturing. The rate of long-term unemployment is, overall, quite low, but highest among older men displaced by industrial restructuring. However, women are much more likely than men to be working involuntarily in part-time jobs and unable to find the hours of work that they want. The biggest gap in unemployment rates is between younger and older workers.

While unemployment in most of Canada fell very significantly between 1996 and 2006, it has to be borne in mind that the average duration of an unemployment spell is fairly short, and that many workers cycle in and out of jobs over the year. Low unemployment is not the same thing as stable employment. Unemployment is experienced by a higher proportion of the total workforce over an entire year than the apparently low average monthly unemployment rate suggests. Despite relatively low unemployment and eligibility provisions that limit access to Employment Insurance (EI) to those who have worked a significant number of hours over the previous year, 2.9 million claims for EI benefits were filed in 2015.[1] Many workers, particularly younger workers and those working in seasonal industries, are in short-term jobs. In 2007, about one in six full-time workers aged 25 to 54 had been in their current jobs for less than one year. In short, even excluding young people who may want short-term jobs, there is a lot of movement in and out of employment and unemployment in any given year. Moreover, a lot of jobs fail to offer very stable hours, and there is a lot of variation in annual hours worked by individuals from year to year. About one-quarter of all regular EI claims are made by so-called frequent claimants (HRSDC 2006a).

The overall Canadian job picture of recent years is marred by some very serious flaws. Most notably, working families have increased their incomes mainly by continuing to work more weeks in the year as unemployment has fallen, as opposed to increases in their real wages, and they have gone deeper into debt. Most of the wage and wealth gains in a period of economic expansion went to those at the very top of the earnings spectrum, rather than to the average worker and average working family, and the top 1 percent or so have pulled away from the rest of the workforce. While jobs have been relatively easy to find in some regions

Box 2.1: Labour Force Restructuring, Austerity, and Widening Inequality in Ontario
By the Ontario Common Front

A generation of Ontarians has grown up in a province that is becoming increasingly unequal. It is hard to imagine how such a rich and beautiful place with so many advantages can see its hard-won gains in equality fall into decline. But Ontario has been first battered by a sea change in the labour force and then slammed by a financial typhoon. As manufacturing work has drained out of our province, the inflow of jobs has not offset the outflow. At the same time, income transfer programs have been eroded, leaving Ontarians more and more vulnerable. Add to this, government cuts that are choking our public services—programs that create equity, boost the standard of living and improve life opportunities—just as the "free market" has restructured many Ontarians out of decent jobs. Not surprisingly, our ability to withstand a tempestuous world economy has been stunted.

The numbers are staggering. A quarter-million jobs have disappeared altogether. Those who can find jobs are working harder but not getting any further ahead. Fully half of Ontarians have seen little or no improvement in their incomes stemming from the periods of economic growth over the last thirty years. The share of the work force earning minimum wage has ballooned more than five-fold since 1997. Almost a third of Ontario's workers—1.7 million people—now earn low or minimum wages. For racialized workers, immigrants, women and youth, that proportion is much higher. Residents in our province face a harder time finding full-time work than our counterparts across the country, and involuntary part-time work is far more common here than elsewhere. Ontario's long-term unemployment has surpassed the rate for the rest of Canada and continues to increase.

At the same time as the labour market is delivering more precarious, low paid and inequitable jobs, Ontario has tumbled to the bottom of the country in rankings measuring access to a wide range of social programs and services—from education to health care and housing to child care. All across Canada it has become harder to raise a young family. But here, costs are higher than anywhere else in the country. While they are working more hours than ever, young families are staggering under education debt loads, housing costs and child care price tags that far exceed those in the other provinces. Seniors and people suffering illness or injury find themselves left on stretchers in hallways of overcrowded hospitals that have suffered more bed cuts than any other province. Funding for all social programs and services is now lower in Ontario than anywhere in Canada. Just when it is most needed, the social infrastructure of our province is being plundered to pay both for the fall-out of a recession that most of us had no hand in creating and for billions in corporate tax cuts from which we are seeing no benefit.

***

We *can* move from backslide to progress and prosperity, but this relies upon a wider sharing of benefits and burdens. We can—indeed we must—insist that in [the] rebuilding of Ontario's economy our government does not replicate the failings of the last thirty years.

Source: Ontario Common Front. 2015. *Backslide: Labour Force Restructuring, Austerity and Widening Inequality in Ontario*. Toronto: Ontario Common Front. http://weareontario.ca/wp-content/uploads/OCF-Backslide-2015.pdf.

of the country, many workers still have very unstable and low-paid jobs, and the overall quality of jobs in terms of forms of employment has not been improving. While Canada has relatively few workers who are unemployed for very long stretches of time, a significant proportion of workers are regularly employed in a series of low-wage and precarious jobs, and survive on low hourly and annual earnings. Large inequalities in the job market continue to exist between women and men, between younger and older workers, and between recent immigrants and racialized minorities and other Canadians. The level of income inequality among Canadian families, as well as rates of poverty, are disturbingly high, particularly when Canada is compared to European countries rather than to the U.S. (Smeeding 2002). Not only has earnings inequality significantly increased, but redistributive economic transfers from government have also been cut, and economic security and access to public and social services have been undermined by government policy changes. These tendencies were all heightened through austerity policies that were implemented post-2008 in response to the financial crisis. In short, the labour market in Canada still falls far short of meeting the needs of many working people.

Precarious Work in the "New Economy"

One of the main employment trends of the past two decades has been the spread of precarious work. Precariousness in employment is a condition that is determined through a combination of factors, including low job security, low wages, low control over the labour process, and a lack of regulatory protection from either collective agreements or labour and employment laws (Vosko 2006). Rather than a dichotomy between "good" and "bad" jobs, precarious work exists on a continuum and includes (but is not limited to) workers who are employed in a range of so-called non-standard employment relationships, such as permanent part-time workers, full- and part-time temporary workers, own-account self-employed workers, and self-employed employers. Moreover, conditions of precariousness are present even in sectors of the labour market that have traditionally been sites of more stable employment (PEPSO 2013; Standing 2011).

Compared to some Western European countries, Canada has long had a job market in which a high proportion of workers are employed in precarious jobs. This marks a move away from what is often defined as the Standard Employment Relationship (SER)—jobs that are full-time and permanent, involving an ongoing and stable relationship between a worker and a single employer (Vosko 2000). While Canada has always had a layer of self-employed workers and a large seasonal workforce, for a period of time there was a norm of full-time, permanent employment among men. In direct contrast to the SER, Non-standard Employment Relationships (NSER) include those that are part-time or temporary, or come in the form of self-employment. As shown in Table 2.2, of those aged 15 and over, in 2015 just under 60 percent of men and just over 40 percent of women were employed in full-time jobs, with 20 percent of men and over 20 percent of women employed in the more precarious forms of self-employment and part-time work.[2] While these types of employment should not be treated as synonymous with precarious work, part-time employment and self-employment are often less secure and lower paid than are permanent, full-time jobs.

The rise of non-standard and precarious work is deeply gendered. As indicated in Table 2.2, women are twice as likely to work part-time than men (gender differences in self-employment are further discussed in Chapter 5). This is partly out of the need to balance paid work with unpaid reproductive labour, and partly because women find it harder to find full-time jobs. About one-third of adult women who work part-time say that they would prefer to work full-time, and this proportion would likely be higher if child care and elder care were more widely available and expanded their choices in balancing work and family. At the same time, part-time jobs allow employers to vary hours of work in line with changing business conditions, which might not at all match worker preferences. Many part-timers do not have much control over the hours that they work, and frequently work at night and on weekends. The shift to temporary jobs has also been driven more by employers' increased desire to have a more flexible workforce, which can be increased or decreased in size on short notice, than by workers' desires for very short-term jobs. Similarly, increased self-employment can partly be explained by

Table 2.2: Trends in Forms of Employment, 1997–2015 (by gender, ages 15 and up)

	Male			Female		
	1997	2007	2015	1997	2007	2015
Full-time	58.6	60.4	57.4	37.2	43.4	42.2
Part-time	6.9	7.5	7.9	15.4	15.5	15.1
Temporary	5.7	6.8	6.9	5.3	7.1	7
Self-employed	13.3	12.9	12.1	7	6.8	6.9

Source: Statistics Canada, *Labour Force Survey* Estimates, CANSIM Tables 282-0002, 282-0012, and 282-0080.

the desire of larger companies and governments to contract out work to outside suppliers of goods and services in order to reduce their costs.

Non-standard jobs are not always so-called "bad jobs." Entry-level, temporary, and part-time jobs for youth can be a good source of experience. Many people, particularly students and some parents, want to work part-time. A layer of self-employed professionals and skilled workers—doctors, lawyers, accountants, architects, building contractors, artists, and so on—do very well. However, part-time and temporary jobs, on average, pay significantly less than comparable full-time jobs, are much less likely to provide health and pension benefits, and offer much more limited access to progressive career ladders. Most temporary workers other than students would rather have permanent jobs. And a layer of self-employed workers—the so-called own-account self-employed, who work by themselves and have no employees—tend to have very low annual earnings (Vosko 2006).

Ongoing restructuring in both the private and public sectors, driven by global-ization, technological and organizational change, contracting out, and government spending cuts, have fuelled increased labour market segmentation and inequality. At one pole, we see a high level of insecure and low-paid precarious work among youth and young adults, recent immigrants, Aboriginal Canadians, persons with disabilities, and a layer of adults with limited education or in-demand skills. Women are more likely to be in precarious jobs than men, but the jobs of many men have become increasingly like the jobs traditionally held by women. Precarious work can include permanent, full-time employment that is low paid or frequently interrupted by unemployment, employment in temporary jobs, underemployment in involun-tary part-time jobs, or employment in low-income, own-account self-employment. Precarious work also carries a high risk of not leading to the development of skills and capacities that increase workers' ability to access better jobs or to start and proceed on lifetime career ladders, and to better handle labour market risks, such as permanent layoffs due to economic change. Job experience and on-the-job train-ing are sources of human capital that enable workers to make upward progression in the job market and better deal with economic uncertainty. Many low-wage and short-term jobs are traps rather than stepping stones to better jobs. Almost by definition, precarious workers are excluded from the internal labour markets of large companies and government organizations, where the norm is for permanent workers to climb job ladders through promotion from within. Research shows that there is a significant widening of longer-term or life-cycle earnings differentials and life chances in the 1990s, particularly among men (Beach et al. 2003). Being trapped in a low-wage job usually also means being unable to derive some meaning and fulfillment from work. Workers value jobs not only for purely economic reasons, but also to the extent that they provide interesting work and opportunities for self-development, all of which may be lacking in precarious work.

At the other end of the job spectrum are jobs that continue to reflect the norm of the SER in that they are reasonably secure, full-time, full-year jobs in larger workplaces, and generally require higher levels of education and skills. These jobs often involve the use of skills and discretion on the job, and provide access to lifetime career ladders. For professionals and skilled workers, work reorganization and new technology can produce more interesting and developmental jobs. However, there was also a great deal of work intensification in the 1990s that took the form of greater production demands, increased work pace, and longer hours. Surveys indicate high and rising levels of stress from very long hours, demands to do more with less in the wake of downsizing, the intrusion of paid work into the home, and reduced ability to balance the demands of paid work with those of family and community.

Looking in more detail at the kinds of jobs held by workers in Canada, there was a significant shift to more precarious forms of employment in the recession and slow recovery of the 1990s, which only modestly reversed itself over the course of the following decade. The recession of the early 1990s saw the loss of many permanent, full-time jobs, particularly for men in manufacturing. As the unemployment rate rose, the employment rate fell, and the proportion of part-timers, temporary workers, and self-employed increased. As the economic recovery gathered steam after 1993, job creation began to shift back to full-time jobs. The part-time rate (or the proportion of workers in part-time jobs) rose sharply from 1989 to the mid-1990s, but job growth mainly tilted toward full-time jobs since that time. The part-time rate fell significantly for adult women, while remaining high for young workers. The proportion of own-account self-employed workers also increased in a slack job market, from 7.2 percent in 1989 to 9.8 percent in 2003, as did the proportion of temporary workers, which rose from 7 percent to 11 percent of the workforce (Vosko et al. 2003). However, since 2008 the self-employment rate in Canada has been decreasing. In 2008, 9.2 percent of Canadians reported being self-employed. This rose to 9.5 percent in 2009, dropping slightly to 8.8 percent by 2014 (OECD 2016b) Meanwhile, temporary employment has continued to increase, reaching 13.4 percent in 2014 (OECD 2016c).

The proportion of workers in the most precarious forms of employment remained high and has grown since the 1990s. Temporary work has become entrenched as the norm for the entry of young workers into the full-time job market (Morissette and Johnson 2005). By 2007, about one in five workers were in forms of employment that offered little security, and usually much lower pay and benefits than permanent jobs. Moreover, of all new jobs created since the economic downturn that began in 2008, three-quarters have been part-time, temporary, or in the self-employed sector (Canadian Labour Congress 2015b).

The Rising Corporate Share

From 1996 to 2006, the Canadian economy grew quite rapidly, and real (that is, inflation-adjusted) GDP (national income) per person rose by a cumulative total of 27 percent. However, income in the hands of households failed to grow at anywhere near the same pace. Real personal income—the total of all before-tax wage, investment, small business, and government transfer income going to households, adjusted for increases in consumer prices—rose by only 17 percent over the same period. One reason for the shrinkage in households' share of national income was that corporate pre-tax profits grew rapidly as a share of the total economic pie. Labour's share of total national income (after taxes) has been on a declining trend ever since the late 1970s, while the corporate profit share has been trending upward over the same period, and hit record highs almost every year after the recovery from the recession of the early 1990s.

While wages and household income used to rise more or less in lockstep with productivity growth—the rise in real business sector output per hour worked, which drives the rise in per-person national income—real wages have basically flatlined for much of the past 30 years. While returns from investments boosted the incomes of very affluent households, wage stagnation in an expanding economy meant that working family living standards essentially stalled despite reasonably strong economic growth (Russell and Dufour 2007). Over the past 30 years, and particularly in the years since the 2008 financial crisis, it is clear that the balance of bargaining power in the economy has tilted against workers in Canada. The same trend has been seen in most other advanced industrial countries since the late 1980s, and probably reflects the impacts of greater international trade and investment links with the rest of the world. Companies are generally free to shift investment and jobs to countries where profitability is higher, and this is certainly a factor when it comes to setting wages.

Stagnant Real Wages

A major study by Statistics Canada on changes in the structure of hourly wages between 1981 and 2004 found that most workers experienced very modest gains in their real (inflation-adjusted) wages over that extended period (Morissette and Johnson 2005). In fact, over this time period, the median male worker—one in the exact middle of the male earnings spectrum, such that half earn more and half less—experienced a 2 percent fall in his real hourly wage. In other words, in 2004, the hourly wage of a median male worker was slightly less than that of a median male worker back in 1981. Over the same period, the median female worker experienced a real wage gain of 10.7 percent. While certainly better than the gain for men, a 10.7 percent cumulative real wage gain over 23 years is hardly a cause for celebration and, as discussed in Chapter 5, this wage gain did not erase the persistent wage gap between men and women workers. Real wages stagnated most in manufacturing (the sector that is the most heavily exposed to international competitive forces) and in the public sector (which is subject to fiscal restraint through neoliberalism), while rising a bit more than average in high-skilled private service industries.

Looking at wage trends from 1997 to 2015 in Table 2.3, there was much higher real wage growth at the very high end of the wage distribution, that is, among very high-income earners. Real wage gains were greatest for managers and professionals in business and finance over this time span. Stagnating real wages for most workers have been matched by cuts in benefits coverage, and by an erosion of the union wage and benefit advantage.

Table 2.3 provides data on real wage gains (in 2015 dollars) from 1997 to 2015, which averaged 14.9 percent over nearly two decades. But higher-paid employees, such as senior managers and professionals in business and finance, experienced

Table 2.3: Change in Real Average Hourly Wage, 1997–2015 (in 2015 constant dollars)

	1997	2007	2015	Increase $	Increase %
All	21.92	23.25	25.19	3.27	14.9
Men	24.03	25.28	27.07	3.04	12.7
Women	19.6	21.19	23.26	3.66	18.7
Age 15–24	12.54	13.44	14.63	2.09	16.7
Full-time	23.25	24.78	26.88	3.63	15.6
Part-time	16	16.3	17.53	1.53	9.7
Selected occupations:					
Senior managers	38.97	44.42	44.77	5.8	14.9
Professional occupations in business and finance	28.34	33.29	34.94	6.6	23.3
Health occupations	25.72	27.68	29.01	3.38	12.8
Trades, transport, and equipment operators	22.43	23.23	25.14	2.71	12.1
Machine operators/ assemblers, including supervisors	20.5	20.95	21.77	1.27	6.0
Clerical occupations, including supervisors	18.9	19.48	20.86	1.96	10.4
Sales and service occupations	15.2	15.53	16.99	1.79	11.8

Source: Statistics Canada CANSIM Table 282-0070.

much larger gains, while real wages were essentially flat for non-professionals, including blue-collar, clerical, and sales and service workers. Average real hourly wages began to increase a bit faster up to 2007, as unemployment fell to quite a low level, but averages can be misleading. Real wage gains were very limited for the bottom 80 percent or so of Canadian workers despite a low unemployment rate in the late 1990s and early 2000s, and supposed labour and skills shortages. Wage gains were a bit higher for ordinary workers in booming parts of the country, but even here it has to be taken into account that inflation, driven up above all by soaring housing costs, is also greatest in the provinces with the lowest unemployment rates.

Rising Wage Inequality—The Top Takes Off

Though gaining widespread public attention post-2008, for the past several decades Canada, like the U.S. and the U.K., has experienced a very marked increase in the proportion of all income and, especially, wages going to the very top income earners, such as senior corporate executives (Saez and Veall 2003). Between 1990 and 2000, the share of all income reported on annual income tax returns by the top 10 percent of individual Canadian taxpayers rose from 35.5 percent to 42.3 percent of the total. The top 10 percent in 2012 were those making more than $86,700 per year. Even within this top group, it was the very top that made the biggest gains. The top 1 percent of taxpayers had an average income of $381,300 in 2012 (Statistics Canada 2011g). Looking at the taxable incomes (i.e., earnings and investment income) of individual Canadians from 2006 to 2013, the share of the top 1 percent rose from 8.6 percent to 12.2 percent of all income, and the real incomes of the top 1 percent grew by over 60 percent while stagnating for the bottom 40 percent, and barely increasing for the bottom 80 percent (Statistics Canada 2015a). The gains of the top 1 percent were, in turn, driven by very high income gains among the very, very affluent, such as the top one-tenth of 1 percent, who earned an average of over $1.6 million. In November 2013, the *Globe and Mail* reported that the annual incomes of top earners more than doubled over the past three decades, while the median taxpayer's income changed very little. Between 2001 and 2011, median pay for CEOs at Canada's 100 largest companies has almost tripled, to $4.1 million from $1.4 million (Grant and McFarland 2013).

In Canada, as in the U.S., rising wage inequality is partly explained by changes in labour market institutions. As stressed by noted U.S. economist and *New York Times* columnist Paul Krugman (2007), the "Great Compression" of wages from the 1940s though the mid-1970s was closely associated with the growth in the numbers and bargaining power of unions, and relatively high minimum wages and other worker-friendly legislation that flowed from governments that were responsive to the demands and interests of labour. Changes in the economy and in politics have since placed workers and unions on the defensive. The most common explanation

Table 2.4: Family Income (Before Tax) and Net Worth (Wealth) by Income Quintile, 1999 and 2012

	Average		
	1999	**2012**	**1999 to 2012**
	dollars		**% Change**
Income	**63,300**	**74,800**	**18.2**
Bottom quintile	12,600	13,600	7.9
Second quintile	30,400	34,600	13.8
Middle quintile	49,900	57,200	14.6
Fourth quintile	76,000	88,100	15.9
Top quintile	147,500	180,600	22.4
Net worth	**319,800**	**554,100**	**73.3**
Bottom quintile	79,500	109,300	37.5
Second quintile	175,100	267,400	52.7
Middle quintile	261,800	453,300	73.1
Fourth quintile	360,700	641,000	77.7
Top quintile	721,900	1,300,100	80.1

Source: Statistics Canada, *Survey of Financial Security,* 1999 and 2012.

offered by economists for rising inequality—increased returns to skills due to globalization and new technologies—does not really explain why even the wages of highly educated workers are lagging well behind those at the very top.

A significant part of the increased share of the very top income earners is likely explained by the very rapid growth of compensation of senior corporate executives, especially CEOs. For example, through the 1990s and into the early 2000s, the pay of the top five senior executives in U.S. public companies doubled from 5 percent to 10 percent of total earnings, driven mainly by the huge increase in low-priced stock options granted to senior managers (Bebchuk and Grinstein 2005). In Canada, by 2008, CEOs were earning about as much in one day as an average worker does in a year (Mackenzie 2007). In 2013, the top 100 CEOs had an average income of $7.96 million, 379 times more than full-time minimum-wage workers in 2012 (Mackenzie 2014). That is up from 105 times more in 1998. Senior corporate executives do very well, in part because they exercise a great deal of control over their own compensation, and their rising share cannot be justified by improved corporate performance (Bebchuk and Grinstein 2005; Gordon and Dew-Becker 2008). In the business world, there have also been huge income increases among top bankers and investment professionals, such as those who run private equity funds and hedge funds.

This growing income polarization became a flashpoint in 2011, with the emergence of the Occupy Wall Street movement (Milkman et al. 2013; Tufts and Thomas 2014). Beginning in lower Manhattan in the fall of 2011, the Occupy movement spread quickly to many major cities across North America and beyond. At the centre of the movement was the determination to highlight the disparity between the 1 percent and the 99 percent. While the movement was dissipating by December 2011, its targeting of the 1 percent had a lasting impact on the growing public awareness and concern over economic inequality. Moreover, the legacy of the movement can be seen in the rise of more recent efforts to contest the effects of low-wage, precarious employment through movements like the Fight for $15 and Fairness.

Wealth and Debt

Parallel with the sharp increase in earnings and income inequality, wealth has become even more concentrated in the hands of the very rich (Morissette and Zhang 2006). Household assets consist mainly of financial assets (worth about one-half of all household assets) and housing, while about three-quarters of all debt consists of mortgage debt. Wealth is defined as assets minus debt, and is much more unequally distributed than income. In 2012, the top quintile of Canadian households owned 47 percent of the wealth and had a median net worth of $1.3 million, reflecting the fact that ownership of financial assets in particular is highly concentrated in relatively few hands. The bottom quintile of households owned essentially no net wealth (Uppal and LaRochelle-Cote 2015). The extreme concentration of wealth is somewhat less skewed if one bears in mind that older households generally have more assets than younger ones, if pension assets are taken into account. Still, it is clear that wealth is very unequally shared and has become significantly more concentrated. For example, the wealth share of the top 10 percent of households rose from 51.8 percent in 1984 to 70 percent in 2013 (Brown 2013). Within the top 10 percent, the share of the top 1 percent rose from 7.6 percent of all wealth in 1984 to 14 percent in 2012 (Broadbent Institute 2012). Between 1999 and 2005, the wealth of the bottom 40 percent stagnated or fell in dollar terms, and almost all of the increase in household wealth took place among the top 40 percent, especially the top 10 percent (Uppal and LaRochelle-Cote 2015).

A study by the Vanier Institute of the Family shows that household spending has been rising at a significantly faster rate than household income ever since 1990 (Sauvé 2007). Personal debt has jumped from 91 percent to 166 percent of personal after-tax income (OECD 2016d). Most of that is accounted for by increased mortgage debt. Canada's personal savings rate has steadily declined, from 10 percent in 1990 to just 1 percent in 2014, and approximately 100,000 households declare insolvency each year. It would seem that many households have taken on a lot of debt and increased their consumption by borrowing.

High and rising levels of debt among ordinary working families represent the flip side of the increased concentration of income and wealth in the hands of the very affluent.

Low Pay

The Organisation for Economic Co-operation and Development defines low pay as earning less than two-thirds of the national median hourly wage, which translates into making less than $13.88 per hour in Canada in 2011. Canada stands out among industrialized countries in terms of having a high proportion of low-paid workers, with only the U.S. showing a higher proportion. This indicates that there is a significant group of Canadian workers who are paid well below the national norm. In recent years, about one in four Canadian workers has been low-paid by this definition. The incidence of low wages is, not too surprisingly, very high among young workers aged 15 to 24 (66 percent) compared to workers aged 25 to 54 (32 percent). Among core-age workers aged 25 to 54, the incidence of low pay is much higher among women (22 percent) than men (10 percent) (Galarneau and Fecteau 2014).[3] The incidence of low pay changed little in the years prior to the 2008 financial crisis, meaning that a period of economic recovery did not bring up the wages of workers at the bottom compared to those in the middle of the earnings spectrum (Morissette 2008). The incidence of low pay is, again unsurprisingly, much higher among clerical, sales, service, and labouring occupations, where average pay is itself low, and generally quite low in occupations outside these clusters. The high incidence of low-paid work in North America helps explain rates of poverty among the working-age population, as it is hard to maintain some equality of family incomes if there are large and growing earnings gaps among workers.

Growing Income Inequality among Families

As individual earnings inequality has increased, so has income inequality among working-age families. The period 1976 to 2013 saw a notable increase in inequality of earnings among economic families.[4] Table 2.5 shows changes in after-tax incomes for such families, ranked by decile. The share of all earnings going to the top decile (the top 10 percent) rose from 22.8 percent to 24.4 percent from 1976 to 2013, at the expense of the bottom 90 percent of families. By 2013, 40 percent of all the earnings of economic families were going to the top 20 percent, while the bottom 80 percent had to share the remaining 60 percent.

How do we explain rising market income inequality among families? This is partly driven by changes in the way in which people form families. The rise of single-parent families from the 1980s on meant that more families with children became dependent on just one person's earnings, usually those of the mother.

Table 2.5: Changing After-Tax Income Shares of Economic Families, by Decile, 1976–2013

Decile	1976	1986	1996	2006	2013	Change
1	2.4	2.8	2.7	2.6	2.6	0.2
2	4.5	4.7	4.6	4.5	4.5	0.0
3	6.1	6.0	5.9	5.7	5.6	-0.5
4	7.4	7.3	7.1	6.9	6.7	-0.7
5	8.6	8.5	8.3	8.1	8.0	-0.6
6	9.7	9.7	9.6	9.3	9.2	-0.5
7	11.0	11.0	11.0	10.8	10.8	-0.2
8	12.6	12.7	12.7	12.6	12.7	0.1
9	14.9	14.9	15.2	15.3	15.6	0.7
10	22.8	22.3	23.0	24.0	24.4	1.6

Source: Statistics Canada, Income Statistics Division, CANSIM Table 206-0031.

Another change has been that higher-income men and higher-income women are more likely to live with each other than in the past. High-income men once often lived with spouses who worked at home or only on a part-time basis, but the norm is now for high-income female and male professionals and managers to live with each other. This compounds the impact of individual earnings inequality on inequality among families.

The main reason for rising inequality among families is increased inequality in the job market itself. Two big factors are at play. Families down the income scale are more likely to be made up of people in lower-paid jobs, and they are less likely to be working full-time hours for the whole year if they are in temporary or own-account jobs. Families at the top end of the income scale now usually combine two well-paid, permanent jobs. While Canada's tax system involves higher tax rates moving up the income scale and transfer payments (such as child tax credits, Employment Insurance benefits, and social assistance benefits), which both contribute to offsetting earnings inequality, these measures have not significantly blunted the big increase in income differences between the very top, the middle, and the bottom.

Despite the economic growth experienced for a time during the late 1990s and early 2000s, the positive impact on the incomes of many working-age households was significantly offset by cuts to government social programs. These cuts were made partly to balance government budgets, but also to enhance labour market "flexibility" and increase peoples' dependence on market processes. While seniors' benefits were largely unaffected by policy changes, government transfers to working-age households—mainly Employment Insurance and social assistance benefits—fell sharply. Both EI and welfare benefits fell in dollar terms because

Box 2.2: Deep and Persistent Wealth Inequality in Canada
By the Broadbent Institute

The new Statistics Canada data show a deeply unequal Canada in which wealth is concentrated heavily in the top 10% while the bottom 10% hold more debts than assets. The majority of Canadians, meanwhile, own almost no financial assets besides their pensions.

- The top 10% of Canadians accounted for almost half (47.9%) of all wealth in 2012.
- In 2012, the bottom 30% of Canadians accounted for less than 1% of all wealth; the bottom 50% combined controlled less than 6%.
- The median net worth of the top 10% was $2,103,200 in 2012. It rose by $620,600 (41.9%) since 2005. In contrast, the median net worth of the bottom 10% was negative $5,100 in 2012, dropping more than 150% from negative $2,000 in 2005.
- The top 10% held almost $6 in every $10 (59.6%) of financial assets, excluding pensions—more than the bottom 90% combined. The bottom half of the population held less than 6% of financial assets and the bottom 70% of the population only 16%.
- The concentration of wealth for the top 10% is highest in British Columbia at 56.2% and lowest in Atlantic Canada (31.7%) and Quebec (43.4%). Wealth inequality is also, on the whole, least pronounced in Atlantic Canada and Quebec.

The top 10% of Canadians own almost half of all wealth. And when one considers this concentration alongside the gap between the wealthiest and poorest 10%, or the gap between the wealthiest 10% and bottom 50%, it is clear that deep wealth inequality remains a marked feature of Canadian society.

Source: Broadbent Institute. 2014. *Haves and Have-Nots: Deep and Persistent Wealth Inequality in Canada.* http://www.broadbentinstitute.ca/haves_and_have_nots. All data in this report are sourced from: Statistics Canada, *Survey of Financial Security*, 1999, 2005, 2012.

of falling unemployment, but the cuts to EI benefits brought about through new legislation in the mid-1990s raised the number of hours of work needed to qualify for benefits, with a major negative impact on part-time and seasonal workers. Also, the EI replacement rate (the proportion of insured earnings replaced by EI benefits) was cut from 60 percent to 55 percent, and the maximum benefit was frozen for a decade, cutting it in real terms by over 25 percent. From the early to mid-1990s, most provinces either froze or cut social assistance (welfare) benefits. As discussed in Chapter 1, post-2008 austerity measures compounded these

Box 2.3: Canada's Inequality Equation: Who's Gaining, Who's Lagging and Why
By James Bagnall

It may be one of the strangest aspects of the federal election campaign to date: Liberal leader Justin Trudeau pledging to hike income taxes for anyone earning more than $200,000 annually. The odd part is not that he is taking aim at people such as himself—the top one per cent of Canadians in terms of income. Rather, it's that the policy would attempt to reverse what happened during the Liberals' lengthy stretch in office from 1993 to 2006. That's when the "One Percenters" substantially improved their relative position, as their share of the country's after-tax income surged from 6.3 per cent to 9.7 per cent—a far bigger jump than any other major income group.

The Liberals, under Jean Chretien and Paul Martin, did not set out to produce this result. They simply pushed ahead with an agenda that favoured economic growth, which was helped along by a dramatic economic recovery in the United States, Canada's largest trading partner. The rise in corporate profits triggered a wave of executive bonuses and increases in stock-based compensation, especially during the 1990s tech boom. All groups enjoyed gains in real income, but the top earners gained the most. Achieving a fair division of economic spoils is one of the most difficult things for a country to get right.

When there's too much equality—if, for example, governments tax top earners too much—entrepreneurs don't see enough incentive. When there's too little equality—if the top earners vastly outstrip everyone else—resentment builds among middle- and lower-income citizens. It's a political vein being tapped to great effect south of the border by Democratic Party presidential hopeful Bernie Sanders. The Vermont Senator's popularity has been climbing sharply along with his attacks on America's One Percenters.

While top earners in the U.S. take home nearly double what their counterparts in Canada do, it's no accident the leaders of Canada's main opposition parties are pushing a similar agenda of income fairness during this election campaign. Liberal leader Justin Trudeau and New Democratic Party leader Tom Mulcair are promising more middle-class jobs by investing in urban infrastructure and clean technologies. Each has also announced measures to help families with childcare expenses—the Liberals through a tax benefit, the NDP with a national childcare program offering spaces at less than $15 per day.

The Liberals have also proposed cutting marginal tax rates for individuals on incomes between $44,700 and $89,400—which will be paid for in part by hiking the marginal rate for anyone earning more than $200,000.

For their part, the Conservatives appear satisfied with the status quo they created. During their decade in office, they trimmed taxes on personal incomes and small businesses, and slashed the goods and services tax to five per cent from seven per cent. More recently, they have introduced or expanded programs—such as the registered education savings account and tax-free savings account—that offer the most benefits to those in higher tax brackets, including many in the middle class....

Rise of the One Percenters

In the last three decades the One Percenters have increased their share of the national income by 2.6 percentage points. This was thanks to a 68 per cent jump in average after-tax incomes to $300,700—compared to income gains of less than 14 per cent for taxpayers in the bottom 90 per cent of income earners. Individual taxpayers in the top one per cent to 10 per cent group saw real incomes rise 33 per cent. Their share of the income pie was up 1.2 percentage points. Clues about why the best paid are outdistancing the others can be found in how they performed during key economic events in Canada's largest cities. There is no better example than Ottawa during the telecom technology boom. In the late 1990s the nation's capital was the epicentre of a global rush to create an Internet capable of handling huge amounts of digital traffic at great speed. JDS Uniphase built the fiber-optic components and Nortel Networks assembled them into works of engineering genius. Ambitious employees exercised generous stock options to finance startups. The result: Ottawa's workforce experienced a burst of wealth—and inequality. The top one per cent, representing fewer than 6,000 people, saw average after-tax incomes surge 70 per cent from 1998 to 2000 to nearly $400,000 (constant 2012 dollars). In 1998, the one per cent club controlled 6.6 per cent of the city's after-tax income. Just two years later, they accounted for 10 per cent. The average was skewed by a small group of insiders. For instance, 50 of the city's top high-tech executives—including JDSU chief executive Josef Straus and former chief financial Zita Cobb—took home more than $1 billion during the two peak years of the boom.

Indeed, incomes for Ottawa's One Percenters grew much faster from 1998 to 2000 than in any other city. In Montreal, Toronto and Vancouver, the top guns saw two-year increases in income ranging between 20 and 26 per cent. In Edmonton and Calgary the One Percenters began winning a disproportionate share of income in 2002, as the oil industry began its recovery. Even after the telecom crash, Ottawa's One Percenters in 2002 still claimed income and capital gains more than 50 per cent higher in real terms than during the years leading up to the 2000 peak. And, with only a few exceptions including the recession year of 2009, the top one per cent has seen its fortunes rise ever since. With the exception of the tech bubble years, Ottawa has exhibited the lowest inequality of the country's largest cities. In 2012, its One Percenters accounted for seven per cent of the city's total after-tax income, compared to roughly 8.5 per cent for Montreal and Edmonton, 9.6 per cent for Vancouver, 11.4 per cent for Toronto and 13.3

per cent for Calgary. Government, with its relatively flat pay scales and lack of stock-based compensation, sets the pace. This is abundantly clear in Gatineau, which, unlike Ottawa, did not experience a tech bubble. Gatineau's one per cent club in 2012 accounted for a relatively paltry 5.3 per cent of the city's income. Like their counterparts in the other large cities, Gatineau's top earners have seen their share of their city's income decline somewhat under the Conservative government of Stephen Harper. For this, the explanation can be found in the aftermath of the 2008–09 financial crisis and an underperforming economy. But in all cities, the One Percenters claim significantly more of the collective income than they did during the 1980s.

Source: Bagnall, James. 2015, September 25. "Canada's inequality equation: Who's gaining, who's lagging and why." *Ottawa Citizen*. http://ottawacitizen.com/news/politics/canadas-inequality-equation-why-more-growth-means-less-equality.

tendencies. Thus, in a time when many jobs continued to offer quite insecure hours and fluctuating earnings, and the incidence of low-wage work remained high, income supports for working families were cut back quite significantly.

The Working Poor

Poverty can be defined in many ways, but the most useful measure in Canada is with Statistics Canada Low Income Cut-Offs, which vary according to family size and the size of the community in which they live. Low income is basically defined as having to spend a much higher than average share of household income on food and shelter. The cut-off line in 2011 for a single person in a big city was $23,398 before tax and $19,307 after tax.[5] For a two-person family, it rose to $29,004 and $23,498, respectively.

As shown in Table 2.6, the percentage of people living in low income (after tax) increased sharply between 1989 and 1996, the years of recession and slow recovery. This then fell back to or near 1989 levels, at a bit above 10 percent for all Canadians by 2006, and declined slightly further by 2011. Of particular note in this table is the high percentage of children in female-headed lone-parent families living in low income (23 percent in 2011).

High rates of poverty among single, working-age people show how hard it is for people at the bottom end of the job market to get enough income from earnings. Low earnings are now by far the most significant factor in explaining poverty among working-age households. Families living on social assistance have incomes well below the poverty line, but, as Campaign 2000 has underlined in its annual *Report Card* on child poverty in Canada, the majority of poor children now live in

Table 2.6: Percentage of Persons Living in Low Income, LICO, After Tax, 1992 Base

	(LICO-AT, 1992, after tax)			
	1989	1996	2006	2011
All	10.2	15.2	10.3	8.8
Children	11.9	18.4	11.1	8.5
Age 18–64	9.3	15	11.1	9.7
Age 65+	11.3	9.7	5.3	5.2
Unattached under age 65				
Men	25	37.7	31.8	29.9
Women	34.1	44.2	37.3	36
Children living in female lone-parent families	46.2	56	31.2	23

Source: Statistics Canada CANSIM Table 202-0802.

working-poor families, and more than 40 percent live in families where at least one person is working full-time for the full year.

Individuals and families move in and out of poverty for two main reasons. Changes in families due to the breakdown or establishment of relationships are important, especially for women with children, who often fall into poverty after a divorce. The second major factor is the quality of jobs. A significant proportion of working families cycle in and out of poverty depending on how many weeks of work they get in a year, and at what wage. The working poor tend to move from welfare to work and back from work to welfare after a job ends, perhaps after a period of using up savings and drawing support from Employment Insurance. In round numbers, a single person had to be working more or less full-time in a full-year job and earning about $11 per hour to escape poverty in 2006. The threshold is obviously higher if a single earner has to support a child or a non-working spouse.

Minimum wages continue to be far too low in all provinces to put working families with even full-time jobs above the poverty line. Detailed calculations by the National Council of Welfare (2003) showed that even low-wage (below two-thirds of the median), full-time, full-year jobs, supplemented by government income supports, put most families in larger cities only very modestly above poverty lines. Yet, among core-age workers aged 25 to 54, about 1 in 10 men and more than 1 in 5 women are in low-wage jobs, as are 2 out of 3 young people (many of whom have left home). Because of the persistence of these conditions, there has been growing pressure in recent years to improve the incomes of those in the lowest-paid jobs, for example, through campaigns to raise the minimum wage, and also to introduce a "living wage."[6]

Most adult low-paid workers (particularly women and those with low levels of education) remain low paid, sometimes moving a bit above the poverty line and sometimes falling below, depending on the state of the economy and their ability to find a steady job. Vulnerability to poverty among adult low-wage workers is particularly great for single adults and single parents, who must rely on one income and one wage, as opposed to two-person families, which can usually combine two wages. As will be discussed in Chapter 6, vulnerability is also much greater than average for recent immigrants and racialized minorities, who often have low earnings despite higher-than-average levels of education.

Conclusion

Jobs clearly matter to the well-being of Canadians. While the record of the economic recovery from the mid-1990s to the mid-2000s showed positive signs, the labour market situation of many took a turn for the worse in the years following the Great Recession. Moreover, the labour market shows a long-term trend toward rising precariousness, with many workers in low-paid and insecure jobs. And while the wages of most workers have been stagnant, the earnings of high-paid workers and families have been pulling away. As noted in a report from the Centre for Policy Alternatives (Yalnizyan 2007), aptly titled *The Rich and the Rest of Us*, Canada has a major and growing problem of surging inequality, and a large underclass of working-poor families.

Recommended Reading

Mackenzie, Hugh. 2014. *All In A Day's Work? CEO Pay in Canada*. Ottawa: CCPA.
Poverty and Employment Precarity in Southern Ontario (PEPSO). 2013. *It's More Than Poverty: Employment Precarity and Household Well-being*. Toronto: United Way.
Standing, Guy. 2011. *The Precariat: The New Dangerous Class*. London & New York: Bloomsbury Academic.
Vosko, Leah (ed.). 2006. *Precarious Employment: Understanding Labour Market Insecurity in Canada*. Montreal and Kingston: McGill-Queen's University Press.

Notes

1. Statistics Canada CANSIM Table 276-0004. Manipulated for 2015 sum.
2. Statistics Canada CANSIM Table 282-0012.
3. See also Statistics Canada 2010a.
4. Statistics Canada defines an *economic family* as a group of two or more persons who live in the same dwelling and are related to each other by blood, marriage, common-law, adoption, or a foster relationship.

5. Accessed at: http://www.statcan.gc.ca/pub/75f0002m/2012002/tbl/tbl02-eng. htm; http://www.statcan.gc.ca/pub/75f0002m/2012002/tbl/tbl01-eng.htm.
6. For resources on the living wage campaign, see http://www.livingwage canada.ca.

CHAPTER 3

Education, Training, and Lifelong Learning: Tensions and Contradictions

Lifelong learning can be important for workers in Canada to obtain better jobs and higher living standards. Yet, for many, just like career opportunities, the opportunities for lifelong learning, or even skills development and upgrading, may be limited. For some, the high-level skills and credentials they have achieved may not be fully utilized, while for others, their skills may not even be recognized in the Canadian workplace. This chapter draws attention to the tensions and contradictions in the connections between work and education, training, and lifelong learning. While outlining the importance of education and skills to individual workers as well as to the growth of the economy as a whole, the chapter also highlights the critical problem of lack of access to workplace-based training for many workers, especially the great majority who are not managers or professionals, and argues that wider access to training could significantly improve the situation and prospects of lower-paid workers. The chapter also investigates the dilemma many workers experience as they find themselves stuck in a labour market that often fails to utilize and recognize the skills they have.

Rethinking the Education and Work Connection

The relationship between work and education is often raised through the question, "In what ways does education prepare one for the workforce?" Yet, thinking somewhat more critically and with one of the key themes of this book in mind, one could ask, "To what extent does one's educational background translate into meaningful work?" Taking an even more critical lens, and thinking in particular of the labour market trends covered in Chapter 2, one might ask, "What kind of work (or labour market) does the education system prepare one for?" These questions about the relationship between work and education point to not only the strong correspondence between the two, but also the multiple ways in which we can understand this connection. While education is generally assumed to provide the means to a better job, the relationship may be less straightforward than is immediately apparent (Livingstone 2004).

There are a variety of ways to interpret the role of the education system in contemporary capitalist society. Taking a highly functionalist perspective, the education system can be seen as a site of preparation for work by socializing children and youth and teaching them skills and knowledge, as well as values and attitudes, that will prepare them for the world of work (Wotherspoon 2000). The education system may also sort individuals through the grading system, preparing them for a differentiated labour market. Based on a liberal vision of equality and meritocracy, this functionalist analysis of education assumes that the education system gives all an equal chance to compete and achieve. In other words, it provides the means for individuals to gain "human capital," which they will then exercise in the search for work. More fundamentally, this presents a very liberal view of the role of education in that it promotes a meritocracy: "a vehicle for nurturing the talents and capacities of each individual in harmony with his or her ability to contribute productively" (Wotherspoon 2000: 254). Prestige and wealth are allocated to individuals in relation to their merits/skills, which they develop through the education system.

A more critical perspective on the connection between work and education, however, points toward the ways in which the education system contributes to patterns of social inequality and the reproduction of the class relations of capitalism (Sears 2003). First, education serves a role in instilling work discipline, in that students "learn" punctuality, deference to authority, and so on. Second, education serves a role in imparting liberal ideologies promoting free markets, meritocracy, and economic liberalism, as students are not taught to question the value system and basic social relationships that underpin capitalism. Third, access to education itself, particularly post-secondary education, is shaped by one's socioeconomic status. Children from wealthier families have greater access to advanced education at more prestigious institutions. Moreover, not only does social class shape access to education, but educational attainment also has class effects, as higher levels of formal education correspond to greater likelihood of employment, less risk of unemployment, and higher income.

There are gendered and racialized dimensions to the paradoxes of the education-work relationship as well. In terms of gender, gender differences in education levels diminished immensely over the course of the 20th century (Wotherspoon 2000). However, gender socialization within the education system may contribute to patterns of occupational segregation and gendered divisions of labour in the workforce. With respect to race/ethnicity, selective immigration policies have contributed to higher levels of formal education among recent immigrants. However, for those coming from non–Western European backgrounds in particular, this does not necessarily translate into work that is reflective of educational background, as quite often foreign credentials are not recognized in Canada and a lack of Canadian experience acts as a major impediment to obtaining work commensurate with level of education.

As the education system in Canada grew through the second half of the 20th century, including the dramatic expansion of the post-secondary system in the 1960s, the educational backgrounds of Canadians grew accordingly. For example, between 1961 and 1996, the proportion of those who received at least some post-secondary education rose from 13 percent to over 47 percent (Wotherspoon 2000). The ways in which Canada's education system prepared this increasingly educated population for the labour market came under greater scrutiny by the mid-1990s.

Education Reform in the 1990s

Children in Canada do relatively well at school, scoring above average in internationally comparable tests of basic competencies, including math, science, literacy, and numeracy (OECD 2014). Moreover, the proportion of children and youth with very low scores is relatively low compared to many other countries. The proportion of Canadian youth who do not complete at least a high school education is still high, at a bit over 1 in 10, but it is falling (OECD 2015). The same is true to a degree of participation in post-secondary education.[1] About one-quarter of 25- to 29-year-olds has graduated from university, and another quarter has graduated from college. By some measures, Canada has the most highly educated generation of young adults in the world, and one of the most well-educated workforces overall (OECD 2005).

Yet, the connections between Canada's growing education system and Canada's workplaces were brought into question with the rise of neoliberalism in the 1990s. Consistent with the overall neoliberal perspective, education reform that began in the 1990s aimed to extend the principles of the market into the education system, affecting how education is delivered, what its aims are, how students access the system, and what they can expect to get out of it (Sears 2003). Using the example of Ontario, but arguing that this approach to education reform was not necessarily unique to any particular province, Sears suggests that the Ontario government, under the leadership of Premier Mike Harris and Minister of Education and Training John Snobelen, sought to "invent a crisis" to convince people that the system was broken. These actions paralleled a process in Britain in the 1980s, where the government proclaimed that education "wasn't working." Specifically, the Ontario government argued that there were multiple factors pushing the need for change. The changing labour market needed graduates to develop new skills, which they weren't getting in the system at the time. Schools in general were out of date, inefficient, and unresponsive to change, with universities being a major culprit. By characterizing the crisis in technical terms and creating a "common sense" discourse that declared education reform to be in the interests of all, government was able to mask the neoliberal goals of its education reform plan, including privatization, corporatization, and the prioritization of areas of study with the greatest "marketability." Set in the context of a broader shift to neoliberalism, as well as the changing landscape of work, this approach to education reform became about socializing students for the new world of increased competition and uncertainty.

Moreover, as educational institutions are also workplaces themselves, neoliberal education reform included "Taylorizing" and "making lean" employment conditions and employment relations in educational institutions, such as through standardizing job responsibilities, emphasizing calculable goals over quality of education, and the increased use of contract teachers, rather than permanent employees. At the post-secondary level, education reform also came with a significant rise in the cost to individual students through increasing tuition levels, as post-secondary education was increasingly cast in neoliberal terms as an individual investment in human capital. Between 1990 and 2002, tuition rates for post-secondary education in Canada rose by 135 percent.

Overall, education reform at the end of the 20th century was part of a broader project of neoliberal policy reform that introduced market principles into all aspects of social life (Harvey 2003). It was designed not only to contribute toward preparing one for a job and to making education programs "job relevant," but also to instill an entrepreneurial and individualist orientation, and to "push the market deeper into every aspect of our lives" (Sears 2003: 3). In other words, education reform was not simply about providing better training, but about reorienting students toward the harsh reality of the labour market and the rise of precarious work.

Lifelong Learning and Workplaces

It is now almost universally recognized that learning is an ongoing process that must take place over the whole life-course. Ideally, people would participate in early childhood education programs and arrive at school ready to learn. They would receive a first-class school education that provides them with basic skills, such as literacy and numeracy, and the capacity to learn and work with others, as well as the knowledge needed to proceed to a post-secondary education appropriate to their particular skills and capacities. Post-secondary education is increasingly needed to acquire reasonably well-paid jobs that also provide career ladders to better jobs. It can span a wide range, from short-term vocational and technical training directly tied to entry-level job requirements, to apprenticeship programs combining classroom and on-the-job instruction, to co-op and advanced technical and business education programs in colleges, to general and career-oriented professional programs in universities.

Learning should be seen as a process that continues rather than ends with employment in a steady job, and the workplace should be seen as an important site for lifelong learning. In a fluid job market marked by constant industrial and firm restructuring, and by rapid technological and organizational change within workplaces, workers need to periodically upgrade their skills. Many will need training to switch jobs and careers. And climbing up job ladders over a working lifetime almost always involves learning new skills.

However, Canada's workplace-based training system is relatively underdeveloped, and falls far short of producing results on par with public education (OECD 2002b, 2003a). Despite all of the rhetoric on the importance of skills and learning in the knowledge-based economy, Canada's performance leaves much to be desired. Many reports comprehensively document poor Canadian performance compared to other countries in terms of employer-provided training, especially for lower-paid workers, and Canada has a very high proportion of adults with weak literacy and numeracy skills (Rubenson et al. 2007; Myers and de Broucker 2006; Goldenberg 2006).

While adult workers can and do seek training, it is mainly employers who determine access. Unfortunately, employer-sponsored training is directed very disproportionately to already highly educated professional and managerial employees. Many average employees with formal qualifications and the willingness to learn more do not get access to the further training they need to upgrade their skills and qualifications. Perhaps most importantly, if equality of opportunity is taken seriously, there is little in the way of a second chance for people who leave the education system with limited qualifications, or who made early career choices that turned out to offer limited job and career prospects.

Many working people are caught in a low-skills trap. An estimated 4 in 10 working-age Canadians have limited literacy and numeracy skills, which makes it very difficult for them to take further skills training (Myers and de Broucker 2006). Many new immigrants to Canada have high formal qualifications, but often their credentials are not recognized or they are not given an opportunity due to a lack of Canadian work experience. They often then find themselves in need of further training to gain Canadian equivalencies and credentials recognition. Most of these workers are on their own when it comes to the difficult task of upgrading their skills to find better jobs and deal with a changing job market. Employers are particularly unlikely to invest in training in basic skills, such as literacy and numeracy, and most likely to invest in skills training for those who already have good basic skills.

Skills, the Economy, and a Changing Job Market

Technological change, especially change that is driven by the use of information and communications technologies, has been pervasive over the last several decades. It has often been accompanied by major changes in the organization of production, such as automation, or the use of work teams and the devolution of more decision-making authority to front-line workers. Many routine clerical and blue-collar production jobs have been eliminated or radically changed, and many new occupations have appeared. There has long been a debate among social scientists as to whether these ongoing technological and organizational changes have fuelled a demand for higher worker skills, or have been introduced so as to deliberately de-skill the workers whose jobs survive automation and outsourcing (see Aronowitz 2010). In practice, there has been change in all directions, depending upon the sector, the occupation, and the characteristics of individual companies. There are many very boring, routine, and stressful jobs working with new technology, such as work in call centres, but also many inter-

Box 3.1: Is It Time to Get Soft on the Skills Debate?
By John MacLaughlin

In the recent paper "95 Months Later: Turbulent Times in Toronto's Labour Market," I wrote about the lack of evidence in relation to skill shortages. I received a number of emails and faced harsh commentaries that questioned the legitimacy of the paper's analysis, which indicated that over time university graduates do comparatively well in terms of earnings and employment. Often this correspondence started off with something to the effect of "we know that someone is better off getting a real skill that employers want than wasting time in University." But what is that real skill?

Every meaningful study trying to find the elusive "skills" missing from our workforce invariably comes up empty. Indeed, in survey after survey conducted by those looking to obtain information about specific technical skill shortages we hear about the lack of soft skills such as teamwork, problem solving, and perseverance. *The Growing Importance of Social Skills in the Labor Market* by David Deming of Harvard University shows that the labor market increasingly rewards social skills. He goes through US data over a thirty year period and discovers that, since 1980, jobs with high social skill requirements have experienced greater relative growth throughout the wage distribution. Moreover, employment and wage growth has been strongest in jobs that require high levels of both cognitive skills and social skills. Occupations that require technical skills, while often perceived to be in demand, have actually had only tepid and uneven growth.

In a small attempt to answer the above, TWIG staff spent the summer meeting with focus groups and conducting interviews with longer term job-seekers. While we are still synthesizing the results of this work, it is clear that the process of defining their challenges to finding stable employment may not be simple. We met with numerous young unemployed people and although work experience and skills seemed to be part of the unemployment equation, their employment challenges appeared to be rooted in far larger problems. We had a similar experience, albeit with significant differences, in talking with older workers. Many of them appear to have the exact sets of skills employers have identified as "in-demand." Furthermore, most of these older workers have experience in a growing Toronto industry sector. How can this apparent contradiction be reconciled or addressed by workforce interventions?

While our conversations with job-seekers may not provide answers to the above, we are inching forward to better defining the problems. And better defining the long term unemployment challenge is a good start to coming up with the right answers.

These findings are supported by the recent paper prepared by The Council of Canadian Academies, Some Assembly Required: STEM Skills and Canada's Economic Productivity (2015)[. This paper] recommended that graduates from

Science, Technology, Engineering, and Math (STEM) needed a better range of social and communication skills. Similar results were gained from a Canadian Association of Career Educators and Employers survey of 920 Canadian employers (Smith & Lam, 2013). From a list of 20 competencies, the most valuable attribute for employers among new graduate hires were analytical skills, communication skills (verbal), problem-solving skills, strong work ethic, and teamwork skills.

With the recent change in federal government (given its commitment to additional labour market funding), and given the findings of David Deming and others, we may want to pause before jumping back on to the bandwagon of skills shortages and skills mismatches. The evidence is mixed and the data is virtually non-existent (except at very local levels). Furthermore, disruptive technology, over time, often renders technical skills obsolete. What we do know is that employers value individuals with grit, problem solving abilities and the ability to learn on the job. This has been true for decades and there is no reason to believe that anything has changed.

Source: MacLaughlin, John. 2015, November 11. "Is it Time to Get Soft on the Skills Debate?" Toronto Workforce Innovation Group. http://workforceinnovation.ca/skills-debate/.

esting new jobs, such as running computer systems, writing complex software, or running advanced diagnostic equipment in hospitals. The concept of skill is itself not neutral and refers to a range of characteristics of jobs, from the need for vocational and educational credentials, to cognitive complexity, to the level of responsibility in the job.

Within the workplaces of many "post-industrial" economies, Canada included, there is evidence pointing out that the skill content of jobs has been slowly rising over time. This can be seen in the growth of professional and technical occupations that usually require advanced qualifications and rising skill content in jobs within a wide range of other occupations (Applebaum et al. 2003; Betcherman et al. 1998). This dynamic is not new, however. Long before the computer revolution, there was indeed a big shift out of relatively unskilled but reasonably well-paid factory jobs into jobs in the service sector. The shift to services has produced many more skilled jobs in some sectors, such as health care, finance, and business services. But the growth in higher-skilled jobs has also been accompanied by a growth in many lower-skilled jobs as well, such as those in personal and consumer services, food service, and retail trade, which is indicative of larger patterns of segmentation in Canada's labour market. Many low-wage, low-skill service jobs are not vulnerable to relocation to lower-wage countries, and many are also not terribly subject to elimination through technological change. The shift of jobs to services, combined with technological and organizational change, greater international competition in manufacturing, and the growth of some high-end service industries, has helped divide the workforce between skilled workers with good jobs and relatively unskilled workers with poor jobs.

While the rise of new technologies in the workforce has long been associated with the hope of a shift toward higher-quality, higher-skilled work (Bell 1973), the reality is that new technologies have also been connected to skills polarization within the labour force (Krahn et al. 2007). Workers in high-skill occupations are more likely to have opportunities to be exposed to new technologies and to then gain skills upgrading through these opportunities. However, at the same time, many employers are not implementing training programs to upgrade the skills of workers whose jobs are eliminated by new technologies. And in lower-skill jobs, often the skills likely to be enhanced are "know-how" skills (how to use new technology), rather than decision-making skills (an indicator of autonomy). Overall, new technologies are contributing to patterns of segmentation by creating a split labour force of highly trained/skilled people who design and implement computer technologies, and unskilled workers who carry out low-skill, low-autonomy, low-tech jobs.

This attention to the skills content of jobs points to the multilayered nature of the divisions present within Canada's labour market and to another factor shaping the kinds of inequalities raised in Chapter 2. It is getting harder and harder for workers with less than a post-secondary education to find steady, well-paid jobs, and the skill requirements in so-called "good jobs" in both the private and public sectors will probably continue to grow. Those with relatively low levels of formal education and skills training are increasingly consigned to precarious and marginal jobs that provide low levels of employment security, low pay, limited career progress, and a high risk of poverty. The increased premium upon education means that there is an increased risk of marginalization. Without broadly based, equitable access to education and skills training, many workers will be left behind. This is especially true of young people who leave school with limited education and skills, of women who leave the workforce for extended periods, and of older workers who fall victim to industrial restructuring that devalues their existing skills. This is a particularly confounding problem for many new immigrants, whose formal skills and credentials are frequently not recognized.

Skills and Better Jobs

At the individual level, higher levels of education strongly influence earnings, and the evidence shows that less educated adults who return to school to gain a formal credential realize significant wage gains (Zhang and Palameta 2006). It is also very widely agreed that national investment in "human capital" is key to productivity growth and good national economic performance in a knowledge-based global economy. Investment in education and skills is central to innovation and, at a minimum, facilitates the introduction of productivity-enhancing new technology and new forms of work organization (OECD 2005). The OECD has found that increased educational attainment of the workforce raises the rate of real economic growth, and employer investment in training has been shown to have significant positive impacts on firm-level productivity (Bartel 2000).

Investment in worker training, in conjunction with changes in work organization that take full advantage of those higher skills, has been found in numerous Canadian and international studies to have positive, if hard to quantify, impacts on firm-level productivity and profitability (Arnal et al. 2001; Lowe 2000). While it is hard to separate out the impacts on productivity of new capital investments, technological change, changes in work organization, and investment in workers' skills, it seems clear that the largest productivity payoff comes from a bundling together of all these elements as part of a coherent, high-value-added business strategy. Knowledge-based firms that adopt these kinds of strategies will tend to grow and expand, replacing good jobs eliminated in the process of technological and organizational change.

Beyond investment in public education at all levels, investments in the skills of employed workers through on-the-job training are particularly critical to the success of new forms of work organization based on employee involvement. However, there is strong evidence that companies, particularly Canadian companies, tend to underinvest in on-the-job training (Goldenberg 2006; Myers and de Broucker 2006). Many firms do provide some training, particularly training for new employees, and occasional computer, marketing, and management training, but this is not the same thing as being systematically committed to constant upgrading of the skills of all employees as part of a comprehensive competitive strategy. According to a 2007 report aimed at employers, Canada's poor productivity record "is rooted in a chronic national blind spot—a lack of awareness that investing in the human capacity of Canada's workforce is paramount to success" (Bailey 2007: 4). The literature review in this report shows the strong positive impacts of business investment in workforce training on business performance, and thus high returns to training investments, but this has not translated into increased investment in training.

There are many reasons why Canada lacks a strong workplace training culture. Traditionally, high levels of immigration of skilled workers kept down the need to train workers from within. High unemployment for much of the 1990s meant that firms could easily hire from outside for needed skills, rather than train and promote from within. And there has been less of an expectation in Canada that firms will train and retrain workers than is the case in some other countries. In Germany and many other European countries, most companies accept that they have an obligation to provide apprenticeship training, and there is a highly formalized system of vocational training for young people who do not go on to an academic education. Canada lacks the works councils that are mandated by law in many European countries to help plan and deliver training. Restrictions on layoffs in many European countries have also encouraged companies to train during downtime, when business is slow. Canadian unions that often press employers for more training are weaker than unions in Europe.

There are more general factors that limit firm investment in skills. Training is costly, particularly for smaller firms, and the gains from training are uncertain and often unknown. It is often easier to pursue a cost-cutting strategy than it is to fundamentally rethink how production is organized. Firms fear the risk of losing newly trained workers to other firms, thus losing out on their investment. Poaching skilled workers is particularly widespread in countries with no training culture, where free-riding firms can get away with behaviour that is damaging to the economy as a whole. Investment in training is thus likely to be greatest in large firms that provide steady employment at decent wages and, as a result, experience low worker turnover. Firms' widespread adoption of outsourcing strategies has driven the growth of more precarious employment relationships in smaller firms that are much less well equipped to invest in training.

The dominant focus of Canadian public policy toward "human capital" has been on public education, including post-secondary education, rather than on adult learning and workplace-based learning. However, research suggests that raising the average level of skills (as measured by literacy and numeracy levels) actually has a stronger impact on productivity than does raising the proportion of the workforce with very high levels of education and skills (Coulombe et al. 2004). This is, perhaps, unsurprising given that the majority of the workforce still has quite modest educational and skills attainments, and that many workers are employed in low-productivity/low-skilled jobs. Coulombe et al. (2004) calculate that a 1 percent increase in mean literacy skills relative to the international average can raise labour productivity by 2 percent.

Yet, it must also be noted that most low-productivity/low-skilled/low-pay jobs are to be found in consumer services, such as retail trade, accommodation, and food services, as well as in some business services (such as security and building cleaning). In combination, such services make up about one-fifth of the private-sector economy. This points toward the fact that if we want to raise productivity, we have to think about how to improve low-pay/low-productivity jobs.

Skills, the Needs of Workers, and Human Development

In Canada today, employer support for the training of employed workers on the job, or through paid courses and leaves, goes disproportionately to managers and professionals with relatively high levels of formal education. Far from equalizing opportunities, the workplace training system increases inequality of income and opportunity based on class background and formal educational attainment. This lack of a good training and adult education system thwarts the goal of human development. We may have the most highly educated generation of young adults in the world, but many Canadians are seriously underemployed (Livingstone 2004; Lowe 2000). At least one in five jobs requires education and skills far below those of the workers who hold these jobs. Underemployment in precarious jobs affects many young people as well as highly educated and skilled recent immigrants.

There is evidence that skills gained in the education system often atrophy from lack of use in the workplace (Krahn et al. 2007).

Training is an essential ingredient in human development. Workers want to develop their individual capacities and capabilities, and work in jobs that allow them to exercise and develop their skills. The workforce has become more highly educated, and has justifiably higher expectations of what work will provide in terms of the ability to use an education and continued opportunities to learn. Higher levels of education and skills are generally associated with higher levels of autonomy at work, more varied and interesting jobs, and higher levels of job satisfaction. Investment in skills is also needed to promote the kinds of work reorganization that create more interesting and less stressful jobs, and give workers more control over the pace and content of work. Management and labour objectives are not always the same when it comes to work reorganization, which too often results in high levels of stress. Investment in training, however, is a major ingredient in jointly determined work reorganization processes that can satisfy the interests of both parties.

Education and training is about much more than meeting the skill needs of employers alone. Workers will usually want to gain general rather than highly firm-specific skills, and skills that are recognized through formal certificates or credentials. These will give them much more leverage as individuals in the job market, and the option of either climbing a job ladder with their current employer or looking around for a new job. Workers with a high level of general, certified skills are less likely to experience prolonged unemployment or a deep pay cut if they lose their current job and are forced to seek another one.

Training programs are likely to be most developed and most likely to meet the different needs of workers and employers when they are developed jointly. This can take place through collective bargaining, European-style works councils established by law to deal with training and other issues, joint training committees, or similar institutions (ILO 2001). A major OECD study concluded that joint employer-employee approaches promote more equitable access to training, increase worker involvement in training activities, and increase the training intensity of firms (Arnal et al. 2001: 48). Close employee involvement in the design and delivery of training can facilitate the introduction of new technology and new work practices by ensuring that the current workforce is provided with the tools to adapt to, and benefit from, change.

New technologies and new forms of work organization can be introduced in very different ways, with very different implications for the skill content of jobs and the quality of work (Applebaum 1997; Krahn et al. 2007). Joint approaches to workplace change and related training are much more likely to generate positive outcomes in terms of both higher employer productivity and worker well-being. Certainly, joint approaches to training are a key feature of the industrial and labour relations systems of some European countries with highly productive and innovative economies, notably Germany and the Scandinavian countries. Joint approaches are also common in unionized workplaces. In the U.S. and Canada,

productivity gains from the introduction of new forms of work and new technologies have been greatest where there has been a comprehensive, negotiated process
of workplace change (Black and Lynch 2000). The key reason for this outcome is,
not surprisingly, that worker buy-in into work reorganization is far greater when
workers have an independent voice, and when firms respond to their needs.

   Joint approaches are also more likely to result in training programs that develop
portable, as opposed to very narrow and firm-specific, skills. Such joint programs
are often developed at the sectoral rather than firm level, raising the skill level
of the workforce as a whole while spreading the costs across all employers in a
sector. The advantages of a joint approach to training have been demonstrated
in Canada through the successes of some sectoral skills councils, such as in the
steel industry. Some unions and employers have negotiated access to training
through collective agreements and joint training committees, as in the automotive
assembly sector. Unions representing workers in the skilled trades have traditionally played a major independent role in the design and delivery of training,
especially through apprenticeship programs. Many construction unions run
their own training centres. In Canada, unionized workers enjoy greater access
to employer-sponsored training because unions have pushed employers to take
on the task of upgrading skills and providing current employees with better
jobs, rather than just hiring from the outside to meet new needs (Sussman 2002;
Livingstone and Raykov 2005).

Who Gets Access to Training?

Statistics Canada's *Adult Education and Training Survey* gathers information on
adult participants (aged 25 to 64) in formal job-related learning. Formal activities are defined as structured courses or programs leading to a certificate or
qualification. Courses are much shorter than programs, and include seminars and
workshops. Overall, in 2008, just over one in three adults participated in formal
job-related training, up slightly from 1997 (Knighton et al. 2009). Participation
is about the same for women and men, declines with increasing age, and rises
with the person's level of education. The average amount of time spent in formal
job-related training over the year was eight days per participant (Knighton et al.
2009), spent mainly in courses rather than programs (see also Peters 2004). A lot of
this learning effort is undertaken by individuals without the support of employers. In addition, about one-third of all adults engage regularly in self-directed,
job-related learning.

   A major Canadian problem is the exclusion of roughly the bottom third of the
workforce from workplace training and involvement in formal lifelong learning.
While Canada scores about average in terms of literacy and numeracy scores
among adults, there are small parts of the workforce where such skills are still lacking (Krahn et al. 2007). Literacy attainment in Canada is below the OECD average
for persons with low levels of formal education (see also Coulombe et al. 2004).[2]

Data from the *International Adult Literacy Survey* and Statistics Canada's Adult *Education and Training Survey* clearly show that, once in the workforce, those with advanced education are the most likely to receive employer-sponsored training. Participation in Canadian adult education is very heavily skewed to those with high literacy skills (77.5 percent of those at Level 4/5 vs. 41 percent at Level 1) (Desjardins 2015; see also OECD 2002b: 14). Just one in five workers participates in formal employer-sponsored education, with much lower levels of participation by workers with low levels of formal education (1 in 10 for those with no post-secondary qualification). Participation is even lower for the less educated in small firms, while the growing ranks of contract workers and solo self-employed are almost entirely excluded from workplace-based training. In short, and as is widely recognized, Canada does not have an effective adult education and training system in terms of reaching the bottom third of the workforce, and provides little in the way of a "second chance" for those who have not completed a post-secondary qualification (OECD 2002b).

Survey research shows that there was no increase at all in participation in adult education courses and programs in Canada between 1994 and 2003 (Rubenson et al. 2007). Indeed, the situation deteriorated among the unemployed and those not in the labour force due to cuts to government training programs. Those least likely to participate in formal and informal adult learning are those who are already disadvantaged in the job market, including those with low literacy skills and low levels of formal education, the unemployed, and recent immigrants.

Table 3.1 and Figure 3.1 provide information on participation in training activities. As shown, approximately 41 percent of employees participated in some form of training in 2008. In line with the pattern by level of education, professional/managerial workers are much more likely to receive employer-supported training than blue-collar and sales and service workers. The participation of women in some form of training activity is slightly higher than that of men across all age groups in workers from 25 to 64. Figure 3.2 provides information on employer support for education programs. Just under half of all surveyed workers in 2008 received some employer support for education. Occupations with the largest proportion of workers receiving employer support were in trade, transport, and machinery, health, and management. Also, those in large workplaces (over 500 employees) were much more likely to receive employer support for education than those in workplaces with fewer than 500 workers. Employer support for education was particularly low in small workplaces (under 20 employees).

In summary, employer-provided training is greatly concentrated in the higher layers of the shrinking core workforce in larger firms and the public sector. The concentration of formal training on well-educated professionals and managers in large firms reflects the fact that such firms are not only more likely to be pursuing high-productivity strategies that require skills, but are also still committed to promoting the skills of their core workers. Even blue-collar workers in large firms get more training than average. Also, larger firms are much more likely to be unionized, and the presence of unions makes a difference to training efforts.

Table 3.1: Participation in Training by Occupation, 2008

Occupation	Participation rate in training (%)	Women (%)	Postsecondary education (%)	Unionization rate (%)
All	41.2	47.2	66.5	29.3
Management	50.6	35.7	70.9	8
Business, finance, and administration	38.9	70.2	64	24.4
Natural and applied sciences and related occupations	51.4	21.5	88.8	25.1
Health occupations	62.3	81.8	89.8	54.6
Social sciences, education, government service, and religion	60.7	68.1	91.1	55.4
Art, culture, recreation, and sport	39.4	55.3	79.4	18.6
Sales and service occupations	29.8	56.5	52.7	22.5
Trade, transport, and machinery	29.6	6.8	51.1	33.7
Occupations unique to primary industry	33.1	17.2	41.6	14.2
Occupations unique to processing, manufacturing, and utilities	24.6	27.2	47	39.2

Source: Statistics Canada. 2008. *Access and Support to Education and Training Survey* (ASETS). Ottawa: Statistics Canada.

Figure 3.1: Participation in Job- or Career-Related Training Activities, 2008

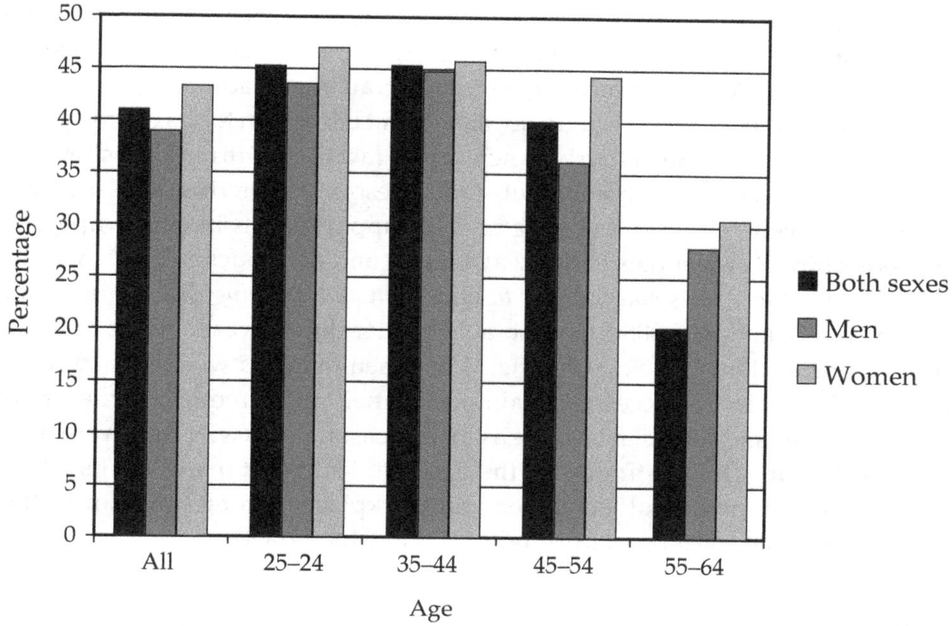

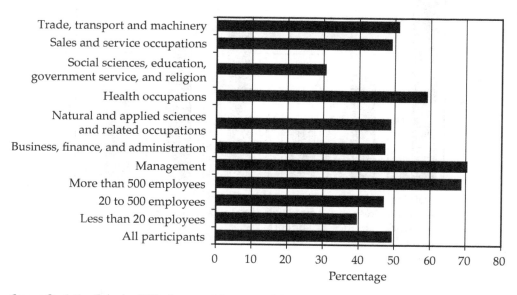

Source: Statistics Canada. 2008. *Access and Support to Education and Training Survey* (ASETS). Ottawa: Statistics Canada.

Figure 3.2: Proportion of Workers Aged 25 to 64 Who Received Employer Support among Those Who Took Education Programs

Source: Statistics Canada. 2008. *Access and Support to Education and Training Survey* (ASETS). Ottawa: Statistics Canada.

Many workers want more training than they are getting from the current system (Sussman 2002; Livingstone 2004). Training participation and the desire for even more participation are both greatest among younger workers who want to embark on developmental job and career ladders. Often, older workers have low expectations of their employers, or have given up. Overall, many adults report that they want more job-related training, but face significant barriers in terms of time, money, or both (Peters 2004).[3] Such barriers include the fact that returning to school (high school or post-secondary) requires substantial resources in terms of both time and finances. As well, there are few programs to support adults intent on upgrading their educational credentials in this way (Myers and de Broucker 2006). As shown in Figure 3.3, the *Access and Support to Education and Training Survey* undertaken by Statistics Canada in 2008 found notable gender differences in terms of the barriers experienced in accessing training. While men reported work-related reasons as the main barriers to accessing training, women most frequently cited family responsibilities and financial barriers as major reasons as to why they were unable to access training. It is testimony to the desire to learn that many adults who are excluded from formal adult education and workplace training programs actively seek out informal learning opportunities (Livingstone 2004).

Figure 3.3: Barriers to Training by Sex

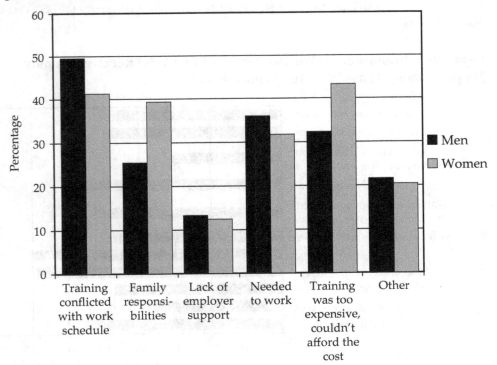

Source: Statistics Canada. 2008. *Access and Support to Education and Training Survey* (ASETS). Ottawa: Statistics Canada.

The weaknesses of the employer-based adult training system have not been adequately compensated for through public policy. Governments do provide some support for adult learning to a small proportion of unemployed workers, mainly funded through the Employment Insurance Act. The fact that eligibility is restricted to current or recent EI recipients, however, means that many of the working poor, as well as recent immigrants, do not qualify. Classroom training for the unemployed was cut back over the 1990s. There are no programs in place to provide paid training leaves for adult workers who want to upgrade their skills or qualifications by returning to school, though some very modest support is provided through the tax system. Over the years, many reports have called for paid educational and training leaves to facilitate the goal of lifelong learning, but individuals are still very much on their own. Governments have also been very reluctant to intervene in employers' training decisions. Of the provinces, only Quebec mandates a minimum employer effort on worker training. Here, an employer who does not spend at least 1 percent of payroll on training must pay that amount to the provincial government. This has had some positive impacts on the overall level of employer-supported training, even though smaller firms are excluded (Peters 2004; see also OECD 2012).

Canada in International Perspective

Countries differ greatly in terms of the extent to which they invest in active labour market policies to promote lifelong learning and labour adjustment, and Canada is a relatively poor performer. While it is hard to compare the training systems of different countries, the Organisation for Economic Co-operation and Development found that the Canadian annual participation rate in adult worker training is, at less than 30 percent, below the industrial country average, and that (at just over 1 percent) we also lag behind the average in terms of employer spending on training as a percentage of payroll costs (OECD 1999; Tuijnman and Boudard 2001). Canada lags behind not only European countries in which there is a very strong emphasis on training, like Germany and the Scandinavian countries, but also the United States. Canada also lags well behind many European countries—but not the U.S.—when it comes to training programs for unemployed workers.

Investing in Skills to Raise the Quality of Low-Paid Jobs

The concept of lifelong learning figures prominently in major policy statements by Canadian governments as a key means to raise productivity and economic performance while also promoting more equal outcomes for individuals. In the economic jargon, investment in human capital is held to simultaneously promote economic efficiency and social equity. However, "supply-side" policies are only one part of the solution to low-wage/low-productivity/low-skill work and increasing wage and income inequality. While it is certainly true that better-educated people fare better as individuals in the job market, education credentials may act more as a sorting device in the job market than as a true indicator of skill demands. The fact that employers often demand higher levels of education and skills than they really need leads to underemployment, and there is overwhelming evidence that many low-wage workers are overeducated, overskilled, or both in terms of literacy and numeracy levels relative to the very limited demands of the routinized jobs they hold (Krahn et al. 2007; Livingstone 2004). A majority of the jobs held by workers in relatively unskilled occupations involve little or no worker discretion or control. Adequate literacy and numeracy skills among younger workers who have recently left the education system often waste away due to lack of use in the workplace. In the Canadian context, there is also strong evidence that many recent immigrants are significantly underemployed relative to their education and skills. In short, the existence of skills does not mean that they are necessarily utilized by employers.

Part of the problem is that employers can and do adopt, consciously or unconsciously, a low-pay/low-skill strategy as opposed to a higher-pay/higher-skill strategy, creating disincentives to invest in labour force development as firms are able to gain competitive advantage through low-wage, low-skill labour (Myers and de Broucker 2006). In fact, there is no automatic translation of higher skills or education supply into higher employer demand for skills, and, while temporary skills shortages can and do exist, the dominant tendency in the job market is for the supply of worker skills to exceed employer demand (Livingstone 2002). Instead, employer demand for skills must be generated through bargaining and other external forces. For example, as noted above, unionized workers, holding all other factors constant, receive more training than do non-union workers (Livingstone and Raykov 2005). About half of all workers covered by collective agreements benefit from (usually permissive rather than mandatory) contract provisions on employer-provided training. While this partly reflects the fact that employers must raise productivity to pay higher union wages, it also reflects the fact that unions can and do push for access to training as a means to improve the quality of jobs and labour market opportunities for workers.

A key policy issue is how to change jobs so that employers develop and use the skills of workers in such a way as to make jobs more interesting and developmental, while also raising productivity and pay. One lever is to raise pay through higher minimum wages or higher unionization in low-pay/low-productivity sectors. Higher wages are likely to push employers to raise productivity by investing in skills. There is some evidence that skills investment and job redesign can indeed raise productivity in otherwise low-pay/low-productivity parts of the job market, such as consumer services.

For example, the Scandinavian countries have a much more equal wage distribution than North American countries, mainly due to widespread collective bargaining even in private services, such as retail trade, restaurants, and hotels. When strong unions push up wages for those at the bottom, it seems that these higher wages do encourage employers to increase productivity by raising skills. Data from the *International Adult Literacy Survey* show that the skills of the bottom third of the workforce (measured by literacy and numeracy) are significantly higher in Sweden and Denmark than those of the bottom third of the workforce in Canada (Schettkat 2002). The percentage of employees with low (Levels 1/2) literacy and numeracy scores is much lower in Sweden than in Canada (e.g., 20 percent vs. 34 percent for quantitative literacy, and 24 percent vs. 38 percent for prose literacy) (Willms 1999). Higher skills at the lower end of the Swedish workforce may partly reflect the impact of higher investment in early childhood learning and a more equal society generally, but workplace-based training jointly delivered by the "social partners" likely plays a major role as well. Moreover, levels of workplace training and labour market training for the temporarily unemployed are markedly higher in Sweden and the Scandinavian countries generally than the European, let alone the Canadian, norm.

In North America, training programs, where they exist, can have a big impact upon the working lives of people employed in traditionally low-wage sectors of the economy. Often, supposedly low-skill and low-wage jobs can be made into better jobs with greater responsibilities if training is provided. The employer often benefits from job enrichment through lower worker turnover. Usually, job ladders from lower- to higher-skilled jobs are few and far between in sectors like hotels, restaurants, building services, and support jobs in health care and social services. This is partly because the better jobs requiring higher skills, including supervisor positions, are filled by hiring people with higher skills or formal qualifications rather than by training current employees to take the better jobs when they open up. In hotels and hospital kitchens, for example, supervisors tend to be hired from college programs. But other approaches that lead lower-skilled/lower-paid workers to better jobs are possible. In some grocery stores in Ontario, employers and unions have agreed to training programs for cashiers that allow them to move into better-paid jobs as meat-cutters. In Las Vegas, there is a large union-run training institute that now does almost all of the training for the huge hospitality industry in that city, allowing workers to gradually climb up the job ladder (Applebaum et al. 2003). Potential job ladders that can be climbed through language and skills training run from housekeeping, to food preparation, to food and beverage service, to desk clerk positions, to supervisory and managerial positions, with pay and job quality improving at each step. Hotels that compete for customers design and deliver training with the union at a sectoral/community level, and recruit from the training centre. The commitment to training in Las Vegas is reported to lower worker turnover and improve service quality and productivity, in turn supporting much higher pay than the hospitality industry norm (Wial and Rickert 2002). Modelled after the training centre in Las Vegas, the Hospitality Workers Training Centre (HWTC) in Toronto formed through a joint venture between UNITE-HERE Local 79 and major hotels in Toronto following the SARS crisis of 2003, which had a signifi-

Box 3.2: Toronto Restaurant Balances Social Mission with Economic Return
By Becky Reuber

The Challenge
Hawthorne, a Toronto restaurant specializing in local cuisine, opened in 2012 as an initiative of the Hospitality Workers Training Centre (HWTC). The HWTC is a non-profit organization with a mission to train and support workers in Toronto's hospitality sector. Hawthorne has two quite different mandates: The first is to provide hands-on real world training for people who are experiencing barriers to employment; the second is to ensure a high quality bistro experience for downtown Toronto diners. Danielle Olsen, the executive director of HWTC, says that "it is essential for us to balance the tension between Hawthorne's social mission and the economic reality of running a restaurant."

But how are they able to do this?

The Background
Founded in 2002, and modelled after similar ventures in Las Vegas, New York and Boston, the HWTC is a partnership between the Hospitality Workers' union, and major hotel chains. The organization provides practical skills training for people who are receiving social assistance, such as people with disabilities, or refugees who lack a social network in Canada and may be living in transitional housing.

Initially, all of the training took place in existing hotels and restaurants, but in 2012 HWTC moved into a building on Richmond St. East, owned by the City of Toronto and designated as part of the Regent Park Redevelopment Initiative. The advisory group decided to develop the space into a full service restaurant—Hawthorne—as a revenue-generating and training initiative.

Around this time, Ms. Olsen was recruited to become the organization's executive director. Previously at Social Capital Partners, she had experience developing and managing public-private partnerships aimed at training objectives, and realized that the key to Hawthorne's success was to find ways to achieve their economic goals while achieving their social goals.

The Solution
Ms. Olsen explains that there are three key practices they follow to achieve the balance they need. The first practice is to make the training relevant by matching it with market demand. From the beginning, the Hawthorne menu has emphasized local, seasonable and sustainable food. All sauces and spreads are made in-house. "Not only is Hawthorne's theme consistent with what our customers want," says Ms. Olsen, "but we are providing our trainees with the knowledge and skills about local Ontario produce that future employers value."

The second practice is to ensure that full-time staff buy into the social mission and are able to incorporate it in their day-to-day work. Ms. Olsen points out that

running a kitchen successfully is difficult. "You have to manage costs, food quality, consistency and the guest experience." And at Hawthorne, added to that
pressure is a work force of inexperienced, albeit, highly motivated trainees, who
have varied life experiences and skills. "It's important to find full-time employees
who thrive in this situation."

The third practice is to be creative in growing training opportunities, because,
as Ms. Olsen emphasizes, "our primary objective is to maximize the number
of people trained and subsequently employed." It would seem that training
opportunities could be limited in a 45-seat bistro, but Hawthorne's founders
were farsighted and constructed a kitchen that is much larger than restaurants
of the same size would have. To take advantage of this excess kitchen capacity,
HWTC has recently launched a catering business in the restaurant. "Catering is
great for training," states Ms. Olsen. "The work is fast-paced and repetitive and
so trainees become quick and consistent, and those are qualities that employers
are looking for."

The Results

Hawthorne is just under two years old, and it has already trained over 40
people, with three-quarters of them successfully transitioning to paid employment within the hospitality sector. Hotel partners are increasingly contacting
HWTC when they have jobs to fill. The goal of the catering business is to
generate profit to re-invest in providing competitive training and work experience for new entrants to the industry. It is only two months old, so these are
still early days, but the preliminary results look encouraging, with revenue
doubling each month.

Source: Reuber, Becky. 2014, November 20. "Toronto restaurant balances social mission with economic
return." *The Globe and Mail.* http://www.theglobeandmail.com/report-on-business/small-business/
sb-growth/toronto-restaurant-balances-social-mission-with-economic-return/article21125089/.

cant impact on the industry. The centre works on a non-profit basis and offers
workers in the industry access to vocational training, workplace education, and
employment support. The HWTC also operates Hawthorne Food & Drink, a
social enterprise training restaurant in downtown Toronto (see Box 3.2).

Conclusion

While the education-work relationship can be a key factor in shaping access
to quality work, this relationship is fraught with tensions and contradictions.
Neoliberal education reform reoriented universities toward supposedly job-
relevant programs and required students to invest heavily in their own human

capital. Yet, while higher education levels improve both employment and earnings potential, the experience in the job market in terms of gaining access to skilled work remains uncertain for many. Moreover, despite the widely noted benefits of lifelong learning and workplace-based training, Canada falls well short of providing adequate access to training opportunities for most workers. This significantly undermines the potential for quality work and is particularly harmful to precarious and low-paid workers. In the face of mounting evidence that investment in training can improve low-wage jobs when combined with strategies to convince employers to shift to a higher-productivity/higher-skill competitive strategy, this lesson seems yet to be learned by many Canadian employers.

Recommended Reading

Canadian Council on Learning. 2007. *Unlocking Canada's Potential: The State of Workplace and Adult Learning in Canada*. Ottawa: Canadian Council on Learning.

Livingstone, David (ed.). 2009. *Education and Jobs: Exploring the Gaps*. Toronto: University of Toronto Press.

Organization for Economic Cooperation and Development (OECD). 2012. *Leveraging Training and Skills Development in SMEs: An Analysis of Two Canadian Urban Regions: Montreal and Winnipeg*. Paris: OECD.

Statistics Canada. 2013. *Skills in Canada: First Results from the Programme for the International Assessment of Adult Competencies*. Ottawa: Statistics Canada.

Notes

1. Data from the *2011 National Household Survey*. Accessed at: https://www12. statcan.gc.ca/nhs-enm/2011/dp-pd/dt-td/Rp-eng.cfm?LANG=E&APATH=3& DETAIL=0&DIM=0&FL=A&FREE=0&GC=0&GID=0&GK=0&GRP=0&PID=10 5910&PRID=0&PTYPE=105277&S=0&SHOWALL=1&SUB=0&Temporal=2013 &THEME=96&VID=0&VNAMEE=&VNAMEF=.

2. Country data from the *2012 Survey of Adult Skills* (PIAAC). Accessed at: http:// gpseducation.oecd.org/CountryProfile?primaryCountry=CAN&treshold=10& topic=AS.

3. In 2008, 68 percent of Canadian adults surveyed reported at least one reason for not undertaking further education or training (Knighton et al. 2009: 21).

CHAPTER 4

The Unhealthy Canadian Workplace

It should come as no surprise to hear that the workplace of early industrial capitalism was a very dangerous place for workers. In Canada, as in all countries experiencing the development of industrial capitalism, workers faced the prospect of serious injury or death on a daily basis and had little government or employer regulation of workplace safety (Marx 1976; Tucker 1990). Despite the fact that working conditions changed substantially over the course of the 20th century through the development of new technologies, the rise of service-sector employment, and the advent of occupational health and safety legislation, for many workers the workplace of the early 21st century remains an unsafe and unhealthy place. Poor ventilation, excessive heat and/or noise, dirt, pollution, and inadequate safety measures continue to characterize manufacturing work. Workers in factories, mines, and construction are exposed to many harmful materials that are linked to serious health problems. Outside manufacturing and resources, workers in white-collar office jobs face problems of repetitive strain injuries and stress. In the contemporary workplace, these problems are often exacerbated by workplace restructuring, which produces speed-up, multitasking, work intensification, and non-standard working hours.

Today, work time lost due to injuries and illness far exceeds time lost to strikes and work stoppages. One in three workers reports exposure to some health hazard (often hazardous materials). In 2012, there were an average of 672 workplace injuries every day in Canada, and close to 977 workplace fatalities (see Box 4.1). These risks are disproportionately experienced by workers in manufacturing and construction, which account for 22 percent and 19 percent of workplace fatalities respectively. While health and safety conditions and standards are always changing, one constant that has remained since the early days of industrial capitalism is that workers face many dangers to both their physical and mental health in the workplace.

Health researchers have demonstrated a clear link between income and socioeconomic status and health outcomes, such that longevity and state of health rise with position on the income scale (Raphael 2008). Given the simple fact that the experience of work dominates the lives of most working-age people, it seems plausible that the close link between socioeconomic status and health may also be closely related to experiences in the workplace. Those at the lower end of the income spectrum are most likely to experience stress from job insecurity and from stress in the workplace itself, and they are also most likely to face hazards to physical health at work. Moreover, research has established strong links from unemployment and precarious employment to poor health outcomes, and from poor working conditions to poor physical and mental health (Lewchuk et al. 2011; Messing 2014). Health risks are created in the workplace due to: dirty and dangerous conditions, which include exposure to harmful substances and hazardous materials; the pace, demands, or repetitive content of the labour process; the exercise of arbitrary power in the workplace, which makes it difficult to refuse dangerous work; employment conditions that create high levels of economic uncertainty; and time pressures that create conflicts with the lives of workers in the home and in the community.

With this broad approach to workplace health in mind, the aim of this chapter is to provide an overview of the impact of employment, working conditions, and the work environment on workers' health. This chapter presents a general overview of current conditions and the overall direction of change, looks at some important cleavages among workers in terms of access to good jobs, and places the situation in Canada in a comparative context with some European countries. As workers and their organizations continue to push for better protection against workplace hazards, workplace health is presented in this chapter as very much a part of the contested terrain of work.

Work and Health

Health researchers have increasingly emphasized the links between work stress and physical and mental health. It has long been recognized that work stress can arise from many sources, including job insecurity, the physical demands of work, the extent of support from supervisors and co-workers, work-life conflict, and job strain (Wilkins and Beaudet 1998). High job strain—a combination of high psychological demands at work combined with a low degree of control over the work process—has been linked to an increased risk of physical injuries at work, high blood pressure, cardiovascular disease, depression and other mental health conditions, and increased lifestyle risks to health.

Work poses physical risks, and is clearly a major source of psychosocial stress, which has been identified as one major cause of increased morbidity and mortality. As leading population health researcher Brian Wilkinson puts it,

> To feel depressed, bitter, cheated, vulnerable, frightened about debts or job or housing insecurity; to feel devalued, useless, helpless, uncared for, hopeless, isolated, anxious. These feelings can dominate peoples' whole experience of life, colouring their experience of everything else. It is the chronic stress arising from feelings like these which does the damage." (Cited in Dunn 2002: 26)

These are conditions endemic of the contemporary world of work, as the shift to a "post-industrial" society with an increasingly well-educated and skilled workforce, as Canada has undergone since the 1960s, is associated with rising levels of stress at work. While a growing body of research has shown some nega-tive consequences for health to date, the full health impacts of work in the 21st century may just be appearing.

Having work that is not detrimental to one's health is widely recognized as a key factor in what makes a "good job." For all of the emphasis (rightly) placed on the fundamental importance of wages, other dimensions of employment are equally important. On the economic front, non-wage benefits, job security, and opportuni-ties for advancement are as important as wages. The content of work and the nature of the labour process are less tangible and measurable, but are also important. A 2007 survey of changing employment relationships in Canada confirmed that a large majority of workers place a high value on having interesting and personally rewarding work, enjoying some autonomy on the job, and having the ability to exercise and develop their skills and capacities. As indicated by the survey, the most important criterion of job quality, cited by 72 percent of workers as being "very important," is being in a healthy and safe workplace. This is followed closely by work-life balance, which 63 percent cited as "very important" (Lowe 2007). For the purposes of this chapter, seven key dimensions of employment with relevance to health and well-being are considered: (1) physical conditions of work; (2) regulatory protection; (3) job security; (4) workplace control and stress; (5) working time; (6) work-life balance; and (7) social relations and participation at work. Before these dimensions are considered in detail, it is useful to briefly summarize some of the wider economic and social forces affecting Canadian workplaces with potential implications for worker health and well-being.

Forces Shaping Workplace Change in Canada

The terms of employment—wages and benefits, hours, working conditions—reflect the relative bargaining power of workers and employers, and the related willingness of governments to establish minimum rights and standards. Since the 1980s, the context has been predominantly defined by growing employment insecurity, increased employer ability to shift production and new investments to lower-cost regions and countries, and an ideologically driven push by govern-ments toward the increased commodification of labour power.

As discussed in Chapter 1, there has been a pervasive and ongoing restructur-ing of employment relationships intended to promote productivity and com-petitiveness, as opposed to a worker-centred agenda of good jobs (Pupo and Thomas 2010). The basic direction of change is best understood as a simultaneous intensification and casualization of work by employers. The most common forms of organizational change have been downsizing, contracting out non-core func-tions, and securing greater flexibility of time worked through a combination of increased overtime and increased part-time and contract work. This restructuring of work has been driven by employers and supported through neoliberal labour market policies and labour laws. With respect to public-sector workplaces, the restructuring of work along these same lines has been led by governments as employers themselves (Ross and Savage 2013). While attention is often given to the impacts of these processes on working conditions such as wages, benefits, and job security, they also have severe implications for job quality, workplace health and safety, and worker well-being.

Factors Affecting Workplace Health

Physical Conditions of Work

One might have thought that dirty and dangerous work was a thing of the past, banished along with the "satanic mills" of the Industrial Revolution. But deaths, occupational diseases, and injuries rooted in the physical conditions of work are still very much a feature of the contemporary workplace. As can be seen in Figure 4.1, of the 919 workplace fatalities in 2014, construction and manufacturing account for a large proportion. As Figure 4.2 indicates, health and social service industries, followed by manufacturing, construction, and retail trade, account for the largest numbers of workplace injuries (that were reported and that resulted in compensation).

Unlike workplace fatalities, the incidence of work-related accidents and injuries appears to be falling. Reported injuries are those that are made known to provincial workers' compensation boards, since they involve time lost from work and payment while off the job. Between 2004 and 2013, reported lost time claims per 100 workers fell from 3.06 to 2.3 in British Columbia, and from 1.88 to 0.95 in Ontario (Ontario MOL 2015). As one might expect, workplace injuries—including fatalities—are heavily concentrated among men in blue-collar industrial jobs. These kinds of jobs

Figure 4.1: Fatalities by Industry, Canada, 2014

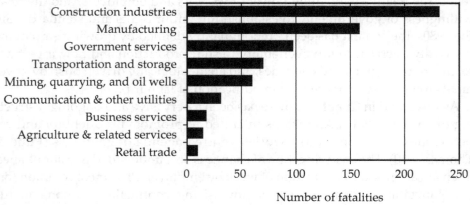

Number of fatalities

Source: Adapted from Association of Workers' Compensation Boards of Canada (AWCBC), National Work Injury/Disease Statistics Program (NWISP). Table 36: Number of Fatalities, by Industry and Jurisdiction, 2013–2015. http://awcbc.org/wp-content/uploads/2016/12/Fatalities-by-Industry-and-Jurisdiction-2013-2015.pdf.

Figure 4.2: Accepted Lost Time Claims by Industry, Canada, 2014

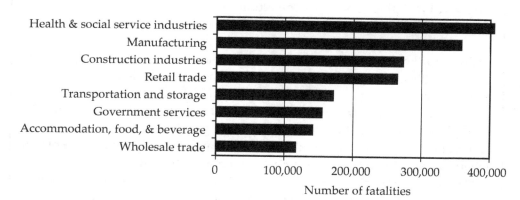

Number of fatalities

Source: Adapted from Association of Workers' Compensation Boards of Canada (AWCBC), National Work Injury/Disease Statistics Program (NWISP). Table 36: Number of Fatalities, by Industry and Jurisdiction, 2013–2015. http://awcbc.org/wp-content/uploads/2016/12/Fatalities-by-Industry-and-Jurisdiction-2013-2015.pdf.

shrank over much of the 1990s, but have recently grown as a result of the resource boom in Western Canada and a strong housing construction market.

The release of a report from the Centre for the Study of Living Standards on growing workplace fatalities in 2006 sparked a major public debate on the real trend in workplace injuries (see Sharpe and Hardt 2006). It is generally recognized that workplace fatalities are the tip of an iceberg, standing above workplace injuries and "near misses," so a decline in injuries combined with an increase in fatalities is curious. In 2007, the CBC Radio program *The Current* ran a program on this issue as part of a series on health and safety in the workplace. Focusing on the situation in Alberta, some argued that workplace accidents are seriously underreported. Troy Ophus, whose hand was crushed against an I-beam by a falling trolley, said that "a lot of injuries don't get reported" because workers feel they will be fired or treated as troublemakers. Dr. Louis Francescutti, an Alberta emergency room physician and university teacher, said that there is "not a shortage of injuries; it's just not being reported."

Part of the problem is that provincial workers' compensation systems have shifted toward experience-rating the premiums paid by employers, so that higher accident rates result in higher costs to them (Lippel 2006). The laudable aim has been to increase the incentive for employers to take workplace health and safety seriously; however, at the same time, it now also makes sense for employers to contract out the most dangerous jobs and try to persuade their own workers not to report injuries. Some employers provide awards for days worked without injuries, increasing pressure on workers not to report an injury.

Box 4.1: Workplace Safety by the Numbers
By Daniel Schwartz

[April 28] is the National Day of Mourning to remember workers injured, killed or afflicted with an occupational illness while on the job. And if it turns out to be an average day for workplace safety in Canada, three workers will die.

In 2012, the most recent year for official statistics, there were 977 workplace-related fatalities in Canada, according to the Association of Workers' Compensation Boards of Canada. But those numbers only cover workplaces where workers can receive provincial compensation benefits.

"Hundreds more die from under-reported illnesses and occupational diseases that go unrecognized in the compensation systems," says the Canadian Labour Congress, which first established the National Day of Mourning exactly 30 years ago this year.

The AWCBC statistics show that the official number of 2012 fatalities was very close to the average of 972 for the years 2000–2012. Construction industries accounted for 22 per cent of fatalities, with manufacturing in second place with 19 per cent.

Health and social service industries accounted for the highest number of injuries on the job, according to the AWCBC. That's 17 per cent of the 245,365 workplace injuries in Canada in 2012.

Work-related injuries falling

The number of work-related injuries has fallen dramatically since the late 1980s, according to federal government and AWCBC statistics. In both 1986 and 1987, there were almost 50 work-related injuries per 1,000 employed workers in Canada, according to federal government calculations. By 2010 that number had fallen to about 15 per 1,000.

The AWCBC numbers, which only cover workplaces under the workers' compensation systems, suggest that ratio likely continued to drop in 2011 and 2012.

The labour movement attributes much of that drop to improving health and safety standards in the workplace.

Nevertheless, an average of 672 workers were injured every day on the job in Canada in 2012, as counted by the AWCBC.

Source: Schwartz, Daniel. 2014, April 28. "Workplace safety by the numbers: National Day of Mourning." *CBC News*. http://www.cbc.ca/news/canada/workplace-safety-by-the-numbers-1.2622466.

Workplace health and safety issues are usually taken most seriously in larger workplaces, which are often unionized, where formal procedures and rules are most often in place, where safety training is most frequently provided, and where government inspections of health and safety conditions in response to worker or union complaints are most likely to take place. The shift of jobs to smaller, usually non-union workplaces and the growth of more precarious forms of employment—such as own-account self-employment and employment with small subcontractors—has thus worked to undermine physical safety on the job. Self-employed workers are generally not covered by government health and safety legislation or by workers' compensation legislation and programs, even though they may be working for large employers, so work-related accidents among this group are not reported (Lippel 2006). Contract employees—who are covered in theory—may not know that they are protected by legislation and workers' compensation programs. This kind of arm's-length employment is quite common in some high-risk industries, such as construction. Also, some quite dangerous jobs—such as farm jobs—may not be covered by health and safety legislation at all. Migrant workers, including seasonal agricultural workers who come to Canada from other countries under special temporary work permits, are especially vulnerable to health and safety risks, and may be the least likely to complain for fear of losing their jobs.

The nature of workplace injuries and conditions is also changing. There has been a disturbing upward trend in repetitive strain and other soft-tissue injuries associated with highly repetitive machine and keyboard work. These account for an upward trend in the proportion of workplace injuries reported by women. As one would expect, physical injuries—sprains and strains to backs and hands, cuts, punctures, lacerations, fractures, and contusions—are associated with physically demanding jobs. Manufacturing and construction account for 17 percent of employment but about 40 percent of injuries. But, as discussed above, injury rates are also high in sectors such as retail trade and health and social services, which involve repetitive physical work. Compounding the changing nature of workplace injuries is that workers' compensation practices, which were designed to address physical trauma in a world of manual, blue-collar, male work, have not changed to sufficiently recognize the growing reality of less visible physical injuries that develop over a period of time (Sullivan 2000). Soft-tissue injuries, such as repetitive strain injuries affecting women clerical and service workers, are under-reported and undercompensated. Many critics of the current workers' compensation system feel that it is inadequate in terms of measuring, let alone compensating for, work-related risks to health in a post-industrial environment.

Musculoskeletal pain and chronic back pain are on the increase (Messing 2014), especially with an aging workforce in physically demanding jobs, and are a major cause of work absence and disability (Shainblum et al. 2000). Many of these conditions have no specific causal event, are slow in onset, and develop progressively over time; thus, it is hard to separate out the specific job-related factors that may be involved. There is a clear link to poor ergonomic conditions in specific kinds of jobs involving heavy work and repetitive tasks, but few workers are able to make successful worker compensation claims. Often, workers will have moved between jobs and even occupations while a condition has been developing, so a condition cannot be attributed to a specific work experience with a specific employer. Similarly, Canada is experiencing a rapidly rising rate of chronic stress–related disability, which often has workplace roots but cannot be identified as solely work-related or solely attributable to a specific job and employer.

Occupational diseases are, of course, also related to workplace risks and exposures. Lung diseases and cancers are linked to physical risks, including inhaling toxic fumes, handling hazardous chemicals, and being exposed to carcinogens. In a limited number of cases, there is a clear causal linkage between occupational exposure and disease onset, which has been recognized by workers' compensation boards. For example, boards recognize that occupational exposure causes asbestosis among asbestos mine workers, and a range of lung diseases among other miners. A handful of highly specific cancers have been demonstrably linked to exposure to specific carcinogens at work. But if we go by the official data, the overall incidence of occupational disease compared to workplace injuries is extremely low.

The workers' compensation system demands high standards of scientific proof of cause and effect in order to keep down costs; however, many carcinogens are present in the workplace. Experts estimate that anywhere from 10 percent to 40 percent of cancers may be caused primarily by workplace exposures; however, only a tiny proportion of cancer victims qualify for workers' compensation. Similarly, though workplace stress and heavy physical exertion are associated with heart conditions, only a tiny proportion of heart attack victims (e.g., firefighters) qualify. The key point is that occupational diseases due to the physical hazards of work are prevalent, but largely unrecognized. Somewhat ironically, employers end up bearing a large share of the costs anyway through employer-funded, long-term disability plans.

Looking beyond Canada, a survey conducted by the European Foundation for the Improvement of Living and Working Conditions (Eurofound) found that "exposure to physical hazards at the workplace and conditions such as musculoskeletal disorders and fatigue caused by intensification of work and flexible employment practises are on the increase" (Eurofound 2000: 10). The survey also provides data on the incidence of repetitive work, showing that in the E.U., 31 percent of workers report continuous, repetitive hand/arm movements, and 23 percent report working at short, repetitive tasks with cycle times of less than one minute. About one in four (24 percent) workers report continuously working at high speed, with the level being highest among machine operators (35 percent), but still high among clerical workers (20 percent) and service workers (23 percent). The incidence of high-speed work due to tight deadlines has been modestly increasing, though there is variation between countries and between different categories of workers. The survey found that those working at high speed were much more likely to report negative health effects, such as muscular pain, stress, and anxiety.

A 2005 Eurofound survey found that intensity of work in the European Union has continued to increase, with a steadily rising proportion of workers expected to work at very high speed and/or to tight deadlines. Between 1991 and 2005, those working at very high speed at least three-quarters of the time rose from just over one in five to about one-third, and the proportion working to tight deadlines at least three-quarters of the time rose from about one-quarter to more than one-third. There was also a modest decrease in the proportion of employees who can exercise autonomy at work, though a majority still reported an ability to change the order of tasks, the speed of work, and the methods of work. Reported job satisfaction declined, with 22.8 percent of workers reporting being not very or not at all satisfied with working conditions in 2005, up from 15.2 percent in 1991. These trends are rather disturbing given the priority that the European Union has accorded to measuring, monitoring, and improving working conditions. On a more positive note, however, only about one in four E.U. workers feels their health and safety is threatened at work, down from about one in three in 1991, and there has been some increase in working-time flexibility and a decline in very long working hours (Eurofound 2007, 2010). Overall, looking at both Canada and the experience in the E.U., despite the transition to "post-industrial" economies, it is clear that occupational health risks remain high.

Regulatory Protection

Workplace health and safety is central to the "contested terrain" of work. When discussing the development of health and safety legislation, it is essential to consider the role of the labour movement, as unions have been central to the social pressure placed on governments to improve health and safety laws. Historically, organized labour played a key role in developing the laws that Canada has today, and unions continue to play an important role in ensuring that workers receive protection under this legal framework.

Around the turn of the 20th century, early health and safety legislation took the form of compensation plans designed to provide workers and their families with some financial compensation for work-related injuries, diseases, and fatalities. Early common law presumed that workers voluntarily assumed the risk of injury in exchange for wages, and there was no legal regulation of workplace conditions that might affect health and safety (Tucker 1990). As workers pressured for reforms in the early 1900s, the system was modified to provide some compensation through either private disability insurance (bargained by workers with their employers) or if an injured worker could prove in court that employer negligence had caused the injury. Neither solution was considered effective by workers. Continued pressure for some protection produced a system of no-fault, employer-funded, state-administered workers' compensation across the provinces, beginning in 1914 in Ontario. The level of compensation was minimal, however, and there was no guarantee that that compensation would provide a family with an income sufficient to alleviate extreme poverty. Widows would lose the compensation upon remarriage, and widowers were only entitled if they were unable to work themselves.

The contemporary occupational health and safety movement emerged in the 1960s, toward the end of the postwar period of economic growth. During this period there was growing awareness and activism around heath and safety dangers within the workplace. The most notable cases were around the carcinogenic effects of asbestos, and the growing protests of miners over "black lung disease" (West Virginia, U.S.), sulphur dioxide gas emissions (INCO, northern Ontario), and silica and radon gas (Elliot Lake, Ontario). The workers' compensation policies, passed early in the 20th century, were recognized as inadequate to proactively address safety conditions within the workplace, giving rise to growing worker protests and wildcat strikes, which were given political support by the New Democratic Party.

In Ontario, this pressure forced the government to call a Royal Commission into health and safety in the province's mines. James Ham, a University of Toronto engineering professor, was appointed to lead the commission. After touring the province and collecting testimony from many workers, Ham issued a report that was particularly critical of the existing "responsibility system" for monitoring health and safety. A major critique he had was that workers and unions were not allowed effective participation in dealing with health and safety issues. For Ham, effective participation should include: knowledge about the conditions of the workplace and the health of workers; the ability to contribute to the assessment of workplace problems; and the ability to make decisions that influence the conditions of work. Ham's recommendations borrowed from health and safety legislation in Saskatchewan, which had been developed under the guidance of Bob Sass, who was responsible for occupational health and safety within the Saskatchewan Ministry of Labour. Sass believed in and pushed for a health and safety system that was built around workers' knowledge of their workplaces and jobs, and that emphasized workers' rights to health and safety protection, including the right to participate, to know, and to refuse. Ham's report to the Ontario government, which was submitted in June 1976, initiated the implementation of occupational health and safety legislation premised on an "internal responsibility system" (IRS) that gave workers and managers the responsibility for the regulation of workplace health and safety. The IRS was premised upon three basic worker health and safety rights: (1) the right to participate (in joint worker/management health, safety, and environment committees); (2) the right to know (about workplace hazards); and (3) the right to refuse (unsafe work). These rights are guaranteed by law (though subject to some variation) in every jurisdiction in Canada.

While this system represented a significant improvement over what existed prior, critics have noted a number of problems (Smith 2000). Workers may not be aware of their legal rights and (especially in the case of non-unionized workplaces) may be fearful of employer reprisals for exercising their rights. Health and safety rights are defined as individual rights, including the right to refuse unsafe work, which means that, technically, health and safety strikes are not permitted (although groups of workers may refuse to work if they feel unsafe individually). Perhaps more significantly, health and safety legislation does not directly address the organization of work processes (for example, job design, workplace, repetitiveness), or of employment relationships (for example, employment form, job security), factors that may be directly related to physical and mental health risks in the workplace. What this means is that although the IRS offers workers some input into the regulation of occupational health and safety in terms of the

most immediate physical dangers, many aspects of work with potentially negative health effects fall outside its scope.

Job Security

In considering the linkages between labour market conditions and health,
researchers have studied both the availability of work and the nature of work. It
is well established from studies of laid-off workers that the state of unemployment is bad for health for both material and psychological reasons. The national
unemployment rate is reported monthly and stood at just over 7 percent in early
2016. Taken at face value, this number considerably understates the true extent of
employment insecurity. To be counted as employed, one need only have worked
for a few hours in a week, so employment numbers include temporary employees, part-time workers who want more hours, and people working in low-wage
survival jobs while looking for regular jobs matching their skills. To be counted as
unemployed, a person has to have been unable to find any work at all and to have
been actively seeking work, even if they knew that no suitable jobs were available. Moreover, there is continual turnover in the ranks of those who are counted
as unemployed over a year. While well down from levels in the early 1990s, a 7
percent unemployment rate counts a significant number of workers experiencing
the stress and uncertainty of unemployment at any given time.

However, as long-term unemployment in Canada is lower than in other
advanced industrial countries, the Canadian job market is marked more by
frequent transitions for many workers, especially women, recent immigrants,
and racialized minorities, between low-paid precarious jobs and relatively short
periods of unemployment. Like longer-term unemployment, frequent short-term
unemployment has also been recognized as a source of stress and anxiety due
to lack of income, uncertain prospects for the future, and its potential to undermine social support networks (WHO 1999). The economic uncertainty generated
through the job insecurity, low wages, lack of control over the labour process, and
lack of regulatory protection characteristic of precarious employment relationships has similarly been identified as a source of stress and anxiety (Lewchuk et
al. 2006; Lewchuk et al. 2011).

Precarious work in Canada is not only widespread, it is also more precarious
than in many other countries. In the European Union, there are often job security
laws and regulations that limit the power of employers to lay off long-tenure
workers. A binding policy directive establishes that there should be limits on
renewals of temporary contracts. Minimum pay laws and widespread collective
bargaining provide a wage and benefit floor to the job market. As a result, there
are far larger pay gaps between precarious and core workers in Canada than in
most E.U. countries.

As inferred above, in addition to stress arising from specific job characteristics
(such as high job demands, fast speed of work, and low degree of control), stress with
adverse implications for health arises from the precarious nature of many employment

relationships in today's job market (Lewchuk et al. 2011; PEPSO 2013). Precarious work—such as temporary and contract work—is stressful in its own right, and also carries a high risk of exclusion from the protections and support networks found in more secure and stable jobs in larger workplaces. Stress from precarious work may stem from lack of secure work, uncertainty about future earnings, lack of ability to provide for basic needs, and lack of control over working time, workload, and the pace of work. A recent survey found that workers in these types of jobs reported poorer overall health and higher levels of stress than workers in permanent jobs. Precarious work includes risks to physical health as well. Studies have found a higher risk of injury and illness, greater workload, greater exposure to dangerous substances among the self-employed and those who work for small contractors, as well as a higher risk of self-reported ill health, and greater incidence of working in pain among precarious workers compared to workers in similar jobs who are in more secure forms of employment. Moreover, those in precarious jobs may not have access to employer-paid health benefits and, without union protection, may experience greater difficulty in exercising their health and safety rights.

Another key difference between relatively secure and more precarious employment with direct implications for health is access to employer-sponsored health benefits. The most important benefit for the working-age population is prescription drug coverage. Governments typically provide drug benefits only to seniors, social assistance recipients, and, sometimes, people leaving welfare for work. Having a low-wage job with no health benefits can mean an inability to buy medically necessary prescription drugs, as well as needed dental and other health services not provided by physicians and hospitals whose costs are covered by Medicare. In 2011, just 63 percent of employees had extended medical, dental, and life/disability coverage, usually provided as a package (Wellesley Institute 2015). While the majority of union members have extended health coverage, coverage is notably lower for the non-unionized, and is typically low in small firms (those with less than 20 employees) and for those in part-time and temporary jobs (see Marshall 2003). Moreover, the rising cost of employer health plans, especially drug costs, has led to reduced coverage for many workers, imposing heavier co-payments and more limitations on allowable prescriptions. The large gaps in our current system mean that there is a tight link between having a good job and having good health-related benefits, and between having a more unhealthy job and having no or very limited benefits. There are also large gaps between secure and more precarious workers in terms of access to paid sick leave. Many precariously employed workers thus face directly higher risks to health because of the quality of their employment, risks that are compounded by lack of access to benefits.

Workplace Stress

Sources of stress at work include the pace and demands of work and the degree of control that workers have over the labour process. Jobs are particularly stressful if high demands on workers are combined with a low level of decision latitude with respect to the use of skills and discretion over how to do the job (Karasek and Theorell 1990). Stress from high-strain jobs (high demands, low control) is greater among women than men, primarily because of lower levels of job control (Wilkins and Beaudet 1998). High-strain jobs are most prevalent among lower-income sales and service workers (Park 2007). Stress may be caused by excessive noise, heat, or cold, work that is too heavy, too fast, or both, harassment by supervisors, and excessive hours of work. Stress can lead to a variety of negative physical, mental, and emotional impacts.

High-stress jobs have been found to be a significant contributing factor to high blood pressure, cardiovascular diseases, mental illness, and long-onset disability. Workers in high-strain jobs are about twice as likely to experience depression as other workers of the same age and socioeconomic status with the same social supports (Shields 2006). There is a link between low levels of control over working conditions and not only stress, but also higher rates of work injuries. Even where work is physically demanding, there is less risk of injury if workers can vary the pace of work, take breaks when needed, and have some say in the design of work stations.

Statistics Canada's *General Social Survey* provides some insight into general levels of workplace stress in Canada. In 2010, 37 percent of workers reported experiencing stress at work from "too many demands or too many hours," up from 33 percent in 1994 and 27.5 percent in 1991. Stress from this source is highest among professionals and managers, at 46 percent and 38 percent, respectively, but it is still high among blue-collar workers (33 percent) and sales and service workers (34 percent) (Crompton 2011a: 47). As one would expect, there is a strong relationship between working long hours and working in jobs that impose high demands. A 2005 survey with a somewhat different question found that one in three workers (32.4 percent) described most days as "quite a bit or extremely stressful," with self-reported work stress being well above average in finance and insurance, and in health care (Lowe 2007: 47).

Women are more likely than men to report high levels of stress from "too many hours or too many demands"—38 percent compared to 36 percent. This partly reflects work-life balance issues considered below. But, it also reflects the high proportion of women working in the high-stress educational, health, and social services sectors, as well as in clerical positions that involve highly routinized, fast-paced work. While we lack detailed information on changes in the overall incidence of work involving high demands and low worker control, high-stress work is common and likely on the increase.

Workplace stress, low control over the labour process, and risk of physical injury may be increased through forms of work reorganization based on the model of "lean production," which involves just-in-time strategies, multitasking, management-by-stress, and an emphasis on a "team" work culture (Moody 1997; Thomas 2008). For example, a study of the impact of the introduction of lean production methods on the auto industry found that: 75 percent reported

Box 4.2: Is the Stress of Your Job Killing You?
By Michael Babad

Workplace stress is killing more than 120,000 Americans a year and driving up health care costs, a new study finds.

It's true that American and Canadian health care systems are different, but such stress spans borders.

"People spend a lot of their waking hours at work," says the report by Joel Goh, an assistant professor of business administration at the Harvard Business School, and his colleagues at Stanford University's Graduate School of Business, professors Jeffrey Pfeffer and Stefanos Zenios.

"Therefore, work environments are consequential not just for stress and feelings of competence and control but also a locus of a person's identity and status," they added in the study, which will be published in Management Science.

"It is, therefore, scarcely surprising that the work environments created by employer decisions can have profound effects on mental and physical wellbeing and, consequently, morbidity, mortality, and health care costs."

The researchers studied 10 stress points, many of which, of course, are similar in Canada.

Having said that, the main problem is a lack of health insurance, so, of course, there's a difference. But unemployment, job insecurity and the heavy demands of the workplace aren't so different.

They researchers also looked at shift work, long working hours, the conflict between work and home and "low organizational justice," among other things.

Recent findings also indicate that "employers can potentially take measures to improve employee health by engaging in managerial practices that mitigate or reduce these stressors," says the report by Mr. Goh.

The researchers note, by the way, that their study is "conservative" on several fronts.

"First it only estimates the costs and morbidity for the individual in the workplace who faces the actual exposure, and does not account for any health consequences to the individual's social network," they write.

"For example, a stressed worker might abuse alcohol or tobacco, which are well-known risk factors for detrimental psychological and physical health in his/her family members."

They also warn of the "overall implication" of their work: "The estimated effect of these workplace stressors is substantially large."

Source: Babad, Michael. 2015, February 3. "Is the stress of your job killing you?" *The Globe and Mail*. http://www.theglobeandmail.com/report-on-business/top-business-stories/is-the-stress-of-your-job-killing-you/article22756664/.

their workload was too fast, was too heavy, had to be done by too few people, or had to be done in too little time; 73 percent reported that their workload had increased, becoming either heavier, faster, or having to be done in less time; 58 percent reported their work pace was too fast; 39 percent reported their physical workload was too heavy; 55 percent reported working in pain or physical discomfort in the month prior to the survey; 51 percent reported working in physically awkward positions at least half of each day; and 53 percent reported that their job was more tense (Lewchuk and Robertson 1999).

Working Time

Changing working time patterns are strongly linked to factors associated with workplace health, stress in particular. A historic goal of the labour movement has been to expand time away from work. Important breakthroughs included the 10- and then the 8-hour working day, the five-day working week and the advent of the weekend, the negotiation of paid days off, and pensioned retirement at progressively earlier ages. By the 1950s, the norm of the standard, five-day, 40-hour workweek with paid annual vacation and retirement with a decent pension was entrenched, though this norm of the Standard Employment Relationship was highly gendered and racialized, and primarily available only to white, male workers (Vosko 2000).

While progress was made through the 1970s and into the 1980s in terms of reduction of weekly hours, annual hours, and the length of a working lifetime, the 1990s saw an increase in daily, weekly, and annual hours for many core workers in full-time jobs, and also a growing hours polarization between these workers and the increasing number of workers in part-time work. These working-time patterns were accompanied and partly facilitated by neoliberal reforms to employment standards legislation that made working time regulation more "flexible" in business-friendly ways (Thomas 2009). Long hours are most prevalent among salaried professional and managerial workers, and among skilled blue-collar workers who frequently work paid overtime. From an employer perspective, overtime helps adjust production to changing market demand, and provides a particularly high cost-saving if the extra hours are not paid for. Even overtime pay premiums are often cheaper than the costs of hiring, training, and providing non-wage benefits to additional workers. Unpaid overtime is increasingly required not just of managers and professionals, but also of public and social services workers attempting to cope with increased workloads. Self-employed workers also tend to work very long hours.

While some workers want to work overtime for higher pay or out of commitment to the job or a career, most have limited ability to refuse demands for longer hours under either employment standards legislation or collective agreements. In most provinces, overtime well in excess of 40 hours can be required, with varying maximum weekly limits. Over one in five workers work overtime in any given week, averaging 8.6 hours, or the equivalent of an extra day's work (Statistics Canada 2007a). About half of this overtime, usually that worked by salaried managers and professionals, is unpaid, suggesting that a large share is the result of too many demands compared to a normal workweek (Lowe 2007: 56).

There was a strong trend to long (and short) working hours for both men and women in the 1980s and 1990s at the expense of the 40-hour workweek norm. The proportion of core-age men aged 25 to 54 working more than 40 hours per week in their main job rose steadily from 15 percent in the early 1980s to about 20 percent in 1994, and continued at that level through the early 2000s. Over the same period, the proportion of core-age women working more than 40 hours per week rose from 5 percent to about 7 percent. About one in three core-age men and one in eight core-age women in paid jobs—those most likely to face work-family time conflicts—now work more than 41 hours per week. Moreover, work is increasingly taken home, especially with the rise of laptops and smartphones, which make electronic work easily portable. By the early 2000s, about one in five workers were working from home in addition to their normal work hours, with this being most prevalent among professionals working in the public sector and for large private-sector employers (Lowe 2007). So-called "good jobs" today make major demands on unpaid time outside of the workplace.

As noted above, working long hours is closely associated with working in high-demand jobs. While these jobs may be interesting and challenging, and give rise to opportunities for advancement, long hours and high demands can be harmful to both physical and mental health. Studies suggest that very long hours are linked to high blood pressure and cardiovascular disease. Long hours of work can contribute directly to physical injury (for example, repetitive strain injuries), as well as mental health problems. Long hours can also contribute to poor health by not allowing for sufficient time to prepare healthy meals, or for sleep and relaxation, and may also contribute to smoking, drinking, and poor diet. Long hours also create a high stress risk in terms of balancing work with domestic and community life.

The shift of core workers to long daily and weekly hours of work is much more characteristic of the U.S. and Canada than the more regulated job markets of continental Europe. The usual weekly hours of full-time paid workers in the E.U. are below 40 (EIRO 2006). Some countries, notably France, Denmark, and Sweden, are now close to a 35-hour norm (Eurofound 2014). Some European countries also provide much more generous paid time off work. In Canada, the minimum vacation entitlement under provincial employment standards is two weeks after a minimum length of service of about one year. Only Saskatchewan provides a minimum of three weeks, though most provinces provide three weeks for workers with higher seniority (between 5 and 15 years). In collective agreements, the norm is three weeks of paid vacation, rising to four weeks after 10 years. By contrast, in the E.U., the minimum statutory entitlement to paid vacation leave is 20 days, or four weeks, and the average provided in collective agreements is 25.7 days, or more than five weeks. Spanish, Austrian, and Portuguese workers get six weeks of paid vacation per year (Eurofound 2014). However, statutory paid holidays on top of paid vacation entitlements are comparable between Canada and European countries.

To summarize, there is a strong trend toward longer hours for some workers, as well as toward more unsocial hours and more variable hours. These conditions all have direct implications for stress, and for physical and mental health.

Work–Life Balance

Longer and more unpredictable hours, combined with high and rising job demands, are particularly likely to cause stress and anxiety in families where both partners work, and for single-parent families. In both cases, women bear the bulk of the burden (Duxbury and Higgins 2002). Nevertheless, faced with a labour market marked by more precarious employment and stagnating wages, increased working time has been a critical factor in maintaining real incomes. Work hours obviously determine both income and the time potentially available to spend with family, children, and in the community. While long hours may result in higher incomes, work-family time conflict may affect the physical and mental health of parents, and also influence the well-being of children. Much of the burden of caring for elderly parents as well as children is borne by working families. These pressures in terms of balancing work and family are greater in Canada than in many other countries because of the relative underdevelopment of publicly financed and delivered early childhood, elder, and home care programs.

Given the working-time patterns discussed above, it is evident that time pressures are steadily increasing (Basso 2003). Several dimensions to this work-life imbalance, or work-life conflict, are becoming common in today's labour market: role overload; work-to-family interference (where work interferes with family responsibilities); and family-to-work interference (where family responsibilities interfere with work) (Duxbury and Higgins 2002). A comparison of data collected on the impacts of work-life conflict in 1991 and 2001 found that high levels of stress at work were twice as prevalent in 2001 than in 1991, and that the absenteeism rates of those with high levels of work-life conflict were three times those of employees with low levels of work-life conflict. Moreover, work-family conflicts arise not just from longer hours, but also from the frequent incompatibility of work schedules with the schedules and needs of children. While a minority of employers offer flex-time arrangements that are responsive to the needs of employees, the great majority of part-time jobs do not offer pay, benefits, and career opportunities comparable to full-time positions, and therefore are not a viable alternative as a means to better construct work-life balance.

Levels of time stress and work-family stress among parents with children are extremely high. Through the 1990s and into 2009, more than one-third of 25- to 44-year-old women who work full-time and have children at home report that they were severely time stressed, and the same is true for about one in four men (Marshall 2009). Twenty-four percent of married fathers, 38 percent of married

Box 4.3: No, It's Not You: Why "Wellness" Isn't the Answer to Overwork
By Zoë Krupka

Many of the people who visit me in my therapy practice spend time talking about work. How much work there is, how they never seem to be able to get it all done, how many hours they spend at work, how tired they are all the time and how fearful they are about losing their jobs. They've read articles telling them how they can improve their work/life balance. They've delegated and relegated, meditated and ruminated.

Women in particular come in suffering the effects of overwork, losing out financially in the longer hours marathon, or perhaps more frighteningly, sacrificing their work to help manage a male partner's crazy schedule. And yet they persist in locating the problem internally. Is there something else they can do, they wonder, to manage it all better? Maybe there's something wrong with them; they just can't seem to live and work at the same time.

We're working longer hours than ever before, and as our employment conditions continue to worsen, they're simply repackaged into a new version of normal in an effort to make the truly pathological state of many of our workplaces appear acceptable. And despite the fact that the very best evidence we have about the causes of work stress and burnout point to factors present in the workplace rather than in us, the stress reduction industry and the helping professions' focus on individual self-care strategies is at an all-time high.

Too busy to be well
Have a look at the lifestyle section of any major newspaper and you'll find a host of articles on how to stay well in a life that's too busy to live in. But the facts are plainer than we're being led to believe. Many of us simply work too much to really be well.

Nothing can alleviate the stress of overwork except working less. Like the road signs say, only sleep cures fatigue. We need to be reminded of this because tired long-haul drivers can be deluded into thinking that coffee, a can of Mother [energy drink] or an upbeat bit of music might help them stay awake. For the madly overworked, we need reminding that the only cure for working too much is to stop. It's as simple as that.

In the last month or so I've had several clients raise the issue of overwork with their managers, with the following results. One had a consultant brought in to assess her team's workloads against their position descriptions. Each member was found to be working at between 130 and 160% of their load. So the load was reset and anyone working at below 150% was told they weren't pulling their weight.

Another workplace appointed an organisational psychologist to assess the team's interpersonal relationships as a way of responding to a workload complaint. As a result, my client was told his personal commitment to reasonable working hours was putting his team at risk and he was put on a program of performance management. Another was simply told not to come in again.

Despite the endless column inches devoted to how we can find balance in our busy working lives, the solution here isn't personal, it's political. Those of us working in the health and wellbeing industries have had our skills hijacked by commercial interests. Employee Assistance Programs, corporate stress management training and the burgeoning multi-billion dollar wellness industry all trade on, support and are supported by the culture of overwork. If we are truly committed to wellbeing, we need to remember who our clients are meant to be and be willing to risk acting in their best interests.

No amount of multivitamins, yoga, meditation, sweaty exercise, superfoods or extreme time management, as brilliant as all these things can be, is going to save us from the effects of too much work. This is not something we can adapt to. Not something we need to adjust the rest of our lives around. It is not possible and it's unethical to pretend otherwise. Like a low-flying plane, the insidious culture of overwork is deafening and the only way we can really feel better is if we can find a way to make it stop.

Source: Krupka, Zoë. 2015, May 21. "No, it's not you: why 'wellness' isn't the answer to overwork." *The Conversation*. https://theconversation.com/no-its-not-you-why-wellness-isnt-the-answer-to-overwork-42124.

mothers, and 42 percent of lone parents report severe time stress (Crompton 2011a: 47; Marshall 2009: 11). Work-family conflict is driven by mounting demands from work, the still largely unchanged division of domestic labour between men and women, and the failure of governments to provide services like child care and elder care on a sufficient scale.

A major 2004 report for Health Canada explored the links between work-life conflict and Canada's health care system (Higgins et al. 2004). The premise was that an employee's ability or inability to balance work and life demands would be associated with key outcomes such as absenteeism, job satisfaction, job stress, family life satisfaction, and level of overall stress in life, and that these outcomes would, in turn, be linked to mental and physical health outcomes. The majority (58 percent) of workers in their sample of employees of medium to large organizations experienced high levels of "role overload," or having too much to do in a given amount of time. They found that, compared to their counterparts with low levels of role overload, employees with high role overload were almost 2.9 times more likely to say their health was just fair or poor, 2.6 times more likely to have sought care from a mental health professional, and about twice as likely to have made frequent visits to a physician. As a result, work-life stress results in high public and private health care costs that could be avoided through better work organization, more family-friendly workplaces, and more supports for working families. The authors concluded that current workloads are not sustainable over the long term. Indeed, in a subsequent study they found that lack of serious progress toward creating more family-friendly workplaces has been a key reason why today's younger workers are putting off having children for many years, if they have children at all. Those who get ahead today are those who put work first.

Social Relations and Participation at Work

Work is a social process, and the social relations of production are an important aspect of the quality of jobs and of a healthy working life. But, little hard information is available on this relatively intangible dimension. In 2000, 15 percent of workers reported stress in the workplace from "poor interpersonal relations," down slightly from 18.5 percent in 1994, but up from 13 percent in 1991. Women report higher levels of stress from this cause than do men. Less than one-half of employees feel that they have much influence on their jobs. A survey by Canadian Policy Research Networks found that only 10 percent of workers feel that they can strongly influence employer decisions that affect their job, and 45 percent feel that they have no influence at all. There were few significant differences by age or gender.

Unionized workers do have some influence through the process of collective bargaining. About one in three paid workers in Canada is covered by the provisions of a collective agreement. As discussed in Chapter 9, coverage is highest by far in the public sector and in large private-sector firms, particularly in primary industries, manufacturing, transportation, and utilities. By definition, collective agreements give access to a formal statement of conditions of employment, such as hours and working conditions, and access to a formal grievance and arbitration process. A formal grievance system militates against the exercise of arbitrary managerial authority, and against harassment by co-workers. Collective agreements also often provide for joint processes to govern working conditions over the life of a contract, such as labour management, training, and health and safety committees. While the great majority of agreements contain a management rights clause clarifying the power of management to assign and direct work, the majority also provide for some advance notification of, and consultation over, technological and organizational change. Many collective agreements also feature detailed job descriptions, meaning that changes in tasks are subject to joint agreement.

Most Canadian unions have adopted formal policies relating to workplace health and safety, work-family balance, work reorganization, and access to training, and have paid some attention to all of these quality-of-work/life issues in bargaining. Improvement of the work environment has been on the agenda, and some unions have made gains. Nevertheless, there are continuous pressures to increase productivity to maintain employment and wages, which tend to militate against an agenda of humanizing work and creating more healthy workplaces. The biggest difference unions make in this area (other than through access to benefits) is through setting limits on hours of work, increasing access to vacations and leaves, and enforcing health and safety laws. However, most commitments to work-life balance and reduced working time tend to be at the level of union policy, rather than actual contractual obligations. It is difficult to bargain these programs and they are often traded off in favour of job security, wage gains, and so on in final bargaining. Employers would generally rather pay a bit more than give up control over scheduling, and unionized workplaces tend to have high rates of overtime hours (Thomas 2006).

While some non-union workers also enjoy access to formalized (if non-binding) processes of dispute resolution and collective consultation, worker "voice" in the Canadian workplace is weak when a union is not present. In terms of the regulation of occupational health and safety, workplace health and safety committees effectively reduce rates of injuries and disability, but are largely absent from the non-unionized precarious labour market (Sullivan 2000). Overall, institutions of collective representation are relatively weakly implanted in Canadian workplaces, undercutting the ability of workers to shape working conditions.

Conclusion

As this chapter has demonstrated, there are many grounds for concern over the potential health impacts of current trends in Canadian workplaces. Workplace threats to physical health in the form of fatalities, injuries, and occupational disease remain significant for many workers. Pervasive job insecurity is a source of stress. In core workplaces, the pace and intensity of work are on the rise, and many are working very long hours in very demanding jobs. The incidence of high-strain jobs that combine high demands and limited control is quite high, particularly among women. The best available evidence suggests that the quality of work along most dimensions valued by workers is deteriorating (Lowe 2007). These negative trends exist across the skills and income spectrum, with well-paid professionals enduring high levels of stress from overwork, while the less skilled and less well paid endure stress from unstable work, physical risks, poor working conditions, and high job demands combined with low levels of control.

More information is needed about the level and trends of workplace determinants of health. This could be remedied if Statistics Canada conducted regular surveys on the quality of the work environment and working conditions. The now-discontinued *Workplace and Employee Survey* provided only very limited information in this area, and the now-discontinued *National Population Health Survey* provided only very limited information on working conditions.

Governments must intervene to help shape and improve workplace conditions. A wide range of relevant recommendations have been made over the years, including through the *Report of the Advisory Group on Working Time and Redistribution of Work* (HRDC 1994) and the *Report of the Collective Reflection on the Changing Workplace* (Canada 1997). The thrust of the first was to regulate working time by limiting long hours and by making precarious work more secure. The thrust of the second—which included a very wide range of options—was to propose changes to employment standards and forms of collective representation. A more recent milestone report was that of a federal task force on employment standards, *Fairness at Work: Federal Labour Standards for the 21st Century*, which called for limits on long hours of work and arbitrary work schedules, more paid time off the job, and measures to secure respect for human rights in the workplace. The report set out a "decency principle," stating that "no worker should be subject to coercion, discrimination, indignity or unwarranted danger in the workplace, or be required to work so many hours that he or she is effectively denied a personal life" (HRSDC 2006b). Similarly, in 2012 the Law Commission of Ontario called for stronger protections for workers in precarious jobs, including better regulation of occupational health and safety (LCO 2012). At the end of the day, it is unlikely that there will be significant positive changes in the workplace if the voices of workers are left out of decisions about how to better create healthy and safe workplaces.

Recommended Reading

Eurofound. 2007. *Report on the European Survey on Working Conditions*. Luxembourg: Eurofound.

Lewchuk, Wayne, Marlea Clarke, and Alice de Wolff. 2011. *Working without Commitments: The Health Effects of Precarious Employment*. Kingston and Montreal: McGill-Queen's University Press.

Smith, Doug. 2000. *Consulted to Death: How Canada's Workplace Health and Safety System Fails Workers*. Winnipeg: Arbiter Ring Publishers.

Raphael, Dennis (ed.). 2016. *Social Determinants of Health: Canadian Perspectives*. 3rd edition. Toronto: Canadian Scholars' Press.

PART II

WORK, INEQUALITY, AND DIFFERENCE

CHAPTER 5

Gender, Work, and Social Reproduction

Despite decades of progress that saw the widespread entry of women into the workplace and a wide range of occupations and professions, gendered inequalities continue to shape the Canadian labour market. The gender wage gap persists in 2016, where on average, women employed full-time, year-round earn 72 percent of what men earn (Lambert and McInturff 2016). The wage gap has been stuck around $0.70 since the mid-1990s—one of the highest levels in the advanced industrial world. Strikingly, the gap has been maintained, even as women have become more educated than men, and even as most women have decided to have fewer children later in life. Women are participating in the paid labour force at higher levels than ever before and very few now drop out of paid work for extended periods of time; yet, the gap persists. Gendered divisions of labour are also persistent and contribute to continued economic inequality, such that women without high levels of education, or whose credentials are unrecognized in Canada, are much more likely than men to be employed in very low-paid and insecure part-time and temporary jobs, especially in private-sector sales and service jobs. When it comes to better-paid jobs, women are still largely excluded from blue-collar jobs, especially in the skilled trades. Though a large and growing layer of women have indeed moved into professional and skilled technical jobs in education, health care, and other community and public services, these women are still paid less than comparable men, and are significantly under-represented in very well-paid jobs.

One of the main causes of the continuing inequality between women and men is that our workplaces and our social and labour market policies fail to reflect the realities of women's lives. Today, the great majority of women, including mothers of young children and women with elderly parents, participate in the paid workforce. But working women still take on most of the responsibility for care and for work in the home. Many employers demand very long hours of full-time workers, fail to provide reasonable and stable work schedules that match family needs, and will penalize women who take temporary leaves. As a result, many women are forced to work in lower-paid and more unstable part-time jobs, pay a big price for dropping out of the workforce for a year or two, or must decide to work very long hours and not to have children at all.

This chapter outlines forms of gender inequality in the Canadian labour market, with particular attention to issues of wages, occupational segregation, job quality, and gendered divisions between paid and unpaid work. While this chapter makes many comparisons between the experiences of women and men, it is also important to emphasize that there are major and growing differences in labour market experiences among women, and that the progress of some women has not been experienced by all. There are also racialized differences in the quality of jobs between women, and differences between women who belong to unions and other women, issues that are considered in more detail in Chapters 6 and 9 respectively.

Participation in the Workforce

Women's participation rates in the workforce increased dramatically through the 20th century, and particularly in the decades following World War II (Armstrong and Armstrong 2010). Women continued to enter the Canadian workforce in increasing numbers in the 1990s and through the 2000s, though at a slower rate than in the past. The labour force participation rate of women aged 15 to 64, which was just over one-half in the mid-1970s, had reached two-thirds by the late 1980s, and stood at an all-time high of almost three-quarters (74.2 percent) in 2015.[1] This is still appreciably below the participation rate of 81.8 percent for men, though the rate for men has been stable or even falling because of a trend toward earlier retirement over most of the 1980s and 1990s. While short periods of time outside the paid workforce remain common, the early years of the 2000s saw a big increase in the participation rate of older women. For women aged 55 to 59, the participation rate jumped from just under one-half in the mid-1990s to 68.6 percent in 2006. Almost half of women aged 60 to 65 are now still in the paid workforce, up from just one-third in the mid-1990s. Unlike earlier generations, most of today's older women have worked for most of their lives.

In almost all OECD countries, the participation rate of women in the workforce has climbed steadily since the 1960s, and the gender gap in employment rates has narrowed considerably. The participation rate of women in Canada (74.2 percent) is now one of the very highest among the OECD countries, as compared to an OECD average of just 62.8 percent. For women aged 25 to 54, the participation rate in Canada was 86.2 percent in 2014, compared to an OECD average of 81.5 percent.[2] Labour force participation in Canada by women lags only (very slightly) behind the Scandinavian countries.

Gender, Work, and Social Reproduction

In all countries, participation rates and employment in full-time jobs tend to be lower for women because women still bear the primary responsibility for *social reproduction*, defined as "the activities required to ensure day-to-day and generational survival of the population" (Luxton and Corman 2001: 29). This includes the wide range of activities and relationships involved in maintaining people on both a daily basis and intergenerationally, such as buying household goods, preparing meals, washing, repairing clothes, cleaning the house, raising children, providing emotional support for children and adults, and so on. These forms of unpaid work, and the ways in which they are socially organized along gender lines, have a deep connection to gender divisions in the labour market (Armstrong and Armstrong 2010). Thus, the gendered organization of unpaid labour in the home is more than simply a "private service for families" that is peripheral to the formal labour market. Rather, it is "socially indispensable labour that contributes to the production of the labouring population and its labour power" (Luxton and Corman 2001: 29).

More specifically, the gendered organization of unpaid labour in households contributes directly to gendered patterns of segmentation and inequality in the labour market (Creese 1999; Pupo 1997; Steedman 1997). First, as it is women who are primarily responsible for social reproduction, gendered divisions of labour within the home have restricted women's access to full-time paid employment. Moreover, gendered assumptions about women's responsibilities in the home (what is "women's work") have shaped the types of occupations available to women workers, and the levels of pay and employment security associated with those occupations. As will be discussed below, women's over-representation in precarious and non-standard employment relationships (especially part-time) is explained in part by their responsibilities for social reproduction. Finally, social reproduction highlights not only the gendered but also the racialized divisions of labour that are connected to the organization of household labour (Glenn 1992). Using an analytical lens that captures intersections of race and gender reveals that social reproduction also involves the (paid and unpaid) labour of racialized, immigrant women under conditions that are highly precarious and exploitative, as discussed in further detail in Chapter 6.

The impact of gendered divisions of unpaid labour on women's experiences and opportunities in the workforce cannot be overstated. Almost everywhere, the gap between the employment rates of women and men increase with the presence and number of children in a family. The especially low participation rates of women in some European countries, such as Germany, Italy, and Spain, reflects the survival of a traditional male breadwinner family model in which men are still the main source of family income, and many married women with children do not participate in paid work at all. This model is eroding as more women have sought economic equality with men, and as cultural norms, including the division of domestic work, have changed. But it is still a significant influence on the job market. It is interesting to note that the number of children born per woman has plummeted most in countries where women have made progress in the educational system and job market, but women are still expected to bear a highly unequal share of caring work and work in the home (Beaujot and Kerr 2007).

The very high participation rates of women in the Scandinavian countries (and, likely, the narrow gender pay gap in these countries) reflect the fact that many of the caring needs of households that were traditionally maintained by women in the home have now been assumed by the whole society through the public and not-for-profit sector. Child care and care for the elderly are readily available at low cost, which has helped women to work outside the home, and also to pursue career paths and climb job ladders without major interruptions in their work experience. Public investment in caring services outside the home has also directly created many good jobs for women.

Canada's very high rate of labour force participation by women does not reflect a well-developed system of government-supported child care. Even in Quebec, a comprehensive system is relatively new. Outside Quebec, quality care is hard to find, and is expensive. There is some evidence that the Quebec program has, as might be expected, helped boost labour force participation by women, while a lack of formal child care has held participation back in other provinces (Roy 2006). It would seem that the major impact in Canada of a lack of organized, quality child care and elder care services is not low labour force participation by women, but rather a heavy tilt toward part-time work, as detailed below. The burden of care does not stop women from working, but it pushes them into lower-paid and more insecure jobs.

Very high rates of participation by Canadian women in paid work undoubtedly reflect the fact that most women want to work to pursue a career, and to enjoy some measure of economic independence, rather than be full-time caregivers at home for extended periods of time or completely dependent on the earnings of a spouse. Cultural norms have shifted much further away from the male breadwinner model of the 1950s than in many European countries, but high participation in paid work by Canadian women also reflects some new and more concerning economic realities. As the real wages of men have stagnated, and for many declined, ever since the mid-1970s, women have entered the labour force to maintain and increase real family incomes. There would have been no real income growth for the great majority of Canadian working families over the past 30-plus years if it had not been for the rising incomes of working women. Incomes of women have increased as more women have joined the workforce, as their hours of work have risen, and as the wage gap between women and men narrowed until the mid-1990s.

The dual-earner family is now very much the Canadian norm, and the earnings of women currently make up approximately one-third of the income of dual-earner families. This proportion has remained steady since the late 1990s, after trending up from 25 percent in the late 1960s (Statistics Canada 2006). About one in four women in dual-earner families now earns more than her male spouse, and the earnings of women are, of course, the main source of income for most single-parent families and for the many women who live alone. Low earnings for many women are a major part of the explanation for very high poverty rates among single-parent families headed by women. They are also a big factor behind low family incomes, since high-earning men now tend to live with high-earning women. Of course, a layer of well-paid men can, and do, support spouses who do not work, or work only part-time, but this is much less common than a generation ago. The key point is that the earnings of women are hugely important to economic well-being, and are now rarely just an add-on to male earnings. This makes the low earnings of many women and the gender pay gap highly problematic for both economic and equality reasons.

Approximately three in four (73 percent) of Canadian two-parent families with children are now two-earner families. While many women (and a few men) with children work part-time, in 2014 69.1 percent of all two-parent families with children had two full-time earners, a significant increase from 1976 (35.9 percent) (Uppal 2015: 2). The domestic responsibilities of women, along with the fact that many women with young children still take some time out of the paid workforce, continue to make a difference. In 2009, one in three women (33.5 percent) with a child under age six and about the same proportion with a child under age three (35.6 percent) were not in paid employment (Ferrao 2010: 9). In the mid-2000s, the participation rates of women who had given birth to a child within the last three years were about 10 percentage points below those of other women in the same age group. The length of maternity and parental leaves increased in the 2000s, partly because of expanded rights to maternity/parental benefits under the Employment Insurance program (Zhang 2007). While more than twice as likely to be in the workforce as 30 years ago, lower-than-average labour force participation rates for women with very young children reflect the choice and opportunity of many women to take short-term or somewhat longer maternity and parental leaves, a choice that has been facilitated by improved maternity/parental benefits and perhaps influenced by problems of access to quality affordable child care. Very long working hours for some men are also likely a factor as to why some couples with children decide to live on one income, at least for a period of time.

Regardless of the reasons, the evidence suggests that giving birth to a child lowers the future earnings of a Canadian woman compared to a comparable woman without children by between 5 percent and 13 percent (Drolet 2002; Zhang 2007). The OECD points out that women who have had children have significantly lower lifetime earnings than women who have not, with the price being lowest in countries with public child care services. In today's job market, periods spent outside of paid work to care for children may be taken voluntarily, but nonetheless come at a price.

Many women, especially those working in part-time jobs, must deal with unstable and unpredictable work schedules. There was an increase in unsocial working hours in the 1990s, with more women working at night and on weekends. More women are also now working very long hours. About one in seven women now works more than 41 hours per week. As women still bear the major responsibility for domestic labour (child care, elder care, household maintenance, etc.), unpredictable or long hours, combined with high and rising job demands, may cause acute stress for many women. While more men are doing some household work, women in dual-earner families continue to take on more of the unpaid housework than men (Marshall 2006; Marshall 2011: 22). Working women are typically more likely than men to be responsible for dropping off and picking up children at child care, and for shopping. As a result, levels of time stress and work-family stress among women with children are extremely high. More than one-third of women in dual-earner families with children at home, as compared to one-quarter of men, report feeling "severely time stressed" (Marshall 2009: 12). Similarly, women report greater dissatisfaction with work-life balance than do men. This acute time conflict for many women likely leads many to "balance" work and family by opting out of jobs with very long hours or very heavy work demands, and this is likely a key factor behind the continuing wage gap.

The Persistent Gender Wage Gap

One striking development in Canada since around the mid-1990s or so has been that the gender pay gap has, after many years of gradual progress toward equality, remained more or less stuck. Continued economic inequality between women and men, despite the fact that the formal educational qualifications of at least younger women now exceed those of men, tells us that women still face discrimination and barriers, and that real equality of opportunity does not yet exist. This in turn means that many women remain, to a significant degree, economically dependent upon the earnings of men to sustain a decent family income, and that many women experience or are especially vulnerable to low income and poverty. This is especially true in an age of unstable families, where about 4 in 10 of all marital unions end in divorce. Wage gaps and low income over the course of a working lifetime condemn many women to low income in old age, with the low income rate of single elderly women significantly exceeding that of men (7.6 percent compared to 3.6 percent in 2008) (Milan and Vézina 2011: 24).

The most commonly cited indicator of the gender wage gap is the annual earnings of full-time, full-year workers. As demonstrated in Table 5.1, by this measure women earned just 71.3 percent as much as men in 2008, or $44,700 compared to $62,600. Breaking this down by educational attainment, it is evident that this gap diminishes as education level rises.

What is striking, as illustrated in Figure 5.1, is that the gender wage gap for full-time, full-year workers closed steadily through the 1980s until the mid-1990s. Over that period, women's annual earnings rose from about two-thirds to about 70 percent of that of men, but the wage gap has since stagnated at that level. As further shown in the chart, the gender wage gap for workers with a university degree also closed steadily until the mid-1990s, and then suddenly rose again in 1997. It has remained stuck at between 66 percent and 68 percent since that time. In short, the long trend toward greater economic equality of women and men stalled by the mid-1990s.

As shown in Table 5.2, the hourly wage gap between women and men narrowed somewhat between 1998 and 2014. The progress here is evident in the shrinking of the gap in the 25 to 54 age group, as the gender wage difference among 15- to 24-year-olds remained relatively stable across this time period. The failure of the gender wage gap to continue to close is particularly surprising given that the educational attainment of women, especially younger women, continued to

Table 5.1: The Pay Gap: Average Annual Earnings of Women and Men Employed Full-Year, Full-Time, by Educational Attainment, 2008

	Men	Women	Earnings Ratio
Less than Grade 9	40,400	20,800	51.5
Some secondary school	43,600	28,600	65.6
Graduated high school	50,300	35,400	70.4
Some post-secondary	50,100	36,400	72.6
Post-secondary certificate or diploma	57,700	41,100	71.2
University degree	91,800	62,800	68.3
TOTAL	**62,600**	**44,700**	**71.3**

Source: Statistics Canada, *Survey of Labour and Income Dynamics*; see also Status of Women Canada 2012.

Figure 5.1: Female/Male Earnings Ratio (%), 1980–2006, Full-Time, Full-Year

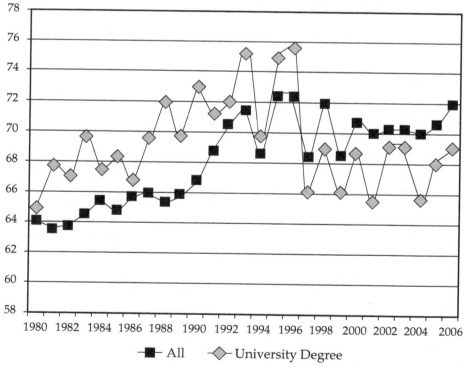

Source: Statistics Canada. Income Trends in Canada, 2006. Cat. 13F0022XIE, Tables 2020102 and 2020104.
Note: Income data are in constant 2006 dollars.

improve compared to that of men (Statistics Canada 2011a). As of 2009, 36.7 percent of women aged 25 to 34 and 37.2 percent of women aged 25 to 54 had some
form of post-secondary certificate or diploma, as compared to 37 percent and
36.8 percent, respectively, of men. For those aged 25 to 34, 34.3 percent of women
as compared to 26 percent of men had attained a university degree. The gap is
narrower for those aged 25 to 54, with 28.1 percent of women and 25.1 percent
of men having achieved a university degree. Yet, despite the high educational
attainments of women, the annual earnings gap has persisted, including among
those with a university education.

**Table 5.2: Average Hourly Wage of Women as a Percentage of Men, 1998–
2014**

	1998	2000	2002	2004	2006	2008	2010	2012	2014
All	81.4%	80.6%	81.8%	83.2%	83.8%	83.6%	85.1%	84.8%	86.0%
Age 15–24	91.0%	89.3%	90.0%	90.4%	90.5%	89.3%	90.4%	91.8%	91.0%
Age 25–54	81.2%	80.4%	81.9%	83.4%	84.0%	83.6%	85.2%	86.1%	86.2%

Source: Statistics Canada, *Labour Force Survey* Estimates, CANSIM Table 282-0072.

Table 5.3 shows average hourly wages for a range of occupations in 2006 and
2014. These show a pure gender gap per hour worked, as opposed to larger pay
gaps for the week and for the year, which reflect not just lower pay rates for
women but also fewer hours worked. Women earned an average of $22.64 per
hour compared to $26.34 for men in 2014, meaning that women earned, on aver-
age, about 86 percent of the male hourly wage. The wage gap tends to be greatest
in the male-dominated blue-collar occupations, and in the low-paid sales and
service sector. Overall, women earned significantly less than men in lower-paid
occupations. By contrast, the wage gap is smaller in better-paid occupations, especially in health occupations. As will be detailed below, the impact of these wage
differences between occupations and wage gaps within occupations is amplified
by the fact that women are disproportionately over-represented in low-wage
occupations. Data for hourly wages, which are consistently available only from
1997, show a slight decrease in the gender wage gap, suggesting that hours of
work play a major role in the annual earnings gap.

Table 5.4 shows a higher proportion of women than men in earnings brackets
for income levels below $20,000. There is a higher proportion of men in all income
brackets starting at $20,000 and over. At an annual earnings level of $75,000 and
over, men predominate in a proportion of just over two to one. At the very top
of the income spectrum, men overwhelmingly dominate. In 2004, the top 5 per-

Table 5.3: Average Hourly Wages, by Occupation, 2006 and 2014

	2006			2014		
	Men	Women	Women as % of men	Men	Women	Women as % of men
All	$21.43	$17.96	83.8%	$26.34	$22.64	86%
Management	$33.33	$27.68	83.0%	$42.12	$35.78	84.9%
Business, finance, administrative	$20.97	$17.95	85.6%	$25.75	$22.57	87.7%
Natural and applied sciences	$28.70	$24.60	85.7%	$34.96	$32.35	92.5%
Health occupations	$23.68	$23.02	97.2%	$29.10	$28.10	96.6%
Social science, education, government services	$28.69	$24.22	84.4%	$34.58	$29.91	86.5%
Art, culture, recreation, sport	$20.69	$18.96	91.6%	$24.89	$23.12	92.9%
Sales and service	$14.91	$11.74	87.7%	$18.52	$14.78	79.8%
Trades, transport, equipment operators	$19.86	$14.67	73.9%	$24.85	$19.05	76.7%
Processing, manufacturing, utilities	$18.79	$13.57	72.2%	$22.24	$16.68	75.0%

Source: Statistics Canada, *Labour Force Survey* Estimates, CANSIM Table 282-0075.

cent of Canadian tax-filers earned $89,000 or more. Of this top group, 76 percent were men, rising to 79 percent in the elite top 1 percent group earning more than $181,000. The disproportionate representation of men in the very highest income groups helps explain the failure of the gender wage gap to continue to close since the mid-1990s, since the proportion of all income going to the male-dominated high-income group has been steadily rising.

Table 5.4: Total Income Level, by Sex (as percentage of total persons with income, all ages), 2013

Income groups	Men (%)	Women (%)
Under $5,000	3.1	4.4
$10,000 and over	42.7	43
$20,000 and over	35.4	31.8
$35,000 and over	26.6	19.9
$50,000 and over	18.8	11.7
$75,000 and over	10.1	5
$100,000 and over	5.4	2.1
$150,000 and over	2	0.6
$200,000 and over	1	0.3
$250,000 and over	0.6	0.2
Median income	$39,290	$26,400

Source: Statistics Canada CANSIM Table 111-0008.

Canada is not alone in these patterns. The gender wage gap exists in all OECD countries, with the median hourly pay of women full-time workers averaging 15.3 percent less than that of men.[3] The gender pay gap in Canada measured by this key international indicator is, however, well above average, with women earning 18.97 percent less than men in full-time jobs. In 2014, the gender pay gap in Canada was the seventh greatest among 35 OECD countries, surpassed only by Turkey, Netherlands, Israel, Japan, Estonia, and Korea.[4]

The Changing Generational Fortunes of Young Women and the Pay Gap

The past several decades have seen a huge shift in the life experiences of younger adults. A generation and more ago, young people left home, entered into marital unions, found stable jobs, and had children at a much earlier age than is now the case. Today, it is not until their mid-twenties that the majority of young people

Figure 5.2: OECD Gender Wage Gap, 2014

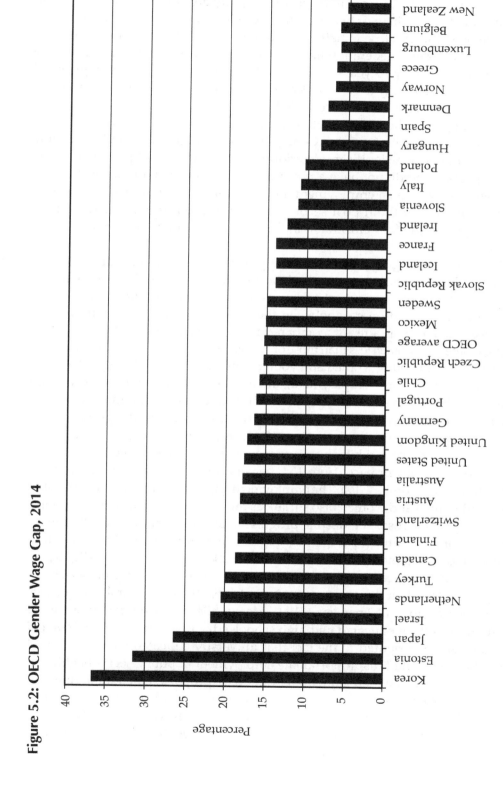

Source: OECD gender gap rating, 2014.

are working full-time. Before that age, the majority are still at school. More than 40 percent of people in their twenties still live at home, up from just one in four in 1981. At age 25 to 29, close to half of all young women are still single, compared to just one-quarter a generation ago. The average age at which a woman has a first child has risen by six years, to age 29.8 (Milan et al. 2011: 13), and single-child families are increasingly the norm (Beaujot 2004). Adding up all of these changes, families have become much more varied.

Key changes in the job market help explain this delayed transition to the adult norm of a generation ago. Good jobs require higher levels of education, and there has been a significant deterioration in the quality of jobs available to young people who do not have a post-secondary education. In the 1990s, wage gaps and differences in employment and unemployment rates between young people with and without post-secondary qualifications greatly increased. As a result, post-secondary enrolment in Canada has soared to one of the highest levels in the world.

On balance, young women have made progress. Compared to earlier generations, families have been prepared to invest in the education of all children, and most young women now expect and want to pursue an education and a career. As noted, the education gap between the sexes no longer exists, and indeed has reversed. Partly as a result, compared to earlier generations, the earnings of young women have fallen less than those of young men (Jackson 2006a). However, the pay gap between young women and young men remains surprisingly intact.

Looking at education, employment, and earnings for young men and women aged 25 to 29 in each of 1981, 1991, and 2001, it can be seen that the educational gap between young women and men continued to widen as the proportion of women in that age group with a university degree rose from 16.2 percent, to 19.1 percent, to 31.3 percent, while the proportion of university-educated young male adults rose at a slower pace, from 15.5 percent, to 16.1 percent, to 26.1 percent (Frenette and Coulombe 2007). The employment gap between university-educated young adult men and women also shrank as the proportion of women graduates working full-time rose. Yet, despite progress in terms of educational attainment and obtaining full-time jobs, the pay gap between university-educated young women and young men persisted from 1991 to 2005, narrowing only slightly. In 2005, university-educated young adult women earned an average of $40,441, or 11.9 percent less than the average earnings of $45,291 for comparable men. This compares to a gap of 12.2 percent in 1991. Meanwhile, the earnings gap remained constant for college-educated and high school–educated young adults. Much of this gap can be attributed to the fact that university-educated women suffered pay cuts as a result of disproportionate employment in public-sector health and education jobs, while men gained pay due to disproportionate employment in private-sector jobs in engineering, computer science, and commerce. The fact remains that it is young adult male university graduates who have had access to the best-paid jobs due to continued occupational segregation, as detailed below.

Box 5.1: Women's Day in Canada: Much to Celebrate, Much More Work to Do

By Emanuela Heyninck

International Women's Day gives us an opportunity to celebrate the many achievements on the journey to gender equality. It also gives us pause to assess where we are in that journey. We are reminded daily that millions of women in developing countries struggle for personal and economic freedom, including the freedom to learn, work, and participate.

Compared to their situation, women in Canada are doing well. Our young men and women may wonder whether the theme for this year's International Women's Day, Inspiring Change, applies to us. When they look around, they see that men and women are attending colleges and universities at equal rates. In some professions, women make up more than half of the graduating classes. Men and women are participating in equal numbers in the work force. In Ontario, we have human rights, pay equity and employment standards laws, in addition to many other services and community organizations that protect the rights of women and continue to advocate for the full integration of women in all areas of public and private life. What, they may ask, needs to change in Canada?

The gender wage gap is one indicator of the fact that progress to economic equality has plateaued. While there are many ways to measure the gap, a common statistic—comparing full-time/full-year average wages—puts the gender gap at 26 per cent. This means that for every $1 earned by a male worker, a female worker is earning only $0.74. In the last decade this figure has barely moved. For women of colour and Aboriginal women, the gap is even wider. Royal Bank has estimated that if the gender wage gap were addressed and women and men in Canada received the same economic opportunities, women would have $168-billion more in disposable income.

The poor representation of women in leadership roles is another indicator. Despite the overwhelming evidence that demonstrates without doubt that companies with more diverse boards are more profitable, women make up only about 16 per cent of corporate board seats.

Business structures and practices have not caught up to modern day realities because stereotypes about women and work persist. Many employers continue to make assumptions about women and their roles as caregivers, consciously or unconsciously overlooking them for advancement and training opportunities or by not considering them for more lucrative projects.

Women have been told to take the initiative by negotiating their pay, but numerous studies show that women who attempt to negotiate for better salaries either don't receive them or are viewed negatively by their managers and co-workers.

Finally, "women's work"—and the so-called "soft skills" that women are respected for—are still being undervalued and under-compensated.

We need to be inspired. We also need to take action—to make use of the laws, strategies and tools that have been developed so that a real and substantive culture shift about women at work becomes the new standard.

Culture shift is never easy. It requires introspection and change at both the organizational and individual level. It takes strong leadership and men and women working together to come up with new ways of doing things. Where gender workplace equality is concerned, it means restructuring our business and compensation practices to mirror the realities of today's world.

By acting to change our own culture to ensure that women are fully integrated into the economic and social fabric of our country, we inspire other jurisdictions and populations and economies to aim for our successes.

Source: Heyninck, Emanuela—Ontario Pay Equity Commission. 2014, March 8. "Women's Day in Canada: Much to celebrate, much more work to do." *The Globe and Mail*. http://www.theglobeandmail. com/opinion/womens-day-in-canada-much-to-celebrate-much-more-work-to-do/article17370856/. For more information, please visit www.payequity.gov.on.ca.

Pay Discrimination and Pay Equity

Economic research has consistently shown that the greatest part of the gender wage gap in Canada, as in other industrial countries, cannot be explained by supposedly objective factors such as the educational level and job experience of women. With careful consideration, it is obvious that the disparity is created through the social relations of gender and the gendering of work (Drolet 2002; OECD 2002a). Pay gaps can and do result from gendered preconceptions regarding the value of particular forms of work, specifically through the devaluing of jobs associated with "women's work." For example, male blue-collar workers are still often paid more than women clerical workers, even though their jobs are no more highly skilled, nor involve greater responsibility, nor are necessarily more demanding. Well into the 1970s, nursing and elementary school teaching were low-paid jobs mainly because these were professions dominated by women, rather than because the skill and responsibility levels of the work were low. Traditionally, male workers were more highly unionized than women, and greater bargaining power helped raise their relative wages. Low unionization for women compared to men is still a major factor shaping wage patterns in the private sector. Until at least the 1960s and 1970s, the social norm was that men should be paid a family-supporting wage, whereas women were viewed as secondary income earners.

Pay gaps can arise from the fact that women are discriminated against when it comes to accessing better jobs and promotions. Such discrimination can be overt—protection of male jobs preserves differences—or more systemic—the devaluing of women's work and the failure to account for unequal responsibilities with respect to social reproduction. While differences in total work experience are not necessarily very large, the perception that a career comes second for women seems to be a major factor behind the glass ceiling that continues to exist in some workplaces and professions.

To counter these tendencies, women in Canada have engaged in longstanding struggles for legislated pay equity. The demand for laws requiring equal pay for women and men doing the same job dates back to the 19th century and, by the 1950s, most Canadian provinces had "equal pay for equal work" legislation forbidding employers from paying women less than men performing the same job. However, expressed in this way, the principle of equality is problematic for the simple reason that women and men mainly work in different jobs, rather than side-by-side for different pay in the same job. Pay discrimination by gender is less discrimination against individuals than systemic, in that the kinds of jobs held by women are undervalued compared to the jobs held by men, and thus pay lower wages (Armstrong et al. 2003).

From the mid-1970s, the federal government and some provinces began to legally require some employers to pay women equal pay for work of equal value, that is, to equalize pay between comparable job groups or classifications within the same establishment. Usually, such legislation has applied to public-sector employers, and application to even large private-sector employers has been much more limited and sporadic. Small employers have almost invariably been excluded.

Proactive pay equity laws covering only the public sector have been introduced in Manitoba, New Brunswick, Prince Edward Island, and Nova Scotia. However, Newfoundland and Labrador, Alberta, British Columbia, and Saskatchewan still have no legislation at all governing equal pay for work of equal value. Only Ontario (1998) and Quebec (1996) have proactive pay equity laws covering both the public and private sectors. Reports on the 10th anniversary of the Quebec Pay Equity Act indicated that one-third of the completed pay equity exercises had resulted in salary adjustments of between 3.9 percent and 8.1 percent. The federal legislation, which requires filing a complaint, is embedded in the Canadian Human Rights Act. Similar human rights provisions also cover the Yukon, the Northwest Territories, and Nunavut. The federal legislation is much less effective. Equal pay for work of equal value can only result from a complaint by employees. When a complaint has been made, employers and unions have had to undertake complex comparisons of job classifications to determine if female-dominated jobs have been undervalued and, if so, to calculate any pay differential that should be eliminated. And employers have used lack of clarity in the legislation to challenge the positive results of pay equity studies, and to tie up the process for years by resorting to the courts.

There have been some significant pay gains for some groups of women under the federal law, as in landmark legal settlements for women clerical and support workers in the federal public service and women workers at Bell Canada. However, these victories came only after years of protracted negotiations and extremely expensive legal struggles. In practice, the legal struggle for pay equity has only benefited women working for large employers, mainly where a union has been prepared to actively press the case. Overall, the principle of equal pay for work of equal value has not been effectively applied outside a few parts of the job market, and has been undercut by the restructuring of work in such a way as to undermine large workplaces where systematic comparisons can readily be made between the jobs of women and men (Armstrong et al. 2003). Pay equity legislation would be much more effective if all employers were required to proactively ensure that their pay classification systems were gender neutral.

Precarious Work

The fact that more women are working is positive from the point of view of the economic independence of women and the incomes of families, but tells us nothing about the quality of the jobs that women are finding. In fact, a significant and disproportionate number of women workers are employed in precarious jobs (Vosko 2006).

Table 5.5 shows the major differences in the kinds of jobs—or "forms of employment"—held by women and men. The biggest difference by far is that women are much more likely to work in part-time jobs. In 2015, more than 1 in 4 women (26.4 percent) worked part-time, compared to just over 1 in 10 men (12.1 percent), and the gap is even greater when young workers are excluded. Men are more likely to be self-employed, but women have been catching up and are more likely to be in the most insecure form of self-employment, working by oneself in an unincorporated business.

Table 5.5: Employment of Women and Men by Form of Employment, 2006 and 2015

	2006		2015	
	Men (%)	Women (%)	Men (%)	Women (%)
Full-time	89.1	73.7	87.9	73.6
Part-time	10.9	26.3	12.1	26.4
Employees	81.3	88.6	81.5	88.1
% of employees in public sector	14.1	25.4	14.2	26.5
% of employees in private sector	67.2	63.2	67.3	61.5
Self-employed	18.7	11.4	18.5	11.9
Self-employed (% of which are unincorporated, with no employees)	43.4	58	41.2	59.8

Source: Statistics Canada, Labour Force Estimates, CANSIM Tables 282-0002 and 282-0012.

Another key dimension of precarious employment is the incidence of low pay, defined as earning less than two-thirds of the median wage (under $12 per hour in 2007). Even steady, full-time jobs can provide little or no economic security if they are in low-paid businesses and sectors. In 2007, 31.4 percent of all women were in low-paid jobs, compared to 20.9 percent of men, and, while the incidence of low pay is highest among young workers, 21.6 percent of women aged 25 to 54 were low paid, compared to just 11.5 percent of men in the same age group.

If we understand precariousness as a combination of unstable, insecure, and low-paid work, it is clear that women are much more precariously employed than men. This translates into a high risk of poverty for single women, especially those with children. Low wages also imply a significant degree of economic dependence upon men for many women in dual-earner families. In 2011, 23 percent of all people in female lone-parent families earned below Statistics Canada's Low Income Cut-off Line (after tax), as did 36 percent of unattached (single) women under 65, compared to 29.9 percent of unattached, non-elderly men.[5]

Racialized women are especially likely to have low earnings. Data from the *2011 National Household Survey* show that while the median employment income for visible-minority women employed full-time was $39,330, women who did not belong to a visible minority group and were employed full-time had a median annual income of $42,848 (Hudon 2016). For first-generation immigrant women who belonged to a visible minority group, the median annual income (with full-time employment) was $38,651. Low earnings of women are clearly one major factor behind very high poverty rates among recent immigrant families. Women from most immigrant groups participate at high levels in the paid workforce, but are often only able to find low-paid and precarious jobs. Many such women have high levels of education, but face difficulty in having international credentials recognized, as well as racial discrimination. Women with disabilities also had lower annual earnings as compared to able-bodied women (Crompton 2011b: 19). These women, like Aboriginal women, experience not just low pay, but also much higher than average rates of unemployment and low levels of employment. Among all equality-seeking groups, women earn significantly less than their male counterparts.

Unemployment

The unemployment rate of women is usually a bit lower than that of men. In 2015, the unemployment rate for women aged 15 to 64 was 6.4 percent, compared to 7.6 percent for men. For core working-age women aged 25 to 54, it was 5.4 percent, compared to 6.2 percent for men.[6] Lower unemployment rates for women mainly result from the fact that a higher proportion of men are employed in seasonal jobs like construction and primary industries, while relatively more women are employed in steadier public and social services jobs. Also, women who lose a job are more likely than men to spend a period of time outside the workforce rather than to actively look for another job right away. That said, many women have experienced unemployment in recent years. The unemployment rate for women topped 10 percent in both 1992 and 1993 before slowly falling over the rest of the decade. Even at a superficially low unemployment rate of 6 percent, it has to be borne in mind that a much higher proportion of workers, about 10 percent, will experience at least one spell of unemployment over the course of a year. Younger women have experienced and continue to experience very high rates of unemployment. In 2015, the unemployment rate for young women aged 15 to 24 was 11.3 percent, still below the 15 percent rate for young men.[7]

While women are unemployed a bit less often than men, they are also less likely to have very stable employment. The average woman worker aged 25 to 54 has been in her job for 94 months, or a bit under eight years, almost one year less than a man in the same age group. Among workers aged 25 to 54, about one in five of both women and men have been in their current job for less than one year. Shorter job tenure is one indicator of more precarious employment, and also reflects periods spent out of the workforce caring for children. There continues to be a significant gap between the proportion of women and men who work full-time hours for a full year—that is, who are steadily employed. In 2015, 57.4 percent of men were engaged in full-time employment, compared to 42.2 percent of women.[8]

Part-Time Work

The paradox of part-time work is that this is a form of employment that can help women balance work and family roles, but one that usually comes at a high cost in terms of job quality (Duffy and Pupo 1992). Certainly, women are much more likely to work part-time than men, and part-time jobs are usually much less desirable than full-time jobs. Some part-time jobs—usually in unionized workplaces, public services, and some larger companies—can offer good pay and benefits, stable and regular shift times, and decent career development prospects. In such contexts, the flexibility of part-time work is welcomed by many, mainly women workers who may choose to work part-time for a few months or even a few years before returning to full-time work.

However, most part-time jobs are low paid, and some employers deliberately create part-time jobs to keep labour costs to a minimum. In 2006, part-time jobs paid an average hourly wage of just $13.80, compared to $20.99 in full-time jobs. Adult female part-timers actually make more on average than male part-timers, but the fact remains that there is a huge hourly wage gap between the two kinds of work. In part, this reflects the fact that many part-time jobs are to be found in relatively low-wage industries, such as retail trade and hospitality, yet studies have also shown that part-time jobs tend to be paid less than comparable full-time jobs. Typically, part-time jobs are also only about half as likely to provide benefits as full-time jobs. Thus, in 1999, just one in five part-timers (18.9 percent) was covered by an employer pension plan, compared to 41.6 percent of full-timers, and

Box 5.2: Women and the Employment Insurance (EI) Program

Despite deep cuts in the mid-1990s affecting who is eligible and the amount of benefits that are paid, EI remains critical to the well-being of workers and working families. In 2010, even with a low overall unemployment rate, the program provided over $13 billion in total regular benefit payments to provide income support to workers between jobs, about $3 billion in maternity/parental benefits to parents (almost all to mothers), and $1 billion in sickness benefits.[9] In 2010, the maximum weekly benefit was $457, representing 55 percent of maximum insurable earnings of $43,200 per year (CEIC 2013).

EI income support during periods of unemployment, maternity/parental leave, and periods of sickness is obviously important in terms of stabilizing and supporting family incomes, and also supports the economic independence of women, since benefits are not based on family income (with the exception of a small supplement for low-income families) but rather on insured individual earnings. However, key EI program rules exclude or unfairly penalize women because they fail to take into account the different working patterns of women compared to men. While the great majority of adult women now engage in paid work, the hours they work exclude many from EI benefits, as do periods of time spent away from work caring for children or others.

A study originally conducted for Status of Women Canada found that only 32 percent of unemployed women qualify for regular EI benefits, compared to 40 percent of men who are unemployed. Over 70 percent of women and 80 percent of men qualified for benefits before major cuts were imposed in the early 1990s. The key reason for the gender gap is that to qualify, a person must have worked in the previous year, and must have put in between 420 and 700 hours of work, depending on the local unemployment rate. At the time of the study, workers in most large urban areas were required to put in 700 hours, roughly the equivalent of 40 weeks of full-time work (Townson and Hayes 2007).

Fewer unemployed women qualify than do men because many women take extended leaves from work to care for children or others. After a two-year absence from paid work, the entrance requirement jumps to 910 hours, or more than six months of full-time work. And, when they work, women are much more likely than men to be employed in part-time and temporary jobs as opposed to full-time, permanent jobs providing steady hours. Because they lack enough qualifying hours, only about half of part-time workers who lose their jobs actually qualify for unemployment benefits. Even when they do qualify, the lower pay of women, combined with more unstable work patterns, means that they usually qualify for lower benefits (an average of $291 per week, compared to $351 for men in 2005–2006). Only about one-third of the total dollar amount of regular EI benefits are paid to women, even though women now participate in the paid workforce at almost the same rate as men.

The EI program also provides up to 15 weeks of maternity benefits and 35 weeks of parental benefits, 90 percent of which are taken by women. The expansion of maternity/parental leaves stands as a major gain for working women in recent years, especially the 2001 increase in parental benefits from 10 to 35 weeks. To qualify, a woman must have worked 600 hours in the previous year. About three-quarters of all women giving birth to a child do qualify, and about 60 percent claim a benefit. But a full year of leave is much more likely to be taken by women who qualify for a reasonable benefit, or whose employer supplements the EI benefit. Quebec has its own EI maternity/parental program, which offers much higher benefits (covered through higher premiums), and also covers self-employed workers for the first time.

The key reforms to the EI program sought by labour and anti-poverty groups are a reduction in the number of qualifying hours for regular benefits to 360 in all regions, a longer duration of up to 50 weeks of regular benefits, and an increase to at least 60 percent in insured earnings replaced by EI benefits.

19.8 percent of part-timers were covered by a supplementary medical insurance plan, compared to 59.5 percent of full-timers.[10]

Work schedules are often extremely variable with part-time work. Four in ten (37.9 percent) non-union part-timers work irregular hours or are on call, compared to one in four unionized part-timers.[11] Irregular part-time hours make it extremely difficult to balance work and family, and work and education. In many stores and restaurants, part-time workers have little or no control over their work schedule. Hours can be posted with little advance notice to meet the fluctuating demands on a business for goods and services, or to fill holes in the work roster. Part-time schedules are usually much more variable than those of full-time workers, who are promised 35 to 40 hours of work per week. It is not uncommon for part-time and casual workers to be obliged to sit at home and wait to be called into work, depending on whether business is good or slow. This practice of varying the hours of part-timers may make business sense, but it makes a mockery of the common idea that part-time work gives women workers the ability to work the hours that they want.

Statistics Canada considers someone to be a part-time worker if he or she works in his or her main job for fewer than 30 hours per week. As noted in Table 5.5, in 2015 more than 1 in 4 (26.4 percent) women worked part-time, compared to only about 1 in 10 men (12.1 percent). Most male part-timers are students. In the core working-age group (age 25 to 54), just 5.5 percent of men worked part-time in 2015, compared to 18.9 percent of women. These proportions have been stable or somewhat declining in recent years. Women with children, especially two or more children, are much more likely to work part-time than other women. As shown in Table 5.6, 5.7 percent of all core-age women are working part-time for

Table 5.6: Part-Time Workers in 2015 among Core-Age Workers (age 25–54)

	2015	
	Men (%)	Women (%)
% of all workers in age group working part-time due to:		
Caring for children, personal and family responsibilities	0.31	5.7
Lack of availability of full-time jobs	0.67	1.80
Personal preference, voluntary, other	1.4	4.9
Total (for all reasons)	**5.5**	**18.9**

Source: Statistics Canada CANSIM Table 111-0008.

reasons related to caring responsibilities, nearly 20 times the proportion of men in the same age group. Women are also nearly three times as likely as men to be working part-time because of problems finding a full-time job.

Significantly more women than men also express a preference for part-time work. Working part-time can, in principle, be desirable, allowing women, and potentially men, to better balance the demands of work, family, and community life. However, this choice must be seen, in part, as socially constructed. Some women "choosing" to work part-time would likely choose to work full-time if they could find high-quality, affordable child care or elder care, or if their spouses took on a greater share of work in the home. The incidence of part-time work for women tends to be much lower in countries like Sweden and Denmark, which offer organized child care and elder care arrangements. Also, the gap between women and men working part-time is more modest in the Netherlands, where it is common for both partners to work part-time and to share child care responsibilities.

Temporary Jobs and Self-Employment

Both corporate and public-sector employers have tried to limit the hiring of more costly full-time, permanent employees with guaranteed hours, and usually benefit by hiring temporary workers to meet spikes in demand and by outsourcing or contracting out some tasks to outside suppliers. Many of these contractors, in turn, contract out work to subcontractors and individuals, with the quality of employment generally declining at each link in the chain. As a result, there has been a steady increase in contract or temporary workers, and also in the number of self-employed workers over the past decade and more. This has come on top of a traditional layer of self-employed workers who run their own businesses.

Contract and temporary work can lead to a permanent job, and some workers enjoy moving from contract to contract or want to work only in a seasonal job. But such employment is rarely a first choice for adult workers, since temporary workers are typically excluded from benefit plans, training programs, and career ladders, and are paid less than comparable permanent employees.

As noted, in 2009, 12.9 percent of all female employees, compared to 12.1 percent of male employees, were in temporary jobs, which are defined as jobs that are casual, seasonal, or most often have a set end date (Ferrao 2010). The incidence of temporary employment for women has about doubled since the late 1980s, and has been inching up even in the low unemployment period since the late 1990s. Female temporary workers are much more likely to work part-time than male temporary workers.

Self-employment is another form of precarious work. A layer of self-employed workers are high-earning professionals—such as doctors, lawyers, architects, engineers, and accountants—who usually work with professional colleagues and employ support workers. Others are owners of small- and medium-sized businesses that employ workers. These people are mainly self-employed by choice, and can earn high and stable incomes. However, a large and growing layer of self-employed workers are running tiny businesses of their own mainly because they cannot find stable, permanent employment. Unincorporated microenterprises with no employees run the whole range from home and building cleaning, to household maintenance, to child care and elder care, to making clothes, to working as freelance writers, editors, and artists. Many of these solo self-employed workers have just a few clients and can, in many cases, be considered to be hidden employees.

The rapid growth of self-employment in the first half of the 1990s was mainly driven by the increasing numbers of so-called own-account workers—that is, self-employed workers who are unincorporated and employ no paid help. About one-half of all own-account workers reported in the mid-1990s that they would rather have regular jobs.[12] A lot of people are self-employed for short periods and many low-paid, precariously employed workers frequently alternate between solo self-employment and temporary jobs. The legal distinction between self-employed and contract workers is not clear-cut, and can even differ from one legal statute to another (Fudge et al. 2002). Also, many disguised employees are covered by minimum labour standards in theory, but are often not aware of that fact (HRSDC 2006b).

Self-employment among women rose in the first half of the 1990s, from 9.9 percent of total women's employment in 1990 to 11.6 percent in 1997, but increased only slightly to 11.9 percent by 2015.[13] Women self-employed workers are also much more likely to have very low earnings than are self-employed men. In 2000, almost half (45 percent) of all self-employed women made less than $20,000 from their businesses, compared to 19 percent of self-employed men. Less than one-fifth of self-employed workers making more than $60,000 per year were women.

Working in the Public Sector

As the welfare state expanded in the 1960s and 1970s, so too did opportunities for women to enter relatively good public-sector jobs. Since public-sector jobs tend to be better paid and more secure than average, the major expansion of employment of women in public and social services helped close the overall pay gap. In OECD countries, women have benefited greatly from the growth of public-sector employment, and the pay gap is lowest in countries with higher levels of employment in public and social services (Fuller 2005).

In the public sector, women are employed in jobs that share many of the characteristics of the best jobs held by men in the private sector. Many public-sector jobs require high levels of education, and many public-sector employers are large employers. As in the private sector, large employers are more likely to offer decent wages, benefits, and working conditions. The public sector is also highly unionized and wages are more equal between different categories of workers, not least men and women, when workers bargain collectively with employers (Ross and Savage 2013; Ross et al. 2015). Public-sector women workers have also benefited from struggles to make governments "model employers" in important areas, such as pay equity and access to maternity and parental leaves. Public-sector employment also tends to be more stable than employment in the private sector. Last but not least, when controlling for occupational differences, men are paid more or less the same whether they work in the public or private sector. Women, however, are better paid if employed in the public sector, while holding other objective factors that govern pay constant. This suggests that outright pay discrimination against women, while certainly still present, is less significant than in the private sector.

It has not gone unnoticed among private-sector employers that the public sector provides better jobs for women, resulting in pressures on them to pay higher wages. For example, the Canadian Federation of Independent Business argues that decent wages in public services "distort" the labour market and make it harder for them to recruit and retain workers at the wages they want to pay (CFIB 2006). While reflecting other factors, the drive by governments at all levels to contract out and privatize public services reflects demands from business employers to reduce cost pressures on them. Privatization and contracting out are also driven by the intent to lower public-sector wage costs to (more discriminatory) private-sector levels, at the expense of mainly women workers.

A large number of women are employed in so-called "ancillary" jobs in health care—everything from clerical support work, to food preparation, to cooking and cleaning, to provision of personal care, such as washing and bathing. This is heavily gendered and frequently devalued work, even though it is actually very important to good health outcomes for patients. In both hospitals and long-term care homes, the quality of care is critically bound up with the quality of ancillary jobs, since it is these kinds of workers with whom most patients and residents come into contact, and since good food and clean facilities are critical to the health of both patients and professional health care workers (Armstrong and Laxer 2006). Nonetheless, in recent years, there have been ongoing attempts by some governments and health care institutions to cut health care costs by contracting out ancillary health care work, shifting it from predominantly unionized hospitals and often unionized long-term care homes to non-union private contractors who pay much lower wages and benefits.

In British Columbia, the provincial government passed legislation in 2002 removing job security and "no contracting out" clauses from the collective agreements of health care and social service workers. Bill 29 permitted regional health authorities and long-term care facilities to lay off support staff and conclude new agreements with global firms such as Sodexho, Aramark, and Compass. Housekeeping services, as well as dietary, security, and laundry services, were contracted out. As a result, more than 8,500 workers who were members of the Hospital Employees' Union (HEU) lost their jobs in less than a year (Stinson et al. 2005). Almost immediately, the unions representing the health care workers launched a court case to challenge the legality of Bill 29—the Health and Social Services Delivery Improvement Act—which had resulted in the largest mass firing of women workers in Canadian history and a protracted struggle in the health care sector (Camfield 2008).

At the time, women who worked in the private sector earned 64 percent of what women in the public sector earned, while men employed in the private sector earned 77 percent of their public-sector counterparts (Fuller 2005: 419). The great majority of HEU members are women, many of whom are workers of colour. As unionized public-sector health care workers, they were much less vulnerable to pay discrimination and low wages than in the private sector. When their jobs were contracted out, these workers experienced large pay cuts. At $10.25 per hour, the newly contracted-out wages were 79 percent lower than the HEU Health Support wage of $18.32 per hour. These workers immediately joined the ranks of the working poor and began to face unsafe working conditions, inadequate training, and planned overwork. The quality of caring services began to rapidly deteriorate due to disruption of teamwork, higher staff turnover, reduced capacity to provide quality cleaning services, and a reduced capacity to respond quickly to urgent requests from doctors, nurses, and unit clerks (Stinson et al. 2005; HEU 2007).

Before the major cuts in British Columbia, 19.3 percent of women were employed by the B.C. government, and 71.3 percent of workers in the broader provincial public sector were women (Fuller 2005: 408). In addition to Bill 29, the B.C. government committed itself to large cuts to public spending and downsizing, and public-sector employment fell by about 10 percent from 2002 to 2005. This drop in public-sector employment resulted in significant downward pressure on wages, which was more pronounced for women than men. As a result of public-sector downsizing, there was a 3.4 percent increase in the gender wage gap in B.C. over these years (Fuller 2005: 436).

In June 2007, five years after the fact, the Supreme Court of Canada ruled that key sections of Bill 29 were unconstitutional and violated the Canadian Charter of Rights and Freedoms. This decision found, for the first time, that rights to collective bargaining are protected to some degree by the Charter's right to freedom of association, marking a significant legal victory for the Canadian labour movement (Faraday and Tucker 2014; Smith 2012).

Occupational Segregation of Women and Men

In Canada, as in all advanced industrial countries, there is still very marked occupational segregation between women and men. In other words, men and women hold very different kinds of jobs, working in almost parallel occupational worlds. This is an important part of the reason for the gender wage gap, because jobs where women predominate still tend to be lower paid than jobs where men predominate, even though the educational and skill requirements may differ very little. Traditionally, men were relatively concentrated in blue-collar industrial occupations, as well as in white-collar management jobs and the professions, while women were relatively concentrated in low-level, pink-collar clerical and administrative jobs in offices, and in sales and services occupations. This division has broken down over time as women have entered professional and managerial jobs in increasing numbers. However, women in better-paid occupations are still mainly to be found in only a relatively few occupational groups, notably in health, education, and social services jobs in the broader public sector. Women are much more likely than men to work in the public sector, defined as working directly for government or in almost entirely government-funded bodies, such as schools, universities, and hospitals. Just over one in four women (26.5 percent) worked in public services in 2015, as compared to just 14 percent of men.[14] The better-paid professional and managerial jobs in the business sector of the economy and, indeed, many of the higher-paid jobs in the public sector, are still held mainly by men.

Table 5.7 provides a fairly detailed picture of the employment of women and men by broad occupational groups in 1995 and 2015. Looking at 2015, it is striking that nearly 4 in 10 men (37.1 percent) are still to be found in blue-collar jobs: the total of the share of all men's jobs to be found in primary industries (4.5 percent), trades, transportation, and equipment operation occupations (26.5 percent), and processing, manufacturing, and utilities jobs (6.1 percent). These kinds of jobs include blue-collar jobs in manufacturing, utilities, trucking, and other transportation industries, as well as in construction. Many of these jobs are in the skilled trades and require an apprenticeship or college-level education, while others are relatively unskilled. While by no means all well paid, these kinds of jobs tend to command above-average pay and are often unionized. By contrast, in 2015, just 5.9 percent of women were employed in these blue-collar jobs, and this small minority of women are mainly to be found in relatively low-paid manufacturing jobs in sectors like clothing rather than in the well-paid skilled trades, which women have barely penetrated. Moreover, nearly 13 percent of women hold

Table 5.7: Distribution of Employment of Women and Men by Occupation (%), 1995 and 2015

	1995		2015		Women as %
	Women	Men	Women	Men	Employment within occupa-tion in 2015
Managers	7.8	12	6.1	9.8	36.3
Business and finance professionals	2.9	2.6	3.8	3.2	51.9
Clerical, including supervisors	14.1	5.3	12.9	5.2	69.2
Sales and service	28.5	19	29.1	20.5	56.3
Primary industry	2.2	6.7	1.2	4.5	19.8
Trades, transport, and equipment operators	2	26.6	2.1	26.5	6.7
Processing, manufacturing, and utilities	2.1	6.6	2.6	6.1	27.6

Source: Statistics Canada, *Labour Force Survey* Estimates, CANSIM Table 282-0010.

office jobs—clerical and administrative (including supervisory)—compared to just 5.2 percent of men. Many of these jobs are quite skilled, certainly involving computer skills, but they tend to pay less than skilled blue-collar jobs. A lot of men and women work in usually low-paid, often part-time, sales and service jobs, a big occupational category that includes salespersons, chefs and cooks, security guards, and child care and home support workers. But more women are employed in these lower-end jobs than are men, explaining why women are much more likely to be low-paid than men. About one in three women (29.1 percent) worked in these occupations in 2015, compared to one in five men (20.5 percent), and the men who work in these kinds of jobs tend to be teens and young adults.

Turning to professional occupations, which usually require formal post-secondary education and qualifications, women now hold a significant edge over men. Over one in three women (36.7 percent) work in these kinds of jobs, a nota-bly higher proportion than for men (24.7 percent). But women are significantly more likely than men to work in professional jobs to be found in public and social services: in health care occupations; in social services and government jobs; and in teaching. As shown in Table 5.8, in 2014, women accounted for 61.4 percent of all professional jobs, but 80.5 percent of jobs in health-related occupations (not including doctors and dentists, where the majority of workers are still men); 74.3 percent of social science, government service, and religion jobs (most of them in public and not-for-profit social services); and 68.1 percent of teaching jobs. Of

Table 5.8: A Closer Look at Professionals, 2014

	%		Women as %
	Women	Men	Employment within occupation
Business and finance	3.6	3.1	51.4
Natural and applied sciences	3.5	11.3	22.1
Health occupations	11.5	2.6	80.5
Social science, government service, and religion	8.3	2.6	74.3
Teachers and professors	5.7	2.4	68.1
Artistic, literary, recreational	4.1	2.7	57.7
Total	36.7	24.7	61.4

Source: Statistics Canada, *Labour Force Survey* Estimates, CANSIM Table 292-0010.

the 36.7 percent of all women who are professionals, two in three are employed in these predominantly public-sector, female-dominated occupations. Clearly, issues of privatization and contracting out of public services work are of particular importance to working women.

By contrast, men still overwhelmingly predominate in natural sciences, engineering, and mathematics professional jobs. In 2014, women accounted for just 22.1 percent of employment in natural and applied sciences. That said, while men still account for nearly half of all professional jobs in business and finance, it is notable that the proportion of women in business and finance occupations has increased rapidly, from 38.3 percent in 1987 to 51.4 percent in 2014. Men are also disproportionately represented in management jobs. In 2009, women made up only 31.6 percent of senior management occupations, and 37 percent of total management positions (SWC 2012). These are the kinds of positions that predominate in the top 1 percent of the workforce, whose share of all earnings exploded in the 1990s.

To summarize, the majority of women still work in the traditional and relatively poorly paid clerical, sales, and services categories, while very few women work in the blue-collar occupations. A high and rising proportion of women work in professional occupations requiring higher levels of education and providing better levels of pay; however, these women are still relatively concentrated in public and social services.

A report of the federal government's Special Committee on Pay Equity notes that despite rising levels of education and labour force participation, as well as making inroads into traditionally male-dominated fields of employment, there remains a persistent gender wage gap (SCPE 2016). As has been detailed throughout this chapter, women are still greatly under-represented in most of the very highest-paying professions, from specialist physicians, to senior private-sector managers, to corporate lawyers, to security dealers. Even in the public sector, where women predominate, men are much more likely to hold senior management jobs. In the federal public service, men are more than twice as likely to be senior managers. These differences persist despite employment equity policies that were intended to increase the proportion of women in management jobs (as in the federal public service).

All that said, there has clearly been some continued progress made by a layer of women who have moved into professional and managerial jobs. Since 1987, the proportion of women in management jobs rose from 30.1 percent to 37 percent. As well, the proportion of women in professional occupations rose from 50.4 percent in 1987 to 56.7 percent in 2009 (Ferrao 2010). This occupational shift has been much more pronounced than for men. The shift of women into professional jobs has been led by the growth of employment for women in health, social sciences, and government jobs, but it has also taken place in professional occupations in business and finance, and in the natural sciences. In short, a small group of women are moving into higher-end jobs in the private as well as the public sector.

Conclusion

As this chapter has shown, the economic inequality between women and men remains quite pronounced, and has failed to close in recent years despite dramatic changes to the education gap between women and men. The gender gap remains large and persistent even among younger, well-educated women workers.

There are many important explanations for the continuing wage gap. Perhaps the most important is that women still bear the greatest responsibility for social reproduction, paying a price for dropping out of the workforce or for working shorter hours in part-time jobs in order to care for children or others. This price seems to exist even if the actual difference in work experience is not all that great, since the majority of women with young children now exit the paid workforce for only brief periods. International experience, as summarized by the OECD (2007a), shows that the availability of high-quality, affordable child care is associated with greater economic equality between women and men, as is the availability of work schedules that help women workers balance the demands of paid work and caring work.

There is still very marked occupational and industrial sector segregation between women and men, with women much more likely than men to be employed in low-wage private services jobs, and much less likely than men to be employed in average-pay blue-collar jobs. While a significant layer of women now work in better-paid professional jobs, these women are relatively concentrated in public and social services. Men still predominate in highly paid and senior management jobs, especially in the private sector.

Public policies that could help close the economic opportunity gap between working women and men span a wide range, from child care programs and pay equity laws, to Employment Insurance and public pension reforms, to improved minimum employment standards. More specifically, these could include rights to unpaid leaves from work, rights to vary hours to meet family needs, equal treatment for part-time workers, improved rights for temporary workers, and higher minimum wages. Though rooted in movements over a century old, the struggle for gender equity continues to define the world of work in the early 21st century.

Recommended Reading

Hudon, Tamara. 2016. "Visible Minority Women." In *Women in Canada: A Gender-based Statistical Report*. Ottawa: Statistics Canada.

International Labour Organization (ILO). 2016. *Women at Work: Trends 2016*. Geneva: ILO.

Lambert, Brittany, and Kate McInturff. 2016. *Making Women Count: The Unequal Economics of Women's Work*. Ottawa: CCPA/Oxfam.

Vosko, Leah. 2000. *Temporary Work: The Gendered Rise of a Precarious Employment Relationship*. Toronto: University of Toronto Press.

Notes

1. Statistics Canada CANSIM Table 282-0002. Accessed at: http://www5.statcan. gc.ca/cansim/a26?lang=eng&retrLang=eng&id=2820002&pattern=&csid=.
2. OECD dataset: LFS – Sex and Age Indicators. Accessed at: http://stats.oecd. org/viewhtml.aspx?datasetcode=LFS_SEXAGE_I_R&lang=en.
3. OECD Gender Data Portal. Accessed at: http://www.oecd.org/gender/data/.
4. OECD Gender Data Portal, gender wage gap. Accessed at: https://www.oecd. org/gender/data/genderwagegap.htm.
5. Statistics Canada summary table: "Persons in low income after tax (in percent, 2007 to 2011)." Accessed at: http://www.statcan.gc.ca/tables-tableaux/sum-som/l01/cst01/famil19a-eng.htm?sdi=low%20income.
6. Statistics Canada CANSIM Table 282-0002. Accessed at: http://www5.statcan. gc.ca/cansim/a26?lang=eng&retrLang=eng&id=2820002&&pattern=&stByVal =1&p1=1&p2=37&tabMode=dataTable&csid=.
7. Statistics Canada CANSIM Table 282-0002. Accessed at: http://www5.statcan. gc.ca/cansim/a26?lang=eng&retrLang=eng&id=2820002&&pattern=&stByVal =1&p1=1&p2=37&tabMode=dataTable&csid=.
8. Statistics Canada CANSIM Table 282-0002. Accessed at: http://www5.statcan. gc.ca/cansim/a26?lang=eng&retrLang=eng&id=2820002&&pattern=&stByVal =1&p1=1&p2=37&tabMode=dataTable&csid=.

9. Statistics Canada CANSIM Table 276-0005. Accessed at: http://www5.statcan. gc.ca/cansim/a26?lang=eng&retrLang=eng&id=2760005&&pattern=&stByVal =1&p1=1&p2=35&tabMode=dataTable&csid.

10. Data from Statistics Canada, *Workplace and Employee Survey* 1999.

11. Data from Statistics Canada, *Survey of Work Arrangements* 1993.

12. Data from Statistics Canada, *Survey of Self Employment* 2000.

13. Statistics Canada CANSIM Table 282-0012. Accessed at: http://www5.statcan. gc.ca/cansim/a26?lang=eng&retrLang=eng&id=2820012&&pattern=&stByVal =1&p1=1&p2=37&tabMode=dataTable&csid=.

14. Statistics Canada CANSIM Table 282-0012. Accessed at: http://www5.statcan. gc.ca/cansim/a26?lang=eng&retrLang=eng&id=2820012&pattern=&csid=.

CHAPTER 6

Race, Racialization, and Racism at Work

Canada's labour market is characterized by deeply racialized divisions rooted in long histories of racism that can be traced back to before the development of the Canadian nation-state. Understanding the dynamics of race, racialization, and racism in the labour market in Canada begins by recognizing Canada's origins as a white settler colony. The settlement of British and French colonists, and the ensuing dispossession of indigenous peoples of land and resources shaped the early economic development of what became British North America. With Confederation in 1867, the economy of Canada was thus built on land acquired through colonial processes and that involved the marginalization of the many Aboriginal peoples who existed for centuries prior to European settlement (Coulthard 2014; Stasiulis and Jhappan 1995). The displacement and racist treatment of Aboriginal peoples that began through land dispossession, the colonialist Indian Act, the reserve system, and residential schools put in place a legacy that continues to shape their experiences in the contemporary labour market.

Canada's economic development was also built through waves of migrant and immigrant labour. In the 19th and early 20th centuries, most immigrants arriving in Canada were from Britain and the United States, but many were also from eastern, central, and southern Europe, and China, Japan, and India. Immigrant workers, particularly those of non-British origin, were employed in labour-intensive resource industries such as mining and logging, or in the life-threatening work of railroad construction, and were also often incorporated into low-wage industrial and service employment (Stasiulis 1997). For those who were non-white/non–Western European, the historical experience of work in Canada was characterized by jobs that were not only low paid, but often also physically demanding and dangerous, and these workers were often subject to intense forms of racism from employers, the Canadian government, trade unions, and the white working class (Creese 2006).

The legacies of these histories continue to shape Canada's labour market today. Recent reports on labour market conditions demonstrate that longstanding patterns of racialized inequality have intensified over the course of several decades of neoliberal labour market restructuring (Block and Galabuzi 2011; Block et al. 2014; Creese 2007), as workers from racialized groups continue to experience barriers to secure employment and labour market mobility, and a double-digit income gap when compared across the Canadian labour force overall. The labour market's shifts toward so-called "flexible" labour have brought about increases in labour market precariousness, disproportionately affecting racialized groups. This growing racialized divide is also set in the context of rising levels of international migration, which are driven, in part, by the economic demand for labour migration, where employers in many sectors have sought to employ migrant workers as a means to secure low-wage and "flexible" workforces, in particular through temporary foreign worker programs (Thomas 2010a).

With a focus on present-day Canada, this chapter looks at employment, earnings, and the incidence of poverty for recent immigrants, members of racialized groups, and Aboriginal peoples. Under the federal Employment Equity Act, four major groups are designated as likely to experience discrimination in employment: women, visible minorities (defined as non-Aboriginal persons who are non-white and non-Caucasian), Aboriginal people, and people with disabilities. These are, of course, very different groups, and each in turn is composed of a very diverse range of individuals. But, on average, all experience poor labour market conditions and outcomes compared to the Canadian norm, and employment, or lack of it, is one of the major factors at play behind lower incomes and higher rates of poverty. Systemic forms of discrimination in the job market are key factors at play in organizing inequality and poverty in Canada today.

In her groundbreaking Royal Commission on Equality in Employment report, which drew attention to the reality of discrimination, Judge Rosalie Abella (1984) stated:

> Discrimination ... means practices or attitudes that have, whether by design or impact, the effect of limiting an individual or group's right to the opportunities generally available because of attributable rather than actual characteristics. What is impeding the full development of potential is not the individual's capacity but an external barrier.

These barriers can be intentional, as in overt racism in hiring and promotion decisions, or they can be the by-product of discriminatory systems and procedures. The failure to properly appraise the foreign skills and credentials or the job experiences of new immigrants is one example. Barriers may include a failure to accommodate differences, as in a refusal to recognize possible conflicts between religious beliefs and workplace practices. Disadvantage in the job market also flows from the frequent but more subtle practice of giving preference in hiring and promotions to job applicants from the same ethnic background or social networks as the person doing the hiring. This is particularly the case in periods of high unemployment, when many qualified applicants are available to fill vacant jobs. Employers may assert that they are without prejudice, but rationalize discriminatory hiring by saying that some potential new hires might not "fit in." Discrimination is at work not only in hiring, but also in pay structures and career paths based on job ladders and promotions to better jobs. This chapter aims to illuminate the impacts of these and other aspects of the racialized divide in Canada's labour market.

Defining Racialization

The term *visible minority* appears frequently in this chapter. This term is used in statistical surveys and legislation, including in the data collected by Statistics Canada. The terms *person of colour* and *worker of colour* are often considered preferable to *visible minority*, in the sense that so-called minorities constitute the vast majority of the world's peoples and are already almost the majority in at least two of Canada's biggest cities: Vancouver and Toronto. To shift the attention to social processes that underlie forms of racial discrimination, anti-racist scholars and activists have adopted the term *racialization*, to signal that race is not an objective biological fact or a valid scientific concept, but is rather a social construct (Thomas 2010b). Specifically, the term racialization refers to *the process of attaching social significance or value to perceived biological, phenotypical, or cultural differences between social groups* (Creese 2007; Murji and Solomos 2005). This definition is premised on a sociological rather than biological conception of race: it treats race as a socially constructed category, in which people are classified on the basis of physical characteristics (Miles 1989), and where racialized groups and racial categories are developed through relationships of power and inequality in ways that produce hierarchical relationships of privilege and exclusion (Galabuzi 2006). In the Canadian context, "racialized groups" are identified as persons other than Aboriginal peoples who are non-Caucasian (Teelucksingh and Galabuzi 2005), a definition that is also based on the Federal Employment Equity Act definition of "visible minorities." Moreover, this sociological understanding of race (and racialization) is based on an intersectional approach to social relations that hinges on the notion that social relationships of race, class, and gender are produced and reproduced through interconnection and interdependence and cannot be treated as separate and essentialist categories (Adib and Guerrier 2003). Where possible, we use the terms *racialization* and *racialized workers*, though when reporting on data collected by government agencies such as Statistics Canada, we retain the categories originally used in the data collection.

Racialized Workers and Recent Immigrants in the Workforce

Since the 1970s, immigration from non–Western European source countries has dramatically changed the face of Canada and the Canadian labour force. Data from the *2011 National Household Survey* (NHS) show that one in five Canadians (20.6 percent) is now foreign-born, up from one in seven in the 1950s (Statistics Canada 2007b, 2007c, 2011b). Immigration now accounts for about two-thirds of overall population growth and almost all net labour force growth (though it should be noted that this does not mean that new immigrants are the only people entering the job market, but rather that the large number of echo baby boomers [born 1972 to 1992] entering the job market just about matches the large number of retiring baby boomers). Since the mid-1990s, the proportion of immigrants coming from outside the U.S. and Western Europe has been well above 80 percent, with 6 in 10 immigrants coming to Canada between 2006 to 2011 arriving from Asia (including the Middle East) (Statistics Canada 2011b). Between 2006 and 2011, the primary source countries for immigrants to Canada were the Philippines (13.1 percent), China (10.5 percent), and India (10.4 percent). The remaining top 10 source countries include the United States, Pakistan, the United Kingdom, Iran, South Korea, Colombia, and Mexico. While Canada as a whole is increasingly diverse, about two-thirds of all immigrants settle in the Toronto, Vancouver, and Montreal greater urban areas, which account for 63.4 percent of Canada's immigrant population and are a destination for over 60 percent of new arrivals (Statistics Canada 2011b).

Since the 1970s, the proportion of immigrants who are also counted as visible minorities rose from 55 percent to over 80 percent. As of 2011, visible minority persons made up one in six of the population (19.1 percent, compared to 11.2 percent in 1996), with approximately 65 percent born outside Canada and arriving through immigration (Statistics Canada 2011b). Comprising 60 percent of visible minorities in 2011, the largest visible minority groups are South Asians, Chinese, and Blacks, followed by Filipinos, Latin Americans, Arabs, Southeast Asians, West Asians, Koreans, and Japanese.

An ever-rising proportion of racialized Canadians are not immigrants but born in Canada, the second generation of families who settled in Canada in the 1980s, 1990s, and earlier. One-third of all visible minority persons in 2011 were born in Canada, and many more are counted as part of the first generation, even though they arrived in Canada as young children, grew up in Canadian communities, and were educated in Canadian schools (Statistics Canada 2011b). Over time, the proportion of racialized Canadians consisting of both recent immigrants and the Canadian-born has grown particularly rapidly among young adults and younger workers. Close to one-half of all racialized Canadian youth were born in Canada, and about one in four young Canadians in their twenties are racialized persons.

The category of racialized workers is, of course, enormously diverse. For example, Chinese communities in Canada include many descendants of 19th-century immigrants, as well as recent immigrants from both Hong Kong and different areas of mainland China. The Black community includes persons who escaped slavery in the U.S. 150 years ago, many West Indian immigrants from the 1950s and 1960s, and, more recently, new immigrants from Africa.

If it were not for new arrivals to Canada, we would see a more rapidly aging workforce and fewer labour force entrants than retirees. New immigrants help fill some shortages of skilled workers and constitute the major contribution to labour force growth. Clearly, our economic future as a country depends on continuing immigration. Even more important, our future depends upon successfully integrating newcomers into the Canadian labour market. Ignoring international skills and experience is very costly. A study by the Conference Board of Canada (2004) found that 540,000 Canadian workers lose between $8,000 and $12,000 per year

Box 6.1: Skilled Immigrants Face Hurdles in Finding Jobs, Government Report Says
By The Canadian Press

The Conservatives have made the recognition of foreign credentials for new immigrants a top priority, but skilled newcomers have told government-commissioned researchers there are "huge obstacles" preventing them from finding jobs even when they're qualified to work here.

In a report prepared earlier this year by Environics Research, newcomers in 12 focus groups across the country said other issues hinder their ability to get work.

The participants—including doctors, pharmacists and engineers—said language barriers and requirements for Canadian experience on some job postings pose the biggest problems.

They said they suspected that Canadian experience requirements were "a coded way for employers to favour the Canadian-born," the report said.

The participants also pointed to a lack of Canadian connections or networks and "difficulty in general social interactions due to language and cultural differences."

The participants didn't feel the issue of formal recognition of credentials was a major barrier to employment. There were also differences of opinion on the value of foreign credentials, depending on the participants' country of origin.

"Many Chinese participants believe their training and work experience from China are of limited use in Canada because they feel that everything in China is so radically different from Canada that there is no way it could be applicable," the report read.

"It was noted that a law degree from China in no way prepares anyone to practise law in Canada."

"Big priority"
A spokesman for Employment Minister Jason Kenney said the government commissioned the study in order to determine why skilled immigrants had trouble finding work. He added that the Tories plan to unveil initiatives soon aimed at tackling the problems.

"It's a big priority for the fall," said Nick Koolsbergen.

Earlier this summer, Kenney announced an agreement with the provinces to recognize 10 new occupations, including welders, carpenters and electricians, to improve foreign-credential recognition.

The government said one of the goals was to help lessen the need for temporary foreign workers by making better use of talent that's already in Canada.

Two years ago, the Conservatives also introduced foreign credential recognition loans. They've issued more than 1,000 of them to foreign-trained professionals to help them pay to have their credentials recognized in Canada through further training and instruction.

But the participants in the Environics report also urged the government to do more about raising awareness on credential issues. They recommended adding an education component to the immigration application process specifically focused on qualifications and working in Canada.

"From the participants' perspective, the more details the better and the sooner they can find out about these details in their immigration process, the better," the report said.

Source: The Canadian Press. 2014, September 8. "Skilled immigrants face hurdles in finding jobs, government report says." *CBC News*. http://www.cbc.ca/news/politics/skilled-immigrants-face-hurdles-in-finding-jobs-government-report-says-1.2759702.

in potential earnings because of unrecognized learning credentials, and that the annual cost of the learning recognition gap is between $4 and $6 billion (Bloom and Grant 2001). The study shows that half (47 percent) of unrecognized learners belong to visible minority groups, and that 340,000 Canadians have unrecognized foreign post-secondary degrees and diplomas. They provide a striking example: only 56 percent of engineers who settled in Canada in the first half of the 1990s found work as engineers.

The Changing Fortunes of Immigrant Workers

There has always been an earnings gap between recent immigrants and the Canadian-born. However, studies show that this gap has grown significantly over the past 30 years (Aydemir and Skuterud 2004; Picot 2008). In 1980, male immigrants earned just 13 percent less than the native-born one year after arrival. In 2011, very recent immigrants (landed immigrants for five years or less) aged 25 to 54 with a university degree earned 67 percent of the weekly wages of Canadian-born counterparts, while recent immigrants (landed immigrants for 5 to 10 years) from this same group earned 79 percent of their Canadian-born counterparts (Yssaad 2011). Immigrants who arrived in Canada in the 1970s caught up to the Canadian average after 15 years, whereas newcomers who arrived in the 1980s may still be below the average (Frenette and Morissette 2003). The gap has grown even though a higher proportion of earlier immigrants came under the family class provisions of the Immigration Act, meaning that immigration officials did not select them for their ability to quickly integrate into the Canadian job market and they often had limited language ability in English or French. More than one-half of immigrants entering the labour force in recent years, by contrast, have been economic immigrants, selected for their educational credentials and language ability. While the gap between economic immigrants and the rest of the workforce is smaller than for all immigrants, it is still significant and growing. The earnings gap has widened and the period of catch-up has grown longer, even though the educational gap between immigrants and the Canadian-born has widened in favour of immigrants, with over one-half of all new immigrants holding a university-level qualification (Frenette and Morissette 2003).

Table 6.1 shows the median (midpoint) annual earnings of the Canadian-born, immigrants, and recent immigrants aged 25 to 54 in 2010. Looking at the data, it is apparent that there is a significant earnings disadvantage for immigrants, especially recent immigrants, compared to the Canadian-born. This is particularly the case for those with university degrees. While there were modest earnings gains over the decade from the mid-1990s to the mid-2000s—years of reasonably strong economic growth and falling unemployment—among the Canadian-born, annual earnings stagnated in real terms over the decade for immigrants, and actually fell among university-educated immigrants. The same was broadly true, though rather less so, for the most recent immigrants. In short, immigrants did not catch up with the Canadian-born over the past decade, and indeed fell even further behind.

There is a pronounced gap between the employment rates of immigrants and the Canadian-born as well, particularly for immigrants who have been in the country for less than 10 years. Looking at the unemployment rates by country of birth also reveals that immigrants born in countries outside Europe or North

Table 6.1: Median Earnings of Immigrants and Canadian-Born in 2010 (age 25–54)

	Canadian-born	Immigrants	Recent immigrants (after 2001)
All			
With post-secondary (certificate, diploma, or degree)	46,435	36,603	29,977
Without post-secondary	23,697	22,259	18,959
Men			
With post-secondary (certificate, diploma, or degree)	55,136	43,340	37,131
Without post-secondary	29,641	27,325	24,201
Women			
With post-secondary (certificate, diploma, or degree)	40,286	31,533	24,370
Without postsecondary	18,628	18,846	15,900

Source: Statistics Canada, *National Household Survey*, Catalogue no. 99-014-X2011041.

Table 6.2: Unemployment Rate, 2014 (%)

	All	Men	Women
All	6.9	7.4	6.4
Country of birth			
Canada	6.6	7.4	5.8
North America	5.9	6.6	5.1
Latin America	8.8	8.7	8.9
Europe	5.7	5.2	6.3
Africa	11.6	10.6	12.9
Asia	8.2	7.8	8.8
Landed immigrants			
All	7.8	7.4	8.2
Landed 5 or less years earlier	12.9	11	15.4
Landed more than 5 to 10 years earlier	9.3	8.1	10.5
Landed more than 10 years earlier	6.4	6.4	6.3

Source: Statistics Canada, CANSIM Table 282-0108.

America have higher rates of unemployment than the Canadian average. This is most notably the case for those born in African countries.

There is a significant and growing gap between immigrants and other Canadians in terms of employment success and incomes (Block et al. 2014; Reitz and Banerjee 2007). Employers tend to undervalue both foreign (i.e., international) educational credentials and foreign work experience, particularly the latter, placing immigrants at a clear disadvantage in the job market. While it is true that credentials from non-traditional countries are not necessarily identical to Canadian credentials, there are relatively few formal channels through which equivalencies can be determined. Even partial recognition would be of value if twinned to bridging programs that led to credentials recognition. As it is, many foreign-trained professionals have to start again in Canada from scratch, and research shows that foreign work experience is given virtually no recognition by Canadian employers (Aydemir and Skuterud 2004). Non-minority immigrants from traditional source countries do gain a small wage premium for their work experience, but this premium does not exist at all for immigrants from non-Western/non-European source countries. Also, the wage premium for higher education is lower for immigrants from non-traditional source countries compared to immigrants from traditional source countries. Thus, a new immigrant doctor, engineer, or architect from India or China fares much worse than a similarly qualified immigrant professional from the U.S., Britain, or France. This is a key factor behind the growth of earnings gaps between immigrant and Canadian-born workers with university qualifications. Also worth noting is the fact that the many immigrants with professional quali- fications who do find work in their field are paid less than their Canadian-born colleagues, and also tend to find it very difficult to move beyond skilled technical and professional jobs to management occupations.

While educational levels among recent immigrants are high, and while recent immigrants are, on average, much more highly educated than the Canadian-born, it is also the case that educational levels have been rising at an even faster pace among the younger Canadian-born population—the echo baby boomers—who have been entering the labour force in large numbers. The relative educational advantage of recent immigrants, then, has been falling. It also has to be taken into account that both recent immigrants and younger workers have been entering a job market that, as shown in other chapters, has been generating more precarious jobs and greater earnings and economic security gaps. In other words, recent immi- grants must enter the new kinds of jobs being created, which are often inferior to the shrinking pool of good jobs held disproportionately by older Canadian-born workers and earlier immigrant groups.

Also worth noting is the fact that many immigrants were permanently affected by coming to Canada in the serious and prolonged economic downturns of the early to mid-1990s and the financial crisis of 2008. Failing to find decent work in the period after entry, they often became and remain trapped in jobs that do not match their credentials and work experience. Immigrant information technology and engineering professionals were also a major part of the workforce in the high-tech sectors that collapsed following the crash of the IT market in 2000. Even high levels of skills were not easily transferable to other jobs, since they were so specialized.

Immigration policy is, in a sense, partly to blame for poor outcomes for many highly qualified immigrants. The most important criterion by far for selecting economic migrants—who now make up the majority of recent arrivals—is for- mal educational qualifications. However, as noted, Canadian employers heavily discount foreign credentials, as well as work experience acquired in non-English- (and non-French-) speaking countries. Barriers to the successful integration of immigrants into the Canadian job market, particularly in the first year or two after settlement, could and should be more systematically addressed by Canadian governments. The federal government maintains a patchwork of agencies for new immigrants, some of which are effective while others are not,[1] but governments have often been reluctant to break down the barriers imposed by professional organizations to keep out qualified newcomers.

Another key barrier to inclusion is lack of English or French language skills appropriate to specific occupations. It is often the case that immigrants have good basic language skills, but not language skills at the level needed to work in a spe- cific occupation, be it a trade, nursing, engineering, or accounting. Government and settlement agency language programs tend to be very short and focused on basic skills, rather than longer and more specialized. Mentoring programs that give newcomers the skills needed to navigate the particularities of Canadian workplaces have proven effective, but funding for settlement agencies running such programs is very limited.

The continuing deterioration of immigrant outcomes has generated very high rates of poverty among families who have recently arrived in Canada (Picot and Hou 2003; Picot et al. 2008). Between one-third and one-half of new immigrants experience poverty in their first year after arrival, and two-thirds experience poverty at least once in their first 10 years in Canada. The low-income rate among immigrants rose through the 1980s and 1990s among recent immigrants (1 to 5 years), as well as among those who had been in Canada for 6 to 10 years and 11 to 15 years. While the low-income rate for immigrant populations has been declining since the mid-1990s, this rate is still about 2.6 times above that of the Canadian-born population (Picot and Hou 2014). While most who enter poverty shortly after arrival do escape, about one in five remains trapped in low income over many years, and the poverty rate for immigrants even after 10 years in Canada remains very high, at almost one in three. The exceptionally low pay and incomes of many recent immigrants help explain the growing earnings gap between immigrants and non-immigrants.

There has been an increased concentration of low-income households in low-income neighbourhoods in big Canadian cities, and many very low-income neighbourhoods have high proportions of recent immigrants and racialized groups (Hou and Picot 2003; Statistics Canada 2011c). Concentrated poverty worsens the already negative impacts of family poverty on individuals, particularly children, and can create very disadvantaged communities, such as inner-city ghettos in the U.S. Low income still remains quite widely dispersed in Canadian cities, as many immigrants live in middle- and high-income communities, and as low-income racialized workers move up the income ladder over time. Still, Canada runs a very serious risk of creating more and more very low-income communities that are also highly racialized if the labour market disadvantages of racialized workers and new immigrants are not seriously addressed.

The Growth of Temporary Foreign Worker Programs

In order to more directly tie immigration to labour market demands, the Canadian government has dramatically expanded the Temporary Foreign Worker Program since the late 1990s (Thomas 2010a). Temporary labour programs, which have become increasingly common over the past several decades in a number of OECD countries, provide governments with the means to address demands for labour while at the same time restricting the settlement of migrants, creating a form of exclusion whereby migrants are granted access to the labour market but not to other aspects of society, such as political citizenship rights (Engelen 2003; Hollifield 2004). This process of exclusion creates a form of labour-force stratification based on legal status, whereby migrant workers are marginalized through the intersection of the need to address labour demands with concerns over the need to protect national resources and culture from "outsiders" (Sharma 2006).

These policies are constructed in relation to patterns of racism. Contemporary foreign-worker programs in Canada build on a history of racial discrimination in the Canadian labour market that includes the employment of temporary foreign workers in jobs that Canadian citizens deem "undesirable" (Satzewich 1991). Racist discourses and ideologies continue to play a central role in the construction of Canada's migrant labour policies, with migrant workers constructed by policy-makers as "problems" for Canadian society (Sharma 2006). For example, in the late 19th and early 20th centuries, male Asian workers who immigrated to Canada were employed in a range of low-wage, labour-intensive occupations, but were denied access to permanent residency and citizenship (Creese 2006). Canada's migrant agricultural labour program, which prohibits migrants from Mexico and the Caribbean from applying for citizenship, emerged, in part, through race-based concerns over the construction of the "national community" (Satzewich 1991). This discursive construction contributes to a differentiation of migrants from Canadian citizens within the Canadian labour force and legitimizes substandard rights for those workers.

Immigration policy in Canada has increasingly emphasized the need for economic priorities in determining eligibility for immigration (see CIC 1994). In 2002, the Immigration and Refugee Protection Act (IRPA) replaced the Immigration Act, which had been implemented in 1976. Under the IRPA, applicants can be admitted to Canada as permanent residents through the Family Class, the Protected Persons Class, or the Economic Class. This latter class of immigrants is the largest, comprising the majority of permanent residents, and includes skilled workers, business immigrants, and the self-employed. In 2008, 247,202 permanent residents landed in Canada. Sixty percent (149,047) came through the Economic Class, while 27 percent came through the Family Class, 9 percent came as Protected Persons, and 4 percent were accepted for exceptional humanitarian, compassionate, or public policy reasons (Alboin 2009). During this period, increasing emphasis was placed on temporary work permits. To be eligible to work temporarily in Canada, a foreign national must have a job offer and a work permit, which is valid for a specific job and for a limited time period and has been approved by Employment and Social Development Canada. While employed in Canada, temporary foreign workers may not undertake full-time studies and may not change jobs or employers unless authorized. The number of foreign workers holding temporary work permits grew from 95,193 to 177,704 between 2005 and 2014, with 62 percent of these employed in some form of low-skill work (including the Live-In Caregivers Program and the Seasonal Agricultural Worker Program). Figure 6.1 illustrates the growth of the temporary foreign workforce from 2005 to 2014.

Those entering Canada on temporary work permits include both skilled, educated professionals with few barriers to restrict their mobility,[2] and lower-skilled workers admitted for limited periods of time, primarily for seasonal work, domestic caregiving work, or lower-tier service-sector occupations.

Figure 6.1: Temporary Foreign Worker Program Work Permit Holders by Program, 2005–2014

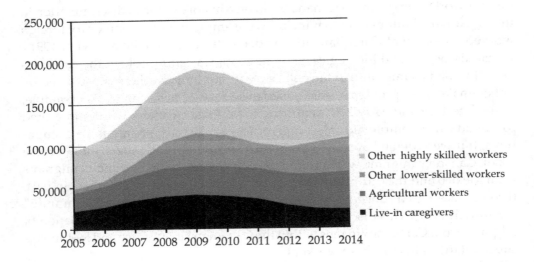

Source: Citizenship and Immigration Canada (CIC). 2015. *Canada Facts and Figures: Immigrant Overview, Temporary Residents*. Ottawa: CIC.

Information technology–related (IT) occupations are a key area for high-skill foreign workers entering Canada. In the late 1990s, the Canadian federal government expanded the opportunities for foreign workers with IT training and work experience to obtain work permits in Canada, facilitating a large inflow of workers during the years of the high-technology boom (Habtu 2003). Following a downturn in that sector, the numbers of foreign workers entering through this stream declined: in 1993, for example, 3,199 workers in this occupational group were admitted; by 2000, this number had risen to 9,500, but then it dropped to 5,689 in 2004. Under the expedited procedures for IT professionals, it is not necessary for an employer to obtain approval for each individual employee in designated IT occupations. Workers who obtain work permits through this stream are not prohibited from applying for permanent residency status, and their spouses and common-law partners are themselves eligible for work permits.

Since the mid-1990s, there has been significant growth in the numbers of workers entering Canada on temporary work permits in low-skill occupational categories, including those employed in "intermediate occupations in primary industries" (Alboin 2009). The key program within this stream is the Seasonal Agricultural Worker Program (SAWP), which operates in nine provinces and facilitates the incorporation of migrant workers from the Caribbean and Mexico into seasonal agricultural production (Preibisch and Binford 2007). This program employs predominantly male workers (97 percent), with the two leading source countries being Mexico and Jamaica, bringing in over 20,000 workers annually (Faraday 2012). The workers in the SAWP are incorporated into agricultural production in Canada as "unfree labour" (Choudry and Thomas 2013). Their period of employment in Canada ranges from 6 to 40 weeks, with a minimum of 40—but often exceeding 60—hours of work per week. The workers are paid an hourly wage that is set through employment agreements negotiated by the countries participating in the program and that slightly exceeds provincial minimum wages. Employers participating in the program must provide accommodation for the duration of the employment contract and cover transportation costs for their employees. SAWP workers are not permitted to seek employment outside their specified contract, and they are not permitted to apply for permanent residence in Canada. Through these restrictions, the Canadian state is able to continually secure a labour force that is both seasonal in nature and static in terms of upward mobility. Thus, the SAWP is shaped not only by the class dimensions of labour migration, but also by the racial/ethnic and gender relations that shape access to Canadian citizenship rights, with denial of access to such rights constituting a central feature of the program. The workers' position as "unfree labour" ensures their temporary status in the country and provides Canadian agricultural producers with a seasonal labour force. Moreover, those who are employed through the SAWP as either "farm workers" or "harvesters" are exempt from minimum employment standards regulating maximum hours of work, daily and weekly rest periods, eating periods, and overtime pay (Thomas 2009; Verma 2003). The threat of deportation, the possibility of "blacklisting," and a lack of alternative employment act to dissuade the workers from registering complaints. The race-based discrimination that was present in the construction of the original program continues to be present in a "systematic fashion," creating a labour force that is willing to undertake physically demanding and dangerous work, but is not welcome to settle permanently in Canada (Suen 2000).

   A second major occupational group in the low-skill temporary foreign worker stream is intermediate sales and service. These workers are primarily employed in child care and domestic service through the Live-In Caregivers Program (LICP) (CIC 2005). Workers in this program, the majority of whom are from the Philippines (Valiani 2012), perform child and elder care, as well as domestic work. Unlike workers in the SAWP, these workers may apply for permanent residence in Canada after completing 24 months of employment over a period of three years. So, while not tied to a cycle of temporary, seasonal employment like agricultural workers, they nonetheless hold a temporary attachment to the Canadian labour market through their employment contract in the program. The LICP is situated in the broader context of what Glenn (1992) describes as a "re-privatization" of domestic work through the employment of economic migrants from the Global South who work as private domestic workers—housekeepers, nannies, and maids—in the homes of professional white women. While historically these jobs have drawn workers from racialized groups already present in the domestic labour market, they are increasingly being filled by migrant workers. For some countries, such as the Philippines, the export of workers is a major industry, as the remittances provide needed income in the home country (Rodriguez 2010). Thus, programs like the LICP contribute to the construction of a transnational race–gender division of labour in the contemporary global economy (Chang 2000).

Overall, the LICP constructs a highly marginalized workforce in several manners. First, those employed in the program are unable to search for other forms of employment for the duration of their contract, which is a minimum of 24 months. While employed as live-in caregivers, they are subject to a highly deregulated and invisible work environment. Regular violations of applicable labour standards, including vacation pay, minimum wages, termination pay, overtime pay, and public holidays, have been widely documented (Arat-Koç 2001). The temporary status of these workers with respect to their residency rights thus places them in a highly vulnerable employment context, severely compromising their capacity to enforce their legal rights.

These two longstanding programs provided a model for the Canadian federal government's expansion of the Temporary Foreign Worker Program. In July 2002, the federal government developed a "Low-Skilled Pilot Project" for occupations requiring at most a high-school diploma or a maximum of two years of job-specific training, which includes occupations in intermediate skills categories in clerical, sales and service, health service, and transportation-related occupations, as well as low-skill labour in the primary resource, construction, and manufacturing sectors. The Low-Skilled Pilot Project initially placed a 12-month time limit on employment contracts for foreign workers, with the requirement that the worker must return home for a minimum of four months before applying for another work permit. Through recent reforms, it is now possible to get work permits for up to four years, and workers must leave the country for four years once the permit has expired. Like the SAWP, workers are prohibited from applying for permanent residence through the program. Moreover, while a spouse may accompany a worker entering through the program, the spouse is not legally entitled to work in Canada, unlike the spouse of a worker who enters on a high-skill temporary work permit (CBA 2006). Foreign workers in the program become effectively tied to and marginalized within a stratum of lower-tier employment and lack effective regulatory mechanisms to enforce basic labour rights (Alboin 2009; Valiani 2007). Furthermore, due to the temporary nature of both the employment contract and their status in the country, they are placed in an employment context characterized by high levels of precariousness created by the lack of both labour-market mobility and capacity for permanent residence, conditions emblematic of the ways in which racialized migrant workers are constructed as a highly exploited labour force.

Race, Racialization, and Racism

It is hard to escape the conclusion that the growing and now acute settlement problems of recent immigrants, as well as rising income and employment opportunity disparities, are closely connected to racism, in individual, systemic, and institutional forms. The significant income and employment disparities experienced by racialized groups that exist between new immigrants and other Canadians are greatest among recent immigrants who belong to racialized groups (Block et al. 2014; Galabuzi 2006; CRRF 2000). The role of racial discrimination is often glossed over or ignored in economic studies, which tend to argue that pay and employment gaps based on race do not reflect discrimination, but rather hidden differences in job qualifications, the supposed inferior quality of education in developing countries, and differences in language skills between immigrants and the Canadian-born.

However, the existence of racial barriers to employment has been well documented in hundreds if not thousands of complaints to human rights tribunals and in public opinion surveys. Aside from the empirical evidence of earnings and employment gaps, surveys—notably Statistics Canada's *Ethnic Diversity Survey*—show that many (36 percent in 2002) racialized Canadians report personal experiences of racial discrimination, with that figure rising to 50 percent among Blacks. The percentage is also high among second-generation racialized Canadians (42 percent). Experiments have shown that job applicants with identical qualifications are treated differently by employers based on racial status (see Box 6.2 below). Racism is systemic, institutional, and cultural within Canadian society, and the evidence demands that Canadians stop denying its reality and take concrete actions to counter exclusion and marginalization (Galabuzi 2006).

The degree of equitable integration of second-generation immigrants into the Canadian labour market and wider society is a key litmus test of whether Canada is truly an inclusive society where genuine equality of individual opportunity exists. The children of visible minority immigrants—as well as the "1.5" generation of immigrants who came to Canada as children—have grown up as part of, if not necessarily fully included in, Canada, and have been educated in Canadian institutions. Differences in outcomes as compared to non-racialized Canadians can be reasonably assumed to indicate the presence of major barriers to inclusion based on racialization. This issue has been widely recognized as a critical one for social stability and the test of equality.

Studies of Census data have shown that rates of high school and university graduation for visible minority second-generation Canadians are generally higher than the average for white native-born Canadians of the same age, and are significantly higher than average for Asians (Boyd 2008; Corak 2008). However, Blacks and Latin Americans have graduation rates well below the average. The same pattern is found in terms of earnings and entry into highly skilled, well-paid occupations. While most of the second generation do relatively well in terms of education, this educational advantage may not be fully reflected in economic outcomes. Research has also shown that many second-generation racialized Canadians do not see themselves as fully belonging to the dominant white society, and that many see racism as a very serious issue (Brooks 2008; Kobayashi 2008). In fact, second-generation Canadians are actually less likely to report that they

Box 6.2: 'Resume Whitening' Doubles Callbacks for Minority Job Candidates, Study Finds
By Ellen Brait

'Discrimination is still a reality' says co-author after two-year study reveals a much higher rate of interest in 'whitened' names for black and Asian Americans

Minority job applicants who resort to "resume whitening" —a practice in which candidates alter any information on their resume that indicates their ethnicity— are more than twice as likely to receive a callback than those who don't, a new study has found.

"It's really a wake-up call for organizations to do something to address this problem. Discrimination is still a reality," said Sonia Kang, co-author of the study and assistant professor at the University of Toronto Mississauga.

During the two-year study, which was published in the *Administrative Science Quarterly Journal*, Kang and her colleagues sent out 1,600 fabricated resumes, based off of real candidates, to employers in 16 different metropolitan areas in the US. Some resumes were left as is, whereas others were "whitened".

While 25.5% of resumes received callbacks if African American candidates' names were "whitened", only 10% received a callback if they left their name and experience unaltered. For Asian applicants, 21% heard back if they changed their resume, and only 11.5% of candidates did if their resumes were not "whitened".

When companies present a pro-diversity image, applicants are less likely to "whiten" their resume, according to the study. Yet Kang said the gap between callbacks for "whitened" resumes and unaltered ones "was no smaller for pro-diversity employers than employers who didn't mention diversity at all".

The researchers also interviewed 59 Asian and African American candidates between the ages of 18 and 25. Thirty-six percent said they "whiten" their resumes, and two-thirds reported knowing someone who does.

"Most studies that have examined racial discrimination in hiring have focused on the employer side," Kang said. "We focused on the job-seeker side too, and found that minorities aren't just passive recipients of discrimination, they're actively trying to do something about this."

The two groups profiled tended to use different techniques in order to disguise their ethnicities. Asian applicants were more likely to change their names or use a middle name instead of their first name; African American interviewees tended to exclude race-focused organizations and awards.

"We interviewed one student who had an extremely prestigious merit-based scholarship which was open only to applicants of a particular racial group," Kang said. "He chose to leave that excellent achievement off of his resume because he knew it would give away his race."

> She added: "Some people have found that whitening helps but I think that the larger message is that it shouldn't be up to minorities to find ways to avoid discrimination."
>
> *Source:* Brait, Ellen. 2016, March 17. "'Resume whitening' doubles callbacks for minority job candidates, study finds." *The Guardian.* https://www.theguardian.com/world/2016/mar/17/jobs-search-hiring-racial-discrimination-resume-whitening-callbacks.

feel they belong to Canada than their parents. Conceptions of identity are quite fluid, with many second-generation racialized minorities feeling themselves to be less "visible minorities" than part of a hidden majority experiencing various forms of racial exclusion, some overt and some very subtle. Discrimination on the basis of race is experienced most by those with very visible racial characteristics, notably skin colour.

It is particularly significant that racialized workers who were born in Canada and educated in Canada still have poorer economic outcomes than otherwise comparable white Canadian workers. The unemployment rate is much higher among Canadian-born racialized groups than the white Canadian-born population (9.8 percent vs. 6.3 percent in 2005), though somewhat lower than for first-generation immigrant racialized workers (Cheung 2006). Canadian-born Blacks, Southeast Asians, and South Asians all do much worse than the average. Similarly, the proportion of Canadian-born racialized workers employed in full-time permanent jobs lags well behind the average.

Reflecting a higher proportion of precarious jobs, higher rates of unemployment, and a higher concentration in lower-wage occupations, there are large gaps between the median annual incomes of racialized and white Canadians, with visible minority men earning median annual incomes of $26,719 in 2010—which is $11,367, or 30 percent, less than non–visible minority men, and visible minority

Table 6.3: Median Annual Income of All Visible Minority Persons in 2010

	$			As % median income of all workers		
	All	Men	Women	All	Men	Women
All	29,878	36,211	24,606	100	121.2	82.4
Not a visible minority	31,286	38,086	25,589	104.8	127.5	85.6
Visible minority	22,951	26,719	20,244	76.8	89.4	67.8

Source: Statistics Canada, *2011 National Household Survey,* Catalogue no. 99-014-X2011041.

women having median incomes of $20,244—which is $5,345, or 21 percent, less than non–visible minority women.

Table 6.4 shows the median annual income in 2010 of persons aged 25 to 44 with a university degree. In other words, age and education are more or less held constant as an explanatory factor. As shown, visible minority workers in this age and educational category earn 35.3 percent less than the median for non–visible minorities. The racial income gap is slightly greater for women (37 percent) than for men (36 percent), and visible minority women have the lowest median annual income. As further shown in the table, second-generation visible minority persons in this age and educational group earn less than non–visible minorities ($58,938 compared to $59,071), though the gap between second-generation visible minority immigrants and non–visible minority men and women is much narrower than the overall gap between visible minorities and non–visible minority persons. Further, the gap is different for different racialized communities, with Chinese and Southeast Asians having higher earnings than those from Arab and Latin American communities. Finally, for all categories shown in Table 6.4, a notable gender income gap is present.

Table 6.4: Median Annual Income in 2010 (persons aged 25–44) with a University Degree

	All	Men	Women
	$		
Not a visible minority	59,071	69,681	52,547
Visable minority			
All	38,195	44,567	33,034
First-generation immigrant	39,561	47,019	33,447
Second-generation immigrant	58,938	69,145	52,221
Third-generation or more	60,142	70,390	54,208
Ethnic background			
Chinese	43,270	49,495	38,849
South Asian	37,778	45,827	30,024
Southeast Asian	44,349	52,866	38,115
Black	41,252	41,771	40,886
Arab	30,397	36,115	23,776
Latin American	33,139	41,040	28,273

Source: Statistics Canada, *2011 National Household Survey*, Catalogue no. 99-014-X2011041.

In sum, recent data show that there are significant and troubling income gaps between racialized and non-racialized Canadian-born university graduates. Some of this may be accounted for by a somewhat lower average age and thus less work experience in the racialized group, and some might, perhaps, be explained by different choices of fields of study. Still, the evidence very strongly suggests the existence of a major economic gap based on race. The intersection of race and economic disadvantage is surely a recipe for increased racial tensions in an increasingly diverse and also more unequal Canadian society.

Canadian population growth and patterns of urban growth have been enormously influenced by new immigration, which now greatly eclipses both natural population growth and internal migration as a source of population change. New racialized immigrants and second-generation racialized workers are highly concentrated in Canada's "majority minority" three largest cities, and are also increasingly concentrated in low-income neighbourhoods in these cities. This gives rise to the disturbing prospect that Canada may be moving in the direction of U.S.-style concentrated urban poverty among racialized communities.

Aboriginal Peoples in the Workforce

Canada is often defined as a "land of immigrants"; while this is true, Canada is also a society founded through settler colonialism. In the land that became named British North America, a process of land appropriation followed the arrival of settlers from Western Europe, which facilitated the early accumulation of capital in the emerging capitalist economy (Coulthard 2014). The British Royal Proclamation of 1763 constituted a critical moment in land appropriation, as it guaranteed Aboriginal title to land not previously ceded to the British Crown. In order to gain further access to land not already surrendered to the colony, British colonialists subsequently had to enter into land treaties with the Aboriginal peoples (many of which were not honoured by the colonizers), covering much of the land that is now Canada. In some parts of the territory, European settlement continued to encroach on Aboriginal land without any treaty agreement in place. Even where Aboriginal peoples entered into agreements with the colonists, there was not necessarily a shared understanding of what was being agreed to between the two parties, leading to many unresolved conflicts over land rights that continue to the present day. Overall, the treaties secured large amounts of land at little cost to the growing European settlement and the expansion of a capitalist economy (Satzewich and Wotherspoon 2000).

Following Canadian Confederation in 1867, the Canadian state exerted control over Aboriginal peoples by constructing the legal category of "Indian," defining who was included and who was excluded from this category, and establishing social and economic policies to govern "Indian" life.[3] Federal responsibility for these lands and peoples was consolidated through the system of Indian reserves, which were lands that were set aside for status Indians through the treaty process (and which subsequently served as a model for the apartheid system in South Africa). The reserves were a site not only for settlement for status Indians, but also for the implementation of a racist policy of assimilation, as the Canadian government considered Indians to be "uncivilized" and to require socialization and education in Euro-Canadian ways. The residential school system, which saw Indian children taken from their families and placed in schools run by Europeans for the purpose of eradicating indigenous languages and cultural practices, was central to this policy (TRCC 2015). The contemporary experiences of Aboriginal peoples in the labour market cannot be separated from this legacy of land dispossession and institutionalized racism.

Today, self-identified Aboriginal people make up just over 4.3 percent of the Canadian population, or more than 1.4 million people (Statistics Canada 2011d). The Aboriginal population is young and grew very rapidly, by 20.1 percent, between 2006 and 2011, as compared to a growth rate of 5.2 percent for the non-Aboriginal population. The category of Aboriginal persons is quite diverse and includes First Nations people (60.8 percent), Métis (32.3 percent), and Inuit (4.2 percent), as well as other Aboriginal identities. Those with registered Indian status comprise approximately 50 percent of the Aboriginal population. The majority of Aboriginal peoples (56 percent) live in urban areas, though this is low compared to the non-Aboriginal population (82 percent) (Indigenous and Northern Affairs Canada 2013). There is a major ongoing movement of Aboriginal peoples to larger cities, and there are large Aboriginal-identity populations in Winnipeg, Edmonton, Vancouver, Saskatoon, and Regina. That said, other big cities, such as Toronto and Montreal, also contain significant numbers of Aboriginal residents. Many people move back and forth between cities and reserves.

The situation of Aboriginal people is incredibly diverse. There are many reserves, especially in rural and remote areas, where the economic base is very limited, very few people have paid work, and incomes are extremely low. In 2010, the labour force participation rate was 75 percent for the Aboriginal population overall, and 71.5 percent for First Nations people living off reserve, as compared to a participation rate of 86.7 percent for the non-Aboriginal population (Statistics Canada 2010b). In 2015, the average weekly wage rate for the Aboriginal population was $860.69, as compared to $924.14 for the non-Aboriginal population.[4] Social conditions on many reserves are appalling, helping account for a massive difference in life expectancy (seven years for men and five years for women) between Aboriginal people and all Canadians. At the other end of the spectrum, there is a small but growing well-educated, urban Aboriginal middle class.

Generalizations are difficult, but Aboriginal people are at a big disadvantage in the job market because many live at a distance from job opportunities, and because average education levels are low. In 2011, nearly half (48.4 percent) of the Aboriginal population had some form of post-secondary credential, though just 9.8 percent had received a university degree, compared to 26 percent of all Canadians (Statistics Canada 2011e). Within the working-age Aboriginal population, 29 percent have less than a high-school level education, compared to 12 percent of the non-Aboriginal population (Indigenous and Northern Affairs Canada 2013). In addition, Aboriginal people often confront discrimination in accessing good jobs, even in resource industries near where they live. The Royal Commission on Aboriginal People of 1996 identified lack of jobs and discrimination as the main barriers to employment (RCAP 1996). Good jobs near reserves, where they exist, tend to be in public services, in Aboriginal enterprises, and in resource industries that have been prepared to hire and train Aboriginal people.

Data from the 2011 NHS show that the employment rate of Aboriginal persons was approximately 63 percent, compared to 76 percent for the non-Aboriginal population, while the unemployment rate for the Aboriginal population (13 percent) was more than double that of the non-Aboriginal population (6 percent) (Indigenous and Northern Affairs Canada 2013). Moreover, as shown in Table 6.5, Aboriginal persons had a median employment income of $20,701 in 2010, which was 28 percent less than the median income for the Canadian workforce overall. The gap for Aboriginal men was 37 percent, while the gap for Aboriginal women was 21.6 percent. Like the rest of the population, there was also a gender income gap within the Aboriginal workforce, with Aboriginal women earning approximately 78 percent of what Aboriginal men earned. High unemployment and low earnings for many Aboriginal peoples contributed to both the high income gap between the Aboriginal and non-

Table 6.5: Median Employment Income of Aboriginal Identity Persons, 2000–2010

	2000	2005	2010
		$	
All	28,123.00	26,852.00	28,878.00
Aboriginal identity	17,991.00	18,982.00	20,701.00
Men			
All	34,103.00	32,867.00	36,211.00
Aboriginal identity	22,407.00	22,452.00	22,924.00
Women			
All	22,447.00	21,545.00	24,606.00
Aboriginal identity	15,154.00	16,089.00	19,289.00

Sources: Statistics Canada, 2006 Census of Canada, Income and Earnings, Topic-based Tabulations, Table 46; Statistics Canada, *2011 National Household Survey*, Catalogue no. 99-014-X2011041.

Box 6.3: 8 Basic Barriers to Aboriginal Employment
By Bob Joseph

There have been massive, comprehensive studies done on this issue for years yet sadly, the barriers identified decades ago are pretty much the same in 2013—not a lot of traction on the ground in terms of change and improvement.

What is the root of the barriers to employment that so many Aboriginal people in Canada face? It can be pretty safely said that the seeds were sown at the time of contact. European settlers viewed Aboriginal people as inferior and savage, and Aboriginal people viewed settlers with distrust, anger and fear.

Move along the timeline to the enactment of assimilation laws and residential schools and we see the ensuing intergenerational fallout of those laws—crushing poverty, poor health, low esteem, broken families and lower than average education achievements. And then there's the Indian Act and its paternalistic laws that further exacerbate the situation.

So, what are the most common barriers?

1. **Literacy and education:** high school and basic literacy skills are requirements for nearly all jobs. The graduation rate of Aboriginal youth in Canada is 24% of 15 to 24-year-olds, compared with 84% in the non-native population;
2. **Cultural differences:** employers and co-workers may not understand or respect the unique cultural differences of Aboriginal people, which can create a worksite atmosphere of disrespect, resentment or distrust;
3. **Racism/discrimination/stereotypes:** this is one of the fundamental barriers to Aboriginal people getting a job and remaining in the job, and it is directly related to the attitudes passed down since European settlers arrived in North America. There are a number of myths and misconceptions about Aboriginal people and perceived special treatment that some non-Aboriginal people still believe are truths;
4. **Self-esteem:** poverty, broken families, racism, stereotypes, discrimination, few role models all contribute to low self esteem. It's hard to present well in a job interview when one is struggling with low self-esteem.
5. **Poverty and poor housing:** fifty percent of First Nations children, living on-reserve, start each day in an overcrowded, inadequate home that likely is in need of repairs, has asbestos, mould, and may not have drinking water. Unhealthy living conditions affect a person's mental and physical well being.
6. **Lack of driver's license:** a real stumbling block in remote communities; just getting to the nearest office to write the initial test can be challenging; taking driver's training is similarly a challenge as there may not be easily accessed training providers or, for that matter, a vehicle on which to learn;

> 7. **Transportation:** few remote communities are serviced by public transit; vehicle insurance is expensive and out of reach for many in pre-employment situations; again, owning a vehicle or having access to a vehicle is frequently not a reality;
>
> 8. **Child care:** safe, affordable child care is a challenge for mainstream Canadians — it is even more of a challenge for parents in Aboriginal communities.
>
> *Source:* Joseph, Bob. 2013, October 1. "8 Basic Barriers to Aboriginal Employment." *Working Effectively With Aboriginal Peoples* (blog). http://www.ictinc.ca/8-basic-barriers-to-aboriginal-employment.

Aboriginal populations, and to a situation where half of status First Nations children are living below the poverty line (Macdonald and Wilson 2013; Wilson and Macdonald 2010).

In sum, Aboriginal people fare very poorly in the job market, largely because they have great difficulty finding permanent, reasonably well-paid jobs. There is some evidence that gaps may be closing with rising educational levels, and as a result of economic development efforts driven by or including Aboriginal peoples. As well, Aboriginal resistance movements that aim to assert indigenous sovereignty over their land offer hope. To a large degree, the job issues facing Aboriginal peoples are inseparable from the wider economic and social problems facing Aboriginal communities, problems that stem from the entrenched patterns of discrimination and marginalization arising from several hundred years of settler colonialism.

Conclusion

This chapter points to a central contradiction in Canadian society. In recent decades Canada has become increasingly multicultural and multiethnic. Yet despite commitments to government policies of multiculturalism, this growth in diversity has been accompanied by the entrenchment of pronounced patterns of racialized inequality in the labour market. The chapter outlined many examples of pervasive patterns of labour market disadvantage for new immigrants, racialized workers, and Aboriginal peoples, with persons from these groups experiencing greater difficulty finding and keeping steady jobs, receiving below-average pay, and being most exposed to poverty. The financial crisis of 2008 created conditions that further intensified these patterns. As unemployment levels increase, racialized groups are particularly hard hit, and those already in precarious employment relationships experience further insecurity.

While the situation is dire, there are many potential strategies to counter these patterns, ranging from minor legislative reforms to much deeper forms of social transformation. These include raising the floor of workplace standards by implementing legal reforms to improve minimum wages, extending legislative protection to broader categories of workers, and improving the enforcement of employment laws. This could also include the expansion and improvement of employment equity laws and policies, which are designed to remedy racial discrimination in hiring practices, but are often insufficient and ineffective. In Canada, employment equity laws are quite limited in scope, mainly covering only public-sector and some very large private-sector employers in a few jurisdictions. Along with reforms to employment laws and policies, migrant workers, specifically, need access to work visas that permit labour-market mobility, ending provisions in programs that tie migrants to a specific employer or sector. In addition to labour-market mobility, processes to enable settlement rights should be made part of labour migration programs, as without settlement rights, migrant workers face the constant threat of repatriation or deportation. For many immigrant workers, establishing mechanisms to ensure the recognition of credentials and foreign work experience is equally essential to countering disparities in the labour market. Finally, contesting the discrimination experienced by Aboriginal peoples in the workplace would be insufficient without attention to the much deeper problems stemming from the institutions of settler colonialism. Combined, such efforts would mark the starting point to challenge the multifaceted conditions of racialized inequality in the labour market, thereby constituting first steps in real movement towards workplace equity.

Recommended Reading

Block, Sheila, Grace-Edward Galabuzi, and Alexandra Weiss. 2014. *The Colour Coded Labour Market By the Numbers*. Toronto: Wellesley Institute.

Choudry, Aziz, and Adrian Smith (eds.). 2016. *Unfree Labour? Struggles of Migrant and Immigrant Workers in Canada*. Oakland: PM Press.

Faraday, Fay. 2012. *Made In Canada: How the Law Constructs Migrant Workers' Insecurity*. Toronto: Metcalf Foundation.

Wilson, Daniel, and David Macdonald. 2010. *The Income Gap Between Aboriginal Peoples and the Rest of Canada*. Ottawa: Canadian Centre for Policy Alternatives.

Notes

1. For example, see the Canadian Information Centre for International Credentials: http://cicic.ca/1293/About-the-Canadian-Information-Centre-for-International-Credentials-CICIC/index.canada.

2. Entry for high-skill occupations is also regulated by the North American Free Trade Agreement (NAFTA), Chapter 16, whereby citizens of Canada, the United States, and Mexico can gain temporary entry into each of the three

countries to conduct business-related activities. Chapter 16 applies to business visitors, professionals, intra-company transferees, and persons engaged in trade or investment activities, and enables each of these to enter Canada without a labour-market test being applied.

3. In 1867, the British North America Act defined Indians and lands reserved for Indians as the responsibility of the federal government. The 1876 Indian Act defined an Indian as "any male person of Indian blood reputed to belong to a particular band, any child of such person and any woman who is or was lawfully married to such a person." This meant that women would lose status if they married a non-Indian man (a form of gender discrimination that did not end until 1985).

4. Statistics Canada CANSIM Table 282-0233. Accessed at: http://www5.statcan.gc.ca/cansim/a26?lang=eng&retrLang=eng&id=2820233&pattern=&csid=.

CHAPTER 7

The Inaccessible Canadian Workplace

The marginalization of people with disabilities is widespread, both within and beyond Canada, with many existing in situations of impoverishment and disenfranchisement. Often the problems experienced by people with disabilities are seen as medical and inherent in the individual's physiology, rather than as produced by social conditions. Reflecting a growing social awareness, largely as a result of disability rights advocates and activism, over the last several decades legal protections against discrimination have been developed and efforts have been made to eliminate barriers that prevent full participation in society. However, many barriers, including those that affect employment, remain firmly entrenched, as poor environmental accessibility serves to limit the labour market participation of people with disabilities (Malhotra 2009). With an emphasis on a "social model," rather than a "medical model," approach to understanding disability, this chapter examines the labour market experiences of people with disabilities. In particular, the chapter draws attention to the many barriers existing in society and the workplace that inhibit the meaningful participation and inclusion of people with disabilities.

Defining Disability

People are considered to have a disability or activity limitation if they have a physical or mental condition or a health problem that restricts their ability to perform activities that are normal for their age. The World Health Organization defines disability as follows:

> *Disabilities* is an umbrella term, covering impairments, activity limitations, and participation restrictions. An *impairment* impacts on body function or structure; an *activity limitation* is a difficulty encountered by an individual in executing a task or action; while a *participation restriction* is a problem experienced by an individual in involvement in life situations.[1]

In this definition, we see that disability is "a complex phenomenon, reflecting an interaction between features of a person's body and features of the society in which he or she lives." Malhotra (2003: 6) notes a definition of disability as "a limitation in the ability to perform an activity of daily living, including an occupation or other social role." This may be related to physical or mental capacities.

Using this broad approach to define disability, Statistics Canada's *Canadian Survey on Disability* tracks persons whose daily activities are limited because of a long-term condition or health-related problem, which may include aspects of agility/dexterity, communication, developmental conditions, emotional conditions, hearing, learning, memory, mobility, pain, and sight. Among adults, the most common types of disabilities are related to pain, mobility, and agility. Among children, the most common types of disabilities are related to learning limitations, communication limitations, and developmental delays. By this definition, which covers a very broad range of limitations in terms of both type and severity, the disability rate in 2012 was 13.7 percent for the total Canadian population (aged 15 or older)—or 3.8 million people—rising to 16.1 percent for those aged 45 to 64, and 26.3 percent for those aged 65 to 74 (Arim 2015: 8). As documented in Table 7.1, the most common forms of disability among adults are those related to pain (9.7 percent), flexibility (7.6 percent), and mobility (7.2 percent), followed by those related to mental health (3.9 percent), dexterity (3.5 percent), and hearing (3.2 percent).

Disability rates rise significantly with age, partly because of health risks due to increasing age alone, and partly due to injuries or an accumulated lifetime exposure to unhealthy working conditions. Many older workers experience chronic pain arising from repetitive or heavy work or from injuries, and mental illness is increasingly prevalent due to the stresses of the contemporary work-

Table 7.1: Prevalence of Disability by Type, Aged 15 Years and Older, 2012

Disability type	Population	Percentage
Total disability	3,775,900	13.7
Pain-related	2,664,200	9.7
Flexibility	2,078,000	7.6
Mobility	1,971,800	7.2
Mental health–related	1,059,600	3.9
Dexterity	953,100	3.5
Hearing	874,600	3.2
Seeing	756,300	2.8
Memory	628,200	2.3
Learning	622,300	2.3
Developmental	160,500	0.6
Unknown	79,500	0.3

Source: Statistics Canada, *Canadian Survey on Disability,* 2012.

place. Disability rates are slightly higher among women than men, and much higher—two to three times the national average—among Aboriginal Canadians, mainly because of high rates of poverty and deprivation. As well, close to one in four adults with a disability reports a severe (22.5 percent) or very severe (26 percent) disability, and many persons with activity limitations report multiple, or co-occurring, conditions (Arim 2015). Roughly one-half of all persons with disabilities experience a continuing, long-term disability, while many more working-age Canadians experience a temporary disability at some time, often as the result of workplace injuries, an accident, or a disease that eventually responds to treatment.

The Medical Model and the Social Model

A common and predominant understanding of disability is the "medical model" approach. Here, the understanding of disability—as well as the understanding of the implications of disability (e.g., inequality)—is linked to the physical impairment of the disabled individual. This explains the marginalization of people with disabilities in relation to a condition (whether physical or mental) that is inherent to the individual (rather than society). This approach emerged with the development of Western science and countered the fear and religious superstition that stigmatized people with disabilities up to the Middle Ages. The medical model places emphasis on the need for medical approaches to treating disability. The medical model—through the use of science—has produced many advancements for people with disabilities (developments that may improve an individual's mobility, etc.). However, in focusing on disability as an individual's medical condition, the model ignores the institutional and social arrangements that may create barriers to participation in society.

The "social model" is premised on the idea that structural barriers in society, such as inaccessible physical structures, transportation systems, communication technologies, and health services, as well as discriminatory and hostile attitudes, marginalize people with disabilities. While there may be a wide range of factors/causes, the common element to this approach is that it places attention on the societal causes of marginalization, rather than the physical or psychological condition of an individual. It aims to denaturalize the social environment that many take for granted in order to critically assess the ways in which that environment may serve to exclude some from meaningful participation. In other words, through this perspective, exclusion due to disability is generally considered to be the result of a failure by society and employers to both accommodate different levels of ability through the provision of appropriate supports and accommodations, and to eliminate discrimination, rather than being due to an individual's medical condition.

Disability and Employment

Lack of access to supports in the workplace is increasingly recognized as a key aspect of exclusion and marginalization for many persons with disabilities

(OECD 2003b). With respect to overall employment, 49 percent of people with disabilities aged 25 to 64 are employed, as compared to 79 percent of people without disabilities (Turcotte 2014). Of those who are employed, 77.7 percent work full-time (Till et al. 2015). As is the case for people without disabilities, gender and age influence employment participation. In 2012, 45 percent of women aged 15 to 64 with disabilities were employed, compared to 70.1 percent of women without disabilities. For men, the percentage was 49.8 percent compared to 77.1 percent.[2] Older workers, those aged 55 to 64, had employment rates notably below the averages. Women with disabilities in this older age group had an employment rate of 34.3 percent, as compared to a rate of 58 percent for women without disabilities, with corresponding rates of 44.2 percent and 70 percent for men in this age group.

Those with severe disabilities and those with lower educational levels were also less likely to be employed. People with disabilities experience higher poverty rates as well, and are more likely to live below the Low Income Cut-off Line (LICO). They are also more likely to live alone and to face food shortages. Primary-income earners with disabilities have a net worth of approximately one-third of those without disabilities. Finally, people with disabilities are less likely to have completed high school: 37 percent have not completed high school, as compared to 25 percent of able-bodied adults. Able-bodied adults are more than twice as likely to have completed a university degree.

The evidence shows, not surprisingly, that working-age persons with disabilities, particularly long-term and severe disabilities, are much less likely to hold paid jobs than are other Canadians (Statistics Canada 2008). This may reflect an inability to work at all or, in many other cases, discrimination and a lack of appropriate supports and accommodations. The employment rate of people with disabilities in Canada is a bit higher than in most other industrial countries, though definitions vary. Canada, however, spends considerably less as a share of the economy on both disability supports and services and disability-related income supports than do many European countries (OECD 2003b). As demonstrated above, the gap in employment rates in Canada between persons with and without disabilities is even higher among older age groups, and is a bit higher among women than among men.

Employment rates are especially low for persons with very severe disabilities. In 2012, only 25 percent of people with severe disabilities were employed, over 20 percent less than the employment rate for all people with disabilities (Arim 2015). While this reflects the fact that some of these people are simply unable to engage in paid work, government support programs also tend to focus on younger persons and on low-cost interventions. Employment rates are lowest for those with disabilities related to developmental conditions (22.3 percent), learning (28.8 percent), memory (30.7 percent), dexterity (31.7 percent), mental/psychological (35.9 percent), mobility (36 percent), and seeing (37.6 percent), whereas employment rates are closer to the 2012 average (47.3 percent) for those with disabilities related to flexibility (39.1 percent), pain (46

percent), and hearing (47.9 percent).[3] It is likely that the latter disability categories are barriers to employment in a narrower range of jobs. Unemployment
rates are also significantly higher for persons with disabilities—11.8 percent
compared to the 7.1 percent national average in 2012[4]—again showing that
exclusion from jobs is partly due to barriers to finding work, and not just due
to inability to work. Despite lower rates of participation in the paid workforce
and higher unemployment, there were still well over one million workers
with disabilities in Canada in 2012, almost evenly divided between women
and men.[5] While such workers are to be found in virtually all industries and
occupations, they are significantly under-represented in managerial, supervisory, and professional occupations. Interestingly, the unionization rates of
workers with and without disabilities are about the same.

The Inaccessible Workplace

A number of major barriers contribute to the marginalization of people with
disabilities (Malhotra 2009). Effective public transportation is essential for people with disabilities, especially those with lower income. It provides access to
employment, medical services, family, recreation, and so on. Public transportation includes local and intercity buses, subways, taxis, trains, aircraft, and fer-
ries. Barriers to accessing these forms of public transportation include physical
impediments to access by people with mobility impairments, failure to make
information on route stops accessible, high cost, and lack of comprehensive
(door-to-door) transit coverage. Many problems persist for wheelchair users who
need access to public transit, particularly in Toronto's subway system. A
random accessibility audit found that on one day, more than one-quarter of
subway elevators were out of service, and none of the subway stations audited
had accessible washrooms. The Toronto streetcar system remains very difficult to access for wheelchair users, and Wheel-Trans—a door-to-door transit
system for people with disabilities—has become increasingly inaccessible. In
1998, the Ontario provincial government downloaded the costs of this system
to municipalities. This has led to increased costs for individual users, and
the services have not been able to keep up with demand; lengthy wait times,
limited hours of service, and higher fares are all common. Increasingly, those
who have service requests that are deemed "minor" are excluded.

    As well, there is a profound shortage of attendant care and home support
services. These services include assisted daily living activities, such as bathing, dressing, and so on, and are essential for many people with disabilities to
fully participate in employment, education, and life in general. They provide an
important alternative to family or institutional care. The demand for attendant
care services greatly exceeds supply, and waiting lists are lengthy. They are classified as "extended health care" under the Canada Health Act and therefore can
be subject to user fees, which makes them inaccessible to many.

While some disabilities preclude regular paid employment, even if community and workplace supports were in place, lack of employment is most often due to a failure by society and by employers to address barriers to employment and to accommodate differences (OECD 2003b; Fawcett 1996). Many persons with disabilities need some help in the home or the community, require assistive aids and devices, have special travel needs, need flexible hours or specially designed and configured workstations, or some combination of these. If these supports and services were in place, rates of employment would be much higher. Participation in the labour market is an important part of life for Canadians seeking personal independence and long-term financial security, and should be promoted as a viable choice for people with activity limitations. In addition to finding employment, people with disabilities may be limited in the amount or kind of work they can do; they may require workplace accommodations, such as modified hours or duties, or structural modifications. In 2012, about one in five Canadians aged 15 to 64 with a disability who was not in the labour force reported that they were completely prevented from working (Till et al. 2015). These non-participants in the paid workforce were much more likely to report a severe or very severe disability. In addition, of those employed, 43 percent described themselves as disadvantaged due to their disability (Arim 2015).

Discrimination is a reality for many people with disabilities seeking to gain employment. Data from the 2012 *Canadian Survey on Disability* indicate that 27.9 percent of potential workers with disabilities reported being denied a job interview, a job, or a promotion because of their disability (Till et al. 2015). Among young workers aged 25 to 34, this rate was even higher, at 36.4 percent. Of potential workers, men with disabilities were more likely to report perceived discrimination than women (22 percent as compared to 12 percent) (Turcotte 2014). Overall, the proportion reporting discrimination increased with the severity of activity limitations.

For those who are employed, persons with disabilities are likely to have lower hourly wages and lower incomes than those without disabilities. Research by the Canadian Council on Social Development (CCSD 2002) shows that the median hourly wage of male workers with disabilities is about 95 percent of the median wage of workers without a disability, while women with a disability earn just 86 percent per hour as much as other women. In 2012, 40 percent of potential workers with disabilities had a household income below $40,000, and 28.6 percent had low-income status (Till et al. 2015). People with disabilities are also less likely to work full-time hours. As a result of both less time worked and lower hourly wages, the annual earnings of workers with disabilities are much lower than for the rest of the population. The low incomes of people with disabilities are further compounded by special rules in provincial employment standards legislation that make allowances for workers with disabilities to be paid wages much lower than the legal minimum in so-called "sheltered workshops" (see Hall and Wilton 2011).[6]

This pay gap partly reflects lower levels of education. Less than one-half of persons with disabilities aged 25 to 54 (46 percent) have completed some kind

Box 7.1: *Garrie v. Janus Joan Inc.*, 2014

Terri-Lynn Garrie is a person with a developmental disability who worked with Janus Joan Inc. as a general labourer. Garrie began to work for Janus Joan Inc. in the late 1990s. The respondent terminated Garrie's employment on October 26, 2009. It is alleged that for more than 10 years, the applicant and other persons with developmental disabilities worked as general labourers on the respondent's work site, and were paid a training honorarium of $1.00 to 1.25 per hour, while general labourers who did not have developmental disabilities were paid the statutory minimum wage in Ontario. In this case it was found that the respondent discriminated against the applicant on the basis of disability by paying her less than employees who did not have developmental disabilities for performing substantially similar work.

Source: The Human Rights Legislation Group, Queen's University. 2014. *Meeting 14—Garrie.* Kingston: Human Rights Office, Queen's University. http://www.queensu.ca/humanrights/hrlg/meeting-headlines/meeting-14/garrie; *Garrie v. Janus Joan Inc.*, 2014 HRTO 272. 2014, February 28. CanLII. http://www.canlii.org/en/on/onhrt/doc/2014/2014hrto272/2014hrto272.html.

of post-secondary education, compared to 57 percent of people of the same age without disabilities. This partly reflects barriers to education for children and youth with disabilities. However, workers with disabilities are also older and more experienced, and those who surmount barriers to gain jobs might be expected to be paid better than average. A number of submissions to a federal government Pay Equity Commission found evidence of discrimination in pay after controlling for differences between workers with and without disabilities, and argued that persons with disabilities should be covered by pay equity laws. Lower wages may reflect employer preconceptions about the capacity of workers with disabilities to perform at higher levels, and it is striking that relatively few workers with disabilities are in professional, supervisory, and management positions.

Among people with disabilities who are prevented from working, some disabled adults are supported by a working spouse or partner, and some collect disability benefits from private insurance. But for many others, exclusion from the job market often means having to live in poverty, with 42.8 percent having a household income of less than $40,000, and 22.7 percent having a low-income status in 2012 (Till et al. 2015). The poverty rate for persons with disabilities aged 16 to 64 is about one in four, or 2.5 times higher than the general population, and persons with disabilities are more than four times as likely to experience long-term poverty as persons without disabilities (HRDC 2001).

Canada provides very modest disability benefits under the Canada/Quebec Pension Plan to some persons with disabilities; however, many disabled persons, particularly those without a long work history, rely on social assistance benefits. These persons almost invariably fall below the poverty line, even though some provinces provide somewhat higher benefits to those who can prove that they are unable to work. Of those excluded from the job market in 2012, 22.6 percent received social assistance, 8 percent received workers' compensation, 39.5 percent received disability benefits under the Canada or Quebec Pension Plan, 17.5 percent received long-term disability benefits, and 2.7 percent received Employment Insurance. A key problem with CPP/QPP disability benefits, and most disability benefits paid by provinces as part of their social assistance programs, is that they require recipients to demonstrate a severe and ongoing disability that precludes paid work. This means that persons with activity limitations who could work part-time or part-year are placed in a catch-22 situation, forced to choose between giving up their benefits (and, often, access to prescription drugs and supported housing) and very insecure and low incomes from employment. If they choose the latter, it is very difficult to re-qualify for disability-related benefits. A better solution would be to supplement the wages of persons with disabilities who want to work, but, for various reasons, can work for only limited hours or periods of time (Cohen et al. 2008; Prince 2008).

The OECD has set as a policy goal the maximum feasible participation of people with disabilities in the job market, and contrasted this with the general reality of marginalization and exclusion from the job market on low benefits, which results from the current structure of income support programs combined with the lack of appropriate supports and services for individuals (OECD 2003b). For the OECD, best practice would involve providing both income supplements and individualized supports to people with disabilities who choose to work. While Canada does provide some tax credits to workers with disabilities, these are very modest and often only cover, at best, the additional costs of working and living. By contrast with other countries, both disability income supports and investments in home, community, and workplace supports are very low.

As discussed in Chapter 3, many workers experience lack of access to training, and this creates an impediment to improving income and gaining access to better employment opportunities. For workers with disabilities, the inaccessibility of training compounds the problem. As illustrated in Table 7.2, which documents barriers to training in the workplace experienced by workers with disabilities, in 2012 at least 20.5 percent of workers with disabilities reported a barrier to training that related directly to their disability. These factors include: location was not physically accessible; courses were not adopted to needs of individual's condition; the individual's condition itself.

Exclusion from the workplace and lack of proper accommodation within the workplace are both major problems for Canadians with disabilities. The major solutions include changes to income support programs to remove the catch-22 choice between low benefits and working in a poverty-wage job (which too often has to be made), employer and government support for accommodations, and supports and services in the workplace as well as in the home and the community.

Box 7.2: Canada Pension Plan Disability Is Failing Many of the Most Vulnerable Canadians
By Canadian Labour Congress

This week, Canada's Auditor General Michael Ferguson released a damning report on the state of the Canada Pension Plan Disability (CPPD) program. Among his findings:

More than one-half of Canadians who initially applied for CPPD benefits were denied. In the 2014-15 fiscal year, that meant 39,707 or 57 percent were denied.

Canadians who wished to appeal their denial of benefits had to wait on average for almost 2.5 years or more than twice as long to get a decision under the Social Security Tribunal (SST) than the previous system. The SST was set up under the Conservatives and has been a disaster. Since it was set up in 2013, backlogged appeals have grown to 10,871 cases.

One in three Canadians who filed appeals to the SST in fact qualified for the CPPD benefits, even though they were denied at the first two levels of decision-making.

Even terminally ill applicants found themselves waiting longer for a decision on benefit eligibility. Only 7 percent of terminally ill applicants had a decision within 48 hours in 2015.

"Many Canadians with long-lasting and severe disabilities are waiting for years to see if they can even access Canada Pension Plan Disability benefits. It's a disgrace," said Canadian Labour Congress President Hassan Yussuff.

Working Canadians, even the self-employed, contribute to the Canadian Pension Plan (CPP). CPP Disability benefits are designed to support CPP contributors who find themselves no longer able to work regularly due to "severe and prolonged disability." The CPPD is not a government income support program funded through taxes but a national, public long-term disability program funded through worker and employer contributions.

Canadians who paid into the CPP should be able to access benefits when they need it most. Among CPPD applicants are Canadians who have terminal illnesses such as stage III or IV cancer, or grave conditions such as Alzheimer's, Parkinson's and paranoid schizophrenia.

However, applying for CPPD takes tenacity. Imagine living with a severe and prolonged disability and having to complete an application kit with eight documents totaling 42 pages.

Even if you are approved, CPPD benefits are modest and is only a partial replacement for income. For 2015, the average monthly CPPD benefit is $928.08 and the maximum monthly amount is $1,264.59, based on CPP contributions during the applicant's working years. If you are also eligible for workers compensation or private disability benefits, the CPPD amount is often deducted from that.

Canadians who have exhausted all options to qualify for CPPD often have to turn to social assistance for help as a last resort.

The long list of flaws in the CPPD program penalizes Canadians who are already vulnerable and need to draw on the national public long-term disability program.

"The CPPD program needs to be fixed. Canadian workers should not be forced through an arduous application process and years of appeals to get the help they need when they need it most," said Yussuff.

Source: Canadian Labour Congress. 2016, February 6. "Canada Pension Plan Disability is failing many of the most vulnerable Canadians." http://canadianlabour.ca/news/news-archive/canada-pension-plan-disability-failing-many-most-vulnerable-canadians.

Accommodations and Accessibility

In Canada there is a "duty to accommodate" workers with disabilities that stems from legal cases on the duty to accommodate workers with religious beliefs and from the development of legal decisions following the Charter of Rights and Freedoms (1982), which prohibits discrimination on the basis of disability (Malhotra 2003, 2009). In 1984, the Royal Commission on Equality of Employment (Abella 1984) stated that

> to achieve equality in the workplace so that no person shall be denied employment opportunities or benefits for reasons unrelated to ability, and in the fulfillment of that goal, to correct the conditions of disadvantage in employment experienced by women, Aboriginal peoples, persons with disabilities, and persons who are, because of their race or colour, in a visible minority in Canada by giving effect to the principle that employment equity means more than treating persons in the same way but also requires special measures and the accommodation of differences.

Provincial Human Rights Codes also prohibit such discrimination. Through the mid-1990s to the early 2000s, complaints based on discrimination against disability were the most frequently filed complaints at the Canadian Human Rights Commission. A key principle underlying disability rights in the courts is the concept of "adverse effect discrimination." This refers to a situation where "a neutral rule is not discriminatory on its face but nevertheless has a disproportionate effect on a group protected by human rights legislation" (Malhotra 2009: 98). This allows for a broad understanding of the need to accommodate workers with disabilities, as many workplace practices (scheduling, job requirements, etc.) may have a discriminatory effect by creating barriers to participation.

Table 7.2: Barriers in the Workplace for Adults with Disabilities, Aged 15–64

Barriers to training	Number of persons	Percentage
Location was not physically accessible	35,880	5.2
Courses were not adapted to needs of individual's condition	23,780	3.4
Courses requested, but were denied (by employer)	24,700	3.6
Because of individual's condition	82,480	11.9
Inadequate transportation	17,800	2.6
Too costly	71,670	10.3
Too busy	74,080	10.7
Other reason	57,950	8.3

Source: Statistics Canada, *Canadian Survey on Disability*, CANSIM Table 115-0010.

Employers are required to provide reasonable accommodation to a qualified individual with a disability who is able to perform the essential functions of a job, unless the accommodation creates "undue hardship" for the employer. An accommodation is largely an "after the fact modification to existing structures that systematically discriminate against people with disabilities" (Malhotra 2009: 104). Statistics Canada defines workplace accommodations as modifications to the job or work environment that can enable a person with an activity limitation to participate fully in the work environment, which can include many things, such as modified hours or duties, software or hardware modifications, job restructuring, work reassignment, additional training, accessible washrooms, and generally making workplace facilities accessible. But this is not unlimited, and an employee who has accommodations must be able to perform the essential duties of the position. Of course, these kinds of accommodations that an employer must undertake do not address the broader barriers to participation related to transportation, attendant care, and so on.

Of those both employed and unemployed, 43 percent reported requiring some form of workplace accommodation (Arim 2015). The 2012 *Canadian Survey on Disability* indicates that the most commonly required modifications include reduced work hours (23.7 percent), special chair or back support (17.2 percent), and job redesign (14.7 percent). The most commonly reported accommodations required by "potential workers" (those not working but available to work) include modified or reduced work hours (41.5 percent), modified or different duties (31.1 percent), special chair or back support (25.4 percent), modified or ergonomic workstation (18.5 percent), or telework (16.3 percent) (Till et al. 2015). The need for supports is generally greater for older workers. Thus, the problem is not just exclusion from jobs, but also lack of accommodations and supports that would allow those who are working to work with less difficulty, and to work at their full potential. For women with disabilities who are not in the workforce, the most commonly required workplace accommodations are modified hours or days (23 percent), job redesign (14 percent), and special chair or back support (20 percent) (Crompton 2011b: 18). Modified hours or days and job redesign are the most commonly required accommodations cited by men with disabilities who are not working or are unemployed (17 percent). Persons with activity limitations who are not in the labour force or who are unemployed tend to have more severe limitations, and thus even greater requirements for workplace accommodations to be able to work.

Many workers do not receive the accommodations they require. As documented in Table 7.3, reduced work hours is the most commonly required accommodation, though nearly one in three workers who require this report that the accommodation was not made available. As also documented in the table, other accommodations that were reported as required but not made available include communication aids (81.1 percent), computer modification (64 percent), technical aids (56 percent), and human support (55.3 percent). Fully one in three workers reported not requesting accommodation due to fear of a "negative outcome" (Till et al. 2015).

Table 7.3: Modifications for Labour Force Participation for Adults with Disabilities, Aged 15–64, 2012

Modifications	Required to work (%)	Have not been made available (%)
Job redesign	14.7	43.4
Reduced work hours	23.7	29
Human support	4	55.3
Technical aids	1.4	56
Computer modification	3.1	64
Communication aids	2.1	81.1
Modified or ergonomic workstation	12.4	52.3
Special chair or back support	17.2	45.3
Accessible parking	4.4	51.5
Accessible elevator	3.7	33.3
Specialized transportation	1.3	43.2

Source: Statistics Canada, *Canadian Survey on Disability*, CANSIM Table 115-0008.

The Canadian Council on Social Development has closely studied the problem of workplace exclusion and the need for accommodation. They report that

> there is a fairly high requirement for some type of workplace accommodation among those with disabilities, but these requirements are often for things that do not seem difficult to provide. Since modified workstations and accessible parking are the most commonly required structures, and modified work hours and job redesign are the most commonly required aids, one might think that these items would be relatively simple to provide. Instead, however, a fairly high number of individuals have unmet needs for these items, and these unmet needs can act as major barriers to their labour force participation and economic security. (Quoted in CLC 2008: 6–7)

Moreover, research by both the Canadian Abilities Foundation (2004) and the Canadian Apprenticeship Forum (2009) has found that while the requirement for workplace accommodations is fairly high, these accommodations are usually not terribly costly. The Canadian Abilities Foundation (2004: 3) estimated that "annual workplace accommodation costs are under $1,500 for almost all workers who have a disability." For just over half of those requiring some type of accommodation, the estimated cost would be less than $500 per person per year; for one-third, the cost would be $500 to $1,500 per year; and for 16 percent, the cost was estimated at over $1,500. For many persons with disabilities, an employer's reluctance to provide accommodation on the job can be extremely disheartening and frustrating, as "employers are still ignorant about what it takes to hire and accommodate a person with a disability" (CCSD 2005).

The struggle for more accessible public transportation provides another important example of how the disability rights movement is pushing to improve access to work for people with disabilities. As a result of successful human rights complaints in Toronto and Ottawa (2007), the announcing of upcoming stops on municipal transit vehicles (buses, subways, streetcars) is now required in Ontario. A second example relates to VIA Rail cars, which have long been an inaccessible form of transportation for people with wheelchairs and people who require the assistance of service animals. In 2007, the Supreme Court upheld a decision that found newly upgraded cars constituted "undue obstacles" to these people. The decision resulted from a longstanding legal battle undertaken by the Council of Canadians with Disabilities.

Finally, while unions can be powerful vehicles for collective empowerment, they may also serve to counteract measures of accommodation (Malhotra 2003). For example, a disability accommodation could conflict with seniority provisions if a more senior employee was required to give up a preferred shift to accommodate a more junior employee. In some cases, arbitrators have ruled that seniority can be overruled in favour of an accommodation, though generally this is not the case. In recent years, some unions have integrated disability

Box 7.3: Manitoba's New Accessibility Rules Welcomed by Disability-Rights Advocate
By CBC News

New rules that require Manitoba businesses and organizations to be more accessible to customers with disabilities are now in effect, which a local advocate says will help open new opportunities.

A new accessibility standard came into effect on Monday, requiring all public and private organizations in the province with one or more employees to identify and remove any barriers to accessible customer service, or find alternatives to benefit clients with disabilities.

The regulations are part of the Accessibility for Manitobans Act, which was established in 2013.

***

Government agencies will have one year to meet the new standard, public-sector organizations will have two years, while private enterprises and non-profit organizations will have three years.

***

Job opportunities to come?
Under the act, the province will set accessibility standards in four other areas: employment, information and communication, transportation and the "built environment."

[Allen] Mankewich said the province's standard on employment for people with disabilities could lead to more job opportunities—a major change from the frustration he's had to deal with in the past.

"I have a communications background. When you first get out of school, there's a lot of communications companies or different arts organizations that are based in, you know, inaccessible spaces—when you think about some of the places in the Exchange District, things like that—so those options weren't there for me," he said.

***

Mankewich said the employment rate is 50 per cent among working-age people with disabilities, and he hopes the new provincial law will help boost that number.

Source: CBC News. 2014, November 2. "Manitoba's new accessibility rules welcomed by disability-rights advocate: Provincial standard requires businesses, organizations to make spaces easier to access." *CBC News*. http://www.cbc.ca/news/canada/manitoba/manitoba-s-new-accessibility-rules-welcomed-by-disability-rights-advocate-1.3300746.

rights into their framework of political action, becoming more active in promoting disability rights (see CLC 2008). An important case is the legal challenge launched by the Canadian Union of Postal Workers to prevent the cancellation of household mail delivery (CUPW 2014). The case was pursued in association with the Disabled Alliance of Women, Canada, and was presented, in part, as an issue of accessibility. This case illustrates another dimension to the ways in which work and disability intersect, as well as the ways in which diverse movements can come together in struggle for a common cause.

Conclusion

There is a pervasive pattern of labour market disadvantage for persons with disabilities. They have greater difficulty finding jobs, receive below-average pay, and are most exposed to poverty. The failure to see beyond a disability to the talents of an individual job applicant is also a barrier to equal opportunity. Barriers include a failure to make available accommodations that would make the workplace more accessible.

While the situation of persons with disabilities in the job market is very poor, there is growing support for positive changes. The federal and provincial governments have begun to advance a more positive agenda, and funding for community and employment supports is slowly increasing (HRSDC 2006c). Due to a series of far-reaching legal decisions, employers are also increasingly obliged to accommodate the special needs of workers with disabilities, which is of particular importance to workers who have stable employment and then become ill or are injured. Disability rights organizations are extremely active in pushing for inclusion, including by pressuring for more accessible workplaces. There would be many more opportunities in the workforce for persons with disabilities if adequate supports and services were provided, and if barriers to access were addressed. This requires changes in the workplace itself, as well as supportive changes to public policies. Interventions in terms of public policy that address discrimination, along with workplace practices that remove barriers and make workplaces more accessible, are needed to promote greater inclusion of people with disabilities. While disability rights groups have put forward an action agenda for an inclusive and accessible Canada, and while progress has been made, many people with disabilities and their families continue to experience major barriers to full and equal participation in Canadian society. Measures to make the workplace more accessible must also be accompanied by initiatives that counter the many barriers to meaningful participation in society that continue to be experienced by people with disabilities.

Recommended Reading

Canadian Human Rights Commission (CHRC). 2012. *Report on Equality Rights of People with Disabilities*. Ottawa: Minister of Public Works and Government Services.

Cohen, Marcy, Michael Goldberg, Nick Istvanffy, Tim Stainton, Adrienne Wasik, and Karen-Marie Woods. 2008. *Removing Barriers to Work: Flexible Employment Options for People with Disabilities in BC*. Vancouver: CCPA-BC.

Malhotra, Ravi, and Morgan Rowe. 2013. *Exploring Disability Identity and Disability Rights Through Narratives: Finding a Voice of Their Own*. London & New York: Routledge.

Till, Matthew, Tim Leonard, Sebastian Yeung, and Gradon Nicholls. 2015. *A Profile of the Labour Market Experiences of Adults with Disabilities among Canadians Aged 15 Years and Older, 2012*. Ottawa: Statistics Canada.

Notes

1. World Health Organization, Disabilities. Accessed at: http://www.who.int/topics/disabilities/en/.
2. Statistics Canada CANSIM Table 115-0005. Accessed at: http://www5.statcan.gc.ca/cansim/a26?lang=eng&retrLang=eng&id=1150005&pattern=&csid=.
3. Statistics Canada CANSIM Table 115-0006. Accessed at: http://www5.statcan.gc.ca/cansim/a26?lang=eng&retrLang=eng&id=1150006&pattern=&csid=.
4. Statistics Canada CANSIM Table 115-0006.
5. Statistics Canada CANSIM Table 115-0005.
6. In November 2015, Ontario announced that it would end the practice of "sheltered workshops" (Welsh 2015).

CHAPTER 8

Troubled Transitions: Into and Out of the Labour Force

Entering into paid work for the first time is a major life transition, which occurs for many during the course of moving from youth to adulthood. Youths—conventionally defined as persons aged 15 to 24—generally participate in the job market on a part-time or part-year basis as they transition from high school to—for most—some form of post-secondary education to full-time paid work. For teens, an entry-level part-time job is usually all that they want, but the level and stability of earnings become increasingly important to young people as they have to finance full- or part-time post-secondary studies, and are even more important as young adults enter the labour force full-time and seek economic independence from their parents. The fact that many jobs held by young workers are low paid, part-time, and insecure should be of concern. The quality of jobs in what can be a long transition from age 15 to the late twenties, and from high school to a permanent job, is important not just in terms of earnings, but also in terms of gaining useful work experience.

Another of the key transitions in life is that from paid work to retirement. Until relatively late in the 20th century, the period of retirement was short because most workers died at a much younger age than today's elderly, and had to work until late in life because of the inadequacy of public and private pensions. Old age was very often spent in poverty. That changed greatly in the latter part of the century as public and private pension systems matured. More of the elderly began to enjoy longer and reasonably secure periods of retirement, and poverty rates among the elderly improved in comparison to rates among Canadian working-age adults and to seniors in other OECD countries (Myles 2000). Until quite recently, Canadian workers were retiring at much earlier ages than was the norm even in the 1960s and 1970s, typically at about age 60, with many people retiring voluntarily and enjoying reasonable income security. While the average age of retirement in Canada has been steadily falling, there is generally very limited provision for a phased-in retirement process, which would allow older workers to voluntarily reduce their hours of work. Indeed, most defined pension plans create an incentive to maximize earnings (and, therefore, hours) just before retirement. However, many older workers did not fare well in the economic restructuring of the 1980s and 1990s and enjoy only modest incomes, and private pension coverage is slipping fast among those now approaching retirement. Perhaps relatedly, older workers are staying in the paid workforce much longer than was the case as recently as 2000. There has also been increasing advocacy for policies that would push older workers to work longer (Townson 2006). It is thus far from clear that the relatively favourable patterns of the recent past in terms of a secure retirement will continue. Indeed, we are likely to see much greater inequality among older workers moving forward, and much greater gaps between the retirement incomes of some and their previous earnings.

With an initial focus on young workers entering the labour market, followed by older workers as they move towards retirement, this chapter examines the complex and troubled transitions faced by many workers at two key moments in the life-course. The chapter begins by looking at the work experiences of young workers, and in particular the obstacles they face as they attempt to establish economic independence and security. The second half of the chapter discusses Canada's retirement income system, the incomes of seniors (which are heavily influenced by their work history), older workers in the job market, and debates over pensions and changing transitions to retirement.

Youth and the Labour Market: Work, School, and Economic Independence

The proportion of youth in Canada's workforce has been falling for much of recent history, for the basic demographic reason that birth rates have been falling. However, the "echo baby boom" generation now moving into the job market is still a large group. In 2015, four and a half million people aged 15 to 24 accounted for 15 percent of the labour force.[1] The fact that all net labour force growth is now coming from immigration still means that many younger workers will be replacing the retiring baby boomers. This younger workforce is itself increasingly diverse, as it includes many second-generation immigrants and those who came to Canada as young children.

The current youth cohort will, on average, take far longer to leave the educational system than did their parents, and will likely face greater difficulties in finding reasonably well-paid and secure jobs. Perhaps the most dramatic change of the past 30 years or more has been the greatly increased rate of young adult participation in full-time education (OECD 2008a). Between the mid-1980s and the early 2000s, the proportion of teens who are full-time students rose from 75 percent to over 80 percent as high school dropout rates fell. More dramatically, the proportion of young adults aged 20 to 24 studying full-time (usually attending college or university) rose from one in five to more than one in three (Gunderson et al. 2000). Increased post-secondary enrolment rates reflect the fact that good jobs not requiring such qualifications have become increasingly difficult to find. The fact that young women now have career aspirations at least equal to those of men underpins the even higher enrolment rates for this group.

The transition from full-time school to full-time work and economic independence has been pushed back for a significant proportion of youth compared to
previous generations (Beaujot and Kerr 2007). About half of all young people now
enter some form of post-secondary education more or less immediately after high
school, and many do not seek a full-time job until their mid-twenties or even later.
Many young people also move back and forth between work and education for
an extended period. At the same time, more and more young adults bear a heavy
burden of student debt. While increased educational attainment is a good thing
and strengthens eventual prospects for stable employment at decent wages—and
young Canadians are probably the best educated in the world—the transition to
work is taking longer and longer, and has been becoming more difficult for those
without good educational qualifications.

Statistics Canada has found that many youth who drop out of high school in
their late teens eventually complete their studies, and that many young adults
move back and forth between work and post-secondary studies. A survey of 18-
and 19-year-olds in 2009/10 found that 76.9 percent were high school graduates
and 14.7 percent had not completed high school, but were still attending school,
while just 8.4 percent had not completed high school and were not attending
(McMullen and Gilmore 2010). Of those 20 to 24 years old, 89.5 percent had graduated high school, 2 percent were not graduates but attending, and 8.5 percent had
not completed high school and were not attending. For those aged 20 to 24, 42.1
percent were enrolled in some form of education, while 43 percent were employed
and not enrolled in education. Thus, in 2012 about the same proportion of young
people were in school as were in work and not studying (Statistics Canada 2015b:
description for Chart C.2.1.2).

Overall, by their mid-twenties, the majority of young adults have completed some
form of post-secondary education (including apprenticeships), very few have still
not completed high school, and many of the remainder have participated in, but not
yet completed, post-secondary education. An Alberta study of persons aged 25 in
2003 found similar patterns, with 60 percent of the group having a post-secondary
qualification, and a very high proportion (88 percent) having been in post-secondary
education at some point, including some who were still studying. This group of
25-year-olds had held an average of 5.6 jobs since age 18 (cited OECD 2008a: 61).

The increasingly common pattern of combining paid work and participation
in post-secondary education over extended periods, rather than moving quickly
from school to a permanent job, is likely explained by a wide range of factors,
including the continued difficulty of finding steady, well-paid work, the cost of
maintaining steady enrolment in full-time studies, and experimentation with
different educational and work options. The good news is that a high proportion
of Canadian young adults do eventually acquire qualifications and make a transition to steady employment, and that relatively few end up with no qualifications
or experience unemployment for very extended periods. Canada has one of the
lowest rates of long-term young adult unemployment among industrial countries,
and relatively few young people are neither studying nor working (OECD 2008a).

Increasingly, young people are also delaying marriage and cohabitation, opting to live with their parents through much of their twenties. Census figures for 2011 show that 42.3 percent of young people aged 20 to 29 were still living at home, either because they had never left or because they had returned home (Statistics Canada 2011f). This was up from 26.9 percent in 1981 and 32.1 percent in 1991. Young men are even more likely than young women to stay at home. Following in lockstep, young people are also delaying having children, and choosing to have fewer children when they do start families. Delayed economic independence likely results from: high levels of student debt; high housing costs, especially in large urban centres; and difficulties finding the stable, well-paid employment needed to establish independence. Parents may also be more willing to share households for longer periods of time than was the case a generation ago (Beaujot and Kerr 2007).

Most students seek paid work of some kind. Many full-time students want part-time work during the school year, and most want full-time summer jobs to finance their studies, maintain some economic independence, and gain relevant work experience. At the same time, post-secondary education has become more and more important as a means to access reasonably well-paid and secure jobs that provide ladders to better opportunities. Young workers who are high school dropouts or who have only a high school education are at increasing risk of being able to find only insecure, low-paid, no-future jobs. There is a very significant wage premium for a university education, and a more modest premium for college graduates and those who complete trade apprenticeships. For example, data from the 2006 Census show that male university graduates aged 25 to 34 earned an average of $46,373, compared to $34,460 for male non-graduates, and women graduates earned an average of $35,970, compared to $23,617 for women non-graduates. Unemployment is also lower for those with higher educational credentials.

The Declining Fortunes of Young Workers

Research by economists has documented a major decline in the fortunes of young workers as compared to other workers (often their parents) who were of the same age in the mid- to late 1970s (Beaudry et al. 2000; Gunderson et al. 2000; Picot et al. 2001). Much of that decline was concentrated in the period of recession and slow recovery from 1989 through the 1990s. In slack labour markets, much of the burden of unemployment falls on new entrants to the job market, who lack experience, even though they may have good credentials. Also, there was very little new hiring into larger workplaces offering better jobs over this period, which left younger workers chasing lower-paid and often temporary and insecure positions. As noted below, somewhat surprisingly, the major gap that opened up between the earnings of younger and older workers has failed to close significantly in recent years, even as the youth unemployment rate has fallen, the educational credentials of young adults have continued to rise, and the size of the youth cohort has fallen.

Figure 8.1: Employment Rates for Young Adults Aged 20–24 (1976–2014)

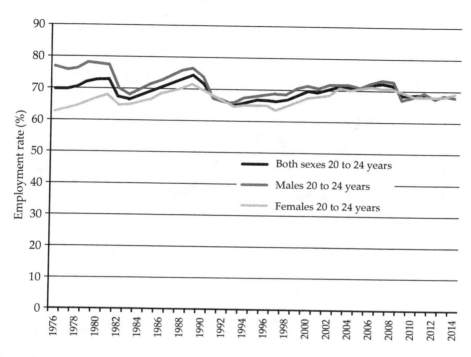

Source: Statistics Canada CANSIM Table 282-0002.

The employment rate for all young workers was 68.5 percent in 2014. The rate fell sharply with the recession of the early 1990s, from 73.9 percent in 1989 to a low of 65.1 percent in 1997, before rising to 71.7 percent in 2007, just before the Great Recession. Employment rates for this age group are a bit higher for young men than for young women, likely because women are spending more time on average in post-secondary education, and some are having children.

In 2014, the youth unemployment rate was 10.7 percent. The rate has been persistently very high since the mid-1970s, never falling much below 10 percent, and reaching a high of 15.9 percent during the recession of the early 1990s. As shown in Figure 8.2, the unemployment rate for those aged 20 to 24 fell sharply from 1992 into the 2000s, then rose again following the 2008 financial crisis. The unemployment rate for men in this age group has been significantly greater than that for women.

Unemployment may be lower among young women, but they continue to earn significantly less than young men. The 2011 Census data indicates that women aged 15 to 24 had an average employment income of $11,638, while men of the same age group earned $14,990.[2] As shown in Table 8.1, in 2014 women aged 15 to 24 had an average hourly wage rate of $11.50, compared to $13.00 for men in the same age group. The wage gaps persist despite the rising relative educational attainment of young women compared to men, as discussed in Chapter 5.

Figure 8.2: Unemployment Rates for Young Adults Aged 20–24 (1976–2014)

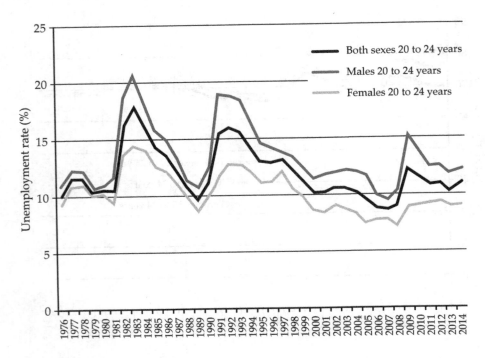

Source: Statistics Canada, CANSIM Table 282-0002.

Table 8.1: Average Hourly Earnings, 1997–2014 (in 2014 dollars)

	1997	2007	2014
Both:			
Age 15–24	10.8	11.2	12
Age 25–54	21.5	22.5	23.8
Men:			
Age 15–24	11.1	12	13
Age 25–54	24.2	24.7	25.5
Women:			
Age 15–24	10.4	10.7	11.5
Age 25–54	19.3	20.2	21.9

Source: Statistics Canada, *Labour Force Survey* Estimates, CANSIM Table 282-0074.

As the table illustrates, in 2014, young workers aged 15 to 24 earned an average of $12.00 per hour, compared to $23.80 per hour for core-age workers aged 25 to 54, or just about half as much. This proportion has been essentially unchanged since 1997, showing that the somewhat improved employment situation for young people has had no impact on their relative hourly earnings. The average hourly earnings of young women compared to women core-age workers have actually fallen slightly since 1997—from 54 percent to 52.5 percent. Young men earn relatively less than core-age men—51 percent as much in 2014, but the gap has narrowed from just 46 percent in 1997.

On top of continuing significant gaps between unemployment rates for younger and older workers, there are large differences in wages between age groups. The other major dimension of the declining fortunes of young workers today compared to earlier generations has been in terms of real wages. Young men aged 15 to 24 earn only about 75 percent as much as did young men in the same age group in the mid-1970s in terms of "real" or inflation-adjusted hourly earnings (Picot et al. 2001). Young women have done slightly better, but they still earn only about 80 percent as much as the young women of the mid-1970s. The pay gap between young women and young men has narrowed slightly, but the gap between youth and adults has greatly increased. By some measures, Canada now has the most highly educated generation of young workers in the world, but young adults have not regained the ground that was lost in the 1990s.

Data from the 2011 Census similarly show that the pay gap between younger and older workers has not been narrowing, and indeed has grown somewhat. In 2010, young workers aged 15 to 24 had an average employment income of just 24 percent as much as workers aged 45 to 54 ($13,353 compared to $55,455),[3] which represented a slight decrease from the 24.5 percent gap in 2000 ($11,358 compared to $46,273). Annual earnings gaps are far larger than hourly earnings gaps, since so many young workers are employed only part-time or part-year. It is notable that the annual earnings of young workers were essentially unchanged between the two Censuses, while they increased for older workers.

As detailed in earlier chapters, one of the dark sides of the post-industrial economy has been the expansion of low-wage, low-skill jobs in private services. These jobs typically provide "ports of entry" to the labour market for young adults, but rather than moving quickly to the bottom rungs of what turn out to be "career jobs," many youth, including well-educated youth, spend several years in a series of low-wage, low-skill jobs in sectors like fast food and retail. Most young people are working in parts of the job market that typically provide low wages, limited, if any, pension or health benefits, and part-time or unstable hours. The majority of young women aged 15 to 24 work in the two lowest-paid broad industrial sectors—retail trade, and accommodation and food services (i.e., in stores, restaurants, and hotels)—as do 4 in 10 young men. One in four young men work in construction or manufacturing jobs—which are more likely than private-sector services to provide full-time hours at decent wages—while 1 in 10 young women work in health and social services.

In looking at falling unemployment rates for youth, it has to be borne in mind that to be unemployed means that a person has been unable to find any kind of job, even a low-paid, temporary, or part-time job. Most teens and young adults who are studying full-time want only a part-time job, at least during the school year; however, the fact that one-third of young adults aged 20 to 24 are working part-time is of concern. It is often assumed that such jobs provide a "flexible" way to balance work and school, but part-time jobs often involve highly variable and unpredictable schedules.

One big change in the job market in recent decades has been the rise of temporary or contract jobs, that is, jobs with a defined end date. As employers have restructured work to make jobs more precarious, they have often done so by making changes that principally affect new hires. In other words, much of the impact falls on young workers entering the job market. In 2015, almost one in three (31.2 percent) young workers were in temporary jobs with a fixed end date.[4] It remains to be seen if the young workers who replace retiring baby boomers will enjoy the same terms and conditions of employment—including an expectation of ongoing employment—or if more contract and temporary jobs have become a permanent feature of the economic landscape.

The fact that young workers are likely to be in part-time and temporary jobs means that they are much less likely than adults to qualify for Employment Insurance benefits when they do become unemployed, even though they pay premiums for every hour worked. To qualify for benefits, new entrants to the workforce must meet an initial threshold of working more than 910 hours in a year (or about six months in a steady, full-time job), and even after that, it is hard for part-time and seasonal workers to qualify. As noted above, one in three unemployed workers is a young worker, though young people under age 25 make up only 8.4 percent of new claims for regular EI benefits.[5]

A very high proportion of young workers who are mainly working full-time and are not students are earning low wages. In 2000, almost half (45 percent) of all young workers aged 15 to 24 working mainly full-time who were not students were low paid (39.9 percent of men and 52.4 percent of women), up from 40.7 percent in 1990, and up from less than one-third (31.2 percent) of young workers in 1980 (Morissette and Picot 2005). While most are protected by family incomes, one in four young low-wage workers lives in a household falling below the poverty line. Low youth wages translate into a very high risk of poverty for young workers who form their own households and live away from home, particularly young families with children. In addition, given the difficulties in entering the labour market, many youth are now compelled to take work without pay in the form of internships and volunteer work in order to develop connections and gain work experience (Perlin 2012).

Some full-time, young, low-wage workers are in entry-level jobs that eventually lead to ladders to better jobs, but many others—especially those who do not complete post-secondary education—face a high risk of being trapped in low-paid jobs for life. Too many of today's young workers—mainly those who fail to gain

Box 8.1: Poloz's Prescription for Unemployed Youth: Work for Free
By Tavia Grant

Bank of Canada Governor Stephen Poloz has sparked controversy by suggesting young people ought to consider unpaid work as a way to gain job experience.

"When I bump into youths, they ask me, you know, 'What am I supposed to do in a situation?' I say, look, having something unpaid on your CV is very worth it because that's the one thing you can do to counteract this scarring effect. Get some real-life experience even though you're discouraged, even if it's for free," Mr. Poloz told reporters Monday in Ottawa.

Testifying before the House of Commons Standing Committee on Finance on Tuesday, he doubled down on that view, saying his advice to young people in this tough job environment was to "volunteer to do something that is at least somewhat related to your expertise set, so it's clear that you are gaining some learning experience during that period."

When asked during the hearing by Liberal MP Scott Brison whether unpaid internships contribute to income inequality—with kids from wealthier families more able to take advantage of those opportunities—Mr. Poloz acknowledged "there are issues like the ones you're raising ... but I still think when there are those opportunities, one should grab them because it will reduce the scarring effect, all other things equal."

Canada's youth unemployment rate is 13.5 per cent, compared with the overall rate of 6.8 per cent, and the percentage of youth who are holding jobs has been little-improved since the recession. Mr. Poloz said the central bank estimates there are about 200,000 young people who are out of work, underemployed or trying to improve their job prospects by extending their education.

***

His main point may have been on the importance of keeping skills up-to-date and gaining real-world experience to plug holes in resume gaps. But the suggestion of unpaid work prompted a scathing response.

"It's extremely frustrating," said Claire Seaborn, founder and president of the Canadian Intern Association. "It's a complete misunderstanding of our employment and workplace laws in Canada ... and it shows a huge devaluing of young people and recent graduates' abilities in the workplace."

She's also concerned the comments "show a lack of understanding of the socioeconomic issues associated with unpaid internships," that can see well-off young people able to do unpaid internships, which gives them better career opportunities, while the less wealthy get "essentially barred from entering certain industries that have made unpaid internships almost a requirement."

Unpaid internships have generated much public debate in the past year. There are no official statistics on numbers of unpaid interns in Canada, though labour lawyer Andrew Langille says estimates put the numbers around 100,000 a year, a level that has grown since the economic downturn.

Mr. Poloz's comments also prompted some scalding comments on social media. Some suggested Mr. Poloz, who earns more than $435,000 a year, give up his salary and try living in his parent's basement. Ivey Business School economist Mike Moffatt noted that unpaid internships are a "non-option" for low-income people.

Several media companies, including *Toronto Life* and *Walrus* magazine, have come under fire in the past year over offering unpaid internships, with both the subject of a crackdown by Ontario's Minister of Labour in March.

Under labour laws, interns are entitled to at least minimum wage unless they are working under certain exemptions, such as through a student program. "Interns have to be paid, unless they're getting school credit," said Ms. Seaborn.

Source: Grant, Tavia. 2014, November 4. "Poloz's prescription for unemployed youth: Work for free." *The Globe and Mail*. http://www.theglobeandmail.com/report-on-business/economy/poloz-having-something-unpaid-on-your-cv-is-very-worth-it/article21439305/.

post-secondary qualifications—will become tomorrow's working-poor adults. Research shows that the probability of young women workers moving up the wage ladder over time is relatively low compared to men, and that the chances of young male workers moving up the job ladder have been falling compared to previous generations (Beach and Finnie 2004). The ongoing polarization of the job market between reasonably secure, well-paid jobs and insecure, poorly paid jobs puts more and more entry-age workers at risk, facing much more unequal futures than did their parents, as does the proliferation of unpaid work. While post-secondary qualifications offer a cushion, many employed graduates find that they are over-qualified for the jobs that they manage to secure (OECD 2008a).

Older Workers in the Canadian Job Market

Shifting the focus to older workers, one of the most notable changes in the early 2000s has been the rising labour market participation rates for both older men and older women. As illustrated in Figure 8.3, the overall pattern is that the participation rate of older men—especially those aged 60 to 64 and 65 to 69—declined until 2000 as the age of retirement fell. Since about 2000, however, the trend has sharply reversed. Labour force participation rates for older women were steadier—and increased for women aged 55 to 59—until 2000, reflecting the fact that women entering older age groups were increasingly likely to have been working at younger ages rather than caring for children. Like men, participation rates for women aged 60 to 64 and 65 to 69 have jumped since about 2000.

Figure 8.3: Participation Rate of Older Men, 1976–2014

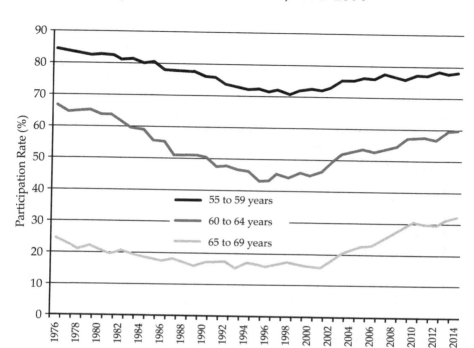

Source: Statistics Canada, CANSIM Table 282-0002.

As of 2000, just 16 percent of men aged 65 to 69 were still active in the paid workforce, down from 21.4 percent in 1980. The participation rate of men aged 60 to 64 fell steadily from the mid-1970s to 2000, from about two-thirds to under one-half, and by 2000, more than one in four men aged 55 to 59 had dropped out of the workforce. This sustained decline in older men's workforce participation mainly reflected decisions to retire earlier than in the past, at an average age of just above 60. This would have been facilitated by the contribution of the pension arrangements described above. However, it also reflected the fact that many older workers lost their jobs in the economic restructuring of the 1980s and the first half of the 1990s. In short, both push and pull factors were at play.

The pattern for women is different. From the mid-1970s to 2000, the participation rate of women aged 55 to 59 rose steadily, from about one-third to more than half, while that of women aged 60 to 64 and 65 to 69 was quite stable, at about one in four and about 1 in 12 respectively. The difference in the trends between women and men basically reflects the fact that older women of the mid-1990s had been more likely to spend most of their lives in the paid workforce than were women of the same age in the mid-1970s. In fact, there is a clear break, with women born after the mid-1950s being much more likely to work than those born before. Women do tend to retire earlier than men, since couples often retire at

Figure 8.4: Participation Rate of Older Women, 1976–2014

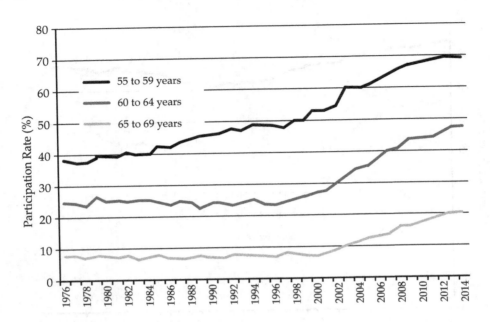

Source: Statistics Canada, CANSIM Table 282-0002.

the same time and married women are typically younger than their spouses, and because family considerations also influence the work decisions of older women. Retirement from paid work is often determined by the need to care for family members. Such pressures to retire are likely to intensify as publicly provided social services are cut.

The increase in the median age of retirement to 64 by 2015 can be seen as a sign of a very pronounced increase in the participation rate of older workers since about 2000, at which point the retirement age was 61. As shown in Figures 8.3 and 8.4, the participation rates of both men and, especially, women aged 55 to 59 have risen significantly, and they have also jumped sharply for those in the older age groups.[6] The respective retirement ages of both men (64.8) and women (63.2) increased at a similar rate between 2000 and 2015, and show only a small difference between them. These increases probably represent, in part, the previous work histories of the current near-elderly women compared to previous generations, and an increase in individual choices to remain at work. More older workers today are in good health and well-educated, and many such workers want to continue to work in some capacity—perhaps in a new job—and jobs have been much more readily available after 2000 than was the case in the 1990s. Delayed withdrawal from the workforce also reflects losses to savings following the stock market collapse of 2000 and the financial crisis.

Older Workers and Transitions toward Retirement

Canada has a rapidly aging population. The proportion of all Canadians aged 55 and over rose from about one in five in 2000, to one-quarter in 2011, and to almost 30 percent in 2015.[7] It is projected that this could reach 35 percent by 2028.[8] The so-called old age dependency ratio—persons aged 65 and over as a proportion of the population aged 15 to 65—will increase from 20 percent in 2000, to 30 percent by 2025, to an expected 40 percent by 2050 (PRI 2005: 7). If people retire at age 65, they will be outside the working population for a good 20 years in the case of men and 25 years in the case of women. The prospect of an aging society enjoying early retirement has caused great concern among many policy-makers. It has been feared that current pension arrangements will become unaffordable, that government expenditures, especially on health care, will surge, and that we will face serious labour shortages, especially shortages of skilled workers. Some commentators have seen it as undesirable that the proportion of a person's total working life spent in the paid workforce should slip so far, from about 74 percent in the 1960s (for men) to below 50 percent (Hicks 2003). However, proposals to raise the age of eligibility for public pensions have been dropped, mainly because the idea of retirement remains very popular. That said, there is widespread support for the idea of facilitating and supporting more choices for older workers, and increased recognition that desirable paths to retirement can be quite different. Many older workers continue in the workforce even as they begin to draw pension income and, as shown above, labour force participation rates for older workers have recently been rising rapidly.

Retirement patterns for baby boomers, who are now mostly in their mid- to late fifties, may be quite different from those of their parents and people now in their seventies. Most significantly, women now entering their fifties and sixties are much more likely than their mothers to have spent all or most of their lives in the paid workforce, and many will continue to work as they grow older. The gradual shift of employment away from very physically demanding jobs may also lead some workers to want to remain in the paid workforce until a later age than in even the recent past. Many of today's older workers are well educated, and such workers tend to retire early from their career jobs, but are also much more likely than average to pursue second careers.

The economic circumstances of people in and approaching retirement vary greatly. Some were victims of economic restructuring, while others have been in steady, full-time jobs with good pensions for most of their working lives. Another factor at play is investment returns. Such returns are quite variable over time, and the sharp decline in share prices in 2000 with the end of the dot-com boom, together with low interest rates, hit the retirement savings of some older workers, and had negative impacts on the assets of many pension plans. One can expect even more individualized paths to retirement, perhaps including a steady rise in the age of retirement after many years of decline, as well as a rise in the proportion of older people who combine pension and employment incomes. Looking further forward, it seems likely that today's young adults will have to work much longer than their parents and grandparents because of declining private pension plan coverage and because other life transitions, including that from education to work, as well as independent family formation, are taking place so much later in life.

Canada's Retirement Income System

Canadian workers gain income in retirement from three main sources: public pensions—the Old Age Security (OAS) program, the Guaranteed Income Supplement (GIS), and the Canada/Quebec Pension Plan (CPP/QPP); private, employer-sponsored pensions; and private savings, including RRSPs. Two of the main sources of income for retirees—CPP/QPP and private pensions—are provided on the basis of earnings and work experience, and are explicitly intended to replace earnings, while the OAS program provides a flat benefit of just $6,880 per year to all Canadians over age 65 (though higher-income taxpayers have some or all of their OAS clawed back) (Government of Canada 2016a). As a very rough rule of thumb, pension experts and policy-makers believe that individuals should be able to obtain 50 percent to 70 percent of their previous earnings in retirement. Public pensions are intended to replace only 30 percent to 40 perent of median earnings, so it follows that employer pensions and private savings must make up a significant share of retirement income, particularly for higher-income earners (Ambachtsheer 2008).

Public Pensions

The GIS, which is linked to the OAS, is an income-tested benefit. In combination, these two programs provide a minimum income floor for older Canadians. For the single elderly (who are overwhelmingly women), the floor amounts to a guaranteed minimum income of just over $17,000 per year (Government of Canada 2016a). This is still below the low-income line in a large urban centre, as established by Statistics Canada. Even so, many working-poor individuals and families experience a substantial income gain when they reach age 65 and qualify for OAS/GIS, and the vast majority of senior households have sufficient income from all sources combined to push them above the poverty line.

The CPP/QPP is a compulsory, earnings-related program, financed from employer and employee contributions, which provides retirement (and disability and death) benefits to the employed and the self-employed and their survivors. The retirement benefit provides 25 percent of pre-retirement earnings, but only for those earning up to the rough equivalent of average wages and salaries with a steady history of employment. Those earning more than average will get a lower benefit as a proportion of their pre-retirement income, while those with short work histories will get less than 25 percent. The average CPP/QPP benefit is only half of the maximum benefit of $13,110 (Government of Canada 2016b). A notable feature of the CPP/QPP is that allowance is made for periods of time women spend outside the workforce to care for children. Benefits are indexed to inflation, while pensionable earnings track average wages. The normal age of entitlement to CPP/QPP retirement benefits is 65, though reduced benefits are available at age 60, and higher benefits can be obtained by delaying retirement up to age 70. The CPP/QPP is explicitly designed to contribute to the goal of replacing pre-retirement earnings, and is not just an anti-poverty program. It is worth noting that CPP/QPP benefits were once entirely financed from current premiums (a pay-go system), but a significant investment fund has now been built up to cover most of the extra costs associated with an aging workforce.

In combination, the OAS and CPP/QPP replace approximately 40 percent of previous wages for an average worker for persons over age 65. Because of the offsetting influences of the GIS and the CPP/QPP, the distribution of public pension benefits among the elderly is actually quite close to a flat amount (Myles 2000; OECD 2001a). Compared to many European countries, Canada's public pension programs are modest in scale, and the labour movement, anti-poverty groups, women's organizations, and others have long advocated significant improvements to public pensions (Townson 2006). Few would see an income replacement rate of 40 percent for an average worker as adequate to secure a comfortable retirement. This is, however, deliberate. In the mid-1960s, when the basic structure of our pension system was put in place, and again after a decade-long debate on pension reform that ended in the mid-1980s, the Canadian government was quite emphatic that it wanted to leave significant room for privately administered retirement income arrangements (Department of Finance 1994; LaMarsh 1968). The expectation has been that Canadians should finance part of their own retirement from savings through pension plans or RRSPs, which in turn are an important source of savings in the economy and a key pillar of the financial sector. Financial interests have traditionally favoured private savings over public pensions since this is a significant source of revenues and profits.

Workplace Pensions

Employers in the private sector are not legally obliged to establish a workplace pension plan, though pensions for government employees are often established by statute and private plans are often created to recruit and retain employees. Generally speaking, employers have seen value in such plans since they foster employee loyalty and discourage workers from quitting to take another job. Pension plans have also been established as a result of pressure from unions. Workplace pensions are undoubtedly of benefit to workers, usually generating a significant and secure pension as a proportion of previous earnings. It is not uncommon for workers with long years of service to draw a good pension well before age 65. In 2014, approximately 59 percent of workplace pension plans, covering approximately 71 percent of all plan members, were of the defined benefit variety, providing benefits based on prior earnings and years of service.[9] Defined contribution-type plans, by contrast, provide much more uncertain benefits based on investment returns. The share of such plans has risen from about 8 percent in the mid-1980s to 37 percent in 2014. The post-retirement benefits provided by workplace pension plans vary greatly. A very good but not typical plan would provide a benefit of 2 percent of earnings multiplied by years of service, indexed to inflation, thus replacing the majority of earnings at retirement for those who have worked for 25 years. Other plans deliver a fixed benefit or lower benefit, and only a minority of pension plans provide even partial adjustments for inflation (Statistics Canada 2000). In combination with public pension benefits, most workplace plans provide an adequate replacement income, and help account for the fact that the great majority of Canadian retirees currently enjoy retirement incomes exceeding 60 percent of their pre-retirement earnings.

That said, very few new defined benefit plans have been established since the 1980s, and many consider them to be a legacy of the more stable economic conditions of the 1960s and 1970s. Employers often complain about the costs and the risks that they bear in sponsoring a pension plan that delivers a defined retirement benefit irrespective of the actual investment returns of the plan. Pension liabilities can indeed loom large in the finances of even large employers, particularly those like the Big Three North American auto companies, which have radically downsized over time and have a large proportion of retirees to current workers. However, pension plans have also often earned large surpluses, which have been used to deliver some combination of reduced contributions or increased benefits. Where they do exist, workers must usually help pay for any deficits, most often in the form of lower wage increases. Defined benefit pension plans are best suited to employers who want to maintain a stable, core workforce, and to workers who stay for many years with one employer. They have thus been undercut by a shift to more precarious and unstable work, and have tended to short-change members who leave their employer before reaching retirement age, whether by choice or because of an involuntary layoff. Employer-sponsored pension plans have delivered income security and a decent retirement to workers and will likely remain a significant, but smaller, feature of the landscape moving forward.

It is clear that employer pension coverage of the workforce is slipping, and that the relative role of employer plans will likely continue to diminish. In 2013, 37.9 percent of employees in Canada belonged to workplace pensions, down from 48.5 percent in 1991.[10] Traditionally, women workers were less likely to be covered than men, but the gender difference had flipped by 2008, and women are now more likely then men to be covered by a registered pension plan (39.4 percent, as compared to 36.6 percent), largely due to the employment of women in the public sector. The chances of being covered by a workplace pension plan increase with income, level of education, and size of employer (Statistics Canada 2000). These numbers exclude self-employed workers, and also include group RRSPs, which offer very variable and uncertain returns.

As illustrated in Table 8.2, the proportion of all employees with a registered pension plan is down from 46 percent in 1977 to 38 percent in 2011. Coverage declined markedly among men through the 1990s, although it increased slightly

Table 8.2: Percentage of Employees with a Registered Pension Plan (RPP), 1977–2011

	All (%)	Men (%)	Women (%)
1977	46	52	36
1991	46	49	41
2004	39	39	39
2011	38	37	40

Source: Drolet, Marie and René Morissette. 2014, December 18. "New facts on pension coverage in Canada." *Insights on Canadian Society.* Ottawa: Statistics Canada.

for women from 1977 to 2011. Only about 20 percent of private-sector workers are members of a defined benefit pension plan, and coverage is minimal in enterprises with less than 100 workers (Ambachtsheer 2008), as there has been a slow erosion of employer pension plan coverage, which has been concentrated entirely in the private sector (Informetrica 2007a). More than half of all couples with husbands aged 35 to 54 have no workplace pension coverage at all, while 14 percent are covered by two pensions. Almost half of all couples in the top 20 percent of earners have two pension plans, while three-quarters of all couples in the bottom 20 percent have no workplace pension plan coverage at all (Morissette and Ostrovsky 2006).

Aside from working in the public sector, where about 80 percent of workers belong to a pension plan, the factor that is most decisive is union membership. Overall, 80 percent of union members belong to workplace pensions, compared to just 27 percent of non-union members. In workplaces of 20 employees or less, 70 percent of union members still belong to workplace pensions, compared to just 13 percent of non-union members (Akyeampong 2002; Informetrica 2007a). Since the end of World War II, the negotiation and improvement of workplace pensions has been an important union bargaining priority and remains so to this day. The launching of Canada's modest public pensions in the 1950s and 1960s allowed some shift in emphasis in collective bargaining from the negotiation of benefits starting at age 65 or later to the negotiation of early retirement programs.

The third major source of retirement income is private savings, notably through tax-supported registered retirement savings plans (RRSPs). Contributions to RRSPs are tax deductible, and investment returns in them accumulate tax-free, which means there is a large subsidy to savings. While of use to the self-employed and those with no or an inadequate pension plan, RRSPs provide the most benefits to higher-income earners, who are in the best position to save significant amounts, and very few people use all of their available RRSP contribution room. RRSP contributions are, unlike workplace pension plan contributions, voluntary, and many people postpone saving until it is too late to generate a decent income in retirement. As a very rough rule of thumb, a person needs about 20 times as much as a desired annual retirement income in savings at age 65 to provide a given amount of annual retirement income to last until death, matching inflation. Thus, one would need about $300,000 in savings to guarantee a continuing real annual income of $15,000 (with the amount varying by life expectancy and real interest rates). In 2014, just 23 percent of tax-filers made a contribution to an RRSP,[11] and the median contribution was $3,000 per tax-filer (Statistics Canada 2016). Contributions have not been keeping pace with either inflation or income growth. A key problem with RRSPs is that investment returns are far from certain; equity values in particular, while rising over the long term, are subject to large fluctuations in the short term and can stagnate over long periods. Even if people do save a lot, RRSPs are a very costly savings instrument. Management and sales-related fees eat up 2 percent to 4 percent of assets every year, cutting deeply into investment returns. Large pension plans and the CPP Investment Fund achieve much higher rates of return on investments than individual investors (Ambachtsheer 2008: 3). Effectively, the decline of workplace pensions has shifted the risk of income insecurity in old age to individuals, at significant cost to most (Townson 2006).

Yet, despite this growing risk of income insecurity in old age, only about one-third of households are saving at sufficient levels on top of public pensions to replace pre-retirement income mainly because of the decline of defined benefit pension plans and insufficient investments in RRSPs (Andrews 2007). Statistics Canada (2000) has also calculated that one-third of households approaching retirement (household head aged over 45) have not saved enough to either replace two-thirds of their income or to have an income above the poverty line. Pension experts now generally agree that Canada's three-pillar pension system is unlikely to work nearly as well moving forward as it has in the past (Ambachtsheer 2008). Middle- and higher-income Canadians in particular are at high risk of facing steep declines in their incomes in retirement—or long working lives—due to the fact that public pensions provide only a very modest replacement income, while workplace pensions do not cover the majority and are in decline.

Incomes of Canada's Elderly

The last quarter of the 20th century was a period of very rapid improvement in the incomes of older Canadians. The real incomes of elderly households increased by 50 percent over the period from 1973 to 1996, and by even more for lower-income seniors. Poverty rates among the elderly fell dramatically. Not only did the incomes of the elderly increase in purchasing power, but the incomes of the elderly compared to younger age groups increased as well. From 1973 to 1996, the average income of elderly households increased from 47 percent to 80 percent of that of non-elderly households, when the numbers are adjusted for differences in household size (Baldwin and Laliberté 1999; Myles 2000). Over this period, two sources of income for the elderly grew particularly rapidly—income from the Canada and Quebec Pension

Plans, and income from workplace pensions. The CPP/QPP share of total income for the elderly grew from 2.8 percent in 1973 to 17.8 percent in 1996. Workplace pension income increased from 10.4 percent to 22.3 percent over the period. By 1996, almost all elderly households received income from OAS/GIS, and 86.5 percent received income from the CPP/QPP, up from only 28.4 percent just 23 years earlier. Just over one-half (53.2 percent) received workplace pension income, 57.9 percent received some investment income (often in very small amounts), and 20.3 percent received some employment income.

Among lower-income senior households, income from public pension programs is of decisive importance. If we divide households into 10 equally sized groups ranked by income, we find that income from OAS/GIS and CPP/QPP accounts for more than half of all income for all households in the bottom 60 percent, while only the top 10 percent receive less than 30 percent of their income from public pensions. Income from workplace pensions is particularly important for those with above-average incomes, with the exception of those at the very top. Public pensions address the poverty issue, while workplace pensions are the key lever for comfortable retirement incomes and sustained economic well-being in the transition from work to retirement.

There is still a substantial and persistent income gap between older men and women. And, there are striking differences in terms of the sources of income for men and women. OAS/GIS and investment income are more important for women, and CPP/QPP and workplace pensions for men. This reflects the working patterns by gender of previous years, and differences may shrink in the future to some degree.

A retirement income system could be judged to be successful if poverty among the elderly is low, and if retirees do not experience a large decline of income compared to their working years. Canada stands out among advanced industrial countries in terms of now having a very low level of poverty among the elderly, though there are still major problems for single elderly women (OECD 2013). In fact, using a common definition of poverty (household income of less than one-half the median), the poverty rate of Canadian seniors is just 7.2 percent, compared to the OECD average of 12.8 percent. Nonetheless, it is important to note that a high proportion of elderly households are still living on incomes that are quite close to the Canadian low-income line, and that single elderly women in particular are vulnerable to poverty.

Turning to income replacement, a Statistics Canada study (LaRochelle-Côté et al. 2008) looked at the incomes of individuals and their families as they moved from age 55 in the mid-1980s through their retirement years. For the average family, income falls after retirement, but by age 68, it stabilizes at about 80 percent of the income that had been earned at age 55. The fall in income compared to prior earnings is less for lower-income families because public pensions replace quite a high share of earned income. Indeed, the majority of the incomes of the bottom 20 percent of retired persons in their late sixties come from public pensions. By contrast, the decline in income in retirement is greater for the more affluent earners at age 55, the majority of whose income in retirement comes from private pensions and investments.

There is a great deal of variation in the levels and sources of retirement income. Table 8.3 shows retirement income for adults 65 and older in 2012. As can be seen in the data, approximately 70 percent have incomes below $30,000, with 89.7 percent of women having retirement incomes at or below this level. Looking at Table 8.4, it can be seen that while most rely on CPP/QPP and OAS/GIS, over half also have income from investments and other private sources. A notably higher proportion of men (25.3 percent) earn income from wages and salaries above the age of 65 than do women (13.7 percent).

Table 8.3: Retirement Income for Adults Aged 65 and up, by Gender, 2012

Retirement income	Men (%)	Women (%)	Both (%)
Under $5,000	20.4	34.7	27.5
$5,000 to $9,999	14.3	21.6	17.9
$10,000 to $14,999	13.8	13.4	13.6
$15,000 to $19,999	10.1	9	9.6
$20,000 to $29,999	16.2	11	13.6
$30,000 to $39,999	12	5.3	8.7
$40,000 to $49,999	5.7	2.3	4
$50,000 to $59,999	3.2	1.4	2.3
$60,000 or more	4.3	1.3	2.8

Source: Statistics Canada, *Canadian Survey on Disability*, 2012, CANSIM Table 115-0022.

Table 8.4: Sources of Income for Adults Aged 65 and up, by Gender, 2012

	Men (%)	Women (%)	Both (%)
Wages and salaries	25.3	13.7	18.9
Investment income	52.5	53.7	53.2
Retirement income from private sources	67	54	59.9
Canada Pension Plan/Quebec Pension Plan benefits	93.3	87.6	90.2
Old Age Security/guaranteed income supplement benefits	90.1	93.4	91.9

Source: Statistics Canada, CANSIM Table 115-0023.

Pension Debates

In the 1970s, there was a major pension debate in Canada, in which the main concern was the income of the elderly. This debate resulted in major pension improvements. In the 1990s, the main issue was seen to be the affordability of pensions in an aging society in which workers will live much longer lives after retirement. The debate was initiated by the World Bank and the OECD, who have favoured later retirement and more individualized pensions based on personal savings (OECD 2000; World Bank 1994). Despite the success of the pension arrangements put in place in Canada, many voices here also called for a return to reliance on individual savings. There was a vigorous campaign by conservative think tanks in the mid-1990s to abolish the CPP/QPP in favour of individual retirement accounts (Lam and Walker 1997; Robson 1996).

The federal government forecast in 1993 that expenditures on Old Age Security and the Canada and Quebec Pension Plans would increase from 5.3 percent of national income in 1993 to more than 8 percent in 2030. While this caused great anxiety for some, it is striking that OAS and CPP/QPP expenditures were projected to increase as a share of GDP by only 50 percent over a period in which the over-65 population was expected to double as a share of the population. One way or another, the costs of aging would have to be borne. The government claimed that if no changes were made to the CPP/QPP, those who came after the baby boomers would be asked to pay two to three times more for the same pensions as those who came before them. While true to a degree, this appeal to fairness between generations tended to ignore the fact that there had been a very large income transfer to the first generation to benefit from the CPP/QPP.

Ultimately, increases in the retirement age and a radical shift to individual accounts were ruled out. Instead, benefits were modestly trimmed and contribution rates were raised from 5.6 percent to 9.9 percent of earnings below the maximum amount, with the aim of building up an investment fund to spread some of the cost of future pensions over a longer period. It is now generally agreed that only minor adjustments will have to be made to ensure that the CPP/QPP is financially sustainable. The federal government eventually abandoned a proposal to replace the OAS/GIS program with a single seniors' benefit, which would have been based on family rather than individual income. Opposition arose because this proposal would have deprived many older women an individual old-age pension, would have resulted in lower benefits for higher-income families, and would also, some feared, erode incentives to save for retirement.

In recent years there has been growing pressure to fundamentally reform Canada's pension system. On top of declining workplace pension plan coverage, some plans, particularly in the private sector, could face serious financial difficulties as workforces shrink while the numbers of retirees grow. Plans are required to accumulate assets to match future liabilities, allowing for short-term fluctuations in financial markets. However, many plans are not fully funded, which could result in reduced benefits. There may be more pressure for pension plan windups or conversions of defined benefit plans to defined contribution plans. The limited nature of the first pillar—public pensions—combined with growing problems for workplace pensions have prompted some recent thinking about alternatives. The labour movement has long advocated a doubling of CPP/QPP benefits to replace a higher share of previous earnings, and thus reduce reliance on often inadequate and usually costly and unstable private savings. Provincial pension plans have been considered, and neutral pension experts have also begun to advocate for new pension alternatives, such as large new quasi-public plans to parallel the CPP/QPP (Ambachtsheer 2008).

Displaced Older Workers and Involuntary Retirement

For many laid-off older workers in the recession and slow recovery of the late 1980s to the mid-1990s, early retirement was an unplanned consequence of a lay-off (Pyper and Giles 2002; Schellenberg 1994). Planned retirements may, in fact, account for only a modest proportion of all supposed "retirements" in times of severe economic downturn (Rowe and Nguyen 2003). While many older workers were pushed out by layoffs in the 1990s, companies that were downsizing also often introduced early retirement incentives funded from then quite healthy pension plan surpluses to maintain jobs for younger workers.

Workers aged 55 to 65 have, on average, held their current job for a considerable period of time (17 years for men and 12 years for women). Many will move from that job into retirement. However, those who lose their job before a planned retirement often experience great difficulty in finding new employment. As a group, displaced older workers are less well educated than average, less likely to have up-to-date skills matching those demanded in new jobs, and less willing and able to move to new jobs. Geographic mobility is not a desirable or realistic option for many such workers, and the potential for moving into a different occupation is often limited by formal education and skill levels. Many employers are unwilling to hire displaced older workers, and governments have, unfortunately, not often been prepared to invest significantly in retraining.

While both unemployment and long-term unemployment rates today are lower than was the case for most of the past 30 years, workers aged 55 and over today still experience significantly longer than average unemployment spells than do younger workers. Between 2006 and 2010, approximately one-third of the unemployed between the ages of 55 and 64 were out of work for 24 weeks or more, which was double the proportion of young workers (aged 20 to 34) (Bernard 2012). Adjustment difficulties are obviously most serious for those with firm-specific or dated skills, or who live in areas with few alternative job opportunities, with long-term unemployment among older workers most serious in Quebec and Atlantic Canada. Further, displaced older workers who find new jobs often experience a significant loss of income. High-seniority displaced workers generally experience wage losses of between one-fifth and one-third (Morissette et al. 2007).

The Retirement Age Debate

As discussed above, concerns about the affordability of pensions and future labour shortages has led to an interest in increasing the age of retirement, and in more complete utilization of the labour force in the "near-retirement" years. The catalogue of policy responses put forward by the OECD and others includes raising the age of eligibility for public pension benefits, removing early retirement incentives in pension plans, and ending mandatory retirement.

Good workplace pension plans create strong incentives to retire at or often before age 65. Few workers will choose to work for a fraction of their former income if this means deferring a decent pension for very long. When early retirement programs are being valued for actuarial purposes, it is common practice to assume that the actual age of retirement will fall halfway between the normal retirement age and the date when the right to early retirement without actuarial reduction is established. Access to good pensions is a major reason why public-sector workers tend to retire at an earlier age than private-sector workers, and why the self-employed tend to work longer than employees. In fact, early retirement is, not surprisingly, concentrated in sectors that tend to have good pension plans, such as public administration, utilities, and education (Kiernan 2001). Moreover, Canadian tax rules make it difficult if not impossible for workers to phase into retirement by combining part-time employment and pension income from the same employer.

Public opinion polling suggests that proposals to delay public pension eligibility are very unpopular. Focus groups conducted by the federal government's Policy Research Initiative found that most Canadians wanted to retire relatively early and were not very supportive of government efforts to encourage them to work longer (PRI 2005). The short shrift given to the possibility of increasing the age of eligibility for Canada Pension Plan benefits in the mid-1990s likely reflected a fair reading by politicians of the public mood. Looking beyond the results of public opinion polls, it is a fair generalization that as societies have grown more affluent, working people have shown a strong desire to take advantage in the form of shorter working hours and pensions. Worker preferences for paid time off may well continue in the face of population aging (Burtless and Quinn 2002).

The preoccupation with the early retirement effects of pensions also oversimplifies individuals' retirement decisions, and the fact that many different factors influence decisions to work or not to work in the older years. There are significant variations in both the trends and levels of the labour force participation of older workers from country to country and within countries. Countries with high levels of older worker participation vary a great deal in terms of other labour market characteristics, including their apparent preference for paid time off as opposed to higher incomes over the entire course of working life (Hayden 2003). One key factor at play is the overall strength of employer demand for workers and the level of unemployment. Germany, with a relatively high unemployment rate, has a very low participation rate for older workers. Sweden and the U.S. have very different labour markets, but both have low unemployment and relatively high participation rates for older workers. It is striking in the case of Canada that provinces with low unemployment rates tend to have higher rates of older worker participation in the labour force, while older people tend not to work in provinces with relatively high unemployment rates.

The preoccupation with pensions' supposed disincentives to work also tends to lead people to ignore negative push factors in the workplace that may play at least as great a role as the pull factor of pensions. As shown in other chapters of this book, for many people, work can involve high levels of stress, long hours, discrimination and harassment, poor physical working conditions, lack of training, and lack of control over the work process itself. And, high job demands are indeed associated with decisions to take early retirement (Turcotte and Schellenberg 2005). It is little wonder that many people choose to retire as soon as they are able to do so.

Many employers do not necessarily wish to retain and use the skills of older workers. Until very recently, the common practice of mandatory retirement in workplaces with pension plans generally reflected union/employer agreement on the desirability of a known path to retirement. From an employer perspective, retirement means that the employment relationship can be ended amicably, and that normal job ladders for younger workers can continue to operate, though some older workers, perhaps as many as one-third, would choose to continue to work at least somewhat longer if they were given attractive options to consider (Lowe 2005).

In the context of declining defined benefit pension coverage, wealth and the returns from financial markets will increasingly influence retirement decisions. As well, it seems very probable that the recent rise in employment rates for older workers partly reflects the fact that some people who were dreaming of "Freedom 55" have decided to work longer simply because they cannot afford not to work. A shift to individual retirement savings will make it more difficult to forecast retirement decisions, since financial returns are so unpredictable. Adding to the affordability issue, older workers are more likely than ever to be supporting children in the post-secondary education system.

The debate over the age of retirement as influenced by pension incentives tends to ignore the complexity of paths out of the paid workforce, and the fact that many older workers combine pension and employment income. Hidden within the overall participation rate numbers for older workers are many transitions from career jobs to second careers. One in five older workers whose career jobs (defined as a job that had been held for more than eight years) ended voluntarily in the mid-1990s continued working in a different full-time job over the next two years (Pyper and Giles 2002). People who continue working after 65, and many aged 60 to 65, seem to be engaged in second careers. They are much more likely to be working part-time than pre-retirement-age workers (Schellenberg et al. 2005). Rates of self-employment are also much higher than among core-age workers—24 percent for workers aged 55 to 64, compared to 15 percent for workers aged 25 to 54 (Marshall and Ferrao 2007: Table 2). They are also likely to be well educated. The employment rates of university-educated seniors over age 65 are double those of people with only a high school education (Duchesne 2004). During the period of rapid economic expansion following the recession of the early 1990s, there was a striking increase in the number of people combining employment and retirement income.

There could be broad support for a later average age of retirement if this arose not from the erosion of income security for older workers, but through policies to expand choices, such as more effective labour adjustment programs for older workers, improvements to social services that reduce the pressure on older women workers to leave paid work to care for family members, and, more generally, improvements in the quality of work that make it less burdensome. Participation rates of older workers could be raised in a positive way not just by recognizing their special needs, but also through more advice and support. Older workers sometimes have difficulty recognizing how their personal work histories might relate to prospects for future employment and training. In some European countries, governments have begun to promote longer working lives more through the use of these kinds of carrot measures than the stick of reduced pensions (Foden and Jepsen 2002).

Conclusion

As illustrated throughout this chapter, transitions into and out of the labour force are complex and often quite troubled. Despite falling unemployment rates, young workers continue to face major problems in the job market, including insecure work and low wages. Governments and policy-makers tend to assume that most young workers are students in transition to better jobs. Some will certainly make this transition, and this may be made easier by the job vacancies opened up as baby boomers retire. However, the trend is now for older workers to remain in the workforce longer, and young adult workers lacking qualifications in demand and desired job experience will face a high risk of insecure, low-paid employment, and sometimes even unpaid labour. There are a number of policies that could improve the situation of youth in the job market. Given very low unionization rates among young workers (approximately 14 percent in 2014) (Statistics Canada 2015c), governments could help even the playing field between employers and young workers by increasing the minimum wage and improving basic employment standards.

In the current discussion on the situation of older workers, the most hotly contested issue is the appropriate age of exit from the labour force. The issue should be approached in a manner that recognizes workers' legitimate needs and desires for a financially secure retirement. Looking beyond the concerns associated with pension financing, and bearing in mind that the overall state of the job market will play a vital role in determining the actual age of retirement, there are clearly some contrary pushes and pulls on the age of retirement. Unsafe, unhealthy, and unsatisfying jobs are likely to drive people to look for a safe haven in retirement. Downsizing of large public and private employers will likely have the same effect.

Clearly, though, if work remains attractive to employees, and employers want to pay for them to remain and to accommodate special needs and circumstances, there will be a growing supply of healthy older workers to draw upon.

Conflicting views about the appropriate age of retirement will continue to fuel political debate in the years ahead. No matter how the age of retirement issue is resolved, there are groups of older workers whose work situation should be a matter of public concern, such as older unemployed and people who have faced discrimination in employment. The situation of older adult immigrants bears particular scrutiny given their low earnings, and many older women still have very low retirement incomes. It is also important that the age of exit issue gets resolved in a manner that creates employment opportunities for older workers who want employment and, at the same time, does minimal damage to the employment prospects of younger workers.

Recommended Reading

International Labour Organization (ILO). 2015. *Global Employment Trends for Youth 2015: Scaling Up Investments in Decent Jobs for Youth*. Geneva: ILO.

Mackenzie, Hugh. 2014. *Risky Business: Canada's Retirement Income System*. Ottawa: CCPA.

Perlin, Ross. 2012. *Intern Nation: How to Earn Nothing and Learn Little in the Brave New Economy*. London & New York: Verso.

Public Policy Forum. 2011. *Canada's Aging Workforce: A National Conference on Maximizing Employment Opportunities for Mature Workers*. Ottawa: Public Policy Forum.

Notes

1. Statistics Canada summary table: "Labour force characteristics by age and sex." Accessed at: http://www.statcan.gc.ca/tables-tableaux/sum-som/l01/cst01/labor20a-eng.htm.

2. Statistics Canada, 2011 *National Household Survey*: Data Tables. Accessed at: http://www12.statcan.gc.ca/nhs-enm/2011/dp-pd/dt-td/Rp-eng.cfm?LANG=E&APATH=3&DETAIL=0&DIM=0&FL=A&FREE=0&GC=0&GID=0&GK=0&GRP=0&PID=106746&PRID=0&PTYPE=105277&S=0&SHOWALL=0&SUB=0&Temporal=2013&THEME=98&VID=0&VNAMEE&VNAMEF.

3. Statistics Canada, 2011 *National Household Survey*: Data Tables. Accessed at: http://www12.statcan.gc.ca/nhs-enm/2011/dp-pd/dt-td/Rp-eng.cfm?LANG=E&APATH=3&DETAIL=0&DIM=0&FL=A&FREE=0&GC=0&GID=0&GK=0&GRP=0&PID=106746&PRID=0&PTYPE=105277&S=0&SHOWALL=0&SUB=0&Temporal=2013&THEME=98&VID=0&VNAMEE&VNAMEF.

4. Statistics Canada, CANSIM Table 282-0080. Accessed at: http://www5.statcan. gc.ca/cansim/a26?lang=eng&retrLang=eng&id=2820080&pattern=temporary+ employment&csid=.

5. Statistics Canada, CANSIM Table 111-0019. Accessed at: http://www5.statcan. gc.ca/cansim/a26?lang=eng&retrLang=eng&id=1110019&pattern=employmen t+insurance&tabMode=dataTable&srchLan=-1&p1=1&p2=-1.

6. Statistics Canada, CANSIM Table 282-0051. Accessed at: http://www5.statcan. gc.ca/cansim/a26?lang=eng&retrLang=eng&id=2820051&pattern=&csid=.

7. Statistics Canada summary table: "Population by sex and age group." Accessed at: http://www.statcan.gc.ca/tables-tableaux/sum-som/l01/cst01/ demo10a-eng.htm.

8. Statistics Canada summary table: "Projected population by age group according to three projection scenarios for 2006, 2011, 2016, 2021, 2026, 2031 and 2036, at July 1 (2026, 2031)." Accessed at: http://www.statcan.gc.ca/tables-tableaux/ sum-som/l01/cst01/demo08c-eng.htm.

9. Statistics Canada summary table: "Registered pension plans (RPPs) and members, by type of plan and sector (Total public and private sectors)." Accessed at: http:// www.statcan.gc.ca/tables-tableaux/sum-som/l01/cst01/famil120a-eng.htm.

10. Statistics Canada summary table: "Percentage of Labour force and employees covered by a registered pension plan (RPP)." Accessed at: http://www.statcan. gc.ca/tables-tableaux/sum-som/l01/cst01/labor26a-eng.htm.

11. Statistics Canada, CANSIM Table 111-0039. Accessed at: http://www5.statcan. gc.ca/cansim/a26?lang=eng&retrLang=eng&id=1110039&pattern=rrsp+contri bution&csid=.

PART III

CONTEMPORARY WORKERS' MOVEMENTS IN CANADA

CHAPTER 9

The Impact of Unions

A defining feature of all capitalist societies, including today's post-industrial societies, is that the great majority of people gain their livelihood through paid work—that is, by selling their labour power (their capacity to work) to employers. The basic terms of any employment relationship are that workers agree to work under the direction of an employer in return for a wage. Unions emerged, in Canada and elsewhere, in response to the alienation and exploitation inherent to the class relations of capitalism and as a means for workers to collectively protect and advance their interests in the capitalist workplace. If it were not for unions, workers would have to negotiate the terms and conditions of their employment (wages, benefits, hours of work, work schedules, conditions of work, etc.) as individuals, protected only by legislated minimum employment standards. And, if it were not for unions, individual workers would be on their own when it came to dealing with arbitrary and unfair treatment by employers, such as dismissal without just cause, harassment, discrimination in hiring, promotion, and layoffs, favouritism by employers and managers in setting pay and assigning jobs, and so on.

While providing a collective vehicle through which to defend workers' interests in the workplace, unions also provide a collective voice for workers in society more broadly and may act as a wider force for social justice by promoting higher levels of social and economic equality. The labour movement has also been a central part of wider movements to make Canadian society more democratic, both inside and outside the workplace, including struggles for women's rights and against racial discrimination. Though many unions work toward broader social justice goals, unions vary a great deal in terms of how internally democratic they are, and in terms of the extent to which they are committed to these social justice goals. This chapter examines the role and impact of unions, focusing on the ways in which unions seek to improve conditions both within and beyond the workplace.

What Are Unions and What Do They Do?

Writing at the turn of the 20th century, two British sociologists, Beatrice Webb and Sidney Webb (1897), argued that working people need unions because, without unions, workers would be subject to the dictatorship of the employer. In the context of industrial capitalism in Western Europe at that time, the Webbs argued that trade unions were key to improving both workplace order and workplace democracy. They believed that the existence of a trade union within a workplace could reduce industrial conflict and ensure the smooth ordering of production through collective bargaining. Unions acted to prevent the "tyranny" of the employer by providing an effective vehicle for workplace reform and regulation within the system of capitalist production. Without unions, capitalist working conditions would tend toward "sweating," or hyper-exploitation. Moreover, unions would not only improve working conditions, wages, and hours, they could also pressure the state towards "economic democracy."

Though recognizing the important role unions play in improving working conditions, Karl Marx and Friedrich Engels (1987) took a somewhat more critical view of some unions. In their early writings, they argued that unions could be a key element in the process of the collective organization of the working class. In and of themselves, unions were not revolutionary organizations, as union concerns tended to be primarily economic, not political, whereas a revolutionary struggle would require political as well as economic focus. However, by facilitating the collective organization of workers and the articulation of their interests against the interests of capitalists, unions could provide a vehicle through which to elevate class consciousness and escalate the collective struggle against capital. Writing during the industrial capitalist era of the mid-1800s in England, they suggested that unions form as a result of two interconnected processes: (1) the increasing centralization of industrial capitalist production into large-scale factories, which brought large numbers of workers together; and (2) the simultaneous impoverishment of the working class, which occurred through the precarious working conditions brought about by industrial machinery and the low wages paid by wealthy industrialists. Thus, the development of industrial capitalism brought workers into contact with one another under shared conditions of exploitation. For Marx and Engels, the expansion of trade unions contributed to laying the groundwork for a coming class struggle. In their later writings (post-1840s), however, Marx and Engels became more critical of the craft unions of higher skilled and better-paid workers, claiming that: (1) unions did not represent the whole working class, but rather a smaller "labour aristocracy" of "privileged workers"; (2) corrupt union leaders derailed or prevented the emergence of revolutionary activity within the unions; and (3) unions contributed to an "enrichment" of the organized working class (British in their writing), making them less willing to engage in revolutionary activity. Thus, while recognizing the role of unions in improving working conditions for the masses of less skilled industrial workers, they noted a *contradictory* tendency of unions, in that while creating a collective voice for (some) workers, unions could act to constrain a broader struggle against capitalism.

While these perspectives indicate a debate over the capacities for unions to effect long-term social change, there is some agreement around the questions of what unions are and what they do. Specifically: unions form in the context of the class relations of capitalism in order to address power imbalance in the workplace; they

Box 9.1: Who's Unionized? Demographic Shift Shows Changes in the Job Market
By Ella Bedard

The makeup of Canada's unionized workforce has changed, according to Statistics Canada.

For most of the 20th Century, the blue-collar male worker was the face of the labour movement. Machinists, miners, auto-workers, steelworkers, construction workers; your average union member was a man working in a manufacturing or trade industry.

But in the last 25 years, that's changed.

Last week Statistics Canada reported that within union memberships women now have a slight majority over men, and are more likely to be working in an office, school or hospital.

"Contrary to the popular cultural image, which assumes that the typical union member is a white male blue-collar worker, the typical union member today is very likely a woman working in the public sector, and that is a major demographic shift," explained Stephanie Ross, Associate Professor in the Department of Social Science and Co-Director of the Global Labour Research Centre at York University.

While this change is precipitated, in part, by the growth in public sector union density—from 70 per cent to 71.4 per cent in the last 15 years—it has more to do with a declining unionization rate in male-dominated private sector industries, which shrunk from 18.1 to 15.2 per cent during that same period, as well as changing dynamics within those industries.

"You have job loss in those sectors rather than job growth, and the jobs that are being created in those sectors are increasingly non-union," said Ross. "And because the public sector is a source of employment for women to a far greater extent than in the parts of the private sector where there are unions, that means that women also constitute an increasing majority of union members."

"It certainly gives a particular character to the labour movement," said Ross, "Women have more and more often been at the forefront to defend public services and the jobs that they deliver those services through."

Statistics Canada first measured unionization through household surveys in 1981, and since then the rate of unionization has fallen from 37.6 per cent to 28.8 per cent in 2014, with more rapid decline taking place in the 1980s and 1990s, but levelling out in recent years.

That decrease has hit men the hardest and the male unionization rate has fallen by almost 15 per cent while the unionization rate among women has held steady around 30 per cent since the 1980s.

But, as Ross explains, that does not necessarily mean that women have increased access to unions.

"The other part of what has driven this shift is that the parts of the private sector that are growing in terms of employment, where women are much more likely to be employed—like food, retail and accommodation—those sectors have very low unionization rates," said Ross, "So insofar as women have access to unions it's primarily through the public sector."

While it's difficult to predict how these trends will progress, Ross says that there needs to be a concerted effort on the part of unions to expand in those parts of the private sector if union density is to increase in this country.

"Unlike auto manufacturers, hotels can't really shut down in the face of a union-ization drive," Ross explained. "They are less mobile and in some ways more poten-tially 'union-izable' because employers don't have that strategy of exit that they do in an economy that allows for manufacturing to be networked across the world."

Ross also noted that there is unmet demand for unions among young workers.

"Most of the research shows that while young workers' unionization rates are low and [for young men] in decline, they are also the age group most interested in and open to unionization," Ross explained. "So there is unmet demand for union-ization here, largely because the sectors that young people work in are tough to organize, and because the kinds of jobs they are more likely in now—temporary, part-time, contract, in any sector—are also tough to organize."

"So that is a key challenge for unions, to figure out out how to unionize the very people that want to be unionized."

Source: Bedard, Ella. 2015, June 12. "Who's unionized? Demographic shift shows changes in the job market." rabble.ca. http://rabble.ca/news/2015/06/whos-unionized-demographic-shift-shows-changes-job-market.

are a reaction against economic exploitation (the extraction of surplus value from workers' labour); and due to the ways in which they may become integrated into capitalist class relations, unions reduce but do not eliminate managerial control and capitalist exploitation. In this way, unions can be seen as organizations that define, promote, and fight for the collective interests and rights of groups of workers. Unions formed out of the fundamental recognition that workers are stronger when they unite and bargain together through a common voice to represent their interests to their employer. Individual workers have less power in determining the content of the employment relationship than employers, particularly when there are many workers capable of doing a given job. The bargaining power of individual workers is particularly weak in times when unemployment is high and many workers are seeking any available job. Historically, unions have been an important force for humanizing and democratizing capitalist workplaces by balancing the power of employers, which results from their control over production. While the workplaces of the early 21st century may look very different in some ways than the workplaces of the times when Beatrice Webb and Karl Marx were writing, the basic social relationships that gave rise to trade unionism remain, and continue to give reason for workers to organize collectively in order to defend and advance their interests.

Limits and Contradictions

While unions act as a force to improve conditions of work, when asking what unions do, the limitations of unions in fully contesting capitalism must be recognized. In Canada, these limitations were created in part through a legal system that, on the one hand, provides workers with the right to unionize and to engage in collective bargaining, but on the other hand, imposes strict limitations and obligations on unions in exchange for these rights (Panitch and Swartz 2008; Fudge and Tucker 2001). Specifically, the labour laws that emerged in the 1940s from an arrangement known as the "postwar compromise" constituted significant gains for workers by ensuring the right to collective bargaining and providing a mechanism for union security (through a mandatory dues checkoff). But the legal framework also created new responsibilities for unions, as, in exchange for certification, bargaining, and dues, unions had to ensure their members behaved "responsibly," which meant not going on strike while a collective agreement was in effect.

In 1944, the Canadian federal government under Prime Minister Mackenzie King introduced Privy Council Order 1003, which provided the basis for compulsory union recognition and the right to free collective bargaining. Under PC 1003, if a majority of employees demonstrated support for a union, the union would become legally certified and the employer must recognize it for the purpose of collective bargaining. Unions received new responsibilities under the legislation as well: strikes during the life of a contract were disallowed, and grievance procedures were bureaucratized to remove the role of shop-floor disruptions in the resolution of grievances. Originally a federal wartime measure, PC 1003 was extended into the years following the war and became a permanent framework for Canadian labour relations in 1948 as part of the Industrial Relations and Disputes Investigation Act. By the 1950s, all provinces had incorporated these principles into provincial labour relations legislation.

The other key element of the postwar labour relations system, the "mandatory dues check-off," was established by Supreme Court Justice Ivan Rand in an attempt to resolve a 1945 strike at the Ford plant in Windsor. Rand ruled that since all workers in a unionized shop benefit from the union contract, all must pay dues through mandatory paycheque deductions. An employee does not have to join the union—participate in meetings, receive newsletters, and so on—but the dues would nonetheless be automatically deducted from his or her paycheque. Through the "Rand Formula," unions were guaranteed a financial base upon which to provide organizational representation to their members, so long as they acted within the bounds of the processes established under PC 1003. Unions were able to pay officials, maintain offices, and service members on an ongoing basis.

PC 1003 and the Rand Formula are generally seen as the cornerstones of the postwar system of labour relations in Canada. They established important labour rights for Canadian workers in the areas of union recognition and collective bargaining. They initially applied to workers in the private sector, but were extended to the public sector in the 1960s. Through this system, unionized workers were able to improve their conditions of work on a regular basis through collective bargaining. These labour rights were not absolute, however, as the postwar system was also designed to ensure stability in labour relations and industrial production. Though establishing a legal right to "free collective bargaining," the scope of bargaining was limited to workplace-based, largely economistic issues. Moreover, if unions did not abide by the prohibition on striking during the life of an agreement, their dues base was jeopardized and they could face legal penalties. This produced what has been termed *industrial hegemony*, involving the securing of capitalist control through forms of worker consent to capital (Burawoy 1985). In the Canadian context, a form of "responsible unionism" emerged, whereby unions were required to police the behaviour of their members and make sure that no actions were taken that violated the collective agreement (including illegal work stoppages) (Fudge and Tucker 2001). Through this system, collective bargaining became a bureaucratic, routine practice that took place between paid union officials and company negotiators, away from the shop floor and out of sight of rank-and-file union members. No shop-floor disruption could be taken until the proper procedures of bargaining were followed. In this way, the system directed unions toward bureaucratized, legalistic processes, entwining them within the institutional framework of capitalism and drawing them away from rank-and-file organizing (Panitch and Swartz 2008). The operation of this framework intensified bureaucratic tendencies within unions, limiting the potential of democratic practices (Michels 1966). This "iron law of oligarchy" pushed unions in conservative directions, turning unions into bureaucracies themselves, limiting their capacity to challenge the power relationships of the workplace and advance workers' struggles (see also Camfield 2011).

In summary, unions provide a collective organization for the working class to improve conditions of work and to challenge the absolute rule of capital. Nevertheless, bureaucratic structures, legal frameworks, and reformist orientations constrain unions in their capacity to fully represent the interests of the working class. In other words, unions both promote and restrain the struggle for better work (Rinehart 2006; Wells 1995). In the contemporary context of globalization and neoliberalism, these tendencies have dampened the capacity for unions to resist aggressive workplace reorganization.

The Impact of Unions

Union strength varies a great deal between countries, including countries in the Global North, where collective bargaining coverage ranges from 80 percent or more of workers in some continental European countries to less than 15 percent in the U.S. Outside of public and social services, where union coverage is typically high, the key bastions of union strength are generally among mainly blue-collar workers in larger companies in primary industries, manufacturing, utilities, communications, transportation, and construction. Union coverage usually extends to only a minority of workers in most private service-sector industries, such as finance, retail trade, accommodation and food, and personal services. The main exception is in some European countries, where unions and employers sign broader-based agreements covering workers in many smaller workplaces.

For unions to be a stronger force for social and economic justice in Canada, union coverage must be extended. As documented in the next chapter, union coverage now extends to just one in three Canadian workers. There is a big difference between very high union coverage in the public sector (over 70 percent) and low coverage in the private sector (15 percent) (Statistics Canada 2015c). Union representation for men and women is about equal, but the great majority of unionized women work in public and social services, while the majority of unionized men work in the private sector. The growing number of workers in low-paid and precarious jobs, many of them women and racialized workers, are currently excluded from the benefits of union representation.

Collective Bargaining

In Canada today, unions are almost always organized on the basis of a certification by a provincial labour board, which allows a union or bargaining agent to represent a specific group of workers in a specific workplace. Those in federally regulated businesses and industries—about 6 percent of workers—are covered by federal labour legislation (the Canada Labour Code) (Government of Canada 2016c). Bargaining units are usually quite narrowly defined, so different groups of workers working for the same employer often belong to different unions or bargaining units. For example, at Air Canada, different unions represent and bargain separately for the pilots, customer service agents, baggage handlers, flight attendants, mechanics, and so on. Managers and even lower-level supervisors are typically excluded from these bargaining units, which are meant to represent communities of interest. The norm is for union locals to belong to one of a few major national or international unions, which, in turn, primarily represent either private- or public-sector workers, but are now usually spread across different industrial sectors. These national unions may or may not coordinate bargaining among the locals they represent, and may or may not cooperate with other unions in bargaining.

It used to be the case, from the 1940s through to the 1970s, that similar kinds of workers in the same industry were represented by the same union. For example, the United Steelworkers (USW) represented workers in the steel industry. Today, most large industrial unions, such as the USW, Unifor, and the United Food and Commercial Workers, are the product of mergers between what used to be separate industrial unions, and represent workers across different sectors of the economy. There are often several unions representing similar kinds of workers in the same industry. For example, there are at least two major unions in the mining sector, and employees in long-term care homes belong to different unions in different provinces, and often to different unions in the same province and even municipality. Unions that used to represent mainly blue-collar men in manufacturing have now branched out into different parts of the private sector and even the public sector. For example, unions that used to represent auto workers (formerly Canadian Auto Workers, now Unifor) and steelworkers (USW) are now general unions. The USW, for example, represents not only miners and steelworkers, as in the past, but also security guards, clerical and support workers at universities, and retail workers. Unifor (formed through a merger of the Canadian Auto Workers union and the Communications, Energy, and Paperworkers union) represents not only auto workers, but also workers in forestry, rail, media, retail, energy, telecommunications, and health care.

After a union is certified to represent a group of workers, its central activity is to bargain and enforce a collective agreement covering such issues as wages, benefits, hours of work, and working conditions with the employer. Literally thousands of such agreements are in force, with most being renegotiated every two or three years. The members of a union local must elect an executive and bargaining committee to take responsibility for bargaining and union affairs, and usually union members also elect stewards to represent members to managers and employers on a day-to-day basis when conflicts arise. Local union officers are typically assisted by full-time, paid union staff, particularly in collective bargaining, and help resolve complaints or grievances arising over the term of an agreement that cannot be resolved at an early, relatively informal stage of discussions. Naturally, the quality of service to members can and does differ between unions, but all have a legal responsibility to bring forward reasonable member grievances against an employer. Unions can and do also differ a great deal in terms of internal democracy and the extent of member involvement; however, collective agreements are almost invariably ratified by a vote of members, and a vote will be held before a strike is conducted. Members are to be closely consulted before bargaining begins so as to identify key issues, and most union locals have regular membership meetings to discuss issues that arise during the course of a collective agreement.

The ultimate source of power for a union lies in the capacity to stop production through a strike (work stoppage). Since the advent of the post–World War II system of labour relations (discussed above), strikes are legally regulated by labour relations legislation and can only be undertaken following a membership vote and once the collective bargaining process has broken down. Wildcat strikes—those that take place outside the legal framework of collective bargaining—happen, though much less frequently, as one of the main impacts of the postwar system of labour relations was to channel union activities away from spontaneous rank-and-file action (Wells 1995).

While a great deal of media coverage of union issues focuses on strikes, these are actually very rare events. As illustrated by Figure 9.1, the number of strikes per year has been on a sharp decline since the mid-1970s. In 2015, in all of Canada, there were just 187 strikes, involving 387,000 workers.

Figure 9.1: Work Stoppages, Canada, 1976–2015

Source: Data provided by the Labour Program, 2016. Ottawa: Government of Canada.

One-third of all employees are union members, but, in a typical year, time lost due to strikes has been well under one-tenth of 1 percent of total working time. That said, the right to strike is a key ingredient in Canada's system of free collective bargaining, and it is often the threat of a strike—and the prospect of lost production for an employer and lost pay for the workers involved—that leads to a negotiated settlement. In Canada, unlike the U.S., employers cannot permanently replace striking workers, and in Quebec and British Columbia, employers cannot replace striking workers during the course of a legal strike. The willingness of or capacity for unionized workers to go on strike may be compromised by economic insecurity and fear of job loss, particularly in industries where employers are geographically mobile, as has been the case in manufacturing. As well, federal and provincial governments have used back-to-work legislation frequently to eliminate (temporarily) the ability of public-sector unions to go on strike (Panitch and Swartz 2008). Given the state of the labour market these days, just like in 1919, it may indeed be time for a general strike. However, the trends in strike activity indicate that this is not likely to happen in the near future.

Most bargaining with employers takes place at the local union level, and some employers bargain with several unions. Industry-wide bargaining was always quite weakly developed in Canada. It remains important in the auto and pulp and paper sectors, and construction agreements are also often negotiated centrally. This very decentralized bargaining system tends to weaken the bargaining power of Canadian unions compared to unions in countries such as Germany and the Scandinavian countries, where bargaining across whole industries is still common, and where there is some coordination of bargaining aims between different unions at the national level. Fragmented bargaining also reflects the reality of very different issues and economic circumstances in different workplaces and sectors of the economy, as well as Canada's diverse regional economies.

Collective agreements are formal and legally binding documents that establish workplace rights for the workers covered by the agreement. Unions are legally obliged to take up (through a grievance) reasonable complaints by members that the terms of an agreement have been violated, and employers are legally obliged to change their practices if they are found to violate the terms of an agreement. Alongside the economic objective of higher wages, workers join unions to ensure this due process in the workplace. Indeed, the ongoing role of unions in workplace governance gives them the capacity to contribute to a form of workplace democratization by acting as a counterbalance to the power of the employer.

Likely the most important aspect of unionization for individual workers is that they have a formal contract of employment that can be readily enforced through the grievance and arbitration process. Members can grieve dismissal, disciplinary actions, and harassment by supervisors, and can often grieve being passed over for promotion, favouritism by managers and supervisors, unwelcome changes in work assignments, hours of work, work schedules, and so on, depending upon the wording of the agreement. By contrast, procedures and processes in non-unionized workplaces are much more highly subject to the exercise of managerial authority. Some large non-union employers do adopt formal, written workplace rules and formal complaint processes and procedures, in effect mimicking union workplace rules, though these do not have the binding legal force of a collective agreement. Minimum employment standards laws provide for minimum wages, maximum hours of work, and safe working conditions in most workplaces (with some important exceptions) (Thomas 2009). However, it is striking that very few complaints about wages or working conditions are filed with government labour standards officials while an employment relationship still exists. The vast majority of individual complaints under employment standards laws, usually well over 90 percent, are lodged only after a worker has left the job in question. Very few complaints are filed against a current employer, most likely due to fear of reprisals, since the evidence shows that many employers do not comply with basic legal standards (WAC 2015). It is union members who generally benefit most from legal protections, since unions have the resources to effectively bring forward and prosecute complaints on behalf of members. For example, pay equity legislation formally applies to all workers, but the large settlements covering federal public-sector workers and Bell Canada workers were the result of years of expensive legal action paid for by unions.

Table 9.1 provides information on the proportion of unionized employees covered by selected provisions in collective agreements. Typically, collective agreements define the following conditions, standards, and processes.

Wages

Wages are usually set by the hour, week, or pay period. Sometimes there is an element of performance pay, but this is much less common than in non-union workplaces, where piecework, commissions, and bonuses based on individual or group performance are more common. Wages are usually set for defined jobs and job classifications, so there is a formal system of pay by position. The union wage advantage is detailed below.

Non-Wage Benefits

Collective agreements commonly specify benefits, such as employer pension plan coverage, health care, and paid or unpaid time off for family and personal reasons. Such benefits are quite expensive and make up a major part of the union advantage in economic terms.

Job Security and Protection

Collective agreements formalize the norm that individual dismissal shall only be for just cause, so individual discipline and dismissal can be appealed through the grievance and arbitration process. There are usually provisions for layoffs for economic reasons to be based upon seniority by date of hiring, so long-tenure unionized workers effectively have a high degree of job security. As shown in Table 9.1, 68 percent of union members are protected from layoff by seniority. Seniority is usually justified by reference to the fact that long-tenure workers have invested a lot in a specific job and employer, and thus deserve greater protection from job loss. In the absence of seniority provisions, there is also greater potential for purely subjective and arbitrary factors to come into play.

Often, agreements have formal provisions to prohibit or limit an employer's contracting out of work to other employers, and to provide advance notice of technological and organizational change. Sometimes there are formal no-layoff provisions for the term of a contract, and often layoffs become subject to formal

Table 9.1: Selected Provisions in Collective Agreements, 2006

	% of union employees covered
Job security and protection	
Layoffs based on seniority	67.8%
Some restriction on contracting out	61.2%
Advance notice to union of technological change	55.6%
Training to deal with technological change	49.2%
Severance on layoff based on years of service	51.4%
Opportunities for job progress	
Promotion based on seniority:	
Primary criterion	20.8%
Tie-breaker	42.2%
Specific to job	50.4%
General	17.0%
Apprenticeship program	29.5%
Employer contributes to training fund	29.9%
Joint committee on training	32.8%
Equity	
Employment equity program	22.8%
Harassment complaint procedure	52.8%
Workplace conditions	
Joint committee:	
Broad mandate	62.6%
Organization of work	38.4%
Working conditions	39.9%
Working time	
Normal hours of work (37.5 hours or less):	
White-collar	48.7%
Blue-collar	15.9%
Some limit on overtime	11.2%
Paid holidays:	
10 days or more	76.8%
12 days or more	32.5%
Annual vacation:	
Four weeks after 10 years or less	74.6%
Four weeks after 5 years or less	34.5%

Table 9.1 (continued)

	% of union employees covered
Five weeks after 15 years or less	33.7%
Provision for job-sharing	15.7%
Provision for flex-time:	
White-collar	23.3%
Blue-collar	6.0%
Compressed workweek:	
White-collar	27.8%
Blue-collar	13.8%

Note: Collective agreement provisions vary widely regarding the precise content.

Source: Human Resources Development Canada, Bureau of Labour Information, 2006.

negotiation. Sometimes unions have even bargained for employers to commit to new investments to maintain and increase employment.

Opportunities for Job Progress

Most, but certainly not all, agreements provide for at least some consideration of seniority in promotions, so that a worker who has the skills and abilities to fill an available job will get the job if she or he is the most senior candidate. Job vacancies usually have to be posted, and are subject to formal competitions. Often, agreements provide defined opportunities for training. These provisions mean that union members are generally able to access better jobs through formalized internal labour markets. Formal structures for promotion can exist in larger non-union firms, but collective agreements typically provide much stronger rights for workers.

Equity and Human Rights

Only a minority of collective agreements provide for formal employment equity programs (sometimes because legislative provisions exist), but harassment complaint procedures have become much more common and now cover a majority of unionized workers. Harassment—often directed at women and racialized workers—is not normally covered by employment standards legislation, though since 2004 Quebec has required employers to maintain anti-harassment workplace procedures. These usually require independent investigation and swift resolution of any complaints.

Workplace Conditions

Many agreements contain provisions—sometimes very detailed—on the content of jobs, workloads, and proper working conditions. Often agreements also set up labour/management committees to informally discuss working conditions. However, almost all agreements also contain management rights clauses that give management the right (subject to specific exceptions) to assign tasks to workers, to direct work, and so on. Unionized workers generally enjoy much higher levels of protection in terms of health and safety, since the collective strength of the union provides the means to ensure that health and safety committees, which are mandated by law for most workplaces, are working effectively.

Working Time and Hours of Work

Agreements usually specify regular hours of work, shift schedules, maximum hours, and provisions for overtime pay, as well as provisions for paid time off. Again, this contrasts with informal schedule arrangements (such as highly variable weekly hours, on-call arrangements, and unpaid overtime) in many non-union workplaces. It is not uncommon for unionized workers in public and social services to work unpaid overtime due to the demands of the job, but unpaid overtime is uncommon among unionized workers outside of professional and managerial job categories. With the rise of part-time work, some unions have begun to direct their attention toward improving the predictability of scheduling and establishing minimum-hours guarantees, as was done in the collective agreement negotiated between the United Food and Commercial Workers and Loblaws in 2015 (Mojtehedzadeh 2015).

Unionized workers generally enjoy far more paid time off the job than do non-union workers. Provincial employment standards legislation gives workers access to a minimum of two weeks of paid vacation (or vacation pay) after one year of service. There is no entitlement at all to a third week in two jurisdictions—Ontario and Yukon—while workers have to put in five or more years of service (15 years in Newfoundland, and 8 years in Prince Edward Island, Nova Scotia, and New Brunswick) to reach three weeks of paid vacation (Payworks 2016). The exception is Saskatchewan, where every worker has access to three weeks after one year of service, and four weeks of paid vacation after 10 years of service. On top of fixed paid holidays (which often add to the list of provincial statutory holidays), the great majority of unionized workers get at least three weeks of paid vacation time, and 70 percent get four weeks, usually after 10 years of service. One in three (31 percent) unionized workers gets five weeks of paid vacation, usually after 15 years of service.

What Are the Impacts of Unions?

Unions Raise Wages

In Canada, as in almost all countries, it is well established that unionized workers earn higher wages than non-union workers. This is referred to as the union wage advantage. Usually the wage advantage is greatest for workers who would otherwise be low paid.

Table 9.2 provides data on the union wage advantage in Canada in 2009. The average union worker earned $26.05 per hour, or $4.80 per hour (22.6 percent) more than the average non-union worker, who earned $21.25 per hour. The difference is somewhat distorted by the fact that non-union workers are a mix of higher-paid professionals and managers, and lower-paid workers. The union average hourly wage advantage is greater for women ($6.71 per hour) than for men ($2.99 per hour). The union advantage, measured in terms of average hourly wages, is greater in the private sector than the much more highly unionized public sector, and tends to be highest in relatively low-paid occupations. As shown in Table 9.2, measured in percentage terms, the union wage advantage is quite significant in many low-wage private service occupations and blue-collar occupations, but is low in some professional occupations.

It is important to take into account that union and non-union workers are different, and also hold different kinds of jobs. Union members are, on average, older and more experienced than non-union members, and are much more likely to work in public and social services and, if they work in the private sector, for large firms. And, more union members are highly trained and educated. Public-sector wages tend to be higher than in the private sector, not just because of higher union coverage, but also because of the high proportion of professional jobs. In other words, the apparently very large union wage advantage reflects many factors other than union coverage. Economists have tried to calculate the union wage advantage for comparable jobs, holding constant all the other factors that determine wages. Calculated this way, the advantage has still been generally estimated to be in the range of 7 percent to 14 percent (Fang and Verma 2002).

It seems that the union hourly wage advantage has fallen since the mid-1990s. Between 1997 and 2007, the average hourly wage of a union member barely increased at all when adjusted for inflation, meaning that the average wage settlements in collective agreements just matched inflation over the course of an entire decade. Meanwhile, the average non-union wage adjusted for inflation rose by about $1.50 per hour over the entire decade. However, this increase mainly reflected high earnings gains by non-union senior managers and professionals. It is also important to note that the cost of a typical union benefits package increased significantly over this period. Holding everything else constant, unions still have a very significant impact on wages. And, wages are only one part of the union pay advantage, which also includes higher benefits and more paid time off than is the case for non-union workers.

The union wage advantage is impossible to determine precisely. It may reflect a compensating differential for more difficult working conditions than those of non-union workers. On the other hand, the union wage advantage may be understated to the extent that it takes no account of the positive impacts of unions on the wages of non-union workers. Many non-union employers more or less match union wages in order to avoid unionization.

Table 9.2: The Union Average Hourly Wage Advantage, 2009

	Union	Non-union	Union advan-tage	Union advantage as % of non-union
All	$26.05	$21.25	$4.80	22.6%
Men	$26.92	$23.93	$2.99	12.5%
Women	$25.17	$18.46	$6.71	36.3%
Age 15–24	$15.84	$12.23	$3.61	29.5%
By occupation:				
Professionals in business, finance	$31.96	$34.16	-$2.20	
Secretary, administration	$24.54	$23.21	$1.33	5.7%
Clerical, supervisors	$22.22	$18.94	$3.28	17.3%
Natural sciences	$32	$30.23	$1.37	5.9%
Health, nursing	$33.95	$39.40	-$5.45	
Assist health occupation	$22.58	$20.11	$2.47	12.3%
Social sciences	$28.82	$22.58	$6.24	27.6%
Teacher, professor	$33.94	$27.61	$6.33	22.9%
Art, culture, recreation	$26.37	$20.07	$6.30	31.4%
Mainly low-wage private services:				
Retail, sales, cashier	$13.12	$12.20	$0.92	7.5%
Chefs, cooks	$15.37	$12.92	$2.45	18.0%
Protective services	$27.52	$20.49	$7.03	34.3%
Child care	$19.78	$12.08	$7.70	63.7%
Sales, service, travel	$15.72	$11.85	$3.87	32.7%
Blue-collar:				
Construction trades	$25.45	$19.41	$6.04	31.1%
Other trades	$28.68	$21.92	$6.76	30.8%
Transport equipment	$22.53	$18.76	$3.77	20.1%
Trades helpers	$22.74	$14.62	$8.12	55.5%

Source: Gender and Work Database, York University. Data from *Survey of Income and Labour Dynamics* (SLID), 2009.

The union wage advantage has been found to be lowest in countries where union density is high, and highest where union density is low. Thus, it is much higher in the U.S. than in Sweden. This reflects the fact that non-union employers will be more likely to be forced to match union wages where unions are very strong. The main impact of unions in countries like Sweden, where the unionization rate is well over 80 percent, is to raise wages for lower-paid workers compared to other workers, rather than to raise union wages compared to the wages of non-union workers.

While wages are obviously a key concern in union bargaining, the key goal of labour movements is—or should be—to expand the range of collective bargaining and to increase union density, with the aim to improve the working conditions of all workers rather than raising the wages of a small union elite. A very high union wage advantage and low union density is likely to promote very strong employer resistance to unions, as in the U.S. and Canada, as opposed to Germany and Sweden, where employers generally take dealing with unions as a given and perhaps even as an advantage. Widespread unionization is likely to promote weaker employer opposition, at least once high density has been established. That is because, in highly unionized environments, wages are effectively taken out of competition, since all employers in a sector or region pay roughly the same union wage and benefits. Employers must then compete with each other on the basis of non-wage costs, productivity, and quality.

The union wage advantage can be paid for from several different possible sources. Part of it may come from lower management salaries and lower profits than in comparable non-union firms. The major part comes from higher productivity, where higher output produced per hour worked supports a higher hourly wage. And, part may come from higher prices that unionized firms charge in order to cover higher wages. The impacts of union wages on jobs and growth are discussed below.

Unions Counter Low Pay and Make Wages More Equal

Economic research has consistently shown that the union wage advantage is greatest for people who would otherwise be lower-paid workers, notably workers with less formal education and skills, younger and less experienced workers, and women and workers of colour who are vulnerable to discrimination. In Canada, unions have been shown to raise the pay of lower-paid workers compared to higher-paid workers, to reduce the incidence of poverty, and to make wages more equal (Chaykowski 1995; Chaykowski and Slotsve 1998). This is partly because unions compress the distribution of wages within unionized firms. For example, highly skilled trades workers in the auto industry make more per hour than regular assembly-line workers, but the difference is not as great as it would be in non-union firms.

As shown in Table 9.2, the union advantage is very significant among low-wage occupations, including those such as child care workers (63.7 percent) and sales and service workers (32.7 percent). By raising the wages of traditionally disadvantaged groups the most, unions typically lower pay differences in the unionized sector between women and men, and between racialized workers and white workers.

Unions and Equity-Seeking Groups

Unions have not only raised pay for low-wage workers, but they have also often attempted to promote pay and employment equity for their members. Many collective agreements contain non-discrimination clauses, and some call for formal pay and employment equity procedures above and beyond those mandated by law. In practice, unionized workers are also most likely to benefit from legislated pay and employment equity laws because unions have been prepared to fight long and costly cases through the courts. For example, after many years, the Public Service Alliance of Canada won a landmark, multi-billion-dollar pay equity settlement for women workers, and, in 2006, the Communications, Energy and Paperworkers Union (now Unifor) concluded a major pay equity settlement with Bell Canada.

While it is clear that unions play a major role in closing the wage gap between women and men, and in countering low pay among working women, this role needs to be strengthened by increasing union representation for women, especially lower-paid women in the private services sector. By 2015, the unionization rate for women (32.4 percent) had risen above that for men (28.9 percent).[1] However, the unionization rate for women in the private sector is, at 13.3 percent in 2015, very low and still well below the 19.5 percent rate for men in the private sector. Unionization is especially low for women working in low-paid private service industries, such as retail trade (12.5 percent) and accommodation and food services (6.3 percent). In contrast, the unionization rate for women in the public sector is high and stable at 76.7 percent. Two-thirds of unionized women work in the public sector, and just one-third in the private sector.

In 2015, unionized women earned an average of $28.01 per hour, or 93.9 percent of the wage of unionized men.[2] Non-union women earned an average of $20.99 per hour, or 80.8 percent of the wage of non-union men. Unions raise the wages of working women and narrow the gender wage gap. In the public sector, union coverage is high for women, raises wages, and significantly narrows the gender wage gap. In the private sector, union coverage is much lower for women than for men, raises wages more modestly (with a greater impact on part-time workers), and does not close the gender wage gap as much as in the public sector. However, unionization does have a major impact on the wages of women in the lowest-paid occupational category, sales and service workers. As shown in Table 9.3, the union wage premium for women in 2015 was $7.02 per hour, or a very substantial 33.4 percent of the wage of non-union women, and unions narrowed the gender wage gap, since the union wage premium is significantly higher for women than men (33.4 percent vs. 14.8 percent). Clearly, the unionization rate of women must be significantly increased if the significant union advantage is to be enjoyed by more working women.

Table 9.3: Union Coverage and Wages in Canada, 2015

	Average hourly wage				Union wage premium	
	Union coverage	All	Union	Non-union	$	%
All	30.6%	$23.57	$28.87	$23.57	$5.30	22.5%
Men	14.6%	$27.07	$29.81	$25.96	$3.85	14.8%
Women	16.0%	$23.26	$28.01	$20.99	$7.02	33.4%

Source: Statistics Canada, *Labour Force Survey* Estimates, CANSIM Table 282-0074.

Unionization among racialized workers is lower than for the Canadian workforce as a whole. Between 1998 and 2003, the unionization rate among racialized workers averaged about 22 percent, well below the 30 percent overall average, with the unionization rate being about the same for racialized women and racialized men. This is significant as unions have a positive impact upon employment outcomes, including closing the wage gap between racialized workers and other Canadians, particularly among men (Cheung 2006; Reitz and Verma 2003).

Table 9.4 illustrates the impact of union coverage on the wages of visible minority workers in 2009. As the table shows, the union wage premium is higher for visible minority workers, at 28.9 percent, as compared to 20.7 percent for workers who are not a visible minority. The union wage premium was particularly great for women, with unionized visible minority women earning a wage 45.6 percent higher than non-unionized visible minority women.

Although unions raise wages for racialized workers, the union wage premium is less than for other workers, and there is a larger racialized gap in unionized workplaces than in the non-union sector. This is probably mainly due to differences in the distribution of racialized workers by sector and occupation, and a relative concentration of unionized racialized workers in lower-paid sectors and jobs. Many racialized workers are relatively recent immigrants, meaning that relatively few are workers with long job tenure. Racialized workers are greatly under-represented in skilled blue-collar jobs and in teaching jobs, both of which are highly unionized occupations. While unions have little direct control over who is hired, some have pushed for more inclusive recruiting and formal employment equity procedures. The racialized pay gap among unionized workers may also reflect lack of sufficient attention to pay and employment equity for racialized workers in collective bargaining.

While working-age persons with disabilities are greatly under-represented in the workforce, the unionization rate for the minority of workers with disabilities who do work on a full-year basis is about the same as for the workforce as a whole. This is probably because workers with disabilities are most likely to find jobs in public and social services and in large firms, where employment equity programs

Table 9.4: Union Impact on Hourly Wages of Visible Minority Workers, 2009

	Visible minority	Not a visible minority
Total	$19.87	$23.14
Covered by a union	$24.10	$26.31
Not covered	$18.70	$21.79
Union premium	$5.40	$4.52
As a %	28.9%	20.7%
Men		
Covered by a union	$25.52	$27.11
Not covered	$21.71	$24.41
Union premium	$3.81	$2.70
As a %	17.5%	11%
Women		
Covered by a union	$22.76	$25.52
Not covered	$15.63	$19.05
Union premium	$7.13	$6.47
As a %	45.6%	33%

Source: Gender and Work Database, York University. Data from Survey of Income and Labour Dynamics (SLID), 2009, Table UN SLID-C5.

are most likely to be in place. Again, unionization helps close the pay gap between people with and without disabilities, and has particularly large impacts on the pay of lower-paid women with disabilities (CCSD 2004).

Unions Provide Much Greater Access to Non-Wage Benefits

In Canada, there are very significant gaps in public programs covering health and welfare issues. Public pensions do provide a minimum income in retirement, but maximum benefits from Old Age Security, plus the Canada/Quebec Pension Plan, fall far below what most pension experts see as reasonable wage replacement levels for average and higher-income workers. Unlike in the U.S., doctor and hospital services are covered by public health care, but this still leaves dental care, drugs, and other services to be paid for privately. Only very limited life and disability insurance is provided through public programs. While advocating broader public programs in all of these areas, unions have also traditionally filled the gap by negotiating employer-provided benefits (sometimes on a cost-shared basis).

A good pension and benefits package can easily make up 20 percent or more of the total compensation package, and this is rising fast with the growing costs of drug plans. Most union pension plans are defined benefit plans, which replace earnings with a guaranteed percentage of previous earnings. Such plans are far superior to RRSPs, since expenses are much lower and there is no uncertainty.

The impact of unions on benefits is far greater than on wages, particularly in smaller firms. As shown in Table 9.5, unionized workers are much more likely to be covered by a medical or dental plan. In addition, virtually all large pension plans in Canada represent the savings of unionized workers, and typically only a small layer of non-union workers are covered by employer-sponsored pension plans. Only one-third of non-union workers are covered by pension plans, and many of these are managers and other excluded workers covered by public sector and large unionized company plans. Pension coverage is extremely rare (and rapidly declining) in the non-union private sector outside very large firms. There has likely been some slippage of pension coverage among both union and non-union workers in recent years, but the very strong union advantage in the pension and benefits area persists (Informetrica 2007a).

Unions are associated with high benefits coverage mainly because this has been given a very high priority in bargaining. Also, some employers recognize that good benefit plans help retain workers. Not all newly unionized workers manage to gain pension and benefits coverage, but the vast majority of new plans are initiated through collective bargaining. Of course, union members differ in their priorities, with younger members with children being most concerned with health benefits, and older workers being most concerned with pensions. Workplace pensions mean that younger workers often gain significant pension entitlements long before they start thinking about this as a serious issue. Unions have sometimes facilitated benefits coverage as well by providing the means for smaller employers to join with larger groups. Construction unions typically directly sponsor pension plans for members who move from employer to employer.

From the point of view of union members, union jobs are good jobs because they generally provide for a decent pension in retirement, and protection against the costs of ill health and disability. However, it also has to be recognized that private benefit plans are expensive and come at the cost of foregone current wages, and

Table 9.5: Benefits Coverage: Union vs. Non-union, 2009

	Medical plan	Dental plan
All employees	61.8%	58.5%
Unionized	82.7%	78.3%
Non-unionized	53.2%	50.4%

Source: Gender and Work Database, York University. Data from Survey of *Income and Labour Dynamics* (SLID), 2009.

have to be paid for out of the total employer wage bill. In some ways, bargaining for income and social security at the workplace is also a second-best solution to public programs, such as good public pensions and public health care. This is particularly the case when jobs become more unstable. The rapid growth of health benefit costs in particular has become a very acrimonious factor in collective bargaining, leading the labour movement to strongly advocate the extension of public health care insurance to prescription drugs.

Unions Improve Job Security and Working Conditions

Unionized workers enjoy greater job security than non-unionized workers. In 2001, 9 percent of men and women non-union workers experienced an involuntary job separation, meaning that they were laid off or dismissed, whereas just 5.5 percent of unionized men and 2.6 percent of unionized women experienced such a separation.[3] This difference reflects the fact that unionized workplaces tend to be either in the public sector, or larger and more stable than small businesses in the private sector. Individual union members also have greater-than-average job security because of the norm of seniority in layoffs, which protects workers who have been in a specific job longer. Unionized members are less likely to be dismissed because of formal grievance procedures, and are also much less likely to quit their jobs. Unionized workplaces thus tend to be more stable, though many have shut down or experienced layoffs due to economic restructuring.

Only limited information is available on the impact of unions on workplace conditions due to a lack of regular government surveys. One might expect that, other things being equal, unions would help improve conditions at work. However, it is also the case that a higher-than-average proportion of unionized workers are employed in jobs with unsocial work schedules (shift work, night work), in jobs with dirty and dangerous working conditions (e.g., exposure to noise, poor air and fumes, dust), and in jobs that are very stressful in terms of the pace and intensity of work and long hours. Manufacturing, resources, and construction jobs, as well as many jobs in social services, can be very stressful and demanding. Surveys suggest that there is little overall difference between union and non-union workers in terms of perceived job stress, though unions may well be making some difference in very demanding workplaces.

In the area of working time, union members are much more likely to be paid for overtime hours than non-union members (though unpaid overtime is on the increase in unionized public services). Some union members work a lot of paid overtime, particularly in blue-collar jobs. Because of the nature of unionized jobs, unions have little impact on the overall incidence of shift work and night work in sectors like manufacturing and public services. About one-third of both union and non-union workers do not work a regular daytime schedule, but work evenings, nights, or weekends, or on an on-call basis. Overall, however, union work schedules are generally more stable and predictable, and there is often premium pay for unsocial hours. More social hours, such as regular day and non-weekend shifts, may be available to higher-seniority workers in unionized workplaces, even where work is organized on a shift basis. As discussed above, some progress has also been made in securing more stability and certainty in the working hours of unionized part-time workers.

Unions and Training

Unions commonly bargain education and training provisions, including paid and unpaid time off for training, apprenticeship programs, and provisions for on-the-job training to help workers deal with technological and organizational change (for example, see Chapter 3, Box 3.2). About one-half of all unionized workers enjoy some rights to training through their collective agreements. Craft unions, such as the construction trades and some industrial unions, have played a major role in the development and delivery of apprenticeship programs, and some unions provide direct skills training to their members. Indeed, unions are increasingly engaged in workplace learning activities, sometimes independently and sometimes in partnership with employers. A number of unions also actively participate in joint employer-union sectoral training bodies. Generally, unions promote training that gives workers formal, portable qualifications, as opposed to training that is very narrowly geared to the needs of a single workplace. In addition, the union wage and benefits advantage pushes employers to invest in work processes that raise productivity and thus skill requirements, which are generally filled by training the current workforce. Data from the *Adult Education and Training Survey* and several studies show that—as a result—unionization helps significantly reduce the major gap in available training opportunities between well-educated workers and those with less formal qualifications (Livingstone and Raykov 2005).

Unions and Political Action

Unions also often engage in various forms of political action, which can range from participating in demonstrations on issues of social policy and social justice, to government lobbying, to formally endorsing political candidates and political parties. Commonly, a distinction is made between business unions—which focus on the interests of their own members in the workplace—and social unions—which seek to broaden the labour movement, to find and build common cause among a broad range of workers in the job market, and to engage in collective political action (Ross 2012). While some unions take a narrow focus on the economic (wages, pensions, benefits) concerns of their members, other unions engage in aspects of social movement unionism, characterized by a commitment to more radical social and economic change through mass mobilization and political action above and beyond electoral politics. This form of unionism connects trade unions to broader social struggles, including those over housing, social services, education, health care, and social citizenship rights for marginalized groups (Seidman 1994). These

Box 9.2: Canadian Labour Congress—What We Do
By Canadian Labour Congress

We are the largest labour organization in Canada, bringing together dozens of national and international unions, provincial and territorial federations of labour and community-based labour councils to represent 3.3 million workers.

For more than 50 years, we have provided research and policy leadership on issues that impact the everyday lives of all working people such as wages, workplace health and safety, pensions and retirement security, social and economic justice and equality, access to public healthcare and childcare.

We advocate in support of our policy goals in the courts and in Parliament, and through public education and political mobilization. Internationally, the CLC is the voice of Canadian workers at the United Nations through the International Labour Organization (the ILO).

Many of the things first won by unions are enjoyed by all workers today—such as minimum wages, overtime pay, workplace safety standards, maternity and parental leave, vacation pay, and protection from discrimination and harassment.

Canadian labour has played a big role in making Canada a better place to work and live. Canada's working class became Canada's middle class as improved wages raised the standard of living. In addition to fair pay, workers and their unions have secured benefits from employers and governments, which has meant greater income security and a better quality of life.

***

Here's how we work to improve Canada for everyone.

Research and analysis
Our economists and researchers are nationally recognized for their skills and expertise, and produce in-depth analysis on issues such as working conditions, health and safety, wages and benefits, healthcare, pensions and retirement security, immigration, training, employment insurance and social and economic equality.

Advocacy
We advocate politically for policies and programs that improve the lives of all Canadians, such as the creation of better and more secure jobs, better public pension plans and retirement security, a stronger public health care system and affordable and accessible child care.

We advocate in Parliament and in the courts to advance legislation that improves the day-to-day lives of all Canadians, such as workplace safety and collective bargaining rights and employment equity.

Community organizing
Working through our labour councils and federations of labour we organize community events such as town hall meetings and rallies to listen to the challenges

facing hard working Canadians and to promote positive social change. We also work through our labour councils to ensure workers' interests are a priority for municipal councils.

Partnering with the United Way

We also partner with organizations on the ground in your communities, such as the United Way in campaigns that raise money for local community and social services and with parents working for improved child care services.

Anti-racism and human rights

We work with Aboriginal workers to strengthen their voices and presence in the Canadian labour movement. We advance women's equality. We promote the full participation of people with disabilities in the union movement and their communities. We fight racism and promote the human rights and equality rights of racialized workers. We also work to end discrimination on the basis of sexual orientation and gender identity.

Education

Our education programs feature state-of-the-art courses in workplace health and safety, fighting racism and discrimination, media and public relations, economics, campaign management, human rights and global solidarity, as well as workplace representation and union steward training.

International solidarity

We also work with unions and workers around the world to advance workers' rights, promote ethical trade, end exploitation of workers, stop violence against trade unionists, and strengthen the fight against HIV and AIDS.

Our structure

The CLC is a democratic organization, driven from the ground up by the needs and aspirations of Canadian workers.

Every three years, thousands of delegates from across the country meet at a weeklong convention—one of the largest regular gatherings of working people in the world. These rank-and-file union members debate issues and adopt policies that set the CLC's agenda. They also elect the CLC leadership by secret ballot: the President, the Secretary-Treasurer and two Executive Vice-Presidents.

Between conventions, the CLC is governed by its Canadian Council, an executive board composed of the Officers, the leaders of every union affiliated to the CLC and the leaders of the provincial and territorial federations of labour. To ensure the broadest possible representation, additional seats on the Canadian Council are filled by women, workers of colour, youth, Aboriginal workers, people with disabilities, retirees and LGBT workers.

Source: Canadian Labour Congress. 2015. *What We Do*. http://canadianlabour.ca/about-clc/what-we-do.

strategies also include efforts to form connections to broader communities and constituencies through coalition-based organizing (Tattersall 2010).

Almost all major unions in Canada belong to the Canadian Labour Congress (CLC). The main exceptions are two labour centrals in Quebec—but not the Quebec Federation of Labour, which is the largest Quebec central labour body—and some smaller professional unions. The CLC tries to make sure that its member unions do not fight each other for members, a practice known as raiding. Unlike central labour bodies in many other countries, the CLC generally leaves collective bargaining and union organizing activities to its affiliated unions. The primary activities of the CLC (and its affiliated provincial federations of labour and local labour councils) involve advancing the interests of members and all workers at the political level, waging broad-based labour movement campaigns, providing services such as research and education to affiliated unions, and representing Canadian workers internationally through the International Labour Organization (ILO) (see Box 9.2).

The Impact of Unions on the Economy and Labour Markets

Studies show that countries with very high levels of collective bargaining coverage have much less pay inequality than lower-union-density countries, such as the U.S., Britain, and Canada. In the social democratic countries of Scandinavia and the social-market countries, such as Germany and the Netherlands, collective bargaining coverage is very high (and generally quite stable) because of high union membership in combination with the de facto or sometimes legal extension of agreements on a sectoral or regional basis. Wage floors set by bargaining protect the great majority of non-professional and managerial workers, including most part-time and even temporary workers. Also, unions and legislatively mandated works councils mean that there are strong elements of joint workplace governance over such issues as training and working conditions in these countries.

Countries with high levels of bargaining coverage have relatively equal wages and high wage floors, so that the incidence of low pay and earnings inequality are much lower than in Canada (OECD 1996, 2006b). In 2012, over one in five (21.8 percent) full-time workers in Canada was low paid—defined as earning less than two-thirds of the median national full-time wage. This figure is much higher than in Denmark (7.6 percent), though notably lower than the United States (25.3 percent) (OECD 2016a). The minimum earnings gap between the top and bottom 10 percent of workers is about three to one in the Scandinavian countries, compared to about four to one in the U.S. and Canada. This is mainly because of institutional differences, notwithstanding common exposure to the forces of globalization and technological and organizational change.

Most mainstream economists see unions as almost exclusively concerned with raising the wages of their members, which they claim distorts wages as compared

Box 9.3: After Paris—A Global Movement for Climate Jobs
By Jonathan Nancy

The Paris Climate Talks

Many have hailed the result of the UN climate talks as a breakthrough, for two reasons. One: all of the countries of the world signed an agreement about climate change. Two: there are some good abstract hopes in that agreement.

But there are also concrete promises about emissions. Some countries have promised to cut emissions by a little in the next fifteen years. They may, or may not, keep their promises. Many more countries, with more emissions, have promised to increase their emissions by a lot. Taken together, these are promises to increase emissions every year between now and 2030. That's the bottom line.

What We Need to do Now

The good news is that we have a growing and increasingly radical global climate movement. And the organisations who think the agreement is a breakthrough also think it is only a beginning. In addition most people in the climate movement saw the result of Paris coming, so we do not have a demoralised movement.

As we return from Paris, it is clear that the leaders of all the countries in the world have failed us. They did so because nowhere did we have the political and social power to make them take decisive action on climate. So now we have to build that power, country by country. The only force we have on our side is seven billion people. We have to mobilise them.

This will not be an easy or quick task. We all know that. After all, we need cuts of 80% in global emissions, as soon as possible. That means deep changes in energy use and society.

Two kinds of campaigns will be central. One is fighting to leave the coal, gas and oil in the soil. There will be a global day of action against fossil fuels in May; national campaigns; local resistance to pipelines, new mines, new drilling, new power stations, extreme energy, fossil fuel sponsorship, and investments in fossil fuels.

The other kind of campaign will be to build an alternative. If we are to leave the fossil fuels in the ground, we have to do four things. We need to replace fossil fuels almost entirely with renewable energy. To do that we need renewable energy for all our electricity. We need a switch from cars to public transport, and almost all transport [to] run on renewable electricity. We need conversions of all homes and buildings to save energy, and then to heat and cool all buildings with renewable electricity. And we need to protect and extend the great forests.

We need to do thousands of other things, but those four things will make most of the difference. All that will take a lot of work—we estimate at least 120 million new jobs worldwide each year for 20 years. This is what we mean by "climate jobs"—jobs that have a direct effect in cutting greenhouse gas emissions.

Moreover, we want government climate jobs programs to ensure a retraining and a permanent job to anyone who loses a high carbon job during the transition. That is only fair, and if we don't do it we will split unions and communities.

***

Seven of the existing campaigns are built on strong union support. Four also have strong support from environmental groups. At Paris two of them took political steps forward. Jeremy Corbyn, the leader of the opposition Labour Party in Britain, publicly endorsed the British One Million Climate Jobs campaign at a rally of 800 people. And the Canadian campaign brought together an impressive coalition of organisations to press Trudeau's new government to hire 200,000 workers a year for five years, to cut Canadian emissions by 25% in 5 years.

***

Global Climate Jobs is the network of all the national climate campaigns. What we want to do is to build national climate jobs campaigns in as many countries as possible. There are two reasons. One is that the more of us there are across the world, the stronger we feel. The other reason is that the key breakthrough for a global solution will come when one country actually wins a government climate jobs program that provides very large numbers of new jobs and cuts emissions by 80% or more. After that, we will all be following a living example. So we need to try everywhere we can...

Source: Nancy, Jonathan. 2015, December 18. "After Paris—A Global Movement for Climate Jobs." *Global Climate Jobs*. https://globalclimatejobs.wordpress.com/2015/12/18/after-paris-a-global-movement-for-climate-jobs/.

to free-market levels. From this perspective, higher union wages force unionized employers to hire fewer workers, pushing more workers into competition for non-union jobs, thus forcing down non-union wages. However, the most authoritative surveys of the economic literature conclude that the positive impacts of unions in terms of reducing low pay and inequality and giving workers a voice in the workplace do not come at a significant economic price. Indeed, there is a strong argument to be made that unions promote economic prosperity as well as social justice. A major study by the World Bank on the economic impacts of unions (Aidt and Tzannatos 2003) found no relationship between union density and the economic or employment performance of countries. A major review of economic studies by the OECD also found no valid statistical relationship between trade union membership and the economic or employment performance of advanced industrial countries in the 1980s and 1990s. Union density is, overall, related neither to higher- nor to lower-than-average rates of unemployment or economic growth (OECD 1996).

The International Labour Organization argues that high employment growth and strong economic growth can be achieved in a very wide range of labour market settings. Studies by the ILO and others (Auer 2000; ILO 2003; Jackson 2000a) have shown that some countries with very high rates of union coverage, notably Denmark, the Netherlands, and Sweden, have also been able to achieve high levels of employment and strong rates of economic growth since the mid-1990s. At the firm level, at which most bargaining in Canada (and, increasingly, elsewhere) is conducted, it is also far from clear that the gains of unionization in terms of higher wages, more benefits, and better working conditions come at the price of fewer jobs. A key problem with the mainstream economic model is that unions do not bargain purely for higher wages without any concern for the jobs of their members. Some elements of the union advantage, such as paid time off the job and restrictions on unpaid overtime, actually increase employment. Research has found that newly organized firms (in the U.S.) are no more likely to go out of business over the long term than are firms in which unions lost representation elections (Dinardo and Lee 2002), and that unionized firms have similar closure and bankruptcy rates to other firms, controlling for other characteristics (Freeman and Kleiner 1999). As noted above, union wages have stagnated in Canada, strongly supporting the case that unions have not imposed major costs on employers.

The union wage premium may be higher than average in highly unionized sectors of the economy. If an industry is highly unionized, such that all employers pay the same union wage and benefit package, the union impact puts no single employer at a significant competitive disadvantage. If union wages are built into the cost structure of all employers, wages are taken out of the competitive equation, forcing firms to compete with one another on the basis of non-cost issues, such as quality and customer service. Indeed, some economists argue that strong unions are a force for positive competition, since they force firms to compete with one another on issues that are positive for consumers, but not negative from the workers' point of view. The high road of firm competition on the basis of high productivity, training, and the production of high-quality goods and services is often contrasted to the low road of competing on the basis of low wages and poor working conditions.

Conclusion

Arising out of class struggle during the early years of industrial capitalism, unions emerged to counter unilateral employer power in the capitalist workplace. Though the transformative power of unions is constrained by the legalistic system of labour relations in Canada, unions are nonetheless an important force for improving conditions inside and outside the workplace, including wages, non-wage benefits, and working conditions, and contribute toward creating a more equal distribution of wages across society. In the context of workplace and labour market change described in this book, however, unions face significant challenges in the struggle to improve work, as examined in the next chapter.

Recommended Reading

Behrens, Matthew, and the Canadian Foundation for Labour Rights. 2014. *Unions Matter: Advancing Democracy, Economic Equality, and Social Justice*. Toronto: Between the Lines.

Camfield, David. 2011. *Canadian Labour in Crisis: Reinventing the Workers' Movement*. Halifax: Fernwood.

Galarneau, Diane, and Thao Sohn. 2013. *Long-Term Trends in Unionization*. Ottawa: Statistics Canada.

Ross, Stephanie, Larry Savage, Errol Black, and Jim Silver. 2015. *Building a Better World: An Introduction to the Labour Movement in Canada*. 3rd Edition. Winnipeg: Fernwood.

Notes

1. Statistics Canada, CANSIM Table 282-0078. Accessed at: http://www5.statcan. gc.ca/cansim/a26?lang=eng&retrLang=eng&id=2820078&pattern=&csid=.
2. Statistics Canada, CANSIM Table 282-0073. Accessed at: http://www5.statcan. gc.ca/cansim/a26?lang=eng&retrLang=eng&id=2820073&pattern=&csid=.
3. Custom data from Statistics Canada, *Survey of Labour and Income Dynamics*, 2001.

CHAPTER 10

Workers' Movements in the New Millennium

Unions face enormous challenges in many advanced industrial countries. There can be little doubt that the power of unions to influence wages, benefits, and working conditions through collective bargaining has been eroded by corporate mobility in many industries, as well as by the hostility of both employers and neoliberal governments to unions in general. In the 1950s and 1960s, strong industrial unions in North America and Europe were able to take wages and labour conditions out of the competitive equation by ensuring that major employers in a specific sector, such as auto, steel, or rubber, provided the same basic conditions of employment. This ability to shape the economics of whole sectors has been greatly eroded by increased international trade and by the deregulation and privatization of sectors like transportation, communications, and health, which were once insulated to at least some degree from the forces of competition. A traditional key bastion of union strength—male blue-collar workers in manufacturing—has been greatly undercut by the shift to a post-industrial, knowledge-based economy, and the restructuring of global production. More recently, public sector unions have been challenged as governments increasingly seek to contract out and privatize the delivery of public services.

As unions have declined in numbers, their political influence has weakened compared to that of employers, and the legislative climate has become much more hostile. In some countries, notably the U.S., unions have been marginalized to a remarkable degree. American unions now represent only one in nine workers, compared to about one in three in the 1960s, and it has become extremely difficult for them to recruit new members due to strong employer resistance and weak labour laws (Bureau of Labor Statistics 2016). In Britain, union strength has also declined greatly, from about one-half to one-quarter of the workforce (DBIS 2016). Even in continental Europe, where the majority of workers are still covered by collective agreements negotiated by unions and employers, individual trade union membership has tended to decline, including in the very high-union-density Scandinavian countries (see Table 10.1 below).[1] Canada has been a modest exception, with the overall unionization rate declining more gradually than elsewhere, holding firm at around 30 percent through the 1990s and 2000s.

Unions have been forced to confront major changes, not just in the economy, but also in the wider society. The emergence of a more diverse and more highly educated workforce—which is now almost equally divided between women and men, and includes many racialized workers—challenges labour organizations to become more inclusive and to shed legacies that include institutionalized racism and sexism. Unions were once a powerful expression of tightly knit working-class communities, but old solidarities and forms of class consciousness declined with industrial change, new immigration patterns, and the feminization of the workforce, all of which began even in the early days of postwar prosperity. What workers expect of unions has also changed, with quality of work and work-life balance issues becoming more important than the traditional (and still important) emphasis on wages and benefits.

Yet, even if employers and governments have become more hostile and the workforce has changed dramatically, unions can and often do adapt to change. Unions change in order to survive and because of pressures from members and activists. The alternative to union decline is union renewal, and there is no shortage of workers in today's new economy who are still attracted to unions, and no shortage of active and engaged union members who want to build a vital labour movement to address the pressing problems of today's workplaces. Against the gradual trend of declining union density, innovations are occurring within the labour movement, which might represent and spark a new move forward. In addition to change within unions, there is growing worker organizing and activism outside and alongside trade unions, as the ranks of non-unionized precarious workers undertake campaigns to improve their conditions of work. This kind of organizing may lead to new forms of worker representation in today's economy.

This chapter looks at some of the challenges facing Canadian unions as a result of economic restructuring and the changing workforce. It analyzes trends in union coverage, especially between women and men and the public and private sectors, and details the sharp decline of unionization among blue-collar men and the much lower but more stable coverage in private services. It concludes with an overview of the process of union change and renewal in Canada, and also discusses some examples of campaigns undertaken by non-unionized workers and the emergence of new forms of worker organizing. Overall, the aim of the chapter is to assess the forces that are challenging the labour movement and the array of strategies that are emerging through worker organizing to counter the neoliberal push toward precariousness.

Trends in Union Density

Union density or coverage refers to the proportion of all employees who are covered by a collective agreement. (Note that a small proportion of workers, usually lower-level supervisors, are not union members, but are still covered by a collective agreement.) Canadian unions today represent about one in three workers (30.4 percent in 2015), though only 16.7 percent of private-sector workers (Statistics Canada 2015c). Table 10.1 indicates high variability in unionization rates in industrialized labour markets, with the U.S. at the low end and the Scandinavian countries showing the highest rates.

Table 10.1: National Trade Union Density, 2013 (percentage)

Country	1999	2005	2013
Canada	28	27.7	27.2
U.S.	13.4	12	10.8
U.K.	30.1	28.4	25.4
Denmark	74	70.7	66.8
Sweden	80.6	76.5	67.7
Australia	25.4	22.3	17
New Zealand	21.7	20.9	19.4

Source: OECD.Stat, Trade Union Density.

Unlike in the U.S., the absolute number of union members in Canada has continued to increase, to a new high of more than 4.5 million union members (ESDC 2015). However, while far from marginal and still a powerful force in many sectors of the economy, union density in Canada has fallen quite sharply from a peak of almost 40 percent in the mid-1980s (Jackson 2006b). In the private sector, less than 1 percent of all non-unionized workers are currently organized into unions each year. While many workers join unions each year because they are hired into already unionized workplaces, new organizing at the current rate is insufficient to stop future decline.

Table 10.2 provides data on union coverage in 1997, 2007, and 2015. Union density overall has fallen slightly since the late 1990s. The decline has been gradual rather than sudden, and was concentrated in the private sector, particularly in the manufacturing sector. The sharp decline from the peak in the 1980s slowed with the economic recovery that began in the mid-1990s and has remained largely stable at around 30 percent since.

The decline in union coverage has been much more pronounced among full-time as compared to part-time workers, though the rate of unionization among part-time workers is much lower than that of full-time workers. Also notable is the very low rate of unionization among young workers (15.3 percent), reflecting the fact that young people entering the workforce have tended to be hired mainly into non-unionized jobs. Table 10.2 shows a large drop in men's unionization rates, as compared to women's rates, which are much more stable. The coverage rate for men is now under 30 percent, down from a high of close to 50 percent in the mid-1980s. The rate for women, after rising rapidly though the 1970s and early 1980s, has slipped much less, and the difference in union coverage between women and men has been reversed, whereby in 2006, for the first time, more women than men belonged to unions.

Table 10.2: Trends in Union Coverage (percentage), 1997–2015

	1997	2007	2015
All	33.7	31.5	30.4
Men	35.2	31.2	28.9
Women	32.1	31.8	31.9
Public	74.6	74.5	74.8
Private	21.3	18.7	16.7
Full-time	36.0	33.0	31.9
Part-time	23.6	24.5	23.7
Age 15–24	13.0	15.0	15.3
Newfoundland/Labrador	40.7	37.7	37.8
PEI	29.1	30.0	32.3
Nova Scotia	30.2	29.4	30.8
New Brunswick	29.9	28.2	28.6
Quebec	41.5	39.7	39.3
Ontario	29.8	28.2	27
Manitoba	37.6	37.1	35.4
Saskatchewan	36.0	34.8	33.3
Alberta	25.8	23.8	22.1
British Columbia	36.3	32.1	30
Utilities	72.1	70.8	64.5
Transportation/warehousing	45.2	42.9	38.2
Construction	32.4	32.6	32
Manufacturing	36.3	29.9	25.7
Trade	14.8	14.3	13.4
Accommodation/food	8.6	8.2	6.5
Finance/insurance/real estate	10.4	11.2	9.3
Education services	73.5	70.7	72.6
Health/social assistance	55.7	55.5	54.7
Public administration	71.4	72.4	72.4

Source: Statistics Canada, *Labour Force Survey* Estimates, CANSIM Tables 282-0078 and 282-0024.

Stable union coverage for women compared to the continued decline among men arises mainly from the fact that women are more likely than men to work in public and social services, where the level of union representation is much higher than in the private sector. As shown by Table 10.2, the majority of all union members are employed in the public sector rather than in the private sector. Union coverage is much higher in the public sector (74.8 percent, compared to 16.7 percent in the private sector), and women in the public sector are even more likely than men to be union members (75.8 percent vs. 72.3 percent). Union coverage in public and social services (public administration, education, and health and social services) has remained high. More than two-thirds of unionized women (68 percent) work in the public sector (defined as direct government employment, plus employment in directly government-funded institutions, such as schools, universities, colleges, and hospitals), and less than one-third work in the private sector. By contrast, 60 percent of unionized men work in the private sector.

As shown in Table 10.2, union coverage is very high in both education (72.6 percent) and public administration (72.4 percent), and also high (54.7 percent) in health and social assistance. Education and health services make up a large and increasing share of total employment, and jobs in these sectors are predominantly

Figure 10.1: Unionization Rates (%) of Employed Individuals Aged 17–64, 1981–2012

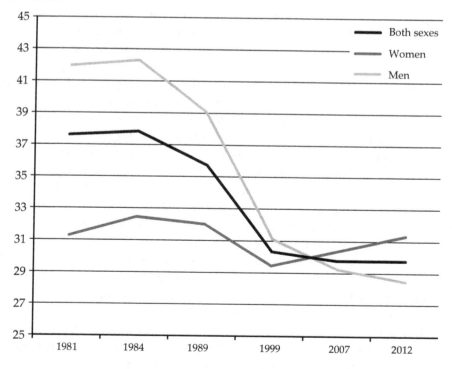

Source: Diane Galarneau and Thao Sohn. 2013. *Long-Term Trends in Unionization.* Ottawa: Statistics Canada.

held by women. Many social services not directly delivered by governments—such as publicly subsidized child care centres, elder care services, and long-term care homes—are often unionized, and the broader public sector has been a key arena for new union organizing.

In sum, the large public and social services labour force has continued to be a key bastion of union strength, partly because the direct public sector is now stable in size, and partly because of union strength in private and non-profit, often contracted-out services, such as long-term care, child care, and home care. Public services unions, such as the Canadian Union of Public Employees, the Public Service Alliance of Canada, and provincial government workers unions (united at the national level in the National Union of Public and General Employees), have actively organized within and outside the formal public sector and have had notable success, particularly among women workers. Some formerly private-sector unions have also organized in this area. For example, one of the largest locals of the United Steelworkers consists of support staff at the University of Toronto. It should be noted that the unionization rate is also very high, at over 70 percent, among part-time workers in public services, contrasting sharply to a unionization rate of around 13 percent among part-time workers in the private sector.

It was sometimes the case in the past that public-sector unions gained voluntary recognition from government employers, but the overall labour relations climate in public services has become much more like the business sector in recent years. In the direct public sector, wage settlements for unionized workers have generally not exceeded private-sector settlements since the early 1990s, despite the enduring myth that public-sector workers enjoy greater bargaining power. Privatization and contracting out of many services, from refuse collection to elder care, means that public-sector wages come under competitive pressure and that employers funded from the public purse have to compete with one another for contracts, putting downward pressure on broader public-sector wages and benefits. Continuing high union density in the direct public sector and broader public sector reflects not so much insulation from market forces as union success in efforts to keep contracted-out jobs unionized, and success in new organizing efforts. For example, the Canadian Union of Postal Workers has organized rural mail route carriers even though they were considered not to be direct employees, and many personal support workers and other staff in long-term care homes working for private employers have been unionized in recent years.

Looking at longer-term changes within the private sector, there has been a marked decline in union density in the traditional bastions of male blue-collar unionism. Density has fallen from about one-half to well under one-third of all workers in manufacturing since the mid-1980s. This is still a big enough sector for the drop to have had a major impact on overall union density as well as on union density in the total private sector. About one-third of the fall of private-sector union density since the late 1980s is explained by the fall within manufacturing. As shown in Table 10.3, in 2014, just 9.1 percent of the unionized workforce was in manufacturing, down from 18.1 percent in 1997, and well down from the 1980s.

Table 10.3: Composition of Union Membership, 1997–2014

Percentage of all union members who are:	1997	2007	2014
Men	54.7%	50.0%	47.9%
Women	45.3%	50.0%	52.1%
Public sector	51.7%	54.4%	57.8%
Private sector	48.3%	45.6%	42.2%
Part-time	87.1%	86.2%	14.4%
Full-time	12.9%	13.8%	85.6%
Age 15–24	6.4%	8.3%	8.0%
Age 25–44	56.7%	46.7%	45.9%
Age 45+	36.9%	45.0%	46.1%
Goods	26.4%	22.4%	19.5%
Services	73.6%	77.6%	80.5%
Manufacturing	18.1%	12.9%	9.1%
Total number of union coverage	3,843,900	4,472,400	4,587,000
Public sector	1,979,100	2,437,900	2,651,100
Private sector	1,855,800	2,034,400	1,935,900

Source: Statistics Canada, *Labour Force Survey* Estimates, CANSIM Tables 282-0020, 282-0024, and 282-0078.

The decline has been pervasive across most subsectors and occupations within manufacturing, and is almost certainly closely linked to a huge turnover in manufacturing establishments since the mid-1980s and the shift of jobs to small and non-union plants. For example, a lot of the job growth in the auto industry has been in non-unionized assembly plants (Toyota and Honda) and in non-unionized parts suppliers (for example, Magna). Widespread industrial restructuring that began in the 1980s likely drove down union density through a combination of large job losses due to plant closures and layoffs, and much greater employer hostility to new organizing in a highly competitive environment. Under free trade (beginning in 1988), workers in Canadian manufacturing were more directly exposed to competition from mainly non-union, lower-cost American and Mexican manufacturing operations. The major shift of manufacturing production to Asia, especially China, has produced even more severe competitive pressures on non-resource-based manufacturing, and consequent pressures on the wages, benefits, and working conditions of unionized workers. Rather little successful new organizing activity took place in the manufacturing sector in the period of recovery from the mid-1990s to 2002, while job losses since then have disproportionately been in unionized plants. Generally speaking, unionized manufacturing workers have seen only very limited gains in wages and benefits. As in the United States, in this context of declining union power, some unions in the manufacturing sector have moved closer to a workplace partnership relationship with employers, and some have adopted two-tiered wages and benefits systems as management has pushed for greater flexibility and cost-savings through collective bargaining.

There has also been a marked decline in union density in other industries that have undergone similar restructuring—primary industries, transportation, and, to a lesser extent, communications and utilities. Deregulation saw the rise of competition from lower-cost non-union airlines and telecommunications companies, forcing unions at union airlines and telephone companies onto the defensive. Many large, unionized companies have contracted out non-core functions to smaller, non-union suppliers, reducing overall union membership and putting intense competitive pressures on their suppliers. By contrast, union coverage in construction has been quite stable at about one-third since the late 1980s. The industrial construction sector remains highly unionized in some provinces, and construction union employment has benefited from the housing and commercial building boom in some cities. Many of the skilled trades have been in high demand, and the pay premium for unionized workers is paid for in significant part by higher skills and higher productivity. Construction unions are typically based on crafts or specific occupations, and the union often plays a major role in directing members to jobs and providing training, pensions, and benefits. Craft unions in construction and in the cultural sector (e.g., unions representing actors, writers, and film technicians) can promote better wages, benefits, and access to training for workers who typically move frequently from one job to another. Their resilience suggests that a very old model of union representation remains quite relevant today.

Union coverage has always been very low in private consumer services like stores, hotels, and restaurants, as well as in financial and business services, but seems to have held up much better than in the traditional high-union-density, blue-collar industries since the late 1980s. As shown in Table 10.2, coverage is low (13.4 percent in 2015) in trade, but fairly stable. Many workers in large grocery stores, alcoholic beverage outlets, and a few department stores are represented by unions. Coverage is very low (6.5 percent), but has always been very low in accommodation and food services (i.e., restaurants and hotels), though many big-city hotels and a few restaurants are organized. Coverage is extremely low in business services, though unions have organized some groups of workers like security guards and building cleaners in recent years. Unions are very weak in the financial sector outside of Quebec, but some insurance companies and a few bank branches and credit unions are unionized. Unlike some European countries, Canada has a very weak tradition of union representation among professional and skilled white-collar workers in the private sector, a relatively fast-growing part of the workforce. Since the mid-1990s, union density has been quite steady, but at low levels in private services. This probably reflects a combination of stable employment in some traditionally unionized sectors and some successful new organizing more or less matching job growth. Union organizing is especially difficult in high-worker-turnover sectors, and many unions in private services, such as the United Food and Commercial Workers Union, typically organize quite a high proportion of their total membership each year. Private service sector organizing has taken place predominantly among lower-paid and more precariously employed workers, especially women and recent immigrants.

Turning to geographical trends in union coverage, Ontario and Alberta, where national job growth was relatively concentrated over the past decade, experienced larger-than-average declines in density from already well below-average levels. Traditionally, union density has been low in the Maritime provinces. In 2015, the highest-union-density provinces were Quebec (39.3 percent), Newfoundland and Labrador (37.8 percent), Manitoba (35.4 percent), Saskatchewan (33.3 percent), and Prince Edward Island (32.3 percent).

Forces Driving Union Density

Canadian union representation is usually achieved through a labour board's certification of a union to represent workers in a particular workplace. Almost always, unionization is a collective rather than an individual choice, and it continues unless and until there is a vote to decertify the union. Most union members become members by being hired into a job in an already unionized workplace rather than by actively joining or supporting a union campaign to organize a non-union workplace. Changing union density is a function of three things: changes in employment in already certified workplaces as a result of establishment closures, layoffs, and new hiring; changes in employment in non-union workplaces; and the rate at which non-union workplaces are organized into unions. Unfortunately, it is impossible to fully separate out these factors.

At a broader level, the growth of union membership will be strongly influenced by structural change in the economy, which influences the relative growth of employment by industrial sector, by occupation, by firm or establishment size, and by form of employment. This is especially true in Canada given that union density varies a lot along all of these dimensions. Union membership is still concentrated among full-time workers in larger private-sector firms in resources, manufacturing, transportation, and utilities, as well as in the public sector. Union density will also be influenced by the changing composition of the workforce, especially by age, gender, and race, which is overlaid upon the changing industrial and occupational mix.

Declining unionization has often been associated with the shift to a post-industrial economy, with a shrinking share of blue-collar jobs, and a rising share of private services jobs, especially for women, in growing but low-union-density sectors like business and consumer services. Structural change has brought into question the continued relevance of the kinds of labour laws and unions that emerged in the postwar era, when a high proportion of the workforce could be found in large industrial workplaces like steel mills and auto assembly plants. The system of labour relations and the form of trade unionism that developed in this context were conducive to organizing industrial workers in large workplaces, but do not easily support organizing workers in small workplaces or in very precarious forms of employment. Industrial unionism also often wins little support from well-educated professionals in the private sector. In the contemporary context, unions thus face the risk of being squeezed by two of the fastest-growing areas of employment.

Other forces of change working against unions include the shifting balance of power between labour and employers in workplaces and the labour market as a result of globalization, as well as the neoliberal restructuring of public and social services through privatization and contracting out. Density is also influenced by the attitudes of individual workers toward unions, and by the capacity of unions and the labour movement to attract and mobilize the unorganized, as well as to retain the loyalties and commitment of the already organized. At a broad, cultural level, collective organizing is undermined by the shift to individualism engendered through decades of neoliberalism.

The idea that declining union density is strongly associated with the changing industrial and occupational composition of employment has some elements of truth, given the extent to which deindustrialization, privatization, and the growth of knowledge-based work have eroded former bastions of union strength. However, as was shown earlier in this book, the total employment share of blue-collar men who traditionally supported unions has not fallen dramatically since the late 1980s. Employment in high-union-density public and social services has been growing as a share of all jobs, and will continue to do so. Looking at sectors of traditional union weakness, it is true that sales and service jobs are a big share of employment, but this has been the case for a long time. One big change that has indeed taken place, however, has been the shift of jobs to business services, partly in professional, scientific, and technical services, which employ mainly white-collar, very infrequently unionized workers. That said, business services include many lower-wage occupations, such as building cleaners and security guards, who have joined unions.

Without denying the long-term trend toward higher-skilled jobs (at least as measured by education) or the emergence of new economy information technology occupations, it is hard to see why occupational and industrial shifts should have had a big negative impact on overall union density. A technically sophisticated analysis of the decline in union density from 1984 to 1998 indeed finds that shifts of employment by industry and by occupation, taken together, have had only a modest impact on the unionization rate, and that the decline is explained more by downward shifts within industries and occupations (Riddell and Riddell 1998). For example, the decline of unions within formerly strong union sectors like manufacturing and blue-collar jobs explains more of the fall in union density than a shift of jobs away from manufacturing and blue-collar jobs. That said, unions will obviously have to reach out to more highly skilled new economy workers, as well as to low-paid private services workers, if continued private-sector decline is to be halted. A few public-sector unions have attempted to organize private-sector professionals, but with limited success to date.

It is often also believed that unions have become weaker because of the decline of large private-sector workplaces and the rise of small business. It is indeed true that the rate of unionization in the private sector is much higher in large than small establishments. About 40 percent of workers in firms with more than 500 workers are unionized, and very large industrial operations are still highly likely to be unionized. It is very difficult to organize and represent workers in smaller businesses under the labour relations practices that generally apply in North America. One problem is that union dues from small workplaces provide less incentive for unions to organize the workers in them. Another is that small- and medium-sized employers tend to be especially hostile to unions. Most importantly, it is very difficult for unions to improve wages, benefits, and working conditions in very competitive sectors dominated by smaller firms, particularly for occupations with potentially large labour pools. High union density in private services in some Northern European countries is made possible mainly by sector-wide agreements, at least at the community or regional level, rather than by North American–style decentralized certification and bargaining. For example, many Scandinavian and German hotel workers are covered by contracts that are bargained centrally and cover almost all hotel workers, placing no single hotel at a competitive advantage, and extending union conditions and protections to workers who are dispersed across many workplaces. Where unions in Canada have gained a foothold among smaller employers, as in the housing construction industry in Toronto or the child care sector in Quebec, it has often been by developing sector-wide rather than employer-by-employer collective agreements and bargaining structures.

All that said, a shift from large to small workplaces does not explain why Canadian union density has declined. In the late 1990s, about 40 percent of private-sector workers were employed in very small workplaces with fewer than 20 workers, and about 30 percent were employed in establishments of more than 100 workers, but this was also the case in the mid-1980s (Drolet and Morrissette 1998). Employment has actually shifted somewhat away from small workplaces. In retailing, for example, there has been a shift from small stores to superstores. In financial services, large call centres have replaced local bank branches. In food services, a lot of food preparation has been contracted out from restaurants to large food processors. If anything, recent union organizing successes have been relatively concentrated in small rather than large establishments, and union density has risen from low levels in small workplaces while falling in larger workplaces.

Changes in the form of employment have also probably had little impact on union density. Self-employment and part-time employment have become more common, but union density has also increased among part-time workers, even in the private sector, since the mid-1990s. The incidence of very low-tenure jobs has not increased since the mid-1980s, and average job tenure has increased. None of this is to deny that many Canadian workers, particularly women, youth, and racialized workers, are employed in precarious and insecure jobs in smaller workplaces, which makes union organization extremely difficult under prevailing labour laws. However, putting all of the emphasis on structural change as a source of union decline, without recognizing the centrality of the changing power dynamics of the workplace through globalization and neoliberalism, can greatly exaggerate its impact.

Variation in labour laws also contributes to union-density rates. As noted above, there is significant provincial variation in union coverage, and this is not unrelated to variability in the legislative climate within each province. Unions generally benefit if labour law requires employers to recognize a union on the basis of a majority of workers in a proposed bargaining unit signing cards, or on the basis of a genuinely free vote, and operate at a significant disadvantage if the law allows employers to fight an active anti-union campaign before a vote. A lot also hinges on whether a first contract can be won through arbitration, and whether employers can replace workers who go on strike for a first or later contract. It is not uncommon for a group of workers to win union certification, but to fail to get a first collective agreement because of employer resistance. Moreover, neoliberal labour law reforms have intensified the challenges faced by workers seeking to organize (Panitch and Swartz 2008). For example, it was more difficult for employers to resist worker support for unionization in Quebec than in the rest of Canada, and was harder for unions to mount successful organizing campaigns in Ontario, Alberta, and much of Atlantic Canada through much of the 1990s, in part due to neoliberal governments in those regions of the country. In Ontario, almost immediately following its election in 1995, the neoliberal Mike Harris government made it more difficult to certify a union and easier to decertify, and lifted the ban on replacement workers. Similarly, one of the first acts of the newly elected Saskatchewan Party government in that province, in 2008, was to change the law to shift from card check certification of unions to votes.

Government attitudes toward unions also matter a lot in terms of representing social services workers. Contracting out services to low-bid, often private-sector providers, as is the case with home care services in Ontario, works against union representation, as opposed to service delivery through the public or non-profit sector. One reason for the strength of Quebec unions has been that recognition was given to unions as the broader public sector expanded into areas like child care services.

New Organizing and Union Renewal

Every year, some non-unionized workers join unions and gain a collective bargaining relationship with their employer through a labour board certification.

Much less commonly, some unions are decertified with the consent of the workers involved. Obviously, if union density is to increase, more workers must be persuaded to build and join unions. Indeed, given that many union employers will shrink or go out of business over time and new businesses will be established, union density will inevitably decline if unions are not organizing many new members. The much slower decline of union density in Canada than in the U.S. in the 1980s and 1990s almost certainly reflects not just more union-friendly labour legislation, but also a greater union commitment to new organizing and movement building. The absolute number of workers organized into Canadian unions each year was, relative to the size of the workforce, probably some five times higher than in the U.S.

Unfortunately, available data from provincial labour boards provide very incomplete information on how many workers are joining unions, and where the new organizing is taking place. From the mid-1970s to the late 1990s, anywhere between 60,000 and 100,000 workers (or as many as 2 percent of all non-union workers) were organized into unions through new certifications (minus decertifications) each year (Johnson 2002; Katz-Rosene 2003; Martinello 1996). There has been a downward trend since the high point of the mid-1980s, with some ups and downs, and by the late 1990s, just under 1 percent of all non-union paid workers were joining unions each year. The organization rate has been consistently much higher than average in Quebec and, until recently, British Columbia.

The average size of new bargaining units is small: 50 to 70 members in Ontario since the mid-1990s, and just 30 to 40 members in B.C. There is evidence of relative success among women workers and racialized workers, and more new organizing in services, especially health and welfare services (Yates 2000, 2003). In B.C. (where the data are most complete), more than 50,000 workers were organized into unions from 1997 to 2002, of whom just one in six worked in the resource and manufacturing sectors. Large private-sector industrial unions, like Unifor and the United Steelworkers, have continued to add new members alongside the Canadian Union of Public Employees, the National Union of Public and General Employees, and other public-sector unions, but many of these new members have been in services, especially the broader public sector, rather than in areas of traditional blue-collar industrial jurisdiction. Large unions have also grown through mergers.

In most years, from the mid-1980s to the mid-1990s, union growth from new certifications offset stagnant or declining union membership in already unionized workplaces, accounting for almost all absolute membership growth. Since the mid-1990s, union membership in already unionized workplaces seems to have grown as well. New organizing in Canada has been far from negligible and has made an important difference to union density, but it has been a case of rowing against the tide of forces working against unions in the job market as a whole.

Observers have often drawn a contrast between an organizing as opposed to servicing model of trade unionism, which is related to a social movement (as opposed to a business union) model of what unions are about (Moody

Box 10.1: Unifor, Canada's Newest Union, Formed as CAW, CEP Merge
By Jeff Mackey

Jerry Dias hopes to use his new position as president of Canada's newest—and largest—private sector union to turn the tide for Canada's labour movement.

The Canadian Auto Workers union and the Communications, Energy and Paperworkers Union of Canada have merged to form a new group called Unifor.

Dias was elected with about 87 per cent support at the new union's founding convention in Toronto on Saturday.

***

"Today is about challenging the status quo and making sure the governments have a formidable foe if in fact they decide to take on the trade union movement."

One early battle between the government and the new union could be brewing in the telecommunications industry. Dias said that he is strongly opposed to Verizon's possible entry into the Canadian market, saying it would put many communication workers' jobs at risk.

Dias, who is from Burlington, Ont., said he would uphold Unifor's promise to dedicate 10 per cent of its revenues to organizing workplaces and adding new members.

He also said that Unifor would welcome workers traditionally excluded from collective bargaining and would seek other ambitious and creative ways to expand membership.

"It is about changing the discussion about workers and how they have to somehow accept less," said Dias.

A major part of this strategy, according to Dias, will have to do with harnessing discontent among unemployed youth.

***

The union will initially represent more than 300,000 workers across roughly 20 sectors of the economy, primarily in manufacturing, communications and transportation.

It will also represent some public sector employees in the health, education and transit sectors.

Dias touched on many current topics in Canada including the Senate scandal, which he views as a serious mismanagement of taxpayers' dollars in which senators found guilty should be kicked from office.

***

Internationally, Dias supported the movement to organize by fast food workers in the U.S. and condemned harsh new laws regarding gay rights demonstrations in Russia.

The CEP and CAW voted last year to join forces, a move they hope will boost the national labour movement.

Officials have said the switch to a non-traditional name—one that goes beyond simply listing occupations or industries—signals the union is looking to branch out.

Source: Mackey, Jeff. 2013, August 31. "Unifor, Canada's Newest Union, Formed As CAW, CEP Merge." *Huffington Post*. http://www.huffingtonpost.ca/2013/08/31/unifor-caw-cep-merger_n_3847388.html.

1997). While overdrawn, the servicing and business union model stands for the bureaucratic, top-down structures, member passivity, and lack of activism and interest in organizing that were often the results of stable industrial relations in long-unionized firms and sectors in the 1960s and 1970s. Some unions were not particularly concerned about an overall fall in union density or about building links to the wider community so long as their own membership was stable and members were making gains at the bargaining table. However, falling overall union strength tends to reach a tipping point, at which time even long-unionized employers will take a much harder line in bargaining or will seek to decertify because of increased competition from lower-cost, non-union employers. In the U.S., the central labour body, the American Federation of Labor–Congress of Industrial Organizations, was quite complacent about union density decline through much of the 1970s and into the 1980s. This turned to alarm as the absolute number of union members began to fall, however, and as slipping density began to turn into a downward spiral. By the mid-1990s, almost all American unions recognized that new organizing was absolutely key to survival.

The commitment of unions to organizing new members will be strongly influenced not just by threats to union security in already unionized sectors, but also by whether leaders, activists, and members see themselves as part of a broader labour movement linked to a wider movement for social and economic change (Fletcher and Gapasin 2009). At their best, unions have been concerned with improving conditions for all workers, not just the narrow union elite. Historically, union expansion has come in big waves as a growing labour move-ment has rapidly expanded into many workplaces over a very short period. In Canada in the 20th century, there were several big waves of union growth (Heron 2012). The first was in the early years of the 20th century, as growing numbers of industrial workers formed new industrial unions such as the auto workers and the steelworkers, taking a more militant approach toward employ-ers than the already established (and often highly exclusionary) craft unions of the 19th century, who mainly represented skilled tradesmen. Indeed, for some years, there were two rival labour central bodies, divided between older craft unions (the American Federation of Labour) and the new industrial unions (the Congress of Industrial Organizations), before they merged in 1955. The ranks of the industrial unions swelled during and just after World War II, when hundreds of thousands of blue-collar workers joined these unions. A third big wave came in the 1960s and into the 1970s, when public services unions grew very rapidly, bringing many women and professional workers, such as teachers and nurses, into the labour movement. One of the big questions today is whether unions are fated to experience a slow and steady decline, or if there will be another big wave of union organizing, this time in the private service sector, perhaps on a very different organizational basis than in the past. The upsurge in activism among non-unionized workers—for example, through campaigns such as the Fight for $15 and Fairness, OUR Walmart, and the fast food workers' strikes—certainly points toward the latter possibility (see Box 10.2).

Since at least the 1980s, there has been a gradual process of union renewal in Canada (Kumar and Murray 2003; Yates 2002; Kumar and Schenk 2006). The process of renewal is about much more than just organizing new members, and is much more complex than just turning from servicing current members to organizing new members. Organizing is important, but unions abandon servicing of current members at their peril, since active and mobilized members are a necessary base for a growing movement. At one level, renewal has been about making unions more democratic internally, as well as more responsive to changes in the workplace, and to the changing needs and interests of workers. This has included an emphasis on making union staff and elected officers more representative of a changing workforce through the inclusion of more women, racialized workers, and younger workers. While the shift has been partial, more women in particular have moved into top leadership and key staff positions.

Though unions themselves are hierarchical and bureaucratic organizations, and this has served to dampen rank-and-file activity (Camfield 2011; Moody 1988), there have also been some changes in structures to make unions more accountable to more active and engaged members. There has been a greater emphasis on internal education and on rank-and-file member involvement in union activities, including bargaining, representing members at the workplace, and sometimes organizing. There has also been at least a limited shift in bargaining priorities and in workplace activities to issues of interest to the new workforce, including training and work-family balance (Kumar and Murray 2003). There has also been a revival of some of the social movement dimensions of unions, which had atrophied to some degree due to the postwar system of labour relations, as discussed. Unions have led major campaigns on issues of interest to all workers—such as the need to protect public health care and public services, pensions, employment and pay equity, and human rights—and have worked to build stronger links with community organizations and other social movements (see Chapter 9, Box 9.2).

Many unions have changed rather dramatically as a result of declining membership in some sectors, offset by mergers with other unions and expansion into other sectors. The former big blue-collar industrial unions, such as the auto workers and steelworkers, have become much more like general worker unions, representing a very broad range of workers, including more women, while the main public-sector unions have expanded from an original base of direct government employees into the much broader social services sector. Many unions now devote significant resources to new organizing within and outside their traditional areas of jurisdiction, though this may still be a relatively small fraction of the total (Kumar and Murray 2003). There is also often intense union rivalry in organizing and bargaining, which can be counterproductive in terms of building a stronger movement. Organizing practices continue to vary a great deal, with some unions relying on rank-and-file members and activists much more than others. While there is no magic formula for success, the evidence shows that successful organizing campaigns tend to be those in which there is a great deal of rank-and-file

Box 10.2: The Fight for $15 Wage in B.C. and Beyond
By Tara Ehrcke

If you find yourself in front of a Walmart or Starbucks in British Columbia on the 15th of any month this year, you just might find yourself amid a new and growing campaign to raise the minimum wage. Activists across B.C. are hitting the streets in the Fight for 15 campaign, endorsed by the B.C. Federation of Labour and supported by individuals and community groups throughout the province. Organizers are planning events for the 15th of every month until the provincial minimum wage is increased to $15 an hour.

B.C. currently has the ninth lowest minimum wage in Canada, at $10.25 per hour. This is below the $13-an-hour poverty level and only half the living wage in the mid-size and large cities, which ranges from $18 to $20 per hour. Like elsewhere in Canada, the U.S. and across Europe, stagnating wages, increasing job precarity and low-wage work are endemic. It is no wonder then, that movements to increase the minimum wage are increasingly popular. B.C.'s campaign joins those in Ontario, and Nova Scotia, and of course the myriad campaigns across the U.S.

The struggles in the U.S. provide inspiration for us north of the border. In B.C., we look south to SeaTac, Wa., a small municipality and the first to vote for an immediate raise to $15. This was followed by another successful campaign in Seattle and in over a dozen municipalities across the states. The American campaigns are becoming so successful that the right-wing lobby group ALEC—the American Legislative Exchange Council—has taken aim at ending the ability of municipalities to set minimum-wage rates. Despite this, the movement keeps growing. Oregon must change its minimum wage at the state level, but this hasn't deterred "15 Now," the vibrant activist coalition of community and labour.

Bridge to Unionization Efforts
The minimum-wage campaigns have been closely tied to the struggle to unionize in low-wage workplaces. Across North America, early attempts at unionization in large retail workplaces such as Walmart and Starbucks have met with draconian corporate responses. Notoriously, the successful organizing drive at a Walmart outlet in Quebec met with the shutdown of the entire store, putting all its employees out of work. Although workers were successful at getting some compensation in court, this type of action deterred new organizing drives.

In response, some unions turned to alternative methods of organizing low-wage workplaces. Unions such as the Service Employees International Union (SEIU) and the United Food and Commercial Workers (UFCW) have put considerable resources into a variety of organizations and campaigns aimed at countering these vulnerabilities. The OUR Walmart campaign attempts to address the vulnerability both of individual workers and also individual worksites by funding campaigns that cross employer and state boundaries. OUR Walmart focuses on direct workplace actions and solidarity actions directed at Walmart stores across the U.S. Jobs with Justice fights for bargaining rights in particular sectors but with multiple employers. The Fight for 15 focuses on a minimum-wage increase, which will affect all low-wage workers in a single jurisdiction. Worker centres provide advocacy and organizational hubs for non-unionized workers. In the best campaigns, the demands are combined, exemplified, for instance, in the slogan "Fifteen and a Union."

***

In the past year, the growth and interplay between these campaigns, and the number of outright successes, has demonstrated the ability of workers to reframe the debate on wages, unions and politics. This is in stark contrast to the "right to work" propaganda, and the false divisions sown by neoliberal politicians between private- and public-sector workers, and union and non-union workers. For too long, and in too many places, the dominant dialogue has been to blame public-sector workers—the last highly unionized sector in both Canada and the U.S.—as the source of debt, deficit, economic woes and cuts to social programs. The new solidarity expressed in campaigns like Fight for 15 is finally breaking down divisions and creating the space amid genuine struggle to revive the labour movement and to push politics left.

***

While the Fight for 15 campaigns may be most visible in retail and fast food, they involve a wide range of workers in a variety of industries. Care aides, housekeepers, receptionists and cashiers span a range of worksites from hospitals to hotels to grocery stores. Not unexpectedly, workers in equity-seeking groups, such as racialized and women workers, tend to be overrepresented statistically in low-wage jobs. Low-wage workers are no longer just the young or poorly educated. They span the age range to include the elderly unable to retire and university grads unable to work in their field. Low-wage work is often accompanied by poor working conditions and unfair employment practices, and this can affect different groups of workers in different ways. The horrific scheduling practices of many low-wage employers, for example, are particularly intolerable for single women workers with children. Working conditions in low-wage jobs are a women's equality issue.

Building Solidarity

There is a tremendous opportunity to build solidarity through the synergy between minimum-wage campaigns, electoral campaigns, the traditional labour movement and anti-oppression activism. We need this solidarity now more than ever. Like elsewhere in Canada, the labour movement in B.C. is plagued by division and trapped in a cycle of bargaining to minimize concessions. The private sector has followed the same decline in unionization rates that we've seen across the globe. In the public sector, neoliberal attacks from government continue to erode wages and working conditions. In response, the public sector has fragmented.

***

Historically, we know that the last union upsurge of the 1960s and '70s did not take place in a vacuum, it was presaged by the civil rights movement, the anti-Vietnam war movement and the generalized upturn in struggle. The upturn of that era shows us that the success of workers in making gains depends on not just the militancy of their own union, but the overall climate of worker and social movements. Employers get scared when strike rates are high, unionization levels are increasing, workers are fighting for racial and gender equity and particularly when there is broad solidarity of workers in action. It is with this context in mind that we should approach the Fight for 15. It is an opportunity not only to right the wrongs of poverty wages, but also to build new movements across old divisions.

Source: Ehrcke, Tara. 2015. "The Fight for $15 Wage in B.C. and Beyond." *Canadian Dimension*, 49, issue 3 (May/June). https://canadiandimension.com/articles/view/the-fight-for-15-wage-in-b.c.-and-beyond.

member involvement, and also where there are close ties to community groups (Bronfenbrenner and Friedman 1998; McAlevey 2014).

A renewal of activism and renewed emphasis on organizing new members help explain some recent successes, particularly among workers in services who would otherwise be in relatively low-paid and precarious jobs. In recent years, there have been notable successes in organizing security guards, hotel workers, workers in long-term care homes, teaching assistants in universities, and even some workers in retail trade and restaurants. Unions have thus had some success in organizing precarious workers, though much more needs to be accomplished.

Future Prospects for Unions

Union density has fallen slowly in the private sector, particularly in the traditional stronghold of male blue-collar industrial workers. It has held up much better among women than among men, mainly because of union strength in public and social services combined with the impact of organizing efforts among lower-paid workers. Unions are weak in some important parts of the knowledge-based economy, but are not doomed to extinction because of structural change or the emergence of a new workforce. There is still substantial worker support for unions as a vehicle for improving pay and benefits and, even more important, for collective representation in the workplace.

A factor in union weakness in terms of recruiting new members has likely been the fact that unions have had great difficulty making major gains at the bargaining table for their current members, and have been forced on the defensive by extensive restructuring and employer hostility in both the private and public sectors. This suggests that if unions are to grow, organizing strategies must be linked to finding a new economic role, and to revitalizing rank-and-file activism. Organizing individual workplaces in low-density sectors is very hard given strong employer resistance, however. Organizing sectorally, across an economically relevant labour market, may result in greater gains and, beyond a certain threshold, less employer resistance. Bargaining of master agreements with groups of employers also makes union representation in small workplaces more viable. Examples in Canada include a handful of master agreements in hotels, restaurants, and the retail sector (Tufts 2007). In community social services in British Columbia and Quebec, organizing success has been achieved in part by promoting sector-wide bargaining between all employers and unions.

Broader-based organizing and bargaining can also be based on unions working with community organizations. In recent years, notable broader-based organizing and bargaining successes in the U.S. have included large groups of low-paid, predominantly racialized workers. For example, the Service Employees International Union has organized downtown office cleaning services in several cities through community-based Justice for Janitors campaigns. The hotel workforce in Las Vegas is highly unionized as a result of union renewal and new organizing across the sector, and wages and benefits are now well above the industrial average (Meyerson 2004). Broader-based organizing and bargaining are generally hindered rather than facilitated by current labour laws based on the norm of workplace-by-workplace certification and bargaining, but successful union organizing can make change happen in any case.

Another possible path forward is community-based activism and organizing. Associations of workers, such as an organization known as ACORN in the U.S., have come into existence to fight for workers' rights and interests outside of collective bargaining. Workers can and do unite to fight for their legal rights under minimum wage and employment standards legislation, and some of these efforts have been supported by unions that also engage in collective bargaining. The Canadian Union of Postal Workers, for example, has supported collective action by bicycle couriers in Winnipeg. In the United States, a wide range of "alt-labour" organizations are growing, as non-unionized workers in sectors with overall low levels of unionization engage in alternative forms of collective organizing and activism, including coalitions and the formation of workers' centres (Eidelson 2013; Fine 2006; Tattersall 2010). In Canada, to date, there have been a small number of experiments along these lines, such as the Community Chapter initiative of Unifor, which offers some of the benefits of unionization to workers who are not certified as a bargaining unit. The Fight for $15 and Fairness campaign, which, as discussed in Box 10.2, is focused on improving the wages of non-unionized, precarious workers, has gained widespread attention through its

Box 10.3: Airport Workers Demand Fair Wages, Better Jobs on May Day
By Teuila Fuatai

It was an afternoon of samba drums, churros and solidarity at Toronto's Pearson International Airport yesterday.

The May Day celebrations, which attracted about 300 workers and labour activists, kicked off around 1:00 p.m. outside the departures block at terminal one.

The crowd marched in support of the Fight for $15 and Fairness along the closed roadway as part of this year's International Workers' Day actions in Canada.

Pearson is the country's largest workplace and employs about 40,000 people.

Its poor health and safety record, endorsement of precarious work and contract flipping practises marks it as a prime battleground in Canada's labour struggle.

Just last week, airport workers said goodbye to 24-year-old ramp worker Ian Henrey-Pervez who was killed when the baggage cart he was driving rolled on April 22.

Sean Smith of the Toronto Airport Workers' Council—a cross-union organization representing workers in dealings with the Greater Toronto Airport Authority (GTAA)—said while the week had been tough on the airport community, yesterday's rally showed the support workers had for gaining change and fairness in their workplace.

"You don't think of the most expensive piece of property in Canada as the bastion of minimum wage precarious work, but it is," Smith said of Pearson.

"These are workers working minimum wage jobs, on-call, no guaranteed hours, and if their wages go above $13 an hour, the next day the company they work for is losing their contract because somebody else is doing it cheaper."

A series of contract changes last year resulted in hundreds of workers in the airport's refuelling, wheelchair assistance and de-icing services being laid off and forced to reapply for jobs at much lower pay rates. According to the involved unions, at least 200 workers were never rehired. Parking attendants were targeted the previous year when the airport's contract providers changed.

"In a completely, deregulated privatised scenario, this is what happens," Smith said.

"You end up with workers competing with each other for fewer and fewer well-paying jobs."

Something has to give eventually, he warned.

"To give an example, at the bottom of the scale you've got minimum wage workers who work two to six in the morning for $40.

"Obviously, the turnover's through the roof, and on the ramp it's even worse because it's physical work.

"The precarious model, it's worse for seniors [experienced workers] too. The seniors are getting burnt out because they've got to do more work to carry the load which leads to worker-on-worker conflict."

One of the key issues at stake is the lack of accountability for oversight of the airport, Smith said.

"Many of the workers here are federally and provincially regulated in the same building—so which government do we turn to when you've got two jurisdictions in the same building and a common issue?"

The workers' council believe the GTAA should implement a sustainable community-orientated model for the airport that prohibits contract flipping and issuing operating licenses to companies willing to provide cheap rates at any cost to workers and their safety. This is what has led to the current "race to the bottom" that workers are trapped in, he said. The GTAA also needs to enforce and regulate proper health and safety standards.

A list of demands for workers at Pearson is due to be presented to the GTAA at its annual general meeting next week. Thousands of signatures in support of the demands, which include a $15 hourly minimum wage and an end to contract flipping, have been collected, Smith said.

Workers' demands at YYZ:

- Equal pay for equal work
- $15 hourly minimum wage for all
- All workers to be allocated a minimum number of sick days
- A guaranteed amount of hours providing workers with sufficient income to live on

Source: Toronto Airport Workers' Council

Source: Fuatai, Teuila. 2016, May 2. "Airport workers demand fair wages, better jobs on May Day." rabble.ca. http://rabble.ca/news/2016/05/airport-workers-demand-fair-wages-better-jobs-on-may-day.

organizing, which includes national days of action. These initiatives remind us that worker organizing is not confined to any one organizational form, and that union strategies, as well as unions as organizations themselves, change over time in relation to changing patterns of work.

Recalling the discussion in Chapter 6 about the growth of the temporary foreign worker program in Canada, the organizing efforts among migrant agricultural workers and their allies provide another example of worker organizing that is taking place both outside the organization boundaries of trade unions, and at times, with the support of unions (Choudry and Hlatshwayo 2015; Choudry and Thomas 2013). In Ontario, farmworkers, including migrant farmworkers employed in the Seasonal Agricultural Workers Program, have historically been exempt from labour relations legislation that facilitates freedom of association and collective bargaining. However, this exclusion has been contested (though unsuccessfully) through a campaign led by the UFCW to win the legal right to organize and bargain collectively for agricultural workers in Ontario. While migrant farmworkers in Ontario continue to lack collective bargaining rights, the UFCW has established community centres to provide services to migrant workers in communities where they are present. Moreover, the UFCW has undertaken organizing campaigns on farms in Quebec, Manitoba, and British Columbia, leading to collective agreements for farmworkers in those provinces (UFCW 2011). In addition, a number of migrant worker justice initiatives have emerged, including the work of both Justicia for Migrant Workers, a grassroots activist collective that promotes the rights of migrant farmworkers, and the Immigrant Workers Centre in Montreal, which provides education on labour rights for migrant and immigrant workers and engages in organizing campaigns (Choudry and Thomas 2013). These initiatives, both those that involve unions and those that do not, illustrate the dynamic nature of worker organizing in the context of the changing labour market.

Conclusion

While business leaders and neoliberal policy-makers sometimes claim that unions are no longer needed in a post-industrial economy, the ongoing social problems of work and the power dynamics of the capitalist workplace make workers' organizations imperative. Historically, as capitalism changed over time, workers developed new organizations (for example, industrial unions, public-sector unions) to represent themselves and engaged in new forms of struggle in response to the changing economic context. In the present day, the strategies, practices, and forms of struggle undertaken by workers and unions may look quite different than in the past, due to changing economic, political, and social conditions. But so long as the conditions of alienation and exploitation that gave rise to unions in the early years of capitalism remain, so too does the need for collective workers' organizations to contest those conditions.

Recommended Reading

Choudry, Aziz, and Mondli Hlatshwayo (eds). 2015. *Just Work? Migrant Workers Struggle Today*. London: Pluto Press.

Fletcher, Bill Jr., and Fernando Gapasin. 2009. *Solidarity Divided: The Crisis in Organized Labor and a New Path toward Social Justice*. Berkeley: University of California Press.

McAlevey, Jane. 2014. *Raising Expectations (and Raising Hell): My Decade Fighting for the Labor Movement*. London and New York: Verso.

Tattersall, Amanda. 2010. *Power in Coalition: Strategies for Strong Unions and Social Change*. Ithaca: ILR Press.

Note

1. OECD.Stat, Trade Union Density. Accessed at: https://stats.oecd.org/Index. aspx?DataSetCode=UN_DEN.

PART IV

THE CANADIAN WORKPLACE IN THE GLOBAL ECONOMY

CHAPTER 11

Globalization and Work in Canada

Writing in *The Communist Manifesto*, Marx and Engels (2002: 223) describe the global reach of capitalism:

> The need of a constantly expanding market for its products chases the bourgeoisie over the whole surface of the globe. It must nestle every-where, settle everywhere, establish connections everywhere.... All old-established national industries have been destroyed or are daily being destroyed. They are dislodged by new industries ... whose products are consumed, not only at home, but in every quarter of the globe. In place of the old wants, satisfied by the productions of the country, we find new wants, requiring for their satisfaction the products of distant lands and climes. In place of the old local and national seclusion and self-sufficiency, we have intercourse in every direction, universal inter-dependence of nations.

While written in the 1840s, this passage is startlingly revealing of the key dynamics of what by the 1990s came to be described as economic "globalization." In this short passage, Marx and Engels note that capitalism involves a constant changing of the way goods and services are produced (the revolutionizing of the means of production), that this is unceasingly disruptive of social and economic life, and that the expansion of capitalism on a global scale is inherent to the system. Perhaps most importantly, the passage points to the fact that what we understand as "globalization" is hardly anything new. Rather, "globalization" can be understood more accurately as part of the global organization, expansion, and reorganization of capitalism that dates back hundreds of years.

While this passage written by Marx and Engels sounds somewhat abstract, perhaps even arcane in some of its terminology, the processes they describe bear direct relevance to the organization of work in Canada in the early 21st century. In the context of globalization, work has been profoundly reorganized as increas-ingly mobile transnational corporations relocate production to capitalize on the potential for lower labour costs, as neoliberal governments negotiate free trade agreements to facilitate foreign direct investment and capital mobility, and as a heightened competitive environment tilts the balance of power between work-ers and employers even more in favour of the latter. As presented in a series of text boxes in this chapter, these forces are directly evident in the case of a group of unionized workers at the Navistar truck manufacturing facility in Chatham, Ontario, who confronted an employer intent on restructuring its workplace in order to cut costs in the competitive global marketplace.

Earlier chapters of this book have detailed the increased precariousness of employment, rising wage inequality, growing income insecurity, and declining union strength. This chapter looks at the impacts on work that have resulted from Canada's increased integration into the North American and global economy in terms of trade and investment flows, and how globalization in this sense has contributed to negative trends in the job market and the wider society. It sets out some reasons why closer trade and investment ties with other countries, particularly low-wage developing countries, would lead to a process of downward harmonization of wages and social standards, and argues that globalization has indeed been a force working against better wages, working conditions, and labour standards. The chapter also builds on the discussion in Chapter 10, highlighting the ways in which the mobile capital and intensified competitive environment of contemporary global capitalism create additional challenges for workers' movements.

Globalization: A Race to the Bottom?

The concept of economic globalization has been used to signify a number of processes that have unfolded within the global economy in recent decades. These include: financial deregulation associated with the breakdown of the Bretton Woods system; rapid rates of technological change and technology transfer, particularly in communications and transportation technologies; and the spatial expansion of capitalist relations into the post-socialist economies of Eastern Europe and across the Global South. Developments related to these general processes include: the geographic fragmentation of systems of production in order to increase profitability; increases in the size, flow, and speed of foreign direct investment; the spread of forms of wage labour across the globe; the predominance of neoliberal approaches to public policy; and new forms of cultural interpenetration and commodification (McNally 2006; Panitch 1998).

While technological developments and free trade agreements are most often associated with globalization, it is the increasing levels of foreign direct investment (FDI) and the growth of transnational corporations (TNCs) that lie at the heart of contemporary globalization, where developments such as free trade agreements are part of a deeper process of reducing the constraints on the free movement of capital (McNally 2006). This drive for a "spatial fix" (Harvey 2003) to a crisis of profitability occurred through the accelerated relocation of manufacturing production that began during the 1970s, a shift that was made possible through new developments in communications and transportation technologies that facilitated the development of global value chains involving labour-intensive, low-cost, export-based manufacturing controlled by TNCs.

In the Global North, the shift of manufacturing to Global South countries resulted in plant closures and increased economic insecurity, facilitating the push toward more precarious working conditions. Jobs that are most vulnerable to these processes are relatively low-skill and in labour-intensive sectors (garment, auto parts, electronics). This has occurred not only through the direct relocation of production, but also through the ideological impact created by the threat of relocation, whereby in the context of increasing levels of capital mobility and international economic competition, employers have pressured unions into concession bargaining, thereby reducing the wages, benefits, and job security of unionized workers. As will be illustrated below, these were the dynamics at play in the case of Navistar.

Globalization and Free Trade

In neoclassical economic theory, increased trade between countries leads each country to concentrate its productive resources in the areas of greatest comparative advantage, and this leads to higher national income. The basic idea is that access to larger markets and increased competition will lead to economies of scale, specialization, and higher productivity, and thus to rising living standards. Certainly trade openness has been sold to Canadians on the promise that it would lead to growth, better jobs, and rising incomes.

However, this theory of free trade is based on a number of assumptions that are not necessarily true in the real world, including the assumption that it is only goods and services that flow between countries, not capital, and that all resources in a country are fully employed. In the real world, a country might be a net exporter of capital, and workers who lose their jobs due to increased imports might not necessarily find comparable or better jobs quickly due to a shortage of expanding sectors. Many economists have noted that the reality of international trade often fails to fit the theory in that governments can and do intervene to shape and create comparative advantage, rather than leave it all to the market. For example, many of today's advanced industrial countries, including the U.S., Germany, and Canada, have industrialized behind high-tariff walls and extended significant government support to the development of infant industries. Many of today's more successful East Asian economies, such as China and South Korea, have similarly industrialized and moved up the value-added ladder, not just by exporting to global markets, but also by actively managing trade and investment flows so as to develop their own industrial capacities.

Further, it could be expected that the impacts of trade and capital flow between countries at similar stages of economic development, such as the OECD advanced industrial countries, might be more favourable than those between such countries and low-wage developing countries. The latter have grown rapidly from quite low levels over the past two decades. Most economists would argue that there are still gains from trade, but concede that there are "losers" as well as "winners" as industries in high-wage industrial countries restructure and jobs in labour-intensive manufacturing are shifted to those countries that have the strong comparative advantage of abundant cheap labour. Many economists now concede that the rise of China, India, Brazil, and so on as major industrial powers over the past 20 years or so has been a contributing factor to the stagnant wages, rising wage inequality, and decline of unions in the advanced industrial economies (Freeman 2007). The fact that national income may rise due to increased openness also does not mean much to working people if most of the gains flow to much higher profits and to the incomes of the very rich. This has been the case in Canada, for example, as inequality has grown significantly since the 1980s (OECD 2011a; see also Broadbent 2014).

Finally, the metaphor of mutually advantageous trade between countries based on specialization and comparative advantage is increasingly misleading in a world economy dominated by large TNCs that have few loyalties to any one country, and allocate different elements of their production chains across countries in order to minimize costs while maximizing productivity and quality. Some one-third of U.S. corporate profits are earned outside of the U.S., meaning that the relatively few Americans who own most U.S. corporate assets and the senior managers of U.S.-headquartered TNCs have a rather different take on the costs and benefits of globalization than do American workers whose jobs are vulnerable to offshoring and to higher U.S. imports from foreign affiliates of U.S.-owned corporations. To ask if increased free trade is good or bad for the United States misses the point that some gain, and others lose.

There have been many important changes in the global economy since the 1970s, driven by new communication and transportation technologies that have sharply cut costs, and by trade and investment liberalization agreements, such as the World Trade Organization (WTO) and the North American Free Trade Agreement (NAFTA). The fundamental principle behind such agreements is that countries (1) should not require companies selling into a national market to produce in that market, and (2) should treat domestic and foreign producers in the same way. While many exceptions still exist, this means that corporations are generally free to produce where they want without losing market access. National economies have become more closely integrated as trade and investment flows across borders have grown much more rapidly than the growth of the world economy as a whole (Glyn 2006). Many of those investment flows take place through TNCs. These may be based in one country, but offshoring means that many services and component inputs to final products are sourced globally, and final product assembly may also be widely dispersed so as to access different national markets at the lowest cost. Markets for most manufactured goods and at least some services (notably business, financial, and information services) have become much more competitive. In the 1960s, the noted U.S. economist John Kenneth Galbraith described a world in which a handful of large companies dominated national markets for auto, steel, and the like, engaged in restrained "oligopolistic" competition with one another, and were generally content to share the wealth generated by their protected market position with workers and, through taxes, with governments. While a very few global industries (such as the production of large passenger jets and pharmaceutical drugs) are similarly dominated by a very few companies, the reality in most manufacturing industries and in some service industries is fiercely contested national and global markets, especially in the advanced industrial countries, which maintain low tariffs and have dropped most significant regulatory barriers to imported goods and services.

Companies facing intense competition for market share (and also under increased pressure from the financial sector to maximize short-term profitability) will try to lower wages and benefits along with other costs to match those of their lowest-cost competitors. They will also seek to raise productivity or output per hour, with potentially negative implications for hours of work and working conditions, and will consider shifting production and new investment to jurisdictions where wages are lower. It is true that wages are only one element of total costs, and that what really counts is the level of wages in relation to worker productivity, which is a function of skills and capital investment. That said, corporations very much seek the lowest cost of labour at a given level of technology and productivity.

Industrial restructuring in response to increased global competition has pushed the manufacturing industries in the advanced industrial countries to become much more capital-intensive and productive, and some market share has usually been lost to imports from new global producers. Globalization has thus been one factor behind the slow shrinkage of the manufacturing sector in almost all advanced industrial countries, including Canada (Informetrica 2007b). It is very hard to estimate the impacts of increased global competition on jobs and wages solely by looking at the level of imports in a given sector in a given country, since wages may have fallen and productivity may have increased by working harder or for longer hours in order to avert a rise in the import share. Increased global competition also results in major incentives for companies to move to jurisdictions that levy low business taxes and impose few costly regulations on business, including strong employment standards. This often means lower levels of social protection for working families. Many observers see so-called liberal globalization as prompting a "race to the bottom" in which mobile global corporations play workers and governments against each other, to the detriment of working people (Ross 2004, 2011; Teeple 2000).

The basic problem of greatly increased competition is compounded by the fact that regulation of the economy at the national level to promote the rights and interests of workers has not been replaced by positive regulation at the international level. To be sure, the conventions of the ILO guide governments in the promotion of labour rights and standards, and the *Universal Declaration of Human Rights*, ratified by most nations, protects a wide range of social rights, but there is no enforcement of these commitments. Many member countries of the ILO, including Canada, have been cited in violation of its labour standards, and experience no penalty for being so (Thomas 2009). When China joined the WTO, the government was not required to recognize the rights of workers to form independent trade unions or, for that matter, to hold free elections. The only requirement was to provide free access to its market to foreign imports and investments. Companies can thus effectively choose to operate under one set of social rules in Canada, or another in China, while governments must apply the same set of economic rules to domestic and foreign corporations and investors alike.

Globalization is often associated with especially strong pressures toward downward harmonization of wages along with labour and social standards because of increased trade and investment ties between high-wage countries of the Global North and low-wage countries of the Global South. There are certainly grounds for concern that increased North-South trade has negatively influenced Canadian jobs and wages. The shift of manufacturing to developing countries in Asia and elsewhere in the Americas has been an important cause of plant closures and layoffs in the manufacturing sector, and there are signs of a growing impact on services as telecommunications technology increases the capacity of countries in the Global South to serve our market from a considerable distance for everything from software, to back-office operations, to call centres. The average industrial wage even in large export-oriented and foreign, transnational-owned plants in China is less than one-tenth of that in Canada, which has direct impacts on the competitive investment climate.

Workers and unions in Canada often face plant closures and layoffs in this environment. The jobs that are most vulnerable to relocation are often considered to be those in relatively low-skill and labour-intensive sectors, such as clothing and light assembly consumer goods industries, which have indeed massively contracted as the share of the Canadian market for these goods accounted for by imports has grown. It is now unusual to find an item of clothing, footwear, or, even more so, a toy, appliance, or consumer electronics product in a Canadian store that is made in North America or Europe as industrial capacity has grown significantly in the Global South. In Brazil, aerospace manufacturer Embraer competes directly with Canada's Bombardier in global markets. Auto assembly and auto engine manufacturing in Mexico competes directly with domestic auto industries in both Canada and the United States. And information technology services and software developers in India service both North American and Western European markets.

To take one concrete example, wages in manufacturing in Mexico average about one-quarter the Canadian and U.S. level. Mexico entered NAFTA with a significant auto assembly and parts industry oriented mostly to its domestic market, including plants operated by the Big Three North American producers, Volkswagen, and some Japanese companies. While wages are far lower, auto assembly plants and many sophisticated parts and engine plants in Mexico employ similar technology and work practices as in Canada. Under NAFTA, the Mexican share of North American auto and auto parts production has grown steadily. In 2008, the shift of the industry to Mexico became even more pronounced when the Mexican unions—in the context of a major wave of threatened North America–wide capacity reduction—agreed to cut the wages of new hires in assembly plants to just

Box 11.1: Chatham Reels Over Navistar Loss—Truck Plant Closing Will Kill 5% of City's Jobs
By Oliver Bertin

Tony Davis has built trucks for 26 years—his entire working life—in this farming city in the fertile flatlands one hour east of Windsor.

But his job and those of his 2,400 co-workers will disappear next June when the Chicago-based owners of Navistar International Corp. pull up the tent pegs in Chatham and move the plant to low-cost, low-wage Mexico.

The closing will deal a resounding blow to this farm and manufacturing centre of 43,000 people, eliminating more than 5 per cent of the jobs in the city and directly affecting nearly one-quarter of the local population.

Navistar is just the latest in a long line of U.S.-based auto manufacturers that have pulled out of Chatham in recent years, leaving behind a work force that is clearly demoralized.

***

Mr. Davis is resigned to his fate, but many of his fellow workers are just plain angry that a U.S.-based industrial giant would close its only Canadian plant after 93 years as the biggest employer in town.

***

The hardest-hit workers are the long-term veterans, the 300 workers who are close to retirement after spending most of their working lives at the plant. They will have to retire early, on a partial pension, with a severance of six months' pay in their pocket.

"Where are we going to go when the plant closes?" asked Linda Larue, a middle-aged woman who drops by the plant every day to pick up her husband, a 55-year-old assembly-line worker with diabetes and a history of heart attacks.

***

Ms. Larue is working part time at the local hospital, the only job she has been able to get. She is trying for a second part-time job to help pay the bills, but she has no pension, no benefits and not much hope for the future.

The bad news came Thursday when Navistar announced that it will shut the plant early next summer, ending the jobs of 1,000 active employees and 1,200 people currently on layoff.

Company executives met with workers in a tense meeting on Thursday.

***

The executive said the decision was "irreversible ... The decision has been made. I never say never, but I wouldn't consider it an option."

Company spokesman Roy Wiley expressed sympathy for the workers in a telephone interview Friday. "We want to be a good corporate citizen," he said, adding that the Chatham workers were building some of the best-quality trucks in North America. "They put their heart and their soul into those trucks. We want to do the right thing for them."

But he offered little hope of keeping the plant open, of jobs elsewhere in Navistar or of raising the severance benefits above the minimum in the union contract. Under that contract, most workers will get one week of salary for every year they have worked.

Source: Bertin, Oliver. 2002, October 21. "Chatham Reels Over Navistar Loss—Truck Plant Closing Will Kill 5% of City's Jobs." *The Globe and Mail*. http://www.theglobeandmail.com/report-on-business/chatham-reels-over-navistar-loss/article25423649/.

$2.50 per hour. It appears that new investment to produce the more fuel-efficient vehicles sought by U.S. and Canadian consumers will disproportionately be undertaken in Mexico, which can produce essentially the same products using the same technologies at a far lower labour cost.

Global capitalism entered a new phase in the 1990s when the global economy grew enormously in scale and space. Until that time, international trade and investment flows took place overwhelmingly between the advanced industrial countries of Western Europe, North America, and Japan, though an increasing role in manufacturing was being played by the East Asian countries—South Korea, Taiwan, Singapore, Hong Kong—as well as Brazil. China and the Soviet Bloc had only modest trade and investment links to the OECD countries, while much of the rest of the world, such as Latin America and Africa, had low levels of both imports and exports, even when they had industrially developed. Beginning in the early 1990s, however, there was a massive increase in effective world labour supply as the Soviet Bloc collapsed and as China in particular liberalized and followed the path of industrialization-driven manufacturing for export (Glyn 2006; Freeman 2007). Even pro-globalization economists, such as former U.S. Federal Reserve Chairman Alan Greenspan, were forced to concede that massively increased foreign production and competition from low-wage countries has resulted in lost jobs and very significant downward pressures on wages. As Greenspan (2007: 382–3) himself states:

Well over a billion workers, many well-educated, all low paid, began to gravitate to the world competitive marketplace from economies that had been almost wholly or in part centrally planned and insulated from global competition.... This movement of workers into the marketplace reduced world wages.... Not only did low-priced imports displace production and hence workers in developed countries, but the competitive effect of the displaced workers seeking new jobs suppressed the wages of workers not directly in the line of fire of low-priced imports.

For over the past two decades, Chinese exports—almost all manufactured goods—grew by about 20 percent per year, driven by huge investments in industrial capacity. China has become the largest machinery producer in the world, with machinery output increasing four-fold between 2000 and 2009, and with over 16 percent of machinery on the world market produced in China, the U.S. being by far the leading destination (Avery 2011). Its exports have grown rapidly (Glyn 2006), as has its share of the global GDP, which in 2015 reached 17.1 percent, with a projection to reach nearly 20 percent by 2021 (Statista 2016). Of course, the global economy has greatly expanded as the Chinese share of that market has grown, but the fact remains that the share of the domestic markets of the OECD countries accounted for by imports from low-wage countries has grown very rapidly, especially in the U.S., which runs huge trade deficits with China and other Asian countries. At least one-half of these Chinese-manufactured exports come from the Chinese operations of TNCs, as assembly and other relatively low-value-added, labour-intensive activities have been shifted from the U.S., Japan, Taiwan, and Korea to China and other low-wage, fast-developing Asian countries.

As China has rapidly industrialized by shifting workers from farms and the old state sector to the export-oriented manufacturing sector in the coastal regions, the economics of entire industries, such as toys, clothing, textiles, consumer electronics, and a wide range of other consumer goods, have changed fundamentally (Prestowitz 2005; Fishman 2006). By 2005, China produced about one-third to one-half of total global production of a significant range of consumer goods. China is not just the world's location of choice for low-cost commodity manufacturing, but it is also rapidly becoming the location of choice for high-tech manufacturing and even research and development (Prestowitz 2005). China is now at the point of developing export capacity in the auto assembly sector and has given birth to indigenous high-tech firms partnered with world-leading companies in aerospace and other high-tech industries.

Limits to Downward Harmonization

All that said, there are limits to the logic of the argument that in a globally integrated economy, production and mobile investment capital will inevitably flow overwhelmingly to those countries where investors and corporations find low wages, weak unions, low taxes, and low social and environmental standards, setting in motion an unrelenting race to the bottom in terms of wages and labour and social standards. This is certainly true to a degree, and very real forces work in this direction. But sometimes the proponents and critics of globalization alike exaggerate the power of TNCs and downplay potential counter-tendencies.

Despite all of the rhetoric of globalization, many areas of the contemporary economy are not very highly exposed to international competition at all, let alone to competition from developing countries. The possibility of relocation of production is largely confined to manufacturing, with a bias toward labour-intensive production of final products. It makes economic sense

Box 11.2: "We Can't Get Too Stubborn and Let the Companies We Work For Fail"—Overseas Competition Sparks New Era in Management-Labour Relations
By Virginia Galt

Doug Deneau has worked at the Navistar truck plant in Chatham, Ont., for almost 29 years. The past three, as plant chairman for the Canadian Auto Workers union, have arguably been the longest years of his life.

Through strike, threat of shutdown and—finally—sacrifice in exchange for long-term job security, Mr. Deneau and his co-workers have been to the brink and back.

In a deal announced last week, the CAW agreed to a contract extension that will freeze wages until the summer of 2009 in exchange for a commitment from Illinois-based Navistar International Corp. to keep the plant open and invest in a new product line. The trade-off saved almost 1,000 union jobs that pay an average of $26.57 an hour.

The deal between Navistar and the union is a sign of the radical change sweeping through management-labour relations as companies strive to change the way they operate in the face of low-cost competition. In many cases, while unions still talk hard-line, they're more willing to compromise than in the past when faced with the stark choice of change or job losses.

As painful as it was to forgo wage increases, a majority of Navistar's production workers ratified the settlement, which contains some pension and benefit improvements over the life of the contract and puts an end to outsourcing of their work. The skilled trades workers, however, were not so acquiescent and rejected the contract extension.

***

While Navistar hailed "the new collaborative culture," the CAW representatives were more restrained.

When the alternative is shutdown or liquidation, "there are times when you just can't fold your arms and say we're not doing anything," CAW president Buzz Hargrove said in a recent interview. He was talking about the restructuring negotiations at Air Canada, but this sense of resigned pragmatism is evident throughout the labour movement.

It is no longer bargaining as usual for management or labour, said Jayson Myers, senior chief economist at Canadian Manufacturers & Exporters.

Companies and, by extension, unions are having to undergo an enormous amount of change to survive in the new global business environment and compete with lower-cost operations in China, Latin America and Eastern Europe, Mr. Myers said in an interview.

Part of the Navistar agreement includes a joint commitment "to create a cost-competitive and high-quality environment in which to produce our new line-haul truck," said Dee Kapur, president of Navistar International's truck group.

***

For labour leaders, this means walking a fine line and not being gulled by exaggerated claims of financial hardship, said Ken Georgetti, president of the Canadian Labour Congress.

"We can't get too stubborn and let the companies we work for fail, because that costs us dearly," Mr. Georgetti said.

***

One e-mail, posted on the CAW website, captures the quandary that many of the members find themselves in.

While expressing "a surge of respect and pride in the CAW for having taken a stand and stuck to our guns for so long," the member goes on to express profound disappointment that laid-off members "will only be able to come back at a reduced wage rate. . ."

***

Mr. Hargrove replied that the union had to find savings somewhere to finance retirement and voluntary separation incentives for the more than 1,000 members who have indicated they would like to leave the company.

This will open up some jobs for laid-off employees who might otherwise never have the opportunity to return, he said.

Given the "awful circumstances," the union leadership decided "the only choice was to agree to lower rates to return some laid-off people and hope that the wage re-opener in 2006 would mean money available that we could use to improve the rates of recalled people," Mr. Hargrove wrote.

Source: Galt, Virginia. 2004, July 5. "'We Can't Get Too Stubborn and Let the Companies We Work For Fail'—Overseas Competition Sparks New Era in Management-Labour Relations." *The Globe and Mail*. http://www.theglobeandmail.com/report-on-business/we-cant-get-too-stubborn-and-let-the-companies-we-work-for-fail/article655567/.

for corporations seeking low labour costs to ship clothing production and electronics assembly to China, but transportation costs and time still count against the offshoring option within complex production chains, which still often take place in a concentrated geographical area. Highly capital-intensive manufacturing is also less vulnerable. If industries like auto and aerospace shift in a major way from North America and Europe, it will be a gradual process, driven by new investments at the margin given the large fixed capital investments already in place. Offshoring of services is happening, but service imports still account for well under 10 percent of the huge markets for private services in advanced industrial countries. Low-wage service sector jobs are better explained by high youth unemployment and low minimum wages than by low wages in China. Most service jobs—from health care to hotels, stores, and restaurants, to business consulting, to public services—can be offshored only with great difficulty, if at all. It is true that India has developed a very fast-growing offshore service industry, and that call centres, data analysis, software development, and the like are being relocated, but the overall impacts on North American wages in these sectors are still modest.

Moreover, the advanced industrial countries continue to hold an overwhelming comparative advantage in many major and growing industries, from software development, to entertainment, to aerospace and biotechnology, to the manufacturing of sophisticated machinery and equipment of all kinds. Computers may be assembled in China, but advanced computer-controlled machinery in Chinese factories is imported from Japan, Europe, and the U.S. Mobile phones are assembled in developing Asian countries, but new generations of communications technology are mainly designed, developed, and often first manufactured in Europe and North America. A lot of manufacturing production in terms of a huge physical volume of cheap goods has shifted to the Global South, but very high-valued goods and services are still overwhelmingly produced in the Global North. While their manufacturing sectors have shrunk in terms of their overall share of employment, Germany, Japan, and, to a lesser extent, the U.S. still dominate global markets for sophisticated capital goods and global technology development. Only a handful of emerging economies, notably Korea and Taiwan, have built genuinely innovative transnational corporations of their own. Because of all of these factors, the volume of North-South trade is still eclipsed by trade among the advanced industrial countries. OECD countries still generate about two-thirds of both world exports and imports, and most long-term investment flows are still among these countries. However, there are big differences within the OECD. Western Europe, Japan, and the growing Asian economies hold a strong edge over North America when it comes to balancing their growing imports with higher sophisticated exports to China.

As production shifts to the Global South, and as workers' movements in the Global South grow and push for better working conditions, living standards and wages should gradually rise, again reshaping the global market as a whole. However, wages in Global South countries could remain at very low levels for some time because of huge reserves of unemployed and rural workers seeking industrial jobs, and because of severe employer and government repression of unions. Still, wages have increased in South Korea and other countries in Asia, including coastal China, and the internal markets of the most successful developing countries have grown more or less in line with exports. As well, despite often intense repression, workers' movements and workers' protests are on the rise in many countries across the Global South, from Brazil, to South Africa, to Bangladesh, to China (Ness 2015). Just as workers' organizing in the Global North reshaped the path of capitalist development through the 20th century, these movements in the Global South hold the capacity to redefine the conditions of the global economy in the 21st century.

The Impacts of Free Trade Agreements and North American Economic Integration

From the earliest days of European settler colonialism, Canada has been very closely integrated with the changing international economy. Economic historians, such as Harold Innis (1999), have seen Canada's national economic development as a process driven mainly by foreign demand for natural resources, from fur and fish, to wheat and forest products, to minerals and energy resources. From the 16th century, European settlers traded with the rest of the world and relied on foreign capital to finance new investment. Over time, close trade and investment links with Great Britain and the British Empire gave way to gradual incorporation into a North American economy. By the 1940s, the U.S. had become by far the most important destination of Canadian exports and source of imports and new investment. From the late 19th century, Canada built up a manufacturing sector behind tariff walls in order to protect domestic employment and to limit dependency upon exports of resources. Moreover, Canadian governments helped shape economic development with policies such as the national energy policy and the auto pact through the 1970s. In fact, the Canadian and U.S. economies were very closely tied through trade and major U.S. corporate investments in Canada long before the Canada-U.S. Free Trade Agreement (FTA) of 1988.

For the Canadian economy, globalization was for the most part, and for many years, more about greater economic integration with the U.S. than increased openness to the Global South. The FTA marked a further and important stage in continental economic integration and liberalization. It not only phased out most remaining tariffs and trade barriers, which were modest, but also explicitly prohibited Canada from ever returning to nationalistic economic policies that had been previously undertaken in order to protect domestic industries. Most notably, the FTA limited the federal government's ability to review, prohibit, or place conditions on U.S. corporate takeovers of Canadian companies, to block new U.S. corporate investments, set up new Crown corporations, or give favourable treatment to Canadians when it came to pricing natural resources or giving out government contracts. While subject to numerous exceptions, the guiding principle of the FTA was that Canadian governments would dismantle barriers to the free flow of goods, services, and investment between the two countries, and treat U.S. and Canadian companies in almost exactly the same way. These same principles were incorporated into the NAFTA, which was created when Mexico joined the FTA in 1993, and also into the rules of the WTO, which now govern Canada's economic relations with most of the rest of the world.

In addition to liberalizing trade and investment flows, NAFTA and WTO rules also restricted the ability of governments to regulate corporations in the public interest and to maintain a public sphere outside of the market economy. Critics of these agreements point out that they form a new constitution that entrenches the principle of non-discrimination against foreign corporations, as well as the neoliberal principle of minimizing government intervention in market relations (Clarkson 2002). Trade rules tend to reinforce the view that governments should not intervene in the decisions of business on where and how to operate, and should not insulate large sectors of the economy from the forces of the so-called free market.

The General Agreement on Tariffs and Trade (GATT), which governed the liberalization of Canadian trade before the FTA, NAFTA, and the WTO agreement (which came into effect 1995), used to be almost exclusively about trade in goods and lowering tariffs, and had few (if any) implications for the boundary between the market and the state outside of a limited set of industrial development policies. But new agreements, such as NAFTA, the WTO (regulating trade negotiations and trade-related disputes), and the General Agreement on Trade in Services (GATS), which is an extension of the WTO, intrude much more deeply into the sphere for democratic choice by restricting the ability of governments to both maintain and expand a non-market sector. Pushed actively by transnational corporations, the fundamental premise of these agreements is that TNCs should, by and large, have the right to establish in national markets and be given the same treatment as domestic companies. NAFTA broke new ground by codifying investment rights and extending trade liberalization rules from goods to services like communications, finance, and culture, and by creating a means through which foreign corporations could directly challenge government decisions outside of domestic legal processes (through investor-state disputes settlement). While GATS does not have investor-state provisions, it does envisage setting up domestic tribunals to which transnational corporations could turn for redress. Agreements have increasingly effective enforcement mechanisms, usually based on narrow constructions of rules arrived at in private sessions of trade specialists. The central point is that privatization and the erosion of the public and not-for-profit sectors are already being promoted through binding trade and investment agreements to some degree, and that the pressures for these processes are mounting.

The Free Trade Debate

The great national debate in the late 1980s over the Canada-U.S. FTA split Canada down the middle. While the Mulroney Conservative government won the 1988 election, which was fought almost entirely on the FTA, a majority of voters backed the Liberals and NDP, who opposed the deal. Supporters of free trade, such as the Business Council on National Issues and many economists and conservative think tanks, argued that there would be significant economic gains from trade and investment liberalization that would be shared with workers in the form of higher wages in better jobs, and that a stronger economy would support and sustain social programs. In line with the neoclassical economic argument, tariff elimination was expected to lead to higher productivity and a stronger manufacturing sector (Department of Finance 1988). Labour adjustment was seen as a small, manageable problem because it was assumed that there would be a small overall job gain as workers moved from shrinking to expanding sectors and firms.

For their part, critics such as unions and the nationalist Action Canada Network feared major job losses and argued that closer trade and investment ties with the U.S., and the reduced power of government to control those ties, would increase the bargaining power of mobile, transnational corporations as compared to workers, unions, and governments. Threats to move investment, production, and jobs to the U.S. would work toward the downward harmonization of social and labour standards. These groups saw free trade as a threat to more equitable economic models (Cameron 1988; CLC 1987). Critics also argued that the FTA risked freezing the status quo of excessive resource dependency and a relatively weak manufacturing sector. It was not a question about whether trade with the U.S. was a good or bad thing; rather, the debate was about what role government should have to manage trade and to shape the economy in the interests of workers and communities.

In the years following the passage of first the FTA in 1988 and then NAFTA in 1993, opposition to free trade included the emergence of transnational-focused labour activism, which tapped into a growing global current of counter-movements, as labour movements and social movements in many countries attempted to resist the intensified labour exploitation brought about by globalization (Munck 2002). In the 1990s, this was evident in the anti-sweatshop campaigns that aimed to raise awareness about labour and human rights abuses by TNCs, and to bring pressure to bear on major brand TNCs such as The Gap, Levi-Strauss, and Nike (Ross 2004). In direct response to NAFTA, there was a growth of labour movement cross-border organizing between Mexico, the United States, and Canada (Carr 1999; Ross 2006; Wells 1998). These activities included union organizing campaigns in the *maquiladora* plants along the U.S.-Mexico border, and the organizing of consumer boycotts to support unionization campaigns. These forms of labour activism around transnational labour issues contributed to the emergence of mass protests organized to coincide with the negotiations of major free trade agreements and meetings of international trade bodies, including the Asia-Pacific Economic Cooperation meetings in Vancouver (1997), the WTO in Seattle (1999), the Free Trade Area of the Americas in Quebec City (2001), and more recently the G20 in Toronto (2010). The mass protests at these events contributed to the birth of the anti-globalization movement in the late 1990s and early 2000s (McNally 2006). At their peak, these gatherings brought together tens of thousands of activists aiming to resist the policies and institutions of neoliberal globalization.

Structural Economic Change

Canada–U.S. economic integration in terms of two-way trade flows proceeded extremely rapidly in the wake of the FTA, far faster than anyone on either side of the debate had anticipated. Exports and imports both almost doubled as a share of the economy over the 1990s. Most manufacturing industries became even more strongly oriented to the North American rather than the domestic market, to the extent that the U.S. is now a larger market for Canadian-based manufacturers than Canada itself, and most of the Canadian demand for manufactured goods is now met with imports. Some industries, such as auto and telecommunications, are now so closely integrated that components cross and re-cross the border as they move between different production sites of the same companies.

The FTA was expected to help close the longstanding Canada–U.S. productivity gap, but at best, the gains were modest in the most heavily liberalized sectors. Many smaller plants went under, and the plants that survived did not necessarily expand. The overall Canada–U.S. gap in terms of productivity or output per worker actually widened since the late 1980s, mainly because Canada has been relatively weak in the knowledge-based sectors where productivity growth has been most rapid. A plethora of reports from the OECD (e.g., OECD 2008b), the Conference Board of Canada, and other business think tanks have documented and lamented the growing Canada–U.S. productivity gap that free trade was expected to narrow, while generally favouring even more trade and investment liberalization.

Because of weak productivity growth, Canada's healthy export position in the U.S. market through the economic recovery of the 1990s until the early 2000s was almost entirely due to stagnant real wages and the continued fall of the Canadian dollar, rather than to building up a more sophisticated industrial economy. The longstanding structural problems of Canadian industry remain: too many small, undercapitalized plants; relatively low business investment in machinery and equipment, research and development, and worker training; and overdependence on the production of resources and low-value-added industrial materials as opposed to finished goods. Deeper integration of the manufacturing sector in the North American economy has done little to decisively shift the structure of the economy toward the more dynamic and faster-growing, higher-wage knowledge-based industries capable of withstanding growing global competition and tapping into markets in the Global South. Canada certainly has some strength in a few high-tech industries like communications, biotechnology, and aerospace, and has a large and important auto industry. However, business investment in research and development is confined to a very few firms and sectors, and is less than half the U.S. level as a share of the economy.

While it was hoped that free trade would support a higher-value-added industrial economy, resources and resource-based, low-value-added products like oil and gas, lumber, pulp and paper, and minerals have continued to make up a large share of Canada's exports, and resource dependency has grown significantly since the early 2000s. Resources are an important and continuing source of wealth and jobs, and help sustain regional economies, but sectors like mining and energy are extremely capital-intensive and provide very few direct jobs. It will be very hard to raise Canadian living standards and to sustain and create well-paid jobs over the long term without a shift in production toward more unique or sophisticated goods and services that can command a price premium in world markets, and that are better placed to withstand competition from producers in low-wage countries.

The immediate labour adjustment costs of the FTA turned out to be much greater than had been forecast, partly because the Canadian dollar was overvalued against the U.S. dollar just as the deal came into effect. Between 1989 and 1991, more than one in five manufacturing workers lost their jobs through a massive wave of layoffs and plant closures that devastated industrial communities throughout Ontario and Quebec. The adjustment programs that had been promised were not delivered, and many older workers were forced into premature retirement. Other workers found new jobs, but at much lower wages. The lost jobs in manufacturing were, over time, more than offset by gains in the firms and sectors that survived restructuring, and eventually began to grow as the Canadian dollar fell against the U.S. dollar after 1992. The scale of change in manufacturing that disrupted the lives of so many working people is underlined by the fact that half of all the plants in existence in 1988—accounting for more than one-quarter of all jobs—had closed by 1997, while 39 percent of all plants in 1997—accounting for 21 percent of all jobs—did not exist at all in 1988 (Baldwin and Gu 2003).

The Resource Boom and the Manufacturing Jobs Crisis

As of 2015, manufacturing continues to be an important direct source of approximately 1.7 million good jobs due to above-average productivity, the result of higher-than-average capital investment per worker, and a strong base of skilled workers.[1] These jobs pay about $21 per hour on average, compared to hourly wages of around $16 per hour in private-sector services, where most of the net new jobs in the business sector are being created.[2] Manufacturing jobs are also more likely to be full-time jobs, to provide pension and health benefits, and to be unionized. Displaced workers must compete for other jobs, lowering wages in other sectors in periods of layoffs, and usually face significant pay cuts in new jobs. Even though the manufacturing sector has been shrinking as a share of employment over time due to rising productivity and increased imports, it still supports many good jobs in both private and public services, and tends to set a wage standard that spills over into other sectors. The state of manufacturing is thus important to the overall health of the job market. While often denigrated as part of an "old economy" that must be replaced by a new "knowledge-based economy," it should also be noted that the majority of all business research and development in Canada, in fact, takes place in manufacturing, especially in industries like aerospace and electrical machinery and equipment (Informetrica 2007b).

After 10 years of relative stability, the manufacturing sector entered a new period of crisis and restructuring in 2002. More than 575,000 direct manufacturing jobs were lost over the 13 years through to 2015.[3] The major cause was a competitiveness squeeze due to the high dollar and a huge and growing trade deficit with Asia. Jobs were lost to plant closures and layoffs caused by lower production, a corporate drive for intensified productivity in remaining opera-

Box 11.3: Navistar to Close Chatham, Ont., Plant—Truck Manufacturing Facility Has Been Idle Since June 2009
By CBC News

Navistar confirmed Tuesday that it intends to close its Chatham, Ont., truck assembly plant.

The company said in a statement Tuesday that the plant has been idled and employees have been on layoff status since 2009 "due to the company's inability to reach a collective bargaining agreement with the Canadian Auto Workers."

"It's not a surprise, but it doesn't take the disappointment away," Canadian Auto Workers president Ken Lewenza said after Tuesday's announcement.

Lewenza criticized the decision to shut the plant and said the proposal put forward by the company "was not ratifiable."

"It's troubling ... without that facility truck manufacturing in Canada is taking another blow," Lewenza said ahead of the announcement.

He said the only good thing about Tuesday's announcement is that it finally brings closure for the workers.

"You can't keep 1,000 people that remain on the seniority list—350 active when we were laid off, but 1,000 total on the seniority list—waiting for another day or waiting for another rumour or waiting for another announcement," Lewenza said. "It's been very, very tough on the community."

The truck plant has been idle for the past two years. At its peak in the late 1990s, the facility employed more than 2,000 workers, he said.

Navistar is building its heavy duty commercial trucks in the United States and Mexico.

The company said the Chatham production has already been absorbed by other truck plants.

Lewenza said the union will meet with company representatives soon to discuss plans to "reduce the pain on the members through retirement and severance options."

Randy Hope, Chatham's mayor, said the real economic impact of the closure was felt in 2009 when the plant was idled.

"Nothing will ever replace the high-paying jobs that were there in that facility," Hope said before the company made the announcement.

Hope wants to have a discussion with the company about the fate of the large site on Richmond Street. The Chatham plant has been around for well over 100 years, he said.

According to the CAW, Navistar benefited from over $60 million in federal and provincial funding over the years, as well as $40 million in contract savings from union members.

Source: CBC News. 2011, August 2. "Navistar to Close Chatham, Ont. Plant—Truck Manufacturing Facility Has Been Idle Since June 2009." *CBC News*. www.cbc.ca/news/canada/windsor/navistar-to-close-chatham-ont-plant-1.1030922.

tions, and increased outsourcing of production inputs, especially services to other countries as part of the creation of global value chains. By sector, job losses have been greatest in auto, forest products, and clothing, and, in the capital goods sector, computers and telecom equipment, which never fully recovered from the dot-com bust of 2000. The impact has been great in the unionized manufacturing sector, which has accounted for half of the job losses, even though only one-third of manufacturing jobs are unionized.

In the early 2000s, the dominant response to a more competitive global market was to shift non-resource production out of Canada, rather than to upgrade production capacity through productivity-oriented innovation within Canada. New Canadian business investment was instead concentrated in the oil and gas and mining sectors, with annual capital investment between 2004 and 2013 increasing at rate of 9.8 percent, rising from $29.9 billion to $69.3 billion (Government of Canada 2016d). Since 2002, Canada's exports became even more dominated by resources and industrial materials, such as ores and concentrates, chemicals, potash, and so on. Though manufactured goods still compose the majority share of Canada's exports (63.8 percent in 2014), this has fallen since the mid-1990s, when the share of manufactured goods was over 80 percent (87 percent in 1999) (Tremblay 2015). The emphasis on resource development shows signs of Canada's traditional role in the global economy as a resource producer.

The conventional wisdom has been that the shrinkage of the manufacturing sector is not a major problem. But good new jobs have not been created in sufficient numbers to replace lost manufacturing jobs. While there are certainly good jobs in the resource sector, mines and oil and gas production are extremely capital-intensive operations that, once built, will require relatively few workers. There are potential problems down the road if manufacturing shrinks too much, especially if growth is driven by an energy sector that is based on non-renewable resources being extracted far too fast in an environmentally unsustainable fashion, with little value added in Canada. Resource-led economies are prone to boom-bust cycles and to having a relatively narrow core of good jobs, as opposed to diversified economies with a strong manufacturing base, which are more stable and have relatively more jobs in higher-productivity sectors.

Harmonization to the U.S. Social Model?

In the free trade debate of the late 1980s, free trade advocates argued that a stronger economy would support better social programs. However, after the deal was signed, business increasingly argued that high social expenditures, financed from progressive taxes, made Canada uncompetitive in a shared economic space. Competitiveness came to be defined as lower taxes, lower social spending, and more flexible labour markets. Experience has shown that there are indeed downward pressures from North American economic integration on progressive, redistributive social policies that arise mainly from the tax side.

Canada used to have a very different social model than the U.S. Among the elements of difference, Canada had—and indeed still has—a significantly more equal distribution of both earnings and after-tax/transfer (disposable) income, which reflects higher unionization, somewhat higher minimum wages, and a smaller pay gap between the middle and the top of the earnings spectrum. More equal after-tax incomes and lower rates of after-tax poverty than in the U.S. also reflect the impacts of a more generous system of transfers acting upon a somewhat more equal distribution of market income. Until the changes of the mid-1990s, the Canadian Unemployment Insurance system was notably more generous than that of the U.S., and Canadian welfare programs benefit a larger share of the non-elderly, non-working poor. All Canadian provinces, but no U.S. states, provide welfare to singles and families without children, and social assistance benefits, while low and falling in real terms, are generally higher than in the U.S. In the mid-1990s, the Canadian poverty rate for all people was just over half the rate in the U.S. (using a common definition of less than half of median household income) and the minimum distance between the top and bottom 10 percent of families ranked by income was 4 to 1, compared to almost 6.5 to 1. The level of services provided on a citizen entitlement basis is also higher in Canada than the U.S., reducing dependence on market income for some basic needs. Medicare is the key example, but Canada also provides a somewhat higher level of community services, such as not-for-profit child care, home care, and elder care services. Greater equality has sustained better social outcomes in terms of health, crime, and educational attainment.

Economic Integration and Income Inequality

As detailed earlier in this book, there has been a significant increase in income inequality among working-age Canadian families over the past decade, driven by stronger wage growth for high-income earners and cuts in social transfers. While many factors have been at play, there is a link between increased global competition and the stagnation of average wages, with part of that linkage running through a weakened labour movement. Real wages have failed to rise in line with productivity, and the decline in unionization and labour bargaining power has been greatest in the manufacturing sector, the most exposed to the reality and threat of disinvestment. There is also a link between continental integration and the increased market incomes of the most affluent Canadians. Closer trade and investment links, along with more investment by Canadian and U.S. TNCs on both sides of the border, have led to a convergence of salary and stock options for highly mobile professionals and managers in the corporate sector upward to U.S. levels. This has driven the increased income share of the top 1 percent. Interestingly, this has not happened in Quebec, where senior corporate executives are, for cultural and linguistic reasons, much less likely to be tempted to move to the U.S.

Economic Integration and Social Programs

Closer integration can be linked to the erosion of income transfers to the working-age population and cuts to social programs. Many people would argue that the Employment Insurance (EI) cuts imposed by the Liberal government in 1995, cuts in federal transfers to the provinces for social programs, and provincial welfare cuts were driven primarily by deficit reduction goals, which is true to a degree. However, the Department of Finance, the OECD, and the International Monetary Fund have long argued that Canada's supposedly generous welfare state is associated with a stronger tendency to wage-driven inflation than in the U.S. The basic argument is that income benefits strengthen the bargaining power of workers and their willingness to hold out for better wages if and when they become unemployed. Cuts to transfers, particularly EI, were consciously intended to promote greater labour market and wage flexibility (Jackson 2000b; Sargent and Sheikh 1996). In short, closer integration with the U.S. and increased low-wage competition made the U.S. model of a more minimalist welfare state attractive to those who worried about the relative strength of Canadian workers.

In the era of free trade, business organizations and neoliberal governments endlessly repeated the argument that economic success will go to countries that most closely copy the U.S. model of weak unions, low taxes, and low social spending. In the years following the implementation of NAFTA, particularly after the elimination of the federal deficit in 1997, the political argument was constantly advanced that taxes had to be cut to U.S. levels to maintain competitiveness and fuel economic growth and job creation. The argument was that Canadian business taxes (corporate income taxes and capital taxes) and personal income taxes on higher earners were too high compared to the U.S., making the U.S. a more attractive location for mobile corporations to invest and produce. A great deal of emphasis was placed on the need to cut corporate taxes and taxes on high-income earners by business lobby groups, such as the Canadian Council of Chief Executives and the Chamber of Commerce, and conservative think tanks, such as the C.D. Howe Institute. This legitimized the drastic levels of "fiscal discipline" imposed in Canada during the 1990s, which was by far the greatest of any major OECD country (Stanford 2004). Between 1992 and 2002, total government program spending in Canada fell by 10 percentage points of GDP, compared to an OECD average of just one percentage point, with about half coming from federal program spending cuts. As a result, the once very significant Canada–U.S. differences in the relative priority given to social spending or lower taxes have been greatly eroded in the era of greater economic integration.[4] This compounded inequality in Canada, particularly at a time when earnings are becoming much more unequal.

Conclusion

Globalization has significantly increased competitive pressures on Canadian corporations, and resulted in the erosion of the bargaining power and living standards of workers in Canada. NAFTA has created major issues for the future capacity of governments to regulate corporations in the public interest and to maintain a public sphere outside the market. The issues posed by these developments will persist for many years to come, given business proposals for still deeper continental integration, plus further liberalization of the international trade and investment rules. In response to these developments, critics have advanced a range of alternatives. The anti-globalization movement encompasses a wide range of views, from supporters of left economic nationalism who want democratic national governments to have greater control over corporations operating within their borders, to progressive internationalists who support a more open, global economy, but want it to operate under an economically and socially just set of international rules. While global capitalism is a powerful force, as the final chapter in this book discusses, the future of work in a global economy remains highly contested.

Recommended Reading

Caulfield, Norman. 2010. *NAFTA and Labor in North America*. Urbana & Chicago: University of Illinois Press.

McNally, David. 2006. *Another World Is Possible: Globalization and Anti-Capitalism*. 2nd Edition. Winnipeg: Arbeiter Ring.

Ness, Immanuel. 2015. *Southern Insurgency: The Coming of the Global Working Class*. London: Pluto Press.

Teeple, Gary. 2000. *Globalization and the Decline of Social Reform: Into the Twenty-First Century*. Toronto: Garamond Press.

Notes

1. Statistics Canada, CANSIM Table 282-0008. Accessed at: http://www5.statcan. gc.ca/cansim/a26?lang=eng&retrLang=eng&id=2820008&&pattern=&stByVal =1&p1=1&p2=37&tabMode=dataTable&csid=.
2. Statistics Canada, CANSIM Table 282-0151. Accessed at: http://www5.statcan. gc.ca/cansim/a26?lang=eng&retrLang=eng&id=2820151&&pattern=&stByVal =1&p1=1&p2=37&tabMode=dataTable&csid=.
3. Statistics Canada, CANSIM Table 282-0008. Accessed at: http://www5.statcan. gc.ca/cansim/a26?lang=eng&retrLang=eng&id=2820008&pattern=&csid=.
4. While Canadian governments still spend more on social programs and public services than U.S. governments, the difference has shrunk dramatically.

Between 1992 and 2001, total Canadian government spending on programs other than defence fell from 42.9 percent to 33.6 percent of GDP, while U.S. government spending on non-defence programs remained almost the same (increasing slightly, from 27.7 percent to 27.9 percent of GDP). Thus, the once very large gap between the two countries fell from about 15 percentage points of GDP in 1992 to just 6 percentage points in just under a decade (Department of Finance 2003). By 2004, government spending, when corrected for accounting differences, was almost exactly the same in both countries, 38.5 percent of Canadian GDP, compared to 37 percent of U.S. GDP (Ferris and Winer 2007). Non-defence-related government spending was still more than 5 percent of GDP higher in Canada than in the U.S. (37.5 percent vs. 32.7 percent in 2004), though that was down very sharply from the huge 16 percent of GDP (50 percent vs. 34 percent) peak gap between the two countries in 1994, reflecting deep cuts to EI and social assistance in Canada.

CHAPTER 12

Improving Work: Reforming or Transforming Wage Labour?

The early years of the 21st century have seen widespread discontent about work. This is evidenced by the rise of protest movements among workers in precarious jobs, such as the Fight for $15 and Fairness, efforts by unions to reorganize themselves to better reflect the new world of work, and in the growing awareness by some governments of the need to establish new workplace protections to counter precariousness in the labour market. These developments reflect a central tenet of this book: that work should be understood as a "social problem." As has been illustrated throughout the chapters, the conditions of inequality and precariousness that are so connected to the workplace have a fundamentally social basis: they are created through the social relations of work; they are conditioned by social context; and they are experienced collectively. In recognizing work as a social problem, we also must ask what to do about it. This final chapter of the book takes up this question by looking at four broad possibilities for improving work.

The chapter begins by comparing Canada's labour market model to the social democratic Scandinavian model, as exemplified by the "flexicurity" approach. It draws on recent European experience to suggest that there is no inevitable trade-off between high employment and job creation on the one hand, and improving the quality of jobs and promoting equality on the other. The chapter then looks at proposals for reducing and controlling working time as a strategy for resolving the social problem of work by creating greater freedom from work and greater control over time. Third, the chapter examines the potential for worker cooperatives as a means to construct a more democratic workplace. Finally, the chapter concludes by considering the possibility of moving beyond wage labour, suggesting that while reforming work through better policies and practices is essential, to ultimately truly address the social problem of work will require much more fundamental social and economic transformations.

The Scandinavian Model and "Flexicurity"

Quite often, neoliberal economists and policy-makers claim that improving working conditions through stronger labour and employment legislation will come at the cost of job loss, as businesses will not be able to sustain the costs of higher wages and better job security. For example, the highly influential *OECD Jobs Study* (1994) argued that more labour market regulation in continental Europe compared to the U.S. and the U.K. was a major factor behind higher unemployment. The view of neoclassical economists is that overly generous unemployment benefits create barriers and disincentives to work by leading workers to expect wages that are higher than those available, particularly for low-skilled workers. Further, it is argued that high wage floors set by minimum wages and collective bargaining mean that low-skilled workers will be priced out of low-productivity jobs. The ideal labour market is one in which wages closely reflect the relative productivity of different groups of workers. The message to governments has been that there is necessarily a trade-off between the quantity and quality of jobs for lower-skilled and vulnerable workers, and that protective measures such as generous unemployment benefits, unions, and minimum wages come at the significant cost of high unemployment. This view has been a major influence on Canadian labour market policy. Employment Insurance and welfare benefits have been substantially cut and entitlements restricted. Minimum wages have fallen behind average wages, basic employment standards have been eroded, and labour laws have generally become much less supportive of providing access to collective bargaining.

As shown in previous chapters, labour market inequality in Canada has increased since at least the mid-1980s, in that earnings growth for some has increased sharply while there has also been a rise in the incidence of precarious and low-paid jobs. Indeed, Canada stands out as an exceptionally high-earnings-inequality and low-wage country among advanced industrial countries, particularly when compared to the Scandinavian countries. Table 12.1 provides some key indicators of earnings inequality, looking at Canada, the U.S., Sweden, the U.K., Australia, and the Netherlands. As shown, the ratio between the 9th decile and the 1st decile—that is, the minimum gap between the top 10 percent and the bottom 10 percent of the workforce (looking only at full-time workers)—was 3.94 in Canada in 2012, meaning that the top 10 percent earned at least 3.94 times as much as the bottom 10 percent. This is lower than the 4.81 ratio in the U.S., but a much greater gap than in Sweden (2.18), and also higher than the U.K., Australia, and the Netherlands. As shown, while the differences

Table 12.1: Earnings Inequality, 2012

	Canada	U.S.	Sweden	U.K.	Australia	Netherlands
Decile ratios						
9:1	3.94	4.81	2.18	3.53	3.14	3.24
9:5	1.94	2.4	1.59	2.07	1.9	1.79
5:1	2.03	2.01	1.37	1.71	1.65	1.81

Source: OECD, *Survey of Adult Skills* (PIAAC), 2012.

between countries in terms of the gap between the top 10 percent and the middle 10 percent of full-time earners, and between the middle 10 percent and the bottom 10 percent, are not as stark, Sweden remains more equal than Canada, as do Australia and the Netherlands, according to this measure. Overall, earnings inequality as measured by the 9:1 ratio has increased in all countries since the 1990s, but less so in the Scandinavian countries as compared to the more deregulated job markets of the U.S., the U.K., and Canada (Pontusson 2005).

Labour market institutions—wage floors set by collective bargaining and legislated minimum wages—play a major role in accounting for different levels of low pay and earnings inequality. Advanced industrial countries differ rather little in terms of the big structural forces shaping job markets. All are exposed to increased international competition from low-wage countries and technological change, widely believed to be tipping the scales against relatively low-skilled workers. But, there is a strong consensus that labour market institutions still significantly shape outcomes for workers (Aidt and Tzannatos 2003; Freeman and Katz 1995; OECD 1996, 1997; Freeman 2007). As has been shown, collective bargaining raises the relative pay of workers who would otherwise be lower-paid—women, minorities, younger workers, the relatively unskilled—and narrows wage differentials. Due to declining unionization, increases in wage inequality from the mid-1980s have been much greater in liberal labour markets such as Canada and the U.S. than in the Scandinavian or continental European countries (Freeman and Katz 1995; OECD 1996).

If the neoclassical view of how the labour market works was correct, generous unemployment benefits, high wage floors, and low earnings inequality would come at the price of jobs. However, looking at the 1980s and 1990s, research by the World Bank and the OECD found that there is no relationship at the country-wide level between collective bargaining coverage and economic or employment performance (Aidt and Tzannatos 2003; OECD 1997). More recently, the OECD concluded that there are, in fact, different routes to high employment and low unemployment, and that some countries with more regulated job markets have done as well or better than highly deregulated countries like the U.S. and the U.K. (OECD 2006a). Union density, generous unemployment benefits, and relatively equal wages are, overall, related neither to higher- nor to lower-than-average rates of unemployment or economic growth (Baker et al. 2002). The European Commission (2001, 2002) has also rejected the idea of a job quality/job quantity trade-off for lower-skilled workers, and also highlighted the experiences of Denmark and the Netherlands as desirable alternatives to the U.S. model. The fundamental message is that the neoliberal labour market gives rise to unacceptable levels of wage inequality and social exclusion, and that a social democratic model can provide high levels of quality employment with low levels of insecurity.

In fact, the experience of Scandinavian social democratic countries in recent decades suggests that a combination of high employment, relatively equal wages, and real opportunities for workers in precarious employment is possible. This requires regulating the labour market to create a strong wage floor and a low level of wage inequality, achieved primarily via collective bargaining. This also involves providing social and economic security through public programs financed from general taxation, and investing in active labour market policies to upgrade the skills of those at greatest risk of engaging in precarious employment. In the Scandinavian experience, this has included building a post-industrial service economy based on a large non-market sector and high-productivity private services. Success in securing high rates of employment in good jobs also depends on appropriate macroeconomic policies and good labour relations. This social democratic labour market model is based on high levels of paid employment for both women and men, high levels of collective bargaining coverage, and universal social welfare programs and public services financed from taxes, which reduce reliance on wages. The model has limited precarious employment by socializing some of the caring responsibilities of households, such as child and elder care. This has reduced the double burden of household and paid work on women, directly created many jobs of reasonably high quality for women in social services, and reduced the importance of low-wage jobs in private consumer services.

The "flexicurity" model has arisen in this context, striking a balance between the security needs of workers and the flexibility needs of employers. For example, the Scandinavian countries have stressed employment security through active labour market policies and high levels of worker training, as well as generous unemployment benefits as workers move between jobs in a constantly changing labour market. Similarly, some European countries have frowned on the creation of part-time jobs, but others have seen part-time jobs as valuable so long as they are taken voluntarily and provide a decent level of pay and benefits. The very strong job creation performance of the Netherlands in the 1990s owed a lot to part-time job creation. Accordingly, the European Union has implemented binding directives mandating member countries to legislate non-discrimination against part-time workers (1997) and temporary workers (1999) with respect to pay and access to permanent jobs and training. The directive on fixed-term work requires countries to set limits on the maximum duration of contracts or the number of renewals.

The extent to which employers are expected to finance social security through payroll taxes or private pension, health, and other benefits is another key factor. The social democratic model of services for all citizens financed from general taxes lowers these levies on employers. Countries also differ greatly in terms of the extent to which they invest in public education and active labour market policies to promote labour adjustment and lifelong learning. Training for the unemployed and workers in precarious employment helps equalize access to job opportunities and also creates a base for higher-quality jobs. As shown earlier, training can be a force for better jobs in low-wage private services. Such active labour market policies directed to the relatively unskilled have long been a major feature of the social democratic model.

Finally, advanced industrial countries differ a lot in terms of the structure of the service sector, depending on the extent to which the caring needs of households, such as child and elder care, and a wide range of community services, such as health, have been assumed by the market or by the state (Esping-Anderson 1999; O'Conner et al. 1999; Pierson 2001). Traditionally, women's low rates of labour force participation in social market countries went hand in hand with the assumption that children and the elderly would be cared for mainly by women in the home. In the Scandinavian countries, state delivery of caring services has expanded the public sector, enabled women to work, and created new jobs that have gone mainly to women. Jobs in social services tend to have higher skill requirements than private consumer services jobs, and working conditions are usually covered by collective bargaining. Thus, a country's decision to tax and spend on social services has had direct implications for the quality of services jobs.

As noted, high rates of collective bargaining coverage do not necessarily lead to poor employment outcomes. Denmark, the Netherlands, and Sweden have done well, partly because widespread bargaining has produced wage outcomes that have preserved cost competitiveness for employers and maintained low inflation. Unions in Denmark and the Netherlands have consciously bargained, within a framework of loose national guidelines, to promote job growth. By bargaining for jobs rather than just for higher wages for employed insiders, some labour movements have helped counter unemployment and precarious employment.

Rather than destroying private service jobs, high labour standards can raise job quality and pay by raising productivity. Wage floors can lower worker turnover and increase experience and skills, reducing employer costs. A common wage standard can also take wage costs out of the competitive equation. If all employers pay the same wage and benefit package, firms must compete with one another on the basis of non–labour cost issues, such as quality and customer service. There is good evidence that decent wages and high labour standards raise productivity. The fact that employers come under pressure to pay good wages will lead them to invest more in capital equipment and training than would otherwise be the case. Further, high labour standards can raise productivity by improving the social relations of production. If workers know that changes in work organization will not cost them their jobs or lead to poorer health and safety or working conditions, and that the gains of higher productivity will be shared with them, then workers will cooperate in workplace change.

Table 12.2 provides comparative data for Canada, the U.S., Sweden, the U.K., and Australia to draw out some key contrasts between the liberal and the social democratic models. As the table indicates, Sweden has achieved a somewhat higher employment rate and has especially high employment rates for women, as well as lower youth unemployment. Notably, employment rates for workers with low levels of formal education are also significantly higher in Sweden than in the U.S. or Canada, disproving the idea that it is low-skilled workers who are squeezed out of jobs if the wage floor is set too high.

Sweden also has a lower rate of poverty compared to Canada and the U.S., reflecting much lower levels of earnings inequality (Table 12.1) and low pay, and also higher levels of publicly funded social investments as a share of GDP. Overall, relative earnings equality combined with high levels of cash transfers by govern-

Table 12.2: Canada in Comparison: Key Economic and Social Indicators

	Canada	U.S.	Sweden	U.K.	Australia
1. Employment performance (%)					
Employment/population ratio in 2014:					
All (15–64)	72.3	68.1	74.9	72.6	71.6
Men	75.2	73.5	76.6	77.6	77.1
Women	69.4	63	73.2	67.6	66.1
Unemployment rate in 2014:					
All	7	6.3	8.1	6.4	6.2
Men	7.5	6.4	8.4	6.6	6.1
Women	6.5	6.1	7.8	6.1	6.3
Youth unemployment or inactive and not in education nor in training (15–24) in 2012	9.6	15	7.2	13.5	12.1
2. Social investment—public expenditure (% GDP)					
Net total social expenditure, 2011	17.1	20.1	22.5	21.4	17.4
Public expenditure on old-age pensions, in 2011	4	6	6.7	4.8	3.3
Unemployment—cash benefits, in 2011	0.7	0.8	0.4	0.4	0.5
3. Social outcomes					
Poverty rate (less than 50% median) in 2010	11.9	17.4	9.1	10	14.4

Source: Except where otherwise noted, data are from OECD, 2014, *Society at a Glance 2014: OECD Social Indicators*, OECD Publishing. Employment performance, excluding youth unemployment category, is from OECD.org.

ments has produced a strikingly more equal distribution of after-tax family income (Pontusson 2005). Because transfers have risen to offset modestly rising earnings inequality, household income inequality in Sweden has remained more or less unchanged over the past decade. Moreover, not only is income much more equally distributed than in Canada and the U.S., Swedish households rely much less on cash income because they receive many social services at more modest costs. For example, taxpayer-funded health expenditures as a share of GDP in 2014 were at

10 percent in Sweden, as compared to 7.4 percent in Canada.[1] In terms of general social services expenditures, much of the difference in spending is accounted for by higher spending on child care, elder care, and community social services, all of which also account for significant areas of employment.

A Closer Look at Denmark

While in very broad terms it is a version of the Scandinavian social democratic model, Denmark differs from Sweden in many ways. It has an economy based much more on small firms in services, food processing, and light industry, and less on large-scale industry. Like Sweden and the Netherlands, recent employment success contrasts with experiences of high unemployment, fiscal crisis, and very strained labour-management relationships at various times in the 1980s and early 1990s. Like the Netherlands, crisis led to a renewal of the social partnership model and major reforms.

The incidence of low-wage work in Denmark is minimal because of the high wage floor set by collective bargaining. In 2013, 80 percent of all workers and about 77 percent of private-sector workers were covered by collective agreements (Eurofound 2015). Coverage is almost universal in community and social services, and collective agreements cover the majority of workers even in normally low-wage consumer services sectors such as retail trade and hotels and restaurants. Bargaining coverage is stable or even increasing, despite erosion among some higher-paid professionals, and there is also high union coverage of potentially vulnerable workers. With a wage determination system characterized as "centralized decentralization," bargaining is conducted on a sectoral basis between employer associations and unions within a loose framework of centrally agreed wage guidelines, with some enterprise flexibility to pay higher wages.

The incidence of non-standard employment in Denmark is in some areas comparable to Canada, though notably better in terms of temporary work (OECD 2016c). Self-employment (which is disproportionately, though not universally, precarious) accounts for 9 percent of total employment, compared to about 8.8 percent in Canada and an E.U. average of 16.5 percent. Similarly, the low incidence of part-time work (at 19.2 percent) is comparable to Canada's 19.1 percent, though higher than the E.U. average overall (17.6 percent). Temporary or fixed-term contract employment accounts for 8.8 percent of employment, as compared to 13.4 percent in Canada and the E.U. average of 13.9 percent. Moreover, the status of temporary workers in Denmark generally compares very well to other E.U. countries and to Canada, as temporary workers are covered by collective agreements and qualify for paid holidays, parental leave, and sick leave (OECD 2002c).

The European Commission judges Denmark to have the highest overall quality of jobs in the E.U. (European Commission 2001). Measured by pay, working conditions, subjective job satisfaction, and opportunities for advancement, 60 percent of Danes are in good jobs (the highest proportion in Europe), 20 percent are in jobs of reasonable quality, and just 20 percent are in jobs of poor quality (of which less than half qualify as really bad, dead-end jobs). There are also very high rates of transition from lower-quality to higher-quality jobs, with 35 percent of workers in low-quality jobs moving to better jobs one year later, and 50 percent in better jobs three years later (compared to 35 percent in the U.K.) (European Commission 2002). Data from the *European Survey on Work Conditions* also suggest that jobs in the Danish services sector are, on average, much better than elsewhere in the E.U. in terms of levels of work autonomy and the incidence of monotonous work (OECD 2001b).

Despite quite high rates of entry into unemployment, perceived employment security is very high. A 2000 survey found that only 9 percent of Danish workers were afraid of losing their current jobs, the lowest in the E.U. (Ploughmann and Madsen 2002). By contrast, one-quarter to one-third of Canadian workers have reported fear of job loss in recent years, according to the CCSD Personal Security Index. The annual incidence of unemployment is as high as one in four workers, but for the majority, unemployment is very short-term (less than 10 weeks). While there is a low level of job protection, which has encouraged job creation, in line with the principle of "flexicurity" and the traditional social democratic model, unemployment benefits replace a high proportion of wages, and there is a strong emphasis on training and active labour market policy to promote employment security.

The great majority of unemployed workers belong to an Unemployment Insurance Fund administered by the unions, and are eligible for benefits if employed for one year in the last three. The OECD calculated the relative generosity of benefits for unemployed workers for different family types and earning levels and found that the Danish and Swedish systems are by far the most generous. The income replacement rate for an average-production worker is at least 70 percent, rising to 90 percent for relatively low-paid workers (Madsen 2003). For an estimated one-third of unemployed men and one-half of unemployed women, benefits just about match prior earnings (Benner and Vad 2000). Moreover, public expenditures on labour market training and other active employment measures are even higher in Denmark than in Sweden, and six times higher than in Canada. The main focus is on training for the unemployed, and about two in three unemployed workers, or 6 percent of the total workforce, receive some public training each year. This can be in private firms with a wage subsidy, with a public-sector employer, or in training or educational programs to fill future labour market vacancies. In addition, about 10 percent of the workforce benefit each year from government training programs is directed to employed workers.

The Danish system also features high levels of education and training for the currently employed. On top of a strong base of universal public education and high participation in post-secondary studies, the rhetoric of lifelong learning in a skill-based economy has been translated into reality through rights to individual education leaves and opportunities to take education leaves funded by unemployment benefits. These were quite popular when used to address high unemployment in the early to mid-1990s. Unions bargain access to training and help run employer-sponsored training. Denmark has been ranked very high among OECD countries in terms of the extent of adult participation in training (OECD 2011b).

In the discussion above, emphasis was placed on the importance of public and social services as a source of quality employment for women. Such services account for about one-third of Danish employment, and fully one-half of employment for women, though private service sector employment has grown faster since the mid-1980s (Madsen 2003). In Denmark, tax reform in the mid-1990s trimmed already low payroll taxes, and sharply reduced employer responsibility for funding active labour market programs. Workplace pensions play a modest role compared to universal state pensions and the state-run, work-based pension system. As a result, the proportion of social expenditures financed by employers is the lowest in the E.U.—8.7 percent, compared to 46.5 percent in France and 37.4 percent in Germany (ILO 2003: 58), and the percentage of non-wage costs in total labour costs is just 6.3 percent, compared to 31.8 percent in France and 20.7 percent in the U.S. (ILO 2003: 61).

Denmark figured as a particularly interesting case study in a major comparative study of low-wage work in advanced industrial countries (Westergaard-Nielson 2008). The study found that a high "wage floor" set by collective bargaining makes a real difference for workers in sectors that are low-wage in other countries. Set at about $20 Canadian per hour (14 Euros per hour in 2005), the minimum wage floor negotiated centrally between employers and unions means that the incidence of low-wage work in Denmark is just 8.5 percent of the workforce, compared to 25 percent in the U.S. While there are generally strong downward pressures on wages and working conditions at the bottom of advanced industrial labour markets, Denmark has managed to improve the quality of jobs that would be low paid in a North American context.

Looking at the Danish model, it can be seen that raising productivity in low-wage sectors can both improve the quality of jobs and increase the output of the whole economy. For example, while food processing is a low-wage industry in the U.S. and Canada in the wake of a frontal attack on unions, Denmark's relatively large food processing sector has pursued a classic "high road" strategy, raising productivity and creating high-quality products by investing in new equipment, processes, and worker skills. There has been a major shift from manual work to automation in meat processing and other subsectors, with skills rising as a result. The workforce—which includes many recent immigrants—is highly unionized, which helps sustain not just decent pay, but also safe working conditions. An industry focus on high quality as well as on high productivity has helped maintain strong national brands, and a large share of the domestic and European market.

In health care, low-wage work has been virtually eliminated, not just through high unionization but also through a concerted strategy to raise worker skills at all levels and to create coherent and well-planned ladders to better jobs. Given shortages of very highly skilled workers, physician work has been shifted to nurses, from nurses to nursing assistants (two levels of which exist), and from nursing assistants to a new category of ancillary workers. At the lowest level of the job ladder, a category of "hospital service assistant" has jobs that combine cleaning and food preparation with some tasks formerly performed by the lower level of nursing assistants. They receive training in a range of duties, and have the opportunity to train so as to take on more basic nursing assistant responsibilities. Many of the workers who were previously employed in the lowest nursing assistant category have been retrained to work at a level requiring higher skills. In short, a serious attempt has been made to create job ladders so those at the bottom of the ladder can and do move up.

The Limits of the Scandinavian Model

It is important to recognize that, while the social democratic labour market model is progressive from the point of view of limiting the incidence of precarious employment, it is still problematic from a wider equality perspective. In terms of gender equity, women still perform a highly unequal share of caring work, and, as in Canada, there is a highly gendered division of paid labour between women and men, with women having only limited access to higher-level jobs in the private sector. For example, Denmark and Sweden have the lowest gaps in employment rates by gender among OECD countries, and a slightly smaller than average gender wage gap (OECD 2002a). The high level of social services means that children or elderly relatives pose few barriers to women's labour market participation. However, there is an even higher proportion of women employed in female-dominated occupations in Sweden and Denmark than in Canada, and women still perform a very unequal share of work in the home.

With regards to race and ethnicity, being socially homogeneous small countries, the values of social solidarity tend to be racially and culturally defined. In Denmark, for example, unemployment is relatively high among recent immigrants from Global South countries, and conservative governments have limited immigrant access to full welfare benefits. Thus, while the social democratic model is progressive from the standpoint of limiting precarious employment generally, it still falls short from the standpoint of promoting racial/ethnic equality.

Looking at the social democratic model more broadly, many observers question if the social democratic countries can continue to create such a large share of new jobs in tax-financed public and social services, as opposed to lower-skilled and usually lower-paid jobs in consumer services. There have recently been some signs of rising inequality in the Scandinavian countries, which are by no means exempt from competitive pressures that prompt employers to demand greater "flexibility." The "flexicurity" model itself has been critiqued for tendencies to prioritize flexibility over security and to favour the interests of employers over those of workers (Keune and Jepsen 2007; Luce 2015). Ultimately, with the balance of social forces tilted so firmly in favour of capital at the global scale, social democratic models of labour market regulation cannot escape the pressures of neoliberalism.

Reducing and Controlling Working Time

Control over working time is at the heart of the organization of wage labour. Central to the exchange of labour power for a wage is the establishment of the working day, whereby the worker agrees to give up control of their time for a period established by their employer (Marx 1976). It is during this period of time that the worker not only produces commodities, but also surplus value, making the length of the working day (alongside the organization of the labour process itself) a crucial element in both the process of capital accumulation and the dynamics of class struggle.

The emergence of the factory system of industrial capitalism, initially in England, and its methods of production involved the imposition of a new time discipline on the growing industrial working class (Thompson 1967). As capitalism developed and spread, how time was "put to use" changed profoundly in conjunction with transformations in the social organization of work. For example, in pre-capitalist forms of work, there was a longstanding association between the measurement of time and the performance of domestic work, such as the feeding of animals and the cooking of food, which involved "task orientation." Here, labour itself was not timed but performed in relation to natural rhythms, with the working day lengthening and decreasing according to the task, and with a constant blurring between "work" and "life." The shift from task orientation to timed labour coincided with the emergence of wage labour and the imposition of a distinction between the employer's time and the worker's time. As industrial capitalism developed, so too did the time sheet and the timekeeper, which were then followed by the widespread development and utilization of machines that monitored shift times, keeping records of when workers "clocked in" to work.

Through the early history of capitalism, the imposition of employer control over work time, and the tendency for employers to seek to maximize the length of the working day, made working time a key site of struggle. As Marx (1976: 382) notes, "the establishment of a normal working day is the result of centuries of struggle between the capitalist and the worker." Similarly, in describing the response of workers to a new time discipline during the transition to industrial capitalism, Thompson (1967: 85) wrote, "So the workers begin to fight, not against time, but about it." As collective worker organizations began to emerge in response to the exploitation of factory work, they too placed their attention on regulating the working day, with early working-class struggles in Western Europe revolving around establishing the 10-hour day.

The demand for a shorter workday thus has long historical roots. In Canada, the struggle for a shorter working day dates to the Nine-Hour Movement, which began in Hamilton in 1872 through the efforts of union members and non-unionized workers to reduce hours of labour from 10 to 9 hours per day (Battye 1979; Kealey 1980; Thomas 2009). The push for shorter hours was an attempt to provide relief from overwork and work intensification, and was also considered necessary to provide time for "moral, social and intellectual improvement." The movement soon spread beyond Hamilton as Nine-Hour Leagues, which cut across craft lines and contributed to the development of cross-occupational solidarity within the early labour movement, formed in a number of larger cities in Ontario and Quebec (Heron 2012). The strategy of the movement was to attempt to obtain a reduction in work time through direct negotiation with employers, rather than pressure the state for legislation. Industrial employers refused to negotiate with their employees over the issue of the nine-hour day. While strike action was undertaken in a number of locales between March and June 1872, including a strike of over 1,500 workers in Hamilton in May, the movement quickly dissipated as these strikes were settled with wage increases rather than reductions in work time. Only small groups of workers—skilled railway workers—actually achieved a nine-hour day during the period of the Nine Hour Movement. While the movement was not successful in achieving its goal of the nine-hour day, it contributed to the early development of the labour movement in Canada and to the pressure for labour legislation that legalized trade unionism.

In the postwar period, the collective bargaining priorities of organized labour in Canada contributed to the normalization of the standard (40-hour) workweek, with additional compensation for overtime hours, primarily for unionized male workers. The first United Auto Workers agreement in Canada, which was negotiated with General Motors in the 1930s, reduced the standard workweek from 50 hours to 44 hours. In the 1970s, unions in the energy, chemical, and paper sectors negotiated a standard workweek of 37 and 1/3 hours, and by the mid-1990s, over 50,000 members of the Communications, Energy and Paperworkers Union had a standard workweek of under 40 hours (White 2002).

Work reorganization, the rise of non-standard work, and several decades of neoliberal labour market reform across Canada have brought about significant change in the organization of working time (Basso 2003; Hermann 2015; Thomas 2006). The push by employers and neoliberal governments for "flexibility" with respect to time has often meant longer and more variable hours, with greater capacity for employers to control scheduling. The growth of part-time work, in conjunction with the erosion of working time regulation due to neoliberal legislative reform, has contributed to work hours polarization, whereby some work excessive hours while others do not work sufficient hours to earn a stable income. The rise of part-time work has also contributed to greater uncertainty in the organization of time, with many part-time workers subject to on-call scheduling, as well as the prospects of highly variable shift times. These changing patterns in working time affect not only job quality, but also broader relations of social reproduction, as the lack of certainty around time, combined with potentially long work hours for some workers, makes balancing the demands of work and home exceedingly difficult.

Figure 12.1 puts hours of work in Canada in comparative perspective, showing annual hours of work across a number of OECD countries. As shown, annual hours are considerably lower in Germany (1,366), Denmark (1,458), and France (1,473) than in Canada, which is not surprising given the stronger working-time legislation (including annual vacation time) for those countries. Hours are also somewhat lower in Sweden (1,611) than they are in Canada (1,703). Though annual hours are higher in Canada than in Western Europe, they are lower than in the U.S. (1,789) and across the OECD on average (1,770).

In this context of multiple working-time pressures, many unions and community groups have argued for reduced work time in order to lessen overwork and promote job creation. In the mid-1990s, the Canadian Labour Congress played an active role in the development of the *Report of the Advisory Group on Working Time and the Distribution of Work,* which called for a standard 40-hour workweek and annual limits on overtime hours. In Ontario in the late 1990s, changes to provincial employment standards legislation that allow for a 60-hour workweek were widely criticized by organized labour, and produced calls for working-time alternatives that could improve work quality (OFL 2000). The model of the 35-hour workweek in France, and the general shift toward reduced work time in Western Europe, was presented by some Canadian unions as an alternative to the shift toward longer hours of work, and a polarization in the distribution in work time (CAW 2000; White 2002). Labour movement scholars and activists argue that efforts to redistribute working time are needed in a progressive bargaining agenda (Gindin and Stanford 2003).

Figure 12.1: Average Annual Hours Actually Worked per Worker, 2014

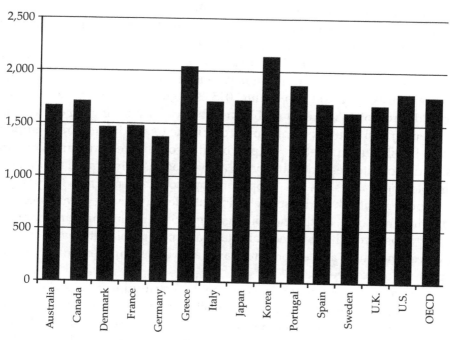

Source: OECD.Stat. 2016. "Average annual hours actually worked per worker." http://stats.oecd.org/Index.aspx?DataSetCode=ANHRS#.

Despite this general commitment, however, reduced daily or weekly working hours have not been widely established across the broader labour movement. By the early 2000s, approximately only one-quarter of collective agreements stipulated a full-time workweek under 40 hours (Thomas 2006). Blue-collar workers were much more likely to have a provision regulating a standard 40-hour workweek than those in white-collar bargaining units. A very clear majority of collective agreements had no provision limiting the use of overtime. Much more common were forms of working-time reduction through additional time off. A large number of agreements provided four or more weeks of vacation for long-service employees. Some form of early retirement, a popular form of lifetime working-hours reduction, was also common.

The growth of part-time work has also raised many working-time pressures, including around scheduling. As discussed in Chapter 9, unions representing part-time workers have recently begun to negotiate collective agreement provisions to provide some certainty to scheduling and to the number of hours worked (Mojtehedzadeh 2015). In the U.S., retail workers in San Francisco won a "Bill of Rights" in 2015 that includes: a minimum hours requirement of two to four hours for on-call shifts that do not happen, or if workers are sent home before a shift ends; two weeks' advance notice scheduling; extra pay for a change made to scheduling; equal treatment between full-time and part-time workers, including for benefits, vacation time, and hourly wages; and the right for part-time workers to have access to full-time employment before additional part-timers or temporary workers are hired (Luce 2015). Establishing these kinds of protections enables part-time workers to have not only a greater degree of economic security, but also a greater degree of control over their time.

Working-time reduction to a 30-hour workweek has been proposed as a solution to the "simultaneous compression, extension, and variation" of work time in contemporary capitalism (Hermann 2015: 3). Reducing full-time work to this level could: promote a more equitable distribution of working time, including greater gender equity in working time; contribute to a reduction in unemployment and involuntary part-time employment through a redistribution of work hours; and promote healthier lifestyles, as well as fostering more ecologically sustainable approaches to work. Approaching working time from the perspective of gender equity should also include strategies to provide greater access to time off for family care, further supplementing existing maternity and paternity leave programs through extended parental leave, compassionate leave, bereavement leave, and child and elder care leave, as well as supplementary income top-ups for those on leave.

As the currently unequal and unsustainable distribution of working time is primarily driven by employer-oriented flexibility, reducing working time should be accompanied with measures to promote greater worker-oriented flexibility in the scheduling of hours in order to better balance work responsibilities with life outside work. In this regard, as Gorz (1999: 96) puts it, it should be possible to "rethink discontinuous working, to rethink the flexibility of working hours and

Box 12.1: Time Is Political: The fight to control the working day remains one of our most important labor struggles
By Stephanie Luce

The struggle over the working day has long been central to Marxist analysis. In chapter ten of *Capital*, Volume 1, Marx chronicles the various ways that capitalists and states worked to extend the working day as much as possible, from the mid-fourteenth century up through the mid-nineteenth century. The reason was simple: the longer the working day, the more capitalists could exploit workers because after paying workers a subsistence wage, all labor done for the rest of the day was a surplus for the employer.

***

Jump ahead to 2015. Many workers are still overworked, enduring lengthy work days and workweeks, and forced overtime. But a growing number of employees also face the problem of underwork: insufficient hours on the job, and erratic schedules that change day to day and week to week.

In some sectors like retail and fast food, workers may be hired for as little as eight hours per week—two shifts of four hours—for a probationary period of two to three months. To make ends meet, they try to pick up extra shifts from coworkers, or find additional jobs. They also agree to "on-call" shifts: making themselves available for work but getting no guarantee that they will actually receive it.

***

This phenomenon is not restricted to low-wage service sector workers. In a 2014 study conducted by University of Chicago researchers, only 62 percent of young adults (ages twenty-six to thirty-two) reported that they know their work schedule more than a week in advance, and among hourly employees, just 59 percent are aware of the shifts they'll be working a week in advance.

This means huge numbers of workers are adjusting their schedules on a weekly basis or less, making it difficult or impossible to plan care work, school, and other family and social commitments. In addition, the researchers found that nearly three-quarters of those surveyed experience fluctuating work hours each month, in some cases significantly—roughly eight hours of variation on average.

In the UK and New Zealand, employers have instituted "zero-hours contracts," meaning the employer has no obligation to provide any work time at all. Instead, the employer schedules work according to weekly needs, which can vary from no time to full-time. Zero-hours contracts spread rapidly after the global financial crisis and today are prevalent in retail, hotels, food service, agriculture, and education. For example, one UK study found that only 4 percent of hotel and restaurant workers had zero-hour contracts in 2004, but 19 percent did by 2011.

***

While erratic scheduling makes it difficult for someone not working a forty-hour week to find and hold a second job, relying on part-time work benefits employers—who can more easily vary hours and schedules, avoid overtime pay, and offer fewer benefits. Many companies have store policies that provide benefits only to full-time workers, and the Affordable Care Act applies only to workers employed thirty or more hours per week.

In the past, unions and policymakers imposed protections that made work more secure and stable. Beginning in 1939, the United Auto Workers included contract language mandating a minimum number of paid hours per shift, and by the 1980s most collective bargaining agreements included call-in and "reporting pay" language. And in Europe, many unions won some protection against irregular scheduling through collective bargaining or industry-wide agreements.

***

In the early 2000s, the European Commission began promoting "flexicurity." First developed by a Dutch academic in the 1990s, flexicurity is designed to make it easier to fire workers and use temp agencies, while generating higher job security for workers in flexible employment arrangements. But research shows that the concept is difficult to realize, particularly when policymakers continue to push and prioritize neoliberal macro policy and labor market reregulation.

In reaction, workers and their organizations in the US and Europe have launched campaigns to win more stable and predictable schedules, ideally with minimum work hours. Activists assert that fighting for a higher hourly wage is limited if workers can't get enough hours, and there are a number of efforts underway to pressure local and state governments, as well as employers, to improve conditions.

Eight states and the District of Columbia already have "reporting pay" laws. These require the employer to pay a minimum number of hours to workers even if they are sent home early. For example, New York State requires employers to pay a minimum of four hours per shift.

Perhaps the biggest victory in the US came last year in San Francisco. There, the county board of supervisors adopted a Retail Workers Bill of Rights that covers the city's chain stores.

***

Activists have also directly pressured employers to improve their practices. OUR Walmart called on the retailer to allow workers access to scheduling software. The company eventually acquiesced and agreed to let workers use the technology to pick up additional shifts of work. Just last month, Victoria's Secret announced that it would end the practice of on-call scheduling after years of pressure from the Retail Action Project to raise pay and improve working conditions.

In New Zealand, the union Unite has been targeting fast-food companies to eliminate zero-hours contracts. They have won agreements from most, and when McDonald's resisted, the union went on strike. McDonald's caved, agreeing to end the practice and give workers a guaranteed minimum of hours.

In the UK, unions and worker organizations are trying to eliminate the zero-hours contracts via legislation. There has been a little progress—but not nearly enough.

The problems of too few hours and lack of schedule control will become more pronounced as the global labor force experiences greater precarity and more "flexibility." Employers will likely keep pushing for more just-in-time scheduling as a way to convert labor from a fixed to a variable cost, from a formal employer–employee relationship with responsibilities to an informal one with no legal restrictions or promises of work.

As workers and worker organizations fight back, it's a good time to think about the bigger picture of what we want. Certainly too few hours is a serious problem, but the solution is not necessarily more hours of work—or a return to a forty-hour workweek. The notion of flexibility has appeal because in reality, there are many employees who want or need an adjustable workweek—either to care for family, go to school, deal with a disability, pursue outside hobbies, or simply because working forty hours per week is too much.

***

Clearly, the labor market is out of balance, as some workers are working too much and others too little. The fight for schedule control should also be a fight to redistribute work hours and shorten the average workweek. This would help spread labor around more evenly, and should allow more space for workers to determine their shifts.

***

Work-sharing policies also involve giving workers the right to request a shorter workweek, amending benefits to eliminate a minimum hours requirement, and increasing the minimum wage and social welfare benefits so that a shorter workweek is more affordable. Austria, Belgium, France, Japan, Turkey, and Uruguay are some of the other countries that have experimented with variations of shorter workhours and work-sharing.

***

Ideally, we would have flexible jobs that allowed each of us some degree of choice over the hours we worked, the schedules we set, and the work we did. But this won't happen through good human resource policy. Instead, we need democratic, worker-run workplaces.

Source: Luce, Stephanie. 2015, July 20. "Time Is Political: The fight to control the working day remains one of our most important labor struggles." *Jacobin*. https://www.jacobinmag.com/2015/07/luce-eight-hour-day-obama-overtime/.

staffing as a source not of insecurity, but of security, and as a form of the right to 'choose one's own working hours,'" where workers have the capacity to "choose and self-manage discontinuity and flexibility." Essentially, establishing worker control over the organization of working time is essential to addressing the current problems of working time. Working-time reduction and increased time sovereignty may provide an alternative to employment insecurity, labour market inequality, and a lack of work-life balance (Beck 2000). Given the continued problems of stress, overwork, and gendered inequalities associated with social reproduction, a broad approach to re-regulating working time in these ways would make a significant contribution to improving the quality of work.

Overall, however, the struggle to control working time has not returned to the historic demands of the labour movement to reduce the hours of the workweek. This reflects a combination of factors, including the normalization of neoliberal labour flexibility and the preponderance of economic insecurity, whereby many working people need as much working time as they can get in order to make ends meet. These factors are reflected in the priorities of the labour movement as well, where there has been a lack of concerted and centralized bargaining efforts around working time in Canada. Research on working time in Western Europe has found that working time is lowest where centralized collective bargaining is strongest (Lehndorff 2000). Canada's highly decentralized collective bargaining system places structural limits on the generalization of progress made by individual unions. The union working-time agenda has also been in many ways shaped by the drive toward working-time "flexibility," as defined on employers' terms. In this context, gains in the area of working time may take the form of simply resisting employer pressures to increase hours of work. Further, making progress on working-time issues has in some cases been traded off in order to prevent monetary concessions. Moreover, related to the broader context of changing employment relationships is the lack of representation in many of the most "flexible" areas of work, including part-time work.

Working-time reduction strategies provide some means to address growing forms of work-life conflict and to place greater control over working time in employees' hands. Working-time reduction may also contribute to greater labour market equity by addressing concerns over social reproduction and the working-time issues faced by part-time workers. However, such practices are still not widespread within the Canadian labour market. Just as it was over 100 years ago, developing a strategy for working-time re-regulation that promotes the goals of balance, equity, and control remains a key challenge for the workers' movements in the 21st century. Moreover, while reduced working time would improve quality of work and quality of life, greater time sovereignty on its own does not address the more fundamental question of workplace democracy.

Worker Cooperatives and Workplace Democracy

The strategies discussed above—both the social democratic approach to labour market regulation and reduced working time—have potential to promote reforms that may make work more bearable. Creating higher-quality work through investment in training improves work experiences. Creating stronger labour laws provides better protection for the most vulnerable. Developing worker-oriented flexibility in working time provides more choice and reduces work-life conflict. But these strategies do not address the more fundamental questions of control and power that underlie the social organization of work in a capitalist economy. Even organizing unions has its limits: as discussed in Chapters 9 and 10, while unions reduce employer power, they do not eliminate it.

The discussion of "improving work" would be incomplete without discussing more fundamental alternatives. One such alternative lies in strategies to make work more democratic through worker cooperatives, which are built around the principles of worker input and decision-making ability. Worker cooperatives emphasize the collective production of goods and services by replacing private ownership with collective ownership, control, and decision-making. As an alternative to employer-directed production, worker-owners work collectively toward common goals. Rather than profit-making as the primary priority (as with private enterprise in capitalist economies), worker cooperatives prioritize collective and democratic principles in their operations, particularly through democratic decision-making processes (one person, one vote), whereby members of the cooperative must work collectively toward common goals.

Currently, there are approximately 300 such worker cooperatives in Canada, with a total of around 6,000 members. They are generally fairly small, but exist in a wide range of sectors of the economy, including construction, small manufacturing, consulting, food services, and daycare. They are often pursued as a form of community economic development in regions that have a difficult time attracting capitalist investment. Given the small scale of worker cooperatives in Canada, it is instructive to look at examples in other parts of the world as well.

The Mondragon cooperative in Spain, founded in 1956, provides a well-established and widely noted case (Gibson-Graham 2003; Morrison 1991). With over 80,000 worker-owners running over 250 manufacturing and service companies, it provides the largest and most successful example of a worker cooperative. It has expanded its operations beyond Spain by establishing worker cooperatives in other countries (especially in automotive parts and domestic appliances). In 2014, it reported revenue of 11.86 billion EUR (Mondragon 2014).

Mondragon operates on the principle of democratic organization, where each firm includes a general assembly made up of all members who establish policies, approve business plans, and elect a supervisory board (which appoints managers). Each worker has an economic stake in the enterprise where they work, meaning that workers make the decisions regarding the distribution of surpluses. The cooperative combines the social goals of cooperative management and democratic decision-making processes within the context of a capitalist enterprise and produces goods for sale in the global marketplace. Worker-owners participate in management and to develop skills for self-management. There are wage ratios between worker-owners who perform executive/management duties and those who work in the factories (with an average of 5:1), and these ratios are decided through democratic processes (voting). In addition to the principles of democratic decision-making, Mondragon involves collective risk-taking through cooperative

Box 12.2: May Day: Workers of the World Unite and Take Over—Their Factories
By Jon Henley, Ashifa Kassam, Constanze Letsch, and Uki Goñi

A 19th-century slogan is getting a 21st-century makeover. The workers of the world really are uniting. At least, some of them are.

The economic meltdown unleashed by the 2008 financial crisis hit southern Europe especially hard, sending manufacturing output plunging and unemployment soaring.

Countless factories shut their gates. But some workers at perhaps as many as 500 sites across the continent—a majority in Spain, but also in France, Italy, Greece, and Turkey—have refused to accept the corporate kiss of death.

By negotiation, or sometimes by occupation, they have taken production into their own hands, embracing a movement that has thrived for several years in Argentina.

In France, an average of 30 mostly small companies a year, from phone repair firms to ice-cream makers, have become workers' co-operatives since 2010. Coceta, a co-operative umbrella group in Spain, reckons that in 2013 alone some 75 Spanish companies were taken over by their former employees—roughly half the total in the whole of Europe.

A gathering in Marseille last year of representatives from worker-controlled factories drew more than 200 delegates from more than a dozen countries—including pioneers from Argentina, whose turn-of-the-century economic crash sparked a wave of fabricas recuperadas that today has left around 15,000 workers in charge at more than 300 workplaces. The fast-developing phenomenon is now a field of academic study; there are websites, such as workerscontrol.net and autogestion.coop, dedicated to it.

No two self-managed ventures launch in the same circumstances, and many face daunting obstacles: bureaucratic inertia and administrative red tape that can delay or even prevent production; legal opposition from former owners; a still-chilly economic climate; outdated machinery, or products no longer in demand. Lifelong union militants can find themselves, for the first time in their lives, making tough commercial decisions.

But many—for the time being at least—are making it work.

Source: Henley, Jon, Ashifa Kassam, Constanze Letsch, and Uki Goñi. 2015, May 1. "May Day: Workers of the World Unite and Take Over—Their Factories." *The Guardian*. http://www.theguardian.com/world/2015/may/01/may-day-workers-of-the-world-unite-and-take-over-their-factories?CMP=share_btn_link.

business ownership (otherwise known as cooperative entrepreneurship) and a community-centred orientation to business, where community concerns are integrated into business decisions. Given the cooperative orientation, membership is open to those who agree to the cooperative principles, and, unlike in private enterprise, organizational information is made available to all.

Another widely cited example is the worker-recuperated enterprises (*empresas recuperadas por sus trabajadores* [ERTs]) in Argentina. ERTs evolved as workers took over their workplaces following the mass unemployment created by the economic crisis in Argentina during the late 1990s and early 2000s. The crisis itself resulted from IMF-directed structural adjustment, neoliberal labour market reforms, and foreign direct investment, which led to large numbers of business bankruptcies beginning in the mid-1990s (Lavaca Collective 2007; Vieta 2010). Under the slogan "Occupy, Resist, Produce," workers occupied abandoned workplaces and turned them into worker cooperatives under the principles of *autogestión* (self-management), effectively placing production under worker control. By 2015, the number of ERTs had grown to about 300 small and medium-sized businesses, involving upward of 15,000 workers. Beginning in small manufacturing, the movement has spread to many sectors of the economy in the years since, including health care, education, and hospitality. Based as they are on the principles of worker self-management, ERTs have shown strong capacity to develop cooperative approaches to work organization within recuperated firms, with the commitment to democratic forms of worker decision-making at the heart of these processes. The model includes horizontal rather than hierarchal work arrangements, as well as egalitarian pay structures, both of which are arranged through elected workers' councils and assemblies. ERTs have also strengthened ties with the communities of which they are a part, and forged "economies of solidarity" between one another (Vieta 2010: 308).

Supporters of the worker cooperative approach cite the potential for combining economic growth, job creation, democratic workplace practices, a less alienating workplace environment, and the potential for building strong links between the workplace and the community (Curl 2009; Novkovic and Webb 2014). Yet, cooperatives continue to operate within the wider environment of capitalism, meaning they are not immune from the competitive pressures felt by any capitalist business enterprise (Fares 2012). In the Argentinian case, ERTs face underproduction as compared to previous levels, in part due to problems securing financing to upgrade machinery and technology. The democratic and cooperative principles of the ERTs also reach limits as a model for social transformation due to their reliance on competitive, capitalist markets, which compel a capitalist production logic—including work intensification, unpaid overtime, repetitive work tasks, and elements of managerial hierarchy—in response to pressures to remain financially viable (Vieta 2010). Worker cooperatives, such as those discussed above, are perhaps best seen as a form of local "economic experimentation," rather than a real alternative to capitalism (Gibson-Graham 2003: 125). While premised on a range of alternative practices and arrangements, they do not in and of themselves create the capacity for systemic transformation.

Beyond Wage Labour

Attention to the social problems that stem from the organization of work raises many fundamental questions, not only about how to concretely address these problems, but also more deeply about the very organization of work itself. Thinking beyond the immediacy of the pressing problems outlined throughout the chapters of this book, the social problem of work points to many short-comings in the larger collective experience of producing and reproducing our conditions of existence.

To truly address these problems would require a thorough reorganization of work. This would include creating work that: provides opportunities to engage in tasks that are fulfilling and meaningful; ensures economic security; fosters health and well-being; is supportive of life outside work; and is based on democratic principles of worker participation in decision-making (see Lowe 2000). At a mini-mum, this would require governments to improve basic employment standards, recognize freedom of association and collective bargaining rights, promote and support training initiatives, encourage investment in healthy work environments, and eliminate the differential treatment accorded to workers through the political category of citizenship when they travel across borders to work (see Sharma 2006; Standing 2011). Though not a call for "abolishing work," this would certainly require abolishing a particular way of organizing and constituting work, and thereby fundamentally reorganizing work to involve democratic decision-making in the workplace, rebalancing time at work and outside work, and providing greater control over work for workers.

While there are many pressures that could lead in this direction, there are of course overwhelming countervailing tendencies: neoliberal governments, powerful transnational corporations, and a highly competitive global economy have destabilized the power relations of the workplace, countering the pressure for alternatives, strong as they may be. Yet, growing labour unrest, whether in workplaces with traditionally high levels of unionization or among non-unionized workers in precarious jobs, continues to demonstrate the contested nature of work in today's economy. Organizing work in ways that create "quality work" conducive to the well-being of workers, and that also overcomes the crisis of work stemming from alienating, exploitative conditions, remains paramount.

To do so requires transforming work beyond the social relations of wage labour to create work that is truly meaningful, sustainable, and democratically consti-tuted. This is a project that begins, as Harvey (2000) describes, with the alienated labouring body as both a site of resistance and the starting point for progressive struggle. In other words, the larger struggle to transform work begins with the particularity of the individual experience of alienation and exploitation, and from there building outwards—recognizing the social basis of that individual experi-ence—in order to construct new forms of collective struggle at local, regional, national, and transnational levels in order to address the conditions of oppression faced by workers in the present day.

Conclusion

In conclusion, this chapter has outlined a number of strategies to address the social problem of work in contemporary Canadian society. Looking at the social democratic model, it can be seen that it is possible to have high levels of employment at decent wages and with decent working conditions and that there is no inevitable trade-off between job quantity and job quality, even at the low end of the job market. The experiences of the Scandinavian model strongly suggest that precarious work is not a precondition for economic success in today's global economy. Another option lies in the strategy of reducing working time and establishing greater worker control over working time. Yet, as discussed, there are limits to both of these strategies, insofar as they retain the hierarchical social conditions of the capitalist employment relationship. More fundamental transformations in the social relations of work are needed to put the organization of work itself under democratic control. With the prevalence of precarious work these days, and the predominance of capitalist power, the prospects for such fundamental transformation may not seem to be on the horizon. However, if anything can be drawn from the contested terrain of the workplace, it is the fact that the future of work is very much unwritten, meaning the possibilities for an alternative to the precarious world of work today remain open.

Recommended Reading

Gorz, Andre. 1999. *Reclaiming Work: Beyond the Wage-Based Society*. Cambridge: Polity.

Hermann, Christoph. 2015. *Capitalism and the Political Economy of Work Time*. London & New York: Routledge.

Lavaca Collective. 2007. *Sin Patrón: Stories from Argentina's Worker-Run Factories*. Trans. Katherine Kohlstedt. Chicago: Haymarket Books.

Serrano, Melisa R., and Edlira Xhafa (eds.). 2012. *The Pursuit of Alternatives: Stories of Peoples' Economic and Political Struggles Around the World*. Germany: Rainer Hampp Verlag.

Note

1. The World Bank, "Health expenditure, public (% of GDP)." Accessed at: http://data.worldbank.org/indicator/SH.XPD.PUBL.ZS.

APPENDIX

Internet Resources

Canadian Centre for Policy Alternatives (www.policyalternatives.ca) is a left-leaning, labour-supported think tank that publishes critical research on public policy and the labour market in Canada.

Canadian Council on Social Development (www.ccsd.ca) is a social research organization that produces studies on a range of issues related to social and economic development, including poverty and employment.

Canadian Labour Congress (www.canadianlabour.ca) is the largest union federation in Canada, representing some three million workers in its affiliated unions, which include all of the largest private- and public-sector unions. The CLC website provides access to a wide range of information on unions and union campaigns, and comprehensive links to the websites of Canadian and international unions.

Canadian Worker Co-op Foundation (canadianworker.coop) is a grassroots membership organization providing resources for those involved in and interested in worker cooperatives.

Colour of Poverty—Colour of Change (colourofpoverty.wordpress.com) is a network aiming to address the social and economic problems of racism and poverty experienced by racialized groups in Canada.

Council of Canadians with Disabilities (www.ccdonline.ca) is an advocacy organization for persons with disabilities in Canada. The council publishes on a wide range of issues covering human rights, income supports, and other matters of concern for people with disabilities.

Employment and Social Development Canada (www.esdc.gc.ca) is the federal government department responsible for Canada's skills agenda and the labour market. The website provides information and research papers on a wide range of issues, including changes in the job market, job training, retirement and pensions, and trends in workplaces and collective bargaining.

European Foundation for the Improvement of Living and Working Conditions (www.eurofound.europa.eu) produces research and provides information, advice, and expertise on living and working conditions and industrial relations.

Gender and Work Database (www.genderwork.ca) is a database portal housed at York University in Toronto that provides a library, interactive statistical database, and thesaurus built around issues of gender inequality, precarious employment, and employment standards.

Global Labour Research Centre (www.yorku.ca/glrc) is a research centre based at York University in Toronto that engages in the study of work, employment, and labour from a global perspective. The centre's website contains a working paper series, a digital archive of recorded talks and presentations, and a series of *Know Your Rights* factsheets about employment law in Ontario.

Immigrant Workers Centre (www.iwc-cti.org) is a Montreal-based centre that defends the rights of immigrant workers, provides education about workers' rights, and works to improve the working conditions of immigrant workers.

International Labour Organization (www.ilo.org) is a United Nations agency that brings together representatives of governments, workers, and employers to develop international labour standards. The website is a portal to statistics, studies, and reports on trends in work and working conditions around the world.

Justicia for Migrant Workers (www.justicia4migrantworkers.org) is an activist-based organization that seeks to promote justice for workers in the temporary foreign worker program in Canada. J4MW provides a great deal of information and analysis on the conditions of migrant workers and on migrant worker policies and programs.

Labour Program of the Government of Canada (www.labour.gc.ca) publishes a wide range of information and studies on unionized workplaces, collective bargaining issues, and employment and labour standards in Canada.

Law of Work (lawofwork.ca) is a labour and employment law blog run by York University professor David Doorey. The blog posts commentary on a wide range of legal issues related to current issues in employment.

Organisation for Economic Co-operation and Development (www.oecd.org) is a Paris-based organization that produces research on many economic and social policy issues, including the *OECD Employment Outlook*, which focuses on labour market issues and summarizes more technical research. The website contains numerous statistics and tables on member countries and comparative research on labour market and social issues.

Statistics Canada (www.statcan.gc.ca), Canada's national statistical agency, provides a wealth of free data on its website, including a wide range of labour market statistics available through CANSIM tables. The website also includes research papers on employment, income, and social issues.

Workers' Action Centre (www.workersactioncentre.org) is a worker-based organization in Toronto that works to improve the working conditions of people in low-wage and precarious work. The website includes many resources on precarious employment.

Youth and Work (www.youthandwork.ca) is a source of information about workplace rights for young people, providing commentaries and resources about public policy, post-secondary education, the labour market, and labour and employment law.

Bibliography

Abella, Rosalie. 1984. *Equality in Employment: A Royal Commission Report*. Ottawa: Minister of Supply and Services Canada.

Adib, Amel, and Yvonne Guerrier. 2003. "The Interlocking of Gender with Nationality, Race, Ethnicity and Class: The Narratives of Women in Hotel Work." *Gender, Work and Organization* 10, no. 4: 413–32.

Aidt, Toke, and Zafiris Tzannatos. 2003. *Unions and Collective Bargaining — Economic Effects in a Global Environment. Directions in Development*. Washington, D.C.: The World Bank. http://documents.worldbank.org/curated/en/831241468740150591/Unions-and-collective-bargaining-economic-effects-in-a-global-environment.

Akyeampong, Ernest. 2002. "Unionization and Fringe Benefits." *Perspectives on Labour and Income* (Autumn): 5–9.

Albo, Greg, Sam Gindin, and Leo Panitch. 2010. *In and Out of Crisis: The Global Financial Meltdown and Left Alternatives*. Oakland: PM Press.

Alboin, Naomi. 2009. *Adjusting the Balance: Fixing Canada's Economic Immigration Policies*. Toronto: Maytree Foundation.

Ambachtsheer, Keith. 2008. *The Canada Supplementary Pension Plan: Towards an Adequate, Affordable Pension for All Canadians*. Toronto: C.D. Howe Institute.

Andrews, Doug. 2007. *Planning for Retirement: Are Canadians Saving Enough?* Ottawa: Canadian Institute of Actuaries.

Applebaum, Eileen. 1997. *The Impact of New Forms of Work Organization on Workers*. Washington, DC: Economic Policy Institute.

Applebaum, Eileen, Annette Bernhardt, and Richard J. Murname (eds.). 2003. *Low Wage America*. New York: Russell Sage Foundation.

Arat-Koç, S. 2001. *Caregivers Break the Silence: A Participatory Action Research on the Abuse and Violence, including the Impact of Family Separation, Experienced by Women in the Live-In Caregiver Program*. Toronto: INTERCEDE.

Arim, Rubab. 2015. *A Profile of Persons with Disabilities Among Canadians Aged 15 Years or Older, 2012*. Ottawa: Statistics Canada.

Armstrong, Pat, and Hugh Armstrong. 2010. *The Double Ghetto: Canadian Women and Their Segregated Work*. 3rd edition. Toronto: Oxford University Press.

Armstrong, Pat, Mary Cornish, and Elizabeth Millar. 2003. "Pay Equity: Complexity and Contradiction in Legal Rights and Social Processes," in L. Vosko and W. Clement (eds.), *Changing Canada: Political Economy as Transformation*. Kingston and Montreal: McGill-Queen's University Press.

Armstrong, Pat, and Kate Laxer. 2006. "Precarious Work, Privatization and the Health Care Industry: The Case of Ancillary Workers," in L. F. Vosko (ed.),

Precarious Employment: Understanding Labour Market Insecurity in Canada. Kingston and Montreal: McGill-Queen's University Press.

Arnal, Elena, Wooseok Ok, and Raymond Torres. 2001. *Knowledge, Work Organization and Economic Growth.* Labour Market and Social Policy Occasional Paper No. 50. Paris: OECD.

Aronowitz, Stanley. 2010. *The Jobless Future.* Minneapolis: University of Minnesota Press.

Auer, Peter. 2000. *Employment Revival in Europe: Labour Market Success in Austria, Denmark, Ireland and the Netherlands.* Geneva: ILO.

Avery, Charles. 2011. "Gearing Up: Engaging China's Globalising Machinery Industry." *The China Analyst* (March). http://www.thebeijingaxis.com/tca/ editions/the-china-analyst-mar-2011/31-gearing-up-engaging-chinas-globalising-machinery-industry.

Aydemir, Abdurrahman, and Mikal Skuterud. 2004. *Explaining the Deteriorating Entry Earnings of Canada's Immigrant Cohorts, 1966–2000.* Ottawa: Statistics Canada, Analytical Studies Branch.

Bailey, Allan. 2007. *Connecting the Dots: Linking Training Investment to Business Outcomes and the Economy.* Ottawa: Canadian Council on Learning.

Baker, Dean, Andrew Glyn, David Howell, and John Schmitt. 2002. "Labor Market Institutions and Unemployment: A Critical Assessment of the Cross-Country Evidence." Center for European Studies Working Paper Series #98. http://aei. pitt.edu/9133/1/Baker.pdf.

Baldwin, Bob, and Pierre Laliberté. 1999. *Incomes of Older Canadians: Amounts and Sources, 1973–1996.* Research Paper No. 15. Ottawa: Canadian Labour Congress.

Baldwin, John, and Wulong Gu. 2003. *Plant Turnover and Productivity Growth in Canadian Manufacturing.* Ottawa: Statistics Canada.

Bartel, A. 2000. "Measuring the Employer's Return on Investments in Training: Evidence from the Literature." *Industrial Relations* 39: 502–24.

Basso, P. 2003. *Modern Times, Ancient Hours: Working Lives in the Twenty-First Century.* London: Verso.

Battye, John. 1979. "The Nine Hour Pioneers: The Genesis of the Canadian Labour Movement." *Labour/Le Travail,* 4: 25–56.

Beach, Charles, Ross Finnie, and David Gray. 2003. "Earnings Variability and Earnings Stability of Women and Men in Canada: How Do the 1990s Compare to the 1980s?" *Canadian Public Policy* XXIX, Supplement: 541–65.

Beach, Charles, and Ross Finnie. 2004. *A Longitudinal Analysis of Earnings Change in Canada.* Statistics Canada Cat. 11F0019MIE, No. 127.

Beaudry, Paul, Thomas Lemieux, and Daniel Parent. 2000. "What Is Happening to the Youth Labour Market in Canada?" *Canadian Public Policy* XXVI, Supplement.

Beaujot, Roderic. 2004. *Delayed Life Transitions: Trends and Implications.* Ottawa: The Vanier Institute of the Family.

Beaujot, Roderic, and Don Kerr. 2007. *Emerging Youth Transition Patterns in Canada.* Ottawa: Government of Canada Policy Research Initiative.

Bebchuk, Lucian, and Yaniv Grinstein. 2005. "The Growth of Executive Pay." *Oxford Review of Economic Policy* 21, no. 2: 283–303.

Beck, U. 2000. *The Brave New World of Work.* Trans. P. Camiller. Cambridge: Polity.

Bell, Daniel. 1973. *The Coming of Post-Industrial Society: A Venture in Social Forecasting.* New York: Basic Books.

Bellamy Foster, John, and Fred Magdoff. 2009. *The Great Financial Crisis: Causes and Consequences.* New York: Monthly Review Press.

Benner, Mats, and Torben Bundgaard Vad. 2000. "Sweden and Denmark: Defending the Welfare State," in F. Scharpf and V. Schmidt (eds.), *Welfare and Work in the Open Economy: Vol. II Diverse Responses to Common Challenges.* Oxford: Oxford University Press.

Bernard, Andre. 2012. *The Job Search of the Older Unemployed.* Ottawa: Statistics Canada.

Betcherman, Gordon, Kathryn McMullen, and Katie Davidman. 1998. *Training for the New Economy: A Synthesis Report.* Ottawa: Canadian Policy Research Networks.

Black, Sandra, and Lisa Lynch. 2000. *What's Driving the New Economy: The Benefits of Workplace Innovation.* National Bureau of Economic Research Working Paper No. 7479.

Block, Sheila, and Grace-Edward Galabuzi. 2011. *Canada's Colour Coded Labour Market: The Gap for Racialized Workers.* Ottawa/Toronto: Canadian Centre for Policy Alternatives/Wellesley Institute.

Block, Sheila, Grace-Edward Galabuzi, and Alexandra Weiss. 2014. *The Colour Coded Labour Market By the Numbers.* Toronto: Wellesley Institute.

Bloom, Michael, and Michael Grant. 2001. *Brain Gain: The Economic Benefits of Recognizing Learning and Learning Credentials in Canada.* Ottawa: Conference Board of Canada.

Boyd, Monica. 2008. "Variations in Socioeconomic Outcomes of Second Generation Young Adults," in A. Kobayashi (ed.), *The Experiences of Second Generation Canadians.* Special Issue of *Canadian Diversity* 6, no. 2: 20–25. Montreal: Association of Canadian Studies.

Broadbent Institute. 2012. *Towards A More Equal Canada.* Ottawa: Broadbent Institute.

———. 2014. *Haves and Have-Nots: Deep and Persistent Wealth Inequality in Canada.* Ottawa: Broadbent Institute.

Bronfenbrenner, Kate, and Sheldon Friedman (eds.). 1998. *Organizing to Win: New Research on Union Strategies.* Ithaca and London: ILR Press.

Brooks, Meghan. 2008. "Imagining Canada, Negotiating Belonging: Understanding the Experiences of Racism of Second Generation Canadians of Colour," in A. Kobayashi (ed.), *The Experiences of Second Generation Canadians.* Special Issue of *Canadian Diversity* 6, no. 2: 75–79. Association of Canadian Studies.

Brown, Mark. 2013, November 25. "CHART: Canada's richest are not as wealthy as you think." *Canadian Business*. http://www.canadianbusiness.com/blogs-and-comment/not-as-wealthy/.

Burawoy, Michael. 1985. *The Politics of Production: Factory Regimes Under Capitalism and Socialism*. London & New York: Verso.

Bureau of Labor Statistics. 2016. "Economic News Release: Union Members—2015." USDL-16-0158. Washington: U.S. Department of Labor. http://www.bls.gov/news.release/union2.nr0.htm.

Burtless, Gary, and Joseph Quinn. 2002. *Is Working Longer the Answer for an Ageing Workforce?* Boston: Centre for Research on Retirement, Boston College.

Cameron, Duncan (ed.). 1988. *The Free Trade Deal*. Toronto: Lorimer.

Camfield, David. 2008. "Neoliberalism and Working-Class Resistance in British Columbia: The Hospital Employees' Union Struggle, 2002–2004," in B. Palmer and J. Sangster (eds.), *Labouring Canada: Class, Gender, and Race in Canadian Working-Class History*. Toronto: Oxford, 444–60.

———. 2011. *Canadian Labour in Crisis: Reinventing the Workers' Movement*. Halifax: Fernwood.

Canada. Advisory Committee on the Changing Workplace. 1997. *Report of the Collective Reflection on the Changing Workplace*. Ottawa: Public Works and Government Services Canada.

Canadian Abilities Foundation (CAF). 2004. *Neglected or Hidden: Connecting Employers and People with Disabilities in Canada*. Toronto: CAF.

Canadian Apprenticeship Forum (CAF). 2009. *Workplace Accommodations for Persons with Disabilities in the Skilled Trades: A Preliminary Investigation*. Ottawa: CAF.

Canadian Auto Workers (CAW). 2000. *New Rights for a New Century: Modern Rights for Ontario Workers*. Toronto: CAW.

Canadian Bar Association (CBA). 2006. *Low Skilled Worker Pilot Project*. Ottawa: CBA.

Canadian Council on Learning. 2007. *Unlocking Canada's Potential: The State of Workplace and Adult Learning in Canada*. Ottawa: Canadian Council on Learning.

Canadian Council on Social Development (CCSD). 2002. *Disability Research Information Sheet No. 4*. Ottawa: CCSD.

———. 2004. *Disability Information Sheet No. 15*. Ottawa: CCSD.

———. 2005. *Disability Research Information Sheet No. 18*. Ottawa: CCSD.

Canadian Employment Insurance Commission (CEIC). 2013. *EI Monitoring and Assessment Report*. Ottawa: CEIC.

Canadian Federation of Independent Business (CFIB). 2006, February 20. *Capitalizing on Canada's Entrepreneurial Spirit: Business Outlook & Budget Priorities for 2006*. www.cfib.ca/legis/national/pdf/5304.pdf.

Canadian Labour Congress (CLC). 1987, December 4. *Canadian Labour Congress Submission to the House of Commons Standing Committee on External Affairs and International Trade*. Toronto: CLC.

———. 2008. *Toward Inclusion of People with Disabilities in the Workplace*. Ottawa: CLC.

———. 2015a, April 4. "Employment Insurance for Women." Ottawa: CLC. http://canadianlabour.ca/issues-research/employment-insurance-women.

———. 2015b, April 10. "Stagnant labour market persists: Part-time job gains overshadowed by loss of full time jobs in today's numbers." Ottawa: CLC. http://canadianlabour.ca/news/news-archive/stagnant-labour-market-persists-part-time-job-gains-overshadowed-loss-full-time.

Canadian Race Relations Foundation (CRRF). 2000. *Unequal Access: A Canadian Profile of Racial Differences in Education, Employment and Income.* Toronto: CRRF.

Canadian Union of Postal Workers (CUPW). 2014, October 14. *Court Challenge Launched Against the Elimination of Door-to-Door Delivery,* media release. http://www.cupw.ca/sites/default/files/legacy_imported_document/10-16-14_MediaRelease_CourtChallenge_E.pdf

Carr, Barry. 1999. "Globalization from Below: Labour Internationalism Under NAFTA." *International Social Science Journal,* no. 159: 49–59.

Chang, G. 2000. *Disposable Domestics: Immigrant Women Workers in the Global Economy.* Cambridge, MA: South End Press.

Chaykowski, Richard. 1995. "Union Influences on Labour Market Outcomes and Earnings Inequality," in K. Banting and C. Beach (eds.), *Labour Market Polarization and Social Policy Reform School of Policy Studies.* Kingston: Queen's University, 95–118.

Chaykowski, Richard, and George Slotsve. 1998, October. "Economic Inequality and Poverty in Canada: Do Unions Matter?" Paper presented to the Centre for the Study of Living Standards Conference on the State of Living Standards and the Quality of Life in Canada. www.csls.ca.

Cheung, Leslie. 2006. "Racial Status and Employment Outcomes." Canadian Labour Congress Research Paper No. 34.

Choudry, Aziz, and Mondli Hlatshwayo (eds.). 2015. *Just Work? Migrant Workers Struggle Today.* London: Pluto Press.

Choudry, Aziz, and Adrian Smith (eds.). 2016. *Unfree Labour? Struggles of Migrant and Immigrant Workers in Canada.* Oakland: PM Press.

Choudry, Aziz, and Mark Thomas. 2013. "From Legal Challenges to Workers' Centres: Migrant and Immigrant Worker Organizing in Canada." *Journal of Industrial Relations* 55, no. 2 (April): 212–26.

Citizenship and Immigration Canada (CIC). 1994. *Into the 21st Century: A Strategy for Immigration and Citizenship.* Hull, QC: Minister of Supply and Services Canada.

———. 2005. *The Monitor.* First Quarter (Summer). Ottawa: CIC.

Clarkson, Stephen. 2002. *Uncle Sam and U.S.: Globalization, Neoconservatism and the Canadian State.* Toronto: University of Toronto Press.

Cohen, Marcy, Michael Goldberg, Nick Istvanffy, Tim Stainton, Adrienne Wasik, and Karen-Marie Woods. 2008. *Removing Barriers to Work: Flexible Employment Options for People with Disabilities in BC.* Vancouver: CCPA-BC.

Conference Board of Canada. 2004. *Making a Visible Difference: The Contribution of Visible Minorities to Canadian Economic Growth.* Ottawa: Conference Board of Canada.

———. 2005. *Work to Retirement Transition: An Emerging Business Challenge*. Ottawa: Conference Board of Canada.

Corak, Miles. 2008. "Immigration in the Long Run." IRPP *Choices* 4, no. 3 (October). Institute for Research on Public Policy.

Coulombe, S., J. F. Tremblay, and S. Marchand. 2004. *Literacy Scores, Human Capital and Growth Across Fourteen OECD Countries*. Statistics Canada Cat. No. 89-552-MIE, No. 11.

Coulthard, Glen. 2014. *Red Skin, White Masks: Rejecting the Colonial Politics of Recognition*. Minneapolis: University of Minnesota Press.

Creese, Gillian. 1999. *Contracting Masculinity: Gender, Class, and Race in a White-Collar Union, 1944–94*. Toronto: Oxford University Press.

———. 2006. "Exclusion or Solidarity? Vancouver Workers Confront the 'Oriental Problem,'" in L. Sefton Macdowell and I. Radforth (eds.), *Canadian Working Class History, Selected Readings*. 3rd edition. Toronto: Canadian Scholars' Press, 199–216.

———. 2007. "Racializing Work/Reproducing White Privilege," in V. Shalla and W. Clement, *Work in Tumultuous Times: Critical Perspectives*. Montreal and Kingston: McGill-Queen's Press, 192–226.

Crompton, Susan. 2011a, October 13. "What's stressing the stressed? Main sources of stress among workers." *Canadian Social Trends*. Statistics Canada Cat. No. 11-008. http://www.statcan.gc.ca/pub/11-008-x/2011002/article/11562-eng.htm.

———. 2011b. "Women with Activity Limitations." In *Women in Canada: A Gender-Based Statistical Report*. Ottawa: Statistics Canada.

Curl, John. 2009. *For all the People: Uncovering the Hidden History of Cooperation, Cooperative Movements, and Communalism in America*. Oakland: PM Press.

Department for Business Innovation & Skills (DBIS). 2016. *Trade Union Membership 2015*. London: DBIS.

Department of Finance. 1988. *The Canada–U.S. Free Trade Agreement: An Economic Assessment*. Ottawa: Government of Canada.

———. 1994. *Action Plan on Pension Reform: Building Better Pensions for Canadians*. Ottawa: Government of Canada.

———. 2003. *Government Spending in Canada and the U.S.* Working Paper 2003–05. Ottawa: Government of Canada.

Desjardins, Richard. 2015. "Participation in adult education opportunities: Evidence from PIAAC and policy trends in selected countries." Background paper for the *Education for All Global Monitoring Report 2015*. UNESCO. http://unesdoc.unesco.org/images/0023/002323/232396e.pdf.

Dinardo, John, and David S. Lee. 2002. "The Impact of Unionization on Establishment Closure." NBER Working Paper No. W8993. www.nber.org.

Drolet, Marie. 2002. "The Male-Female Wage Gap." *Perspectives on Labour and Income* (Spring): 29–37.

Drolet, Marie, and René Morissette. 1998. *Recent Evidence on Job Quality by Firm Size*. Ottawa: Statistics Canada.

Duchesne, Doreen. 2004. "More Seniors at Work." *Perspectives on Labour and Income* (Spring): 55–67.

Duffy, Ann, and Norene Pupo. 1992. *Part-Time Paradox: Connecting Gender, Work and Family*. Toronto: McClelland & Stewart.

Dunn, James R. 2002. *A Population Health Approach to Housing*. Ottawa: Canada Mortgage and Housing Corporation.

Duxbury, Linda, and Chris Higgins. 2002. *The 2001 National Work-Life Conflict Study*. Ottawa: Health Canada.

Duxbury, Linda, Chris Higgins, and Sean Lyons. 2007. *Reducing Work-Life Conflict: What Works? What Doesn't?* Ottawa: Health Canada. http://www.hc-sc.gc.ca/ewh-semt/pubs/occup-travail/balancing-equilibre/index-eng.php.

Economic and Social Development Canada (ESDC). 2015. *Union Coverage in Canada—2014*. Ottawa: ESDC.

Edwards, Richard. 1979. *Contested Terrain: The Transformation of the Workplace in the Twentieth Century*. New York: Basic Books.

Eidelson, Josh. 2013. "Alt-Labor." *The American Prospect* 24, no. 1 (February). http://prospect.org/article/alt-labor.

Engelen, E. 2003. "How to Combine Openness and Protection? Citizenship, Migration, and Welfare Regimes." *Politics and Society* 31, no. 4: 503–36.

Esping-Anderson, Gosta. 1999. *Social Foundations of Post-Industrial Economies*. Oxford: Oxford University Press.

European Commission (Employment and Social Affairs). 2001. *Employment in Europe*. Brussels: European Commission.

———. 2002. *Employment in Europe*. Brussels: European Commission.

European Foundation for the Improvement of Living and Working Conditions (Eurofound). 2000. *Report on the European Survey on Working Conditions*. Luxembourg: Eurofound.

———. 2007. *Report on the European Survey on Working Conditions*. Luxembourg: Eurofound.

———. 2010. *Fourth European Working Conditions Survey: Contribution to Policy Development*. Eurofound: Luxembourg.

———. 2014. *Developments in Collectively Agreed Working Time 2013*. Luxembourg: Eurofound.

———. 2015. *Denmark: Working Life Country Profile*. Luxembourg: Eurofound.

European Industrial Relations Observatory (EIRO). 2007. *Working Time Developments: Annual Update 2*. https://www.eurofound.europa.eu/observatories/eurwork/comparative-information/working-time-developments-2006.

Fang, Tony, and Anil Verma. 2002. *The Union Wage Premium: Perspectives on Labour and Income* (Winter). Ottawa: Statistics Canada.

Faraday, Fay. 2012. *Made In Canada: How the Law Constructs Migrant Workers' Insecurity*. Toronto: Metcalf Foundation.

Faraday, Fay, and Eric Tucker. 2014. "Who Owns Charter Values? A Mobilization Strategy for the Labour Movement," in M. Behrens (ed.), *Unions Matter: Advancing Democracy, Economic Equality, and Social Justice*. Toronto: Between the Lines, 125–38.

Fares, Lygia Sabbag. 2012. "Flasko: A Worker-run Factory," in M. Serrano and E. Xhafa (eds.), *The Pursuit of Alternatives: Stories of Peoples' Economic and Political Struggles Around the World*. Germany: Rainer Hampp Verlag, 55–74.

Fawcett, Gail. 1996. *Living with Disability in Canada: An Economic Portrait*. Ottawa: Human Resources Development Canada.

Ferrao, Vincent. 2010. "Paid Work." In *Women in Canada: A Gender-based Statistical Report*. Ottawa: Statistics Canada.

Ferris, J. Stephen, and Stanley L. Winer. 2007. "Just How Much Bigger Is Government in Canada? A Comparative Analysis of the Size and Structure of the Public Sectors in Canada and the United States, 1992–2004." *Canadian Public Policy* 33, no. 2: 173–206.

Fine, Janice. 2006. *Worker Centers: Organizing Communities at the Edge of the Dream*. Ithaca: ILR Press.

Fishman, Ted. 2006. *China Inc*. New York: Scribner.

Fletcher, Bill Jr., and Fernando Gapasin. 2009. *Solidarity Divided: The Crisis in Organized Labor and a New Path Toward Social Justice*. Berkeley: University of California Press.

Foden, David, and Maria Jepsen. 2002. "Active Strategies for Older Workers in the European Union: A Comparative Analysis of Recent Experiences," in D. Foden et al. (eds.), *Active Strategies for Older Workers in the European Union*. Brussels: European Trade Union Institute.

Freeman, Richard B. 2007. *America Works: Critical Thoughts on the Exceptional US Labour Market*. New York: Russell Sage Foundation.

Freeman, Richard B., and Lawrence F. Katz (eds.). 1995. *Differences and Changes in Wage Structures*. Chicago: University of Chicago Press.

Freeman, Richard, and Morris M. Kleiner. 1999. "Do Unions Make Firms Insolvent?" *Industrial and Labor Relations Review* 52, no. 4 (July): 510–27.

Frenette, Marc, and Simon Coulombe. 2007. "Has Higher Education among Young Women Substantially Reduced the Gender Gap in Employment and Earnings?" Statistics Canada Analytical Research Paper 11F0019MIE2007301. Ottawa: Statistics Canada.

Frenette, Marc, and René Morissette. 2003. *Will They Ever Converge? Earnings of Immigrant and Canadian Born Workers over the Last Two Decades*. Ottawa: Statistics Canada, Analytical Studies Branch.

Fudge, Judy, and Eric Tucker. 2001. *Labour Before the Laws: The Regulation of Workers' Collective Action in Canada, 1900–1948*. Don Mills, ON: Oxford University Press.

Fudge, Judy, Eric Tucker, and Leah Vosko. 2002. *The Legal Concept of Employment: Marginalizing Workers*. Report for the Law Commission of Canada. Ottawa.

Fuller, Sylvia. 2005. "Public Sector Employment and Gender Wage Inequalities in British Columbia: Assessing the Effects of a Shrinking Public Sector." *Canadian Journal of Sociology* 30, no. 4 (Autumn): 405–39.

Galabuzi, Grace-Edward. 2006. *Canada's Economic Apartheid*. Toronto: Canadian Scholars' Press Inc.

Galarneau, Diane, and Eric Fecteau. 2014. *The Ups and Downs of Minimum Wage*. Ottawa: Statistics Canada.

Gellatly, Mary, John Grundy, Kiran Mirchandani, Adam Perry, Mark Thomas, and Leah Vosko. 2011. "'Modernizing' Employment Standards? Administrative Efficiency, Market Regulation, and the Production of the Illegitimate Claimant in Ontario, Canada." *Economic and Labour Relations Review* 22, no. 2: 81–106.

Gibson-Graham, J. K. 2003. "Enabling Ethical Economies: Cooperativism and Class." *Critical Sociology* 29, no. 2: 123–61.

Gindin, Sam, and Jim Stanford. 2003. "Canadian Labour and the Political Economy of Transformation," in W. Clement and L. F. Vosko (eds.), *Changing Canada: Political Economy as Transformation*. Montreal & Kingston: McGill-Queen's University Press, 422–42.

Glenn, Evelyn Nakano. 1992. "From servitude to service work: Historical continuities in the racial division of paid reproductive labor." *Signs* 18, no. 1: 1–43.

Glyn, Andrew. 2006. *Capitalism Unleashed: Finance, Globalization and Welfare.* Oxford: Oxford University Press.

Goldenberg, Mark. 2006. *Employer Investment in Workplace Learning in Canada.* Ottawa: Canadian Policy Research Networks.

Gordon, Robert J., and Ian Dew-Becker. 2008. *Controversies about the Rise of American Inequality: A Survey.* NBER Working Paper No. 13982: www.nber. org/papers/w13982.

Gorz, Andre. 1999. *Reclaiming Work: Beyond the Wage-Based Society.* Cambridge: Polity.

Government of Canada. 2016a. *Old Age Security payment amounts.* Ottawa: Government of Canada. http://www.esdc.gc.ca/en/cpp/oas/payments.page.

– – –. 2016b. *Canada Pension Plan—How much could you receive.* Ottawa: Government of Canada. http://www.esdc.gc.ca/en/cpp/benefit_amount.page.

– – –. 2016c. *Federally Regulated Businesses and Industries.* Ottawa: Government of Canada. http://www.esdc.gc.ca/en/jobs/workplace/human_rights/employment_equity/regulated_industries.page.

– – –. 2016d. "Mining, Quarrying, and Oil and Gas Extraction (NAICS 21): Capital Investment." Ottawa: Government of Canada. https://www.ic.gc.ca/app/scr/sbms/sbb/cis/capitalInvestment.html?code=21&lang=eng.

Grant, Tavia, and Janet McFarland. 2013, November 13. "How Globalization Has Left the 1 Per Cent Even Further Ahead." *The Globe and Mail.*

Green, Francis. 2006. *Demanding Work: The Paradox of Job Quality in the Affluent Economy.* Princeton and Oxford: Princeton University Press.

Greenspan, Alan. 2007. *The Age of Turbulence: Adventures in a New World.* New York: Penguin Press.

Gunderson, Morley, Andrew Sharpe, and Steven Wald. 2000. "Youth Unemployment in Canada, 1976–1998." *Canadian Public Policy* XXVI (Supplement).

Habtu, R. 2003. "Information Technology Workers." *Canadian Economic Observer* (September). Ottawa: Statistics Canada.

Hall, Edward, & Robert Wilton. 2011. "Alternative spaces of 'work' and inclusion for disabled people." *Disability & Society* 26, no. 7: 867–80.

Harvey, David. 2000. *Spaces of Hope.* Berkeley: University of California Press.

– – –. 2003. *The New Imperialism.* Oxford: Oxford University Press.

Hayden, Anders. 2003. "International Work-time Trends: The Emerging Gap in Hours." *Just Labour: A Canadian Journal of Work and Society* 2 (Spring): 23–35.

Hermann, Christoph. 2015. *Capitalism and the Political Economy of Work Time.* London & New York: Routledge.

Heron, Craig. 2012. *The Canadian Labour Movement—A Short History.* 3rd edition. Toronto: Lorimer.

Hicks, Peter. 2003. "The Policy Implications of Aging." *Horizons* 6, no. 2.

Higgins, Chris, Linda Duxbury, and Karen Johnson. 2004. *Exploring the Link between Work-Life Conflict and Demands on Canada's Health Care System.* Ottawa: Health Canada. http://publications.gc.ca/collections/Collection/H72-21-192-2004E.pdf.

Hollifield, J. 2004. "The Emerging Migration State." *International Migration Review* XXXVIII, no. 3: 885–912.

Hospital Employees' Union (HEU) Newsletter. September 14, 2007. www.heu.org.

Hou, Feng, and Garnett Picot. 2003. *Visible Minority Neighbourhood Enclaves and Labour Market Outcomes of Immigrants.* Ottawa: Statistics Canada.

Hudon, Tamara. 2016. "Visible Minority Women." In *Women in Canada: A Gender-based Statistical Report.* Ottawa: Statistics Canada.

Human Resources Development Canada (HRDC). 1994. *Report of the Advisory Group on Working Time and Redistribution of Work.* Ottawa: HRDC.

———. 2001. *Disability in Canada: A 2001 Profile.* Ottawa: HRDC.

Human Resources and Skills Development Canada (HSRDC). 2006a. *Employment Insurance Monitoring and Assessment Report.* Ottawa: Government of Canada.

———. 2006b. *Fairness at Work: Federal Labour Standards for the 21st Century.* Ottawa: Government of Canada.

———. 2006c. *Advancing the Inclusion of People with Disabilities.* Ottawa: Government of Canada.

Indigenous and Northern Affairs Canada. 2013. *Fact Sheet—2011 National Household Survey: Aboriginal Demographics, Educational Attainment and Labour Market Outcomes.* https://www.aadnc-aandc.gc.ca/eng/1376329205785/13763 29233875.

Informetrica. 2007a. *Occupational Pension Plan Coverage in Ontario Statistical Report.* Prepared for Ontario Expert Commission on Pensions. Ottawa: Informetrica.

———. 2007b. *Structural Changes in Manufacturing.* Ottawa: Informetrica.

Innis, Harold. 1999. *The Fur Trade in Canada: An Introduction to Canadian Economic History.* Toronto: University of Toronto Press.

International Labour Organization (ILO). 1995. *World Employment Report.* Geneva: ILO.

———. 2001. *World Employment Report.* Geneva: ILO.

———. 2002. "Towards a Policy Framework for Decent Work." *International Labour Review* 141, no. 1–2: 161–74.

———. 2003. *Decent Work in Denmark: Employment, Social Efficiency and Economic Security.* Geneva: ILO.

———. 2016. *Women At Work: Trends 2016.* Geneva: ILO.

Jackson, Andrew. 2000a. *The Myth of the Equity-Efficiency Trade-Off.* Ottawa: Canadian Council on Social Development.

————. 2000b. "The NAIRU and Macro-Economic Policy in Canada." *Canadian Business Economics* (August): 66–82.

————. 2006a. *A Statistical Portrait of Young Workers in Canada.* Ottawa: Canadian Labour Congress.

————. 2006b. "Rowing Against the Tide: The Struggle to Raise Union Density in a Hostile Environment," in P. Kumar and C. Schenk, *Paths to Union Renewal: Canadian Experiences.* Toronto: Broadview Press, Garamond Press, and CCPA, 61–79.

Johnson, Susan. 2002. "Canadian Union Density 1980 to 1998 and Prospects for the Future." *Canadian Public Policy* XXVIII, no. 3: 333–49.

Karasek, Robert, and Tores Theorell. 1990. *Healthy Work: Stress, Productivity and the Reconstruction of Working Life.* New York: Basic Books.

Katz-Rosene, Ryan. 2003. "Union Organizing: A Look at Recent Organizing Activity through Analysis of Certification across Canadian Jurisdictions." CLC Research Paper No. 26. Ottawa: Canadian Labour Congress.

Kealey, Gregory S. 1980. *Toronto Workers Respond to Industrial Capitalism, 1867-1892.* Toronto: University of Toronto Press.

Keune, Maarten, and Maria Jepsen. 2007. "Not Balanced and Hardly New: The European Commission's Quest for Flexicurity." Working Paper 2007.01. Brussels: European Trade Union Institute.

Kiernan, Patrick. 2001. "Early Retirement Trends." *Perspectives on Labour and Income* (Winter): 7–13.

Knighton, Tamara, Filsan Hujaleh, Joe Iacampo, and Gugsa Werkneh. 2009. *Participation in Lifelong Learning Among Canadians Aged 18 to 64 Years: First Results from the 2008 Access and Support to Education and Training Survey.* Ottawa: Statistics Canada.

Kobayashi, Audrey (ed.). 2008. *The Experiences of Second Generation Canadians.* Special Issue of *Canadian Diversity* 6, no. 2. Montreal: Association of Canadian Studies.

Krahn, Harvey J., Graham S. Lowe, and Karen D. Hughes. 2007. *Work, Industry & Canadian Society.* 5th edition. Toronto: Nelson.

Krugman, Paul. 2007. *The Conscience of a Liberal.* New York and London: Norton.

Kumar, Pradeep, and Gregor Murray. 2003. "Strategic Dilemma: The State of Union Renewal in Canada," in P. Fairbrother and C. A. B. Yates, *Trade Unions in Renewal: A Comparative Study.* New York: Continuum, 200–221.

Kumar, Pradeep, and Christopher Schenk (eds.). 2006. *Paths to Union Renewal: Canadian Experiences.* Toronto: Broadview Press, Garamond Press, and CCPA.

Lam, Karen, and Michael Walker. 1997. "The Next Step in Changing the Canada Pension Plan." *Fraser Forum.* www.fraserinstitute.ca.

LaMarsh, Judy. 1968. *Memoirs of a Bird in a Gilded Cage.* Toronto: McClelland & Stewart.

Lambert, Brittany, and Kate McInturff. 2016. *Making Women Count: The Unequal Economics of Women's Work*. Ottawa: CCPA/Oxfam.

LaRochelle-Côté, Sébastien, John Myles, and Garnett Picot. 2008. *Income Security and Stability during Retirement in Canada*. Statistics Canada Analytical Studies Research Paper No. 306.

Lavaca Collective. 2007. *Sin Patrón: Stories from Argentina's Worker-Run Factories*. Trans. Katherine Kohlstedt. Chicago: Haymarket Books.

Law Commission of Ontario (LCO). 2012. *Vulnerable Workers and Precarious Work*. Toronto: LCO.

Lehndorff, S. 2000. "Working Time Reduction in the European Union: A Diversity of Trends and Approaches," in L. Golden and D. Figart (eds.), *Working Time: International Trends, Theory and Policy Perspectives*. London and New York: Routledge, 38–56.

Lewchuk, Wayne, Marlea Clarke, and Alice de Wolff. 2011. *Working Without Commitments: The Health Effects of Precarious Employment*. Kingston and Montreal: McGill-Queen's University Press.

Lewchuk, Wayne, and David Robertson. 1999. "Listening to Workers: The Reorganization of Work in the Canadian Motor Vehicle Industry," in C. Schenk and J. Anderson (eds.), *Re-Shaping Work 2: Labour, the Workplace, and Technological Change*. Toronto: Garamond, 83–109.

Lewchuk, Wayne, Alice de Wolff, Andrew King, and Michael Polanyi. 2006. "The Hidden Costs of Precarious Employment: Health and the Employment Relationship," in L. Vosko (ed.), *Precarious Employment: Understanding Labour Market Insecurity in Canada*. Montreal and Kingston: McGill-Queen's University Press, 141–62.

Lippel, Katherine. 2006. "Precarious Employment and Occupational Health and Safety Legislation in Quebec," in L. Vosko, *Precarious Employment: Understanding Labour Market Insecurity in Canada*. Montreal and Kingston: McGill-Queen's University Press, 241–55.

Livingstone, D. W. 2002. *Working and Learning in the Information Age: A Profile of Canadians*. Ottawa: Canadian Policy Research Networks.

Livingstone, D. W., and M. Raykov. 2005. "Union Influence in Worker Education and Training in Canada." *Just Labour* 5 (Winter): 50–64.

Livingstone, David. 2004. *The Education Jobs Gap: Underemployment or Economic Democracy?* Toronto: Garamond.

——— (ed.). 2009. *Education and Jobs: Exploring the Gaps*. Toronto: University of Toronto Press.

Lowe, Graham. 2000. *The Quality of Work: A People Centred Agenda*. Toronto: Oxford University Press.

———. 2005. *Work Retirement Decisions: A Synthesis Report*. Prepared for Human Resources and Skills Development Canada.

———. 2007. *21st Century Job Quality: Achieving What Canadians Want*. Canadian Policy Research Networks (September).

Luce, Stephanie. 2015, July 20. "Time Is Political: The fight to control the working day remains one of our most important labor struggles." *Jacobin*. https://www.jacobinmag.com/2015/07/luce-eight-hour-day-obama-overtime/.

Luxton, Meg, and June Corman. 2001. *Getting By in Hard Times: Gendered Labour at Home and On the Job*. Toronto: University of Toronto Press.

Macdonald, David, and Daniel Wilson. 2013. *Poverty or Prosperity: Indigenous Children in Canada*. Ottawa: Canadian Centre for Policy Alternatives.

Mackenzie, Hugh. 2007. *The Great CEO Pay Race: Over Before It Begins*. Ottawa: CCPA.

— — —. 2014. *All In A Day's Work? CEO Pay in Canada*. Ottawa: CCPA.

Maclean, Brian, and Lars Osberg (eds.). 1996. *The Unemployment Crisis: All for Nought?* Montreal and Kingston: McGill-Queen's University Press.

Madsen, Per Kongshoj. 2003. "'Flexicurity' through Labour Market Policies and Institutions in Denmark," in P. Auer and S. Cazes, *Employment Stability in an Age of Flexibility*. Geneva: ILO, 59–105.

Malhotra, Ravi. 2003. "The Duty to Accommodate Unionized Workers with Disabilities in Canada and the United States: A Counter-Hegemonic Approach." *Journal of Law & Equality* 2, no. 1.

— — —. 2009. "A Tale of Marginalization: Comparing Workers with Disabilities in Canada and the United States." *Journal of Law and Social Policy* 22: 79–113.

Marshall, Katherine. 2003. "Benefits of the Job." *Perspectives on Labour and Income* (May). Statistics Canada Cat. 75-001-XIE.

— — —. 2006. "Converging Gender Roles." *Canadian Economic Observer* (August). Statistics Canada Cat. 11-010.

— — —. 2009. "The Family Work Week." *Perspectives on Labour and Income* (April): 5–13. Ottawa: Statistics Canada.

— — —. 2011, July 12. "Generational change in paid and unpaid work." *Canadian Social Trends*. Statistics Canada Cat. 11-008-X.

Marshall, Katherine, and Vincent Ferrao. 2007. "Participation of Older Workers." *Perspectives on Labour and Income* (Autumn).

Martinello, Felice. 1996. *Certification and Decertification Activity in Canadian Jurisdictions*. Kingston: Industrial Relations Centre, Queen's University.

Marx, Karl. 1964. "Alienated Labour," in T. Bottomore (ed.), *Karl Marx: Early Writings*. New York: McGraw Hill, 120–34.

— — —. 1976. *Capital: A Critique of Political Economy*, Volume One. Trans. Ben Fowkes. Harmondsworth: Penguin.

Marx, Karl, and Friedrich Engels. 1987. *Marx and Engels on the Trade Unions*. Ed. Kenneth Lapides. New York: Praeger.

— — —. 2002. *The Communist Manifesto*. London: Penguin.

McAlevey, Jane. 2014. *Raising Expectations (and Raising Hell): My Decade Fighting for the Labor Movement*. London and New York: Verso.

McBride, Stephen, and John Shields. 1997. *Dismantling a Nation: The Transition to Corporate Rule in Canada*. Halifax: Fernwood.

McMullen, Kathryn, and Jason Gilmore. 2010. "A Note on High School Graduation and School Attendance, by Age and Province, 2009/2010." *Education Matters: Insights on Education, Learning and Training in Canada* 7, no. 4. Ottawa: Statistics Canada.

McNally, David. 2006. *Another World is Possible: Globalization and Anti-Capitalism.* 2nd edition. Winnipeg: Arbeiter Ring.

Messing, Karen. 2014. *Pain and Prejudice: What Science Can Learn about Work from the People Who Do It.* Toronto: Between the Lines.

Meyerson, Harold. 2004. "Las Vegas as a Workers' Paradise." *The American Prospect* (January). www.prospect.org.

Michels, Robert. 1966. *Political Parties: A Sociological Study of the Oligarchical Tendencies of Modern Democracy.* New York: Free Press.

Milan, Anne, Leslie-Anne Keown, and Covadonga Robles Urquijo. 2011. "Families, Living Arrangements and Unpaid Work." In *Women in Canada: A Gender-Based Statistical Report.* Ottawa: Statistics Canada.

Milan, Anne, and Mireille Vézina. 2011. "Senior Women." In *Women in Canada: A Gender-Based Statistical Report.* Ottawa: Statistics Canada.

Miles, Robert. 1989. *Racism.* London: Routledge.

Milkman, R., S. Luce, and P. Lewis. 2013. *Changing the Subject: A Bottom-Up Account of Occupy Wall Street in New York City.* New York: CUNY Murphy Institute.

Mills, C. Wright. 1959. *The Sociological Imagination.* New York: Oxford University Press.

Mishel, Larry, Jared Bernstein, and Heather Boushey. 2003. *The State of Working America 2002–03.* Washington: Economic Policy Institute and M. E. Sharpe.

Mojtehedzadeh, Sara. 2015, August 22. "Loblaws rings in better scheduling for part-time workers." *Toronto Star.*

Mondragon. 2014. *Annual Report 2014.* Mondragon, Spain: Mondragon.

Moody, Kim. 1988. *An Injury to All: The Decline of American Unionism.* London & New York: Verso.

———. 1997. *Workers in a Lean World: Unions in the International Economy.* London and New York: Verso.

Morissette, René. 2008. "Earnings in the Last Decade." *Perspectives on Labour and Income* (February). Ottawa: Statistics Canada.

Morissette, René, and Anick Johnson. 2005. *Are Good Jobs Disappearing in Canada?* Ottawa: Statistics Canada. Cat. 11F0019 No. 239.

Morissette, René, and Yuri Ostrovsky. 2006. *Pension Coverage and Retirement Savings of Canadian Families, 1986 to 2003.* Statistics Canada Cat. 11F0019MIE, No. 286.

Morissette, René, and Garnett Picot. 2005. *Low Paid Work and Economically Vulnerable Families over the Last Two Decades.* Statistics Canada Cat. 11F0019MIE, No. 248.

Morissette, René, and Xuelin Zhang. 2006. "Revisiting Wealth Inequality." *Perspectives on Labour and Income.* Ottawa: Statistics Canada. Cat. 75-001-XIE. December.

Morissette, René, Xuelin Zhang, and Marc Frenette. 2007. *Earnings Losses of Displaced Workers: Canadian Evidence from a Large Administrative Database on Firm Closures and Mass Layoffs.* Statistics Canada Analytical Research Paper.

Morrison, Roy. 1991. *We Build the Road as we Travel: Mondragon, A Cooperative Social System*. Philadelphia: New Society Publishers.

Munck, Ronaldo. 2002. *Globalization and Labour: The New 'Great Transformation.'* London: Zed Books.

Murji, Karim, and John Solomos. 2005. *Racialization: Studies in Theory and Practice*. Oxford: Oxford University Press.

Myers, Karen, and Patrice de Broucker. 2006. *Too Many Left Behind: Canada's Adult Education and Training System*. Research Report W 34. Ottawa: Canadian Policy Research Networks.

Myles, John. 2000. *The Maturation of Canada's Retirement Income System: Income Levels, Income Inequality and Low Income among the Elderly*. Ottawa: Statistics Canada.

National Council of Welfare. 2004. *Income for Living?* http://publications.gc.ca/collections/Collection/SD28-1-2004E.pdf.

Ness, Immanuel. 2015. *Southern Insurgency: The Coming of the Global Working Class*. London: Pluto Press.

Novkovic, Sonja, and Tom Webb. 2014. *Co-operatives in a Post-Growth Era: Creating Co-operative Economics*. London: Zed.

O'Conner, Julia, Ann Orloff, and Sheila Shaver. 1999. *States, Markets, Families*. Cambridge, UK: Cambridge University Press.

Ontario Federation of Labour (OFL). 2000. *Submission By the Ontario Federation of Labour On the Consultation Paper 'Time For Change: Ontario's Employment Standards Legislation.'* Toronto: OFL.

Ontario Ministry of Labour (MOL). 2015. *Occupational Health and Safety in Ontario 2014-15 Annual Report*. Ottawa: MOL.

Organisation for Economic Co-operation and Development (OECD). 1994. *The OECD Jobs Study: Facts, Analysis, Strategies*. Paris: OECD.

———.1996. "Earnings Inequality, Low Paid Employment and Earnings Mobility," in *OECD Employment Outlook*. Paris: OECD, 59–108.

———. 1997. "Economic Performance and the Structure of Collective Bargaining," in *OECD Employment Outlook*. Paris: OECD, 133–75.

——— 1999. "Training of Adult Workers in OECD Countries," in *OECD Employment Outlook*. Paris: OECD, 133–75.

———. 2000. *Reforms for an Ageing Society*. Paris: OECD.

———. 2001a. *Ageing and Income: Financial Resources and Retirement in 9 OECD Countries*. Paris: OECD.

———. 2001b. "The Characteristics and Quality of Service Sector Jobs," in *OECD Employment Outlook*. Paris: OECD, 89–127.

———. 2002a. "Women at Work: Who Are They and How Are They Doing?" in *OECD Employment Outlook*. Paris: OECD, 61–125.

———. 2002b. *Thematic Review on Adult Learning: Canada*. Paris: OECD.

———. 2002c. "Taking the Measure of Temporary Employment," in *OECD Employment Outlook*. Paris: OECD, 127–83.

———. 2003a. *Beyond the Rhetoric: Adult Learning Policies and Practises*. Paris: OECD.

———. 2003b. *Transforming Disability Into Ability: Policies to Promote Work and Income Security for Disabled People*. Paris: OECD.

———. 2005. *Education at a Glance*. Paris: OECD.

———. 2006a. *OECD Employment Outlook, Boosting Jobs and Incomes*. Paris: OECD.

———. 2006b. *Society at a Glance: OECD Social Indicators*. Paris: OECD.

———. 2007a. *Babies and Bosses: Reconciling Work and Family Life*. Paris: OECD.

———. 2007b. *Employment Outlook*. Paris: OECD.

———. 2008a. *Jobs for Youth: Canada*. Paris: OECD.

———. 2008b. *Economic Survey of Canada*. Paris: OECD.

———. 2011a. *An Overview of Growing Income Inequalities in OECD Countries: Main Findings*. Paris: OECD.

———. 2011b. *Education at a Glance*. Paris: OECD.

———. 2012. *Leveraging Training and Skills Development in SMEs: An Analysis of Two Canadian Urban Regions: Montreal and Winnipeg*. Paris: OECD.

———. 2013. *Pensions at a Glance: Canada*. Paris: OECD.

———. 2014. *PISA 2012 Results: What Students Know and Can Do—Student Performance in Mathematics, Reading and Science (Volume I, Revised edition)*. Paris: OECD, PISA. http://dx.doi.org/10.1787/9789264208780-en.

———. 2015. *Education at a Glance 2015: OECD Indicators*. Paris: OECD. http://dx.doi.org/10.1787/eag-2015-en.

———. 2016a. "Wage levels (indicator)." Paris: OECD. doi: 10.1787/0a1c27bc-en.

———. 2016b. "Self-employment rate (indicator)." Paris: OECD. doi: 10.1787/fb58715e-en.

———. 2016c. "Temporary employment (indicator)." Paris: OECD. doi: 10.1787/75589b8a-en.

———. 2016d. "Household debt (indicator)." Paris: OECD. doi: 10.1787/f03b6469-en.

Panitch, Leo. 1998. "The State in a Changing World: Social-Democratizing Global Capitalism?" *Monthly Review* 50, no. 5.

Panitch, Leo, and Donald Swartz. 2008. *From Consent to Coercion: The Assault on Trade Union Freedoms*. 3rd edition. Toronto: Garamond.

Park, Jungwee. 2007. "Work Stress and Job Performance." *Perspectives on Labour and Income* (December). Statistics Canada Cat. 75-001-XIE.

Payworks. 2016. "Canadian Payroll Legislation: Vacation Pay." Winnipeg: Payworks. http://www.payworks.ca/payroll-legislation/VacationPay.asp.

Peck, Jamie. 2001. *Workfare States*. New York & London: The Guilford Press.

Perlin, Ross. 2012. *Intern Nation: How to Earn Nothing and Learn Little in the Brave New Economy*. London & New York: Verso.

Peters, Valerie. 2004. *Working and Training: First Results of the 2003 Adult Education and Training Survey*. Ottawa: Statistics Canada.

Picot, Garnett. 2008. "Immigrant Economic and Social Outcomes in Canada: Research and Data Development at Statistics Canada." Analytical Studies Research Paper No. 319.

Picot, G, A. Heisz, and A. Nakamura. 2001. *Job Tenure, Worker Mobility and the Youth Labour Market during the 1990s*. Statistics Canada Cat. 11F0019MPE, No. 155 (March).

Picot, Garnett, and Feng Hou. 2003. *The Rise in Low Income among Recent Immigrants to Canada*. Ottawa: Statistics Canada.

———. 2014. *Immigration, Low Income and Income Inequality in Canada: What's New in the 2000s?* Ottawa: Statistics Canada.

Picot, Garnett, Feng Hou, and Simon Coulombe. 2008. "Poverty Dynamics among Recent Immigrants to Canada." *International Migration Review* 42, no. 2: 393–424.

Pierson, Paul (ed.). 2001. *The New Politics of the Welfare State*. Oxford: Oxford University Press.

Ploughmann, Peter, and Per Madsen. 2002. "Flexibility, Employment Development and Active Labour Market Policy in Denmark and Sweden in the 1990s." CEPA Working Paper 2002-04. New York: Centre for Economic Policy Analysis, New School University.

Policy Research Initiative (PRI). 2005. *Encouraging Choice in Work and Retirement Project Report*. Ottawa: Government of Canada.

Pontusson, Jonas. 2005. *Inequality and Prosperity: Social Europe vs. Liberal America*. Ithaca and London: Cornell University Press.

Poverty and Employment Precarity in Southern Ontario (PEPSO). 2013. *It's More than Poverty: Employment Precarity and Household Well-being*. Toronto: United Way.

Preibisch, K., and L. Binford. 2007. "Interrogating Racialized Global Labour Supply: An Exploration of the Racial/National Replacement of Foreign Agricultural Workers in Canada." *Canadian Review of Sociology and Anthropology* 44, no. 1: 5–36.

Prestowitz, Clyde. 2005. *Three Billion New Capitalists: The Great Shift of Wealth and Power to the East*. New York: Basic Books.

Prince, Michael. 2008. *Canadians Need a Medium-Term Sickness/Disability Income Benefit*. Ottawa: Caledon Institute of Social Policy.

Pupo, Norene. 1997. "Always Working, Never Done: The Expansion of the Double Day," in A. Duffy, D. Glenday and N. Pupo (eds.), *Good Jobs, Bad Jobs, No Jobs: The Transformation of Work in the 21st Century*. Toronto: Harcourt, 144–65.

Pupo, Norene, and Mark Thomas (eds.). 2010. *Interrogating the New Economy: Restructuring Work in the 21st Century*. Toronto: University of Toronto Press.

Pyper, Wendy, and Philip Giles. 2002. "Approaching Retirement." *Perspectives on Labour and Income* (Spring): 5–12.

Raphael, Dennis (ed.). 2008. *Social Determinants of Health: Canadian Perspectives*. 2nd edition. Toronto: Canadian Scholars' Press Inc.

Reitz, Jeffrey G., and Rupa Banerjee. 2007. *Racial Inequality, Social Cohesion and Policy Issues in Canada*. Montreal: Institute for Research on Public Policy.

Reitz, Jeffery, and Anil Verma. 2003. "Immigration, Race and Labour: Unionization and Wages in the Canadian Labour Market." Mimeo.

Riddell, Chris, and W. Craig Riddell. 1998. "Changing Patterns of Unionization: The North American Experience, 1984 to 1998." Department of Economics Working Paper. Vancouver: University of British Columbia.

Rinehart, James. 2006. *The Tyranny of Work: Alienation and the Labour Process*. 5th edition. Toronto: Nelson.

Robson, William. 1996. *Putting Some Gold in the Golden Years: Fixing the Canada Pension Plan*. Toronto: C. D. Howe Institute.

Rodriguez, Robyn Magalit. 2010. *Migrants for Export: How the Philippine State Brokers Labor to the World*. Minneapolis: University of Minnesota Press.

Ross, Robert. 2004. *Slaves to Fashion: Poverty and Abuse in the New Sweatshops*. Ann Arbor: University of Michigan Press.

———. 2006. "A Tale of Two Factories: Successful Resistance to Sweatshops and the Limits of Firefighting." *Labor Studies Journal* 30, no. 4: 65–85.

———. 2011. "The rag trade as the canary in the coal mine: The global sweatshop, 1980-2010." *New Labor Forum* 20, no. 1: 42–49.

Ross, Stephanie. 2012. "Business Unionism and Social Unionism in Theory and Practice," in S. Ross and L. Savage (eds.), *Rethinking the Politics of Labour in Canada*. Halifax: Fernwood, 33–46.

Ross, Stephanie, and Larry Savage. 2013. *Public Sector Unions in the Age of Austerity*. Halifax & Winnipeg: Fernwood.

Ross, Stephanie, Larry Savage, Errol Black, and Jim Silver. 2015. *Building a Better World: An Introduction to the Labour Movement in Canada*. 3rd edition. Winnipeg: Fernwood.

Rowe, Geoff, and Huan Nguyen. 2003. "Older Workers and the Labour Market." *Perspectives on Labour and Income* 15, no. 1 (Spring): 23–26.

Roy, Francine. 2006. "From She to He: Changing Patterns of Women in the Canadian Labour Force." *Canadian Economic Observer* (June). Statistics Canada Cat. 11-010.

Royal Commission on Aboriginal Peoples (RCAP). 1996. *Report of the Royal Commission on Aboriginal People*. Ottawa: Indian and Northern Affairs Canada.

Rubenson, Kjell, Richard Desjardins, and Ee-Seul Yoon. 2007. *Adult Learning in Canada: A Comparative Perspective*. Statistics Canada Cat. 89-552-MIE, No. 17.

Russell, Ellen, and Mathieu Dufour. 2007. *Rising Profit Shares, Falling Wage Shares*. Ottawa: Canadian Centre for Policy Alternatives.

Saez, Emmanuel, and Michael Veall. 2003. *The Evolution of High Incomes in Canada, 1920 to 2000*. National Bureau of Economic Research Working Paper. www.nber.org/papers.

Sargent, Timothy C., and Munir A. Sheikh. 1996. *The Natural Rate of Unemployment: Theory, Evidence and Policy Implications*. Department of Finance, Economic Studies and Policy Analysis Division (August).

Satzewich, V. 1991. *Racism and the Incorporation of Foreign Labour: Farm Labour Migration to Canada Since 1945*. London and New York: Routledge.

Satzewich, V., and Terry Wotherspoon. 2000. "The State and the Contradictions of Indian Administration," in *First Nations: Race, Class and Gender Relations.* Regina: Canadian Plains Research Center, 15–41.

Sauvé, Roger. 2007. *The Current State of Canadian Family Finances.* Ottawa: Vanier Institute of the Family. www.vifamily.ca/library/cft/famfin07.pdf. Link no longer active.

Schellenberg, Grant. 1994. *The Road to Retirement: Demographic and Economic Changes in the '90s.* Ottawa: Canadian Council on Social Development.

Schellenberg, Grant, Martin Turcotte, and Bali Ram. 2005. "Post Retirement Employment." *Perspectives on Labour and Income* (Winter).

Schettkat, Ronald. 2002. *Regulation in the Dutch and German Economies at the Root of Unemployment?* Center for Economic Policy Analysis, New School University. Working Paper 2002-05.

Schumpeter, Joseph A. 1975. *Capitalism, Socialism, and Democracy.* New York: Harper & Row.

Sears, Alan. 1999. "The 'Lean' State and Capitalist Restructuring: Towards a Theoretical Account." *Studies in Political Economy* 59: 91–114.

— — —. 2003. *Retooling the Mind Factory: Education in a Lean State.* Toronto: Garamond.

Seidman, Gay W. 1994. *Manufacturing Militance: Workers' Movements in Brazil and South Africa, 1970–1985.* Berkeley: University of California Press.

Shainblum, Esther, Terrence Sullivan, and John W. Frank. 2000. "Multicausality, Non-traditional Injury and the Future of Workers' Compensation," in M. Gunderson and D. Hyatt (eds.), *Workers' Compensation: Foundations for Reform.* Toronto: University of Toronto Press, 58–95.

Shalla, Vivian. 2007. "Theoretical Reflections on Work: A Quarter Century of Critical Thinking," in V. Shalla and W. Clement (eds.), *Work in Tumultuous Times: Critical Perspectives.* Montreal and Kingston: McGill-Queen's University Press, 3–29.

Sharma, Nandita. 2006. *Home Economics: Nationalism and the Making of "Migrant Workers" in Canada.* Toronto: University of Toronto Press.

Sharpe, Andrew, and Jill Hardt. 2006, December. *Five Deaths a Day: Workplace Fatalities in Canada, 1993–2005.* Centre for the Study of Living Standards, Research Paper 2006-04.

Shields, M. 2006. "Stress and Depression in the Employed Population." *Health Reports* 17, no. 4. Ottawa: Statistics Canada.

Smeeding, Timothy. 2002. *Globalization, Inequality, and the Rich Countries of the G-20: Evidence from the Luxembourg Income Study (LIS).* Center for Policy Research, Paper 112. http://surface.syr.edu/cpr/112.

Smith, Charles. 2012. "Labour, Courts and the Erosion of Workers' Rights in Canada," in S. Ross and L. Savage (eds.), *Rethinking the Politics of Labour in Canada.* Halifax: Fernwood, 184–97.

Smith, Doug. 2000. *Consulted to Death: How Canada's Workplace Health and Safety System Fails Workers*. Winnipeg: Arbiter Ring Publishers.

Special Committee on Pay Equity (SCPE). 2016. *It's Time To Act: Report of the Special Committee on Pay Equity*. Ottawa: House of Commons.

Standing, Guy. 2011. *The Precariat: The New Dangerous Class*. London & New York: Bloomsbury Academic.

Stanford, Jim. 2004. "Paul Martin, the Deficit, and the Debt: Taking Another Look," in T. Scarth (ed.), *Hell and High Water: An Assessment of Paul Martin's Record and Implications for the Future*. Ottawa: Canadian Centre for Policy Alternatives, 31–54.

Stasiulis, Daiva. 1997. "The Political Economy of Race, Ethnicity, and Migration," in W. Clement (ed.), *Understanding Canada: Building on the New Canadian Political Economy*. Kingston & Montreal: McGill-Queen's University Press, 141–71.

Stasiulis, Daiva, and Radha Jhappan. 1995. "The Fractious Politics of a Settler Society: Canada," in D. Stasiulis and N. Yuval-Davis (eds.), *Unsettling Settler Societies: Articulations of Gender, Race, Ethnicity and Class*. London: SAGE, 95–131.

Statista. 2016. "China: Share of global gross domestic product (GDP) adjusted for purchasing-power-parity (PPP) from 2010 to 2021." http://www.statista.com/statistics/270439/chinas-share-of-global-gross-domestic-product-gdp/.

Statistics Canada. 2000. *Pension Plans in Canada, 1999*. Ottawa: Statistics Canada.

———. 2006. *Women in Canada: Fifth Edition*. Cat. 89-503XIE.

———. 2007a. *The Labour Market At A Glance*. Ottawa: Statistics Canada.

———. 2007b. "Immigration in Canada: A Portrait of the Foreign Born Population." 2006 Census.

———. 2007c. "Canada's Ethnocultural Mosaic." 2006 Census.

———. 2008. *Participation and Activity Limitations Survey 2006: Labour Force Experiences of Persons with Disabilities*. Cat. 89-628-X, No. 007.

———. 2010a. "Minimum wage." *Perspectives on Labour and Income*, March: 14–22. Ottawa: Statistics Canada.

———. 2010b. *Aboriginal People and the Labour Market: Estimates from the Labour Force Survey, 2008–2010*. Ottawa: Statistics Canada.

———. 2011a. *Women in Canada: A Gender-based Statistical Report*. Ottawa: Statistics Canada.

———. 2011b. *Immigration and Ethnocultural Diversity in Canada: National Household Survey, 2011*. Ottawa: Statistics Canada.

———. 2011c. *Persons Living in Low-Income Neighbourhoods—National Household Survey, 2011*. Ottawa: Statistics Canada.

———. 2011d. *Aboriginal Peoples in Canada: First Nations People, Metis and Inuit— National Household Survey, 2011*. Ottawa: Statistics Canada.

———. 2011e. *The Educational Attainment of Aboriginal Peoples in Canada—National Household Survey, 2011*. Ottawa: Statistics Canada.

———. 2011f. *Living Arrangements of Young Adults aged 20 to 29.* Ottawa: Statistics Canada.

———. 2011g. *Education and Occupation of High-Income Canadians: National Household Survey, 2011.* Ottawa: Statistics Canada. https://www12.statcan. gc.ca/nhs-enm/2011/as-sa/99-014-x/99-014-x2011003_2-eng.cfm.

———. 2013. *Skills in Canada: First Results from the Programme for the International Assessment of Adult Competencies.* Ottawa: Statistics Canada.

———. 2015a, November 3. "High-income trends among Canadian taxfilers, 1982 to 2013." *The Daily.* Ottawa: Statistics Canada. http://www.statcan.gc.ca/daily-quotidien/151103/dq151103a-eng.htm.

———. 2015b. *Education Indicators in Canada: An International Perspective.* Ottawa: Statistics Canada. http://www.statcan.gc.ca/pub/81-604-x/81-604-x2014001-eng.pdf.

———. 2015c, May 28. "Unionization rates falling." *Canadian Megatrends.* Ottawa: Statistics Canada. http://www.statcan.gc.ca/pub/11-630-x/11-630-x2015005-eng.htm.

———. 2016, February 26. "Registered Retirement Savings Plan Contributions, 2014." *The Daily.* Ottawa: Statistics Canada.

Status of Women Canada (SWC). 2012. *Women In Canada: At A Glance.* Ottawa: Status of Women Canada.

Steedman, Mercedes. 1997. *Angels of the Workplace: Women and the Construction of Gender Relations in the Canadian Clothing Industry, 1890–1940.* Toronto: Oxford University Press.

Stinson, Jane, Nancy Pollak, and Marcy Cohen. 2005. *The Pains of Privatization: How Contracting Out Hurts Health Support Workers, Their Families, and Health Care.* Vancouver: Canadian Centre for Policy Alternatives. https://www.policyalternatives.ca/publications/reports/pains-privatization.

Suen, R. L. W. 2000. "You Sure Know How to Pick' Em: Human Rights and Migrant Farm Workers in Canada." *Georgetown Immigration Law Journal* 15, no. 1: 199–227.

Sullivan, Terrence (ed.). 2000. *Injury and the New World of Work.* Vancouver and Toronto: UBC Press.

Sussman, Deborah. 2002. "Barriers to Job-Related Training." *Perspectives on Labour and Income* (Summer): 5–12.

Tattersall, Amanda. 2010. *Power in Coalition: Strategies for Strong Unions and Social Change.* Ithaca: ILR Press.

Teelucksingh, Cheryl, and Grace-Edward Galabuzi. 2005. *Working Precariously: The Impact of Race and Immigrant Status on Employment Opportunities and Outcomes in Canada.* Toronto: Canadian Race Relations Foundation.

Teeple, Gary. 2000. *Globalization and the Decline of Social Reform into the Twenty-first Century.* Toronto: Garamond Press.

Thomas, Mark. 2006. "Union Strategies to Re-Regulate Work Time." *Just Labour: A Canadian Journal of Work and Society* 9: 1–15.

— — —. 2008. "Working Time and Labour Control in the Toyota Production System," in R. O'Brien (ed.), *Solidarity First: Canadian Workers and Social Cohesion*. Vancouver: University of British Columbia Press, 86–105.

— — —. 2009. *Regulating Flexibility: The Political Economy of Employment Standards*. Montreal & Kingston: McGill-Queen's University Press.

— — —. 2010a. "Labour Migration and Temporary Work: Canada's Foreign Worker Programs in the 'New Economy,'" in N. Pupo and M. Thomas (eds.), *Interrogating the New Economy: Restructuring Work in the 21st Century*. Toronto: University of Toronto Press, 149–72.

— — —. 2010b. "Neoliberalism, Racialization, and the Regulation of Employment Standards," in S. Braedley and M. Luxton (eds.), *Neoliberalism and Everyday Life*. Montreal & Kingston: McGill-Queen's University Press, 68–89.

Thomas, Mark, and Steven Tufts. 2016. "Austerity, Right Populism and the Crisis of Labour in Canada." *Antipode* 48, no. 1 (January): 212–30.

Thompson, E. P. 1967. "Time, Work, Discipline, and Industrial Capitalism." *Past and Present* 38: 56–97.

Thompson, Paul. 1989. *The Nature of Work: An Introduction to Debates on the Labour Process*. Basingstoke: Macmillan.

Till, Matthew, Tim Leonard, Sebastian Yeung, and Gradon Nicholls. 2015. *A Profile of the Labour Market Experiences of Adults with Disabilities Among Canadians Aged 15 Years and Older, 2012*. Ottawa: Statistics Canada.

Townson, Monica. 2006. *Growing Older, Working Longer: The New Face of Retirement*. Ottawa: Canadian Centre for Policy Alternatives.

Townson, Monica, and Kevin Hayes. 2007. *Women and the Employment Insurance Program*. Ottawa: Canadian Centre for Policy Alternatives.

Tremblay, Pascal. 2015. *Trade and Investment: Canada's Merchandise Trade with the World*. Ottawa: Parliamentary Information and Research Service.

Truth and Reconciliation Commission of Canada (TRCC). 2015. *Honouring the Truth, Reconciling for the Future: Summary of the Final Report of the Truth and Reconciliation Commission of Canada*. Winnipeg: TRCC.

Tucker, Eric. 1990. *Administering Danger in the Workplace: The Law and Politics of Occupational Health and Safety Regulation in Ontario, 1850–1914*. Toronto: University of Toronto Press.

Tufts, Steven. 2007. "Emerging labour strategies in Toronto's Hotel Sector: Toward a Spatial Circuit of Union Renewal." *Environment and Planning A* 39, no. 10: 2383–404.

Tufts, Steven, and Mark Thomas. 2014. "Populist Unionism Confronts Austerity in Canada." *Labor Studies Journal* 39, no. 1 (March): 60–82.

Tuijnman, A., and E. Boudard. 2001. *Adult Education Participation in North America: International Perspectives*, Statistics Canada Cat. 89-574-XPE. Ottawa: Statistics Canada and Human Resources Development Canada.

Turcotte, Martin. 2014. *Persons with Disabilities and Employment*. Ottawa: Statistics Canada.

Turcotte, Martin, and Grant Schellenberg. 2005. "Job Strain and Retirement." *Perspectives on Labour and Income* (Autumn).

United Food and Commercial Workers (UFCW). 2011. *The Status of Migrant Farmworkers in Canada, 2010–11*. Toronto: UFCW.

Uppal, Sharanjit. 2015, June 24. "Employment patterns of families with children." *Insights on Canadian Society*. Ottawa: Statistics Canada. http://www.statcan. gc.ca/pub/75-006-x/2015001/article/14202-eng.htm#a3.

Uppal, Sharanjit, and Sebastien LaRochelle-Côté. 2015. *Changes in Wealth Across the Income Distribution, 1999 to 2012*. Ottawa: Statistics Canada. http://www. statcan.gc.ca/pub/75-006-x/2015001/article/14194-eng.pdf.

Valiani, S. 2007. *Briefing Note — The Temporary Foreign Worker Program and its Intersection with Canadian Immigration Policy*. Ottawa: Canadian Labour Congress.

— — —. 2012. *Rethinking Unequal Exchange: The Global Integration of Nursing Labour Markets*. Toronto: University of Toronto Press.

Verma, V. 2003. *The Mexican and Caribbean Seasonal Agricultural Workers Program: Regulatory and Policy Framework, Farm Industry Level Employment Practices, and the Future of the Program Under Unionization*. Ottawa: North-South Institute.

Vieta, Marcelo. 2010. "The Social Innovations of Autogestión in Argentina's Worker Recuperated Enterprises: Cooperatively Reorganizing Productive Life in Hard Times." *Labor Studies Journal* 35, no. 3: 295–321.

Vosko, Leah. 2000. *Temporary Work: The Gendered Rise of a Precarious Employment Relationship*. Toronto: University of Toronto Press.

— — — (ed.). 2006. *Precarious Employment: Understanding Labour Market Insecurity in Canada*. Montreal and Kingston: McGill-Queen's University Press.

Vosko, Leah, Nancy Zukewich, and Cynthia Cranford. 2003. "Precarious Jobs: A New Typology of Employment." *Perspectives on Labour and Income* (October): 16–26. Ottawa: Statistics Canada.

Webb, Beatrice, and Sidney Webb. 1897. *Industrial Democracy*. London & New York: Longmans, Green, and Co.

Wellesley Institute. 2015. *Low Wages, No Benefits: Expanding Access To Health Benefits for Low Income Ontarians*. Toronto: Wellesley Institute.

Wells, Don. 1995. "Origins of Canada's Wagner Model of Industrial Relations: The United Auto Workers in Canada and the Suppression of 'Rank and File' Unionism, 1936-1953." *Canadian Journal of Sociology* 20, no. 2: 193–224.

— — —. 1998. "Fighting the Mexico Mantra: Labour's New Internationalism." *Out Times* 17, no. 6 (November/December): 20–27.

Welsh, Moira. 2015, November 29. "Ontario's Sheltered Workshops to Close Forever." *Toronto Star*. https://www.thestar.com/news/canada/2015/11/29/ ontarios-sheltered-workshops-to-close-forever.html.

Westergaard-Nielson, Neils (ed.). 2008. *Low Wage Work in Denmark*. New York: Russell Sage Foundation.

White, Julie. 2002. "A New Look at Shorter Hours of Work in the Communications, Energy and Paperworkers Union." *Just Labour* 1: 41–49.

Wial, Howard, and Jeff Rickert. 2002. *US Hotels and Their Workers: Room for Improvement*. Washington, DC: Working for America Institute.

Wilkins, Kathryn, and Marie P. Beaudet. 1998. "Work Stress and Health." *Health Reports* 10, no. 3 (Winter).

Willms, J. Douglas. 1999. *Inequalities in Literacy Skills among Youth in Canada and the United States*. Statistics Canada Cat. 89-552 MIE, No. 6.

Wilson, Daniel, and David Macdonald. 2010. *The Income Gap Between Aboriginal Peoples and the Rest of Canada*. Ottawa: Canadian Centre for Policy Alternatives.

Workers' Action Centre (WAC). 2015. *Still Working on the Edge: Building Decent Jobs from the Ground Up*. Toronto: WAC.

World Bank. 1994. *Averting the Old Age Crisis: Policies to Protect the Old and Promote Growth*. Washington: World Bank.

World Health Organization (WHO). 1999. *Labour Market Changes and Job Insecurity*. Regional Publications/European Series No. 81.

Wotherspoon, Terry. 2000. "Transforming Canada's Education System: The Impact on Educational Inequalities, Opportunities, and Benefits," in B. S. Bolaria (ed.), *Social Issues and Contradictions in Canadian Society*. Toronto: Thomson Nelson, 250–69.

Yalnizyan, Armine. 2007. *The Rich and the Rest of Us: The Changing Face of Canada's Growing Gap*. Toronto: Canadian Centre for Policy Alternatives.

Yates, Charlotte. 2000. "Staying the Decline in Union Membership: Union Organizing in Ontario, 1985–1999." *Relations Industrielles/Industrial Relations* 55, no. 4: 640–74.

— — —. 2002. "Expanding Labour's Horizons: Union Organizing and Strategic Change in Canada." *Just Labour* 1.

— — —. 2003. "The Revival of Industrial Unions in Canada," in P. Fairbrother and C. Yates (eds.), *Trade Unions in Renewal: A Comparative Study*. New York: Continuum, 221–44.

Yssaad, Lahouaria. 2011. *The Immigrant Labour Force Analysis Series: The Canadian Immigrant Labour Market*. Ottawa: Statistics Canada.

Zhang, Xuelin. 2007. "Returning to Work after Childbirth." *Perspectives on Labour and Income* (December). Statistics Canada Cat. 75-011XIE.

Zhang, Xuelin, and Boris Palameta. 2006. *Participation in Adult Schooling and Its Earnings Impact in Canada*. Statistics Canada Analytical Studies Branch Research Paper No. 276.

Copyright Acknowledgments

Box 6.2: Brait, Ellen. 2016, March 17. "'Resume whitening' doubles callbacks for minority job candidates, study finds." Copyright © The Guardian. https://www. theguardian.com/world/2016/mar/17/jobs-search-hiring-racial-discrimination-resume-whiteningcallbacks.

Box 6.3: Joseph, Bob. 2013, October 1. "8 Basic Barriers to Aboriginal Employment." *Working Effectively With Aboriginal Peoples* (blog). Copyright © Robert Joseph. http://www.ictinc.ca/8-basic-barriers-to-aboriginal-employment.

Box 7.2: Canadian Labour Congress. 2016, February 6. "Canada Pension Plan Disability is failing many of the most vulnerable Canadians." Copyright © Canadian Labour Congress. http://canadianlabour.ca/news/news-archive/canada-pension-plan-disability-failing-many-most-vulnerable-canadians.

Box 7.3: CBC News. 2014, November 2. "Manitoba's new accessibility rules welcomed by disability rights advocate: Provincial standard requires businesses, organizations to make spaces easier to access." Copyright © CBC News. http://www.cbc.ca/news/canada/manitoba/manitoba-s-new-accessibility-ruleswelcomed-by-disability-rights-advocate-1.3300746.

Box 8.1: Grant, Tavia. 2014, November 4. "Poloz's prescription for unemployed youth: Work for free." Copyright © The Globe and Mail. http://www.theglobeandmail.com/report-on-business/economy/poloz-having-something-unpaid-on-your-cv-is-very-worth-it/article21439305/.

Box 9.1: Bedard, Ella. 2015, June 12. "Who's unionized? Demographic shift shows changes in the job market." Copyright © *rabble.ca*. http://rabble.ca/news/2015/06/whos-unionized-demographic-shift-shows-changesjob-market.

Box 9.2: Canadian Labour Congress. 2015. *What We Do*. Copyright © Canadian Labour Congress. http://canadianlabour.ca/about-clc/what-we-do.

Box 9.3: Nancy, Jonathan. 2015, December 18. "After Paris—A Global Movement for Climate Jobs." *Global Climate Jobs*. https://globalclimatejobs.wordpress.com/2015/12/18/after-paris-a-global-movement-for-climate-jobs/.

Box 10.1: Mackey, Jeff. 2013, August 31. "Unifor, Canada's Newest Union, Formed As CAW, CEP Merge." *Huffington Post*. Copyright © The Canadian Press. http://www.huffingtonpost.ca/2013/08/31/unifor-caw-cep-merger_n_3847388.html.

Box 10.2: Ehrcke, Tara. 2015. "The Fight for $15 Wage in B.C. and Beyond." *Canadian Dimension* 49, issue 3 (May/June). Copyright © Canadian Dimension. https://canadiandimension.com/articles/view/the-fight-for-15-wage-in-b.c.-and-beyond.

Box 10.3: Fuatai, Teuila. 2016, May 2. "Airport workers demand fair wages, better jobs on May Day." Copyright © rabble.ca. http://rabble.ca/news/2016/05/airport-workers-demand-fair-wages-better-jobs-on-may-day.

Box 11.1: Bertin, Oliver. 2002, October 21. "Chatham Reels Over Navistar Loss—Truck Plant Closing Will Kill 5% of City's Jobs." Copyright © The Globe and Mail. http://www.theglobeandmail.com/report-on-business/chatham-reels-over-navistar-loss/article25423649/.

Box 11.2: Galt, Virginia. 2004, July 5. "'We Can't Get Too Stubborn and Let the Companies We Work For Fail'—Overseas Competition Sparks New Era in Management-Labour Relations." Copyright © The Globe and Mail. http://www.

Index